ACKNOWLEDGMENTS

Revising and re-illustrating the manuscript of *Looking Good In Print* for this fourth edition has been an exciting task—and an exhausting one. At Ventana, thanks go to Amy Hayworth, who first suggested me for the project; Chris Grams, who seconded the motion, handled all of the pesky details, and became my most enthusiastic supporter; and Lisa Gill, who drew some of the new illustrations for the color section (the good-looking ones!). Many thanks also to my brother Steve (a.k.a. "Mr. B"), who acted as an unofficial proofreader and copyeditor whenever I got stuck. (I got stuck fairly often.)

Thanks also to my new friends at The Coriolis Group, who will be overseeing the publication of this edition (and, if all goes well, future editions).

—Patrick Berry

LOOKING GOOD IN PRINT

About The Authors

Roger C. Parker is the author of several design titles, including *Newsletters from the Desktop* and *Desktop Publishing With WordPerfect*. He has conducted numerous seminars and workshops on desktop publishing design. He is president of The Write Word, Inc., an advertising and marketing firm based in Dover, New Hampshire.

Patrick Berry is a freelance puzzle creator and desktop publisher living in Carrboro, North Carolina. Before pursuing a freelance career, he was in charge of layout design at Ventana Communications Group. His puzzles have appeared in *The New Yorker*, *Harper's*, and *GAMES*.

Looking Good In Print

FOREWORD

Welcome to the latest edition of *Looking Good In Print*. For a decade, *Looking Good In Print* has been helping readers like you make the most of their ads, brochures, newsletters, and training materials. More important, for over ten years *Looking Good In Print* has been helping people advance their careers.

The desktop publishing revolution, which *Looking Good In Print* has paced, broke down the barriers between writers and designers. Today, you can't depend on writing alone to get your message across. To succeed in today's economy, you need to not only choose and use the right words, you have to *format them*—you have to choose the right typeface and design the page on which they'll appear. Newsletter editors have had to become graphic designers and typesetters—and so have business owners, departmental managers, and consultants.

Ten years ago, the first edition of *Looking Good In Print* helped non-designers, searching for an easy way to master graphic design, quickly locate the information they needed. Today, *Looking Good In Print* not only serves the same function, it also serves as a review guide for those who have already mastered design but need a *design refresher* to brush up on the details and improve their skills.

It's interesting to compare the similarities and differences between the first edition of *Looking Good In Print* and the copy in your hand. I'm pleased that the emphasis on message and basics like attention to detail remains. However, like desktop publishing itself, the *Looking Good In Print* in your hands is light-years ahead of what it was when the book first appeared. The sections on photography and color, for example, reflect the technological advancements of the past decade. Who, ten years ago, would have dared to predict the impact that Adobe Photoshop would have on design?

Other improvements include new illustrations to keep the present edition abreast with an increasingly sophisticated market. The new appendix also includes entirely new sections on image databases, prepress, file preparation, and color management.

Writers write to make a difference. One of the most satisfying aspects of writing *Looking Good In Print*—aside from the friends I have made who contacted me as readers—is the feeling that "this book has made a difference." I first realized this when, at a Seybold Publishing Conference in New York City, I met the art director of one of the nation's leading cable networks. I introduced myself and said how I enjoy the network's beautiful art direction and he replied: "Thank you, but I should be thanking you—I read *Looking Good In Print* the night before my first interview there and it helped me get the job!"

After you finish this volume—and, perhaps—share it with your friends, I hope you'll drop me an email letting me know what you think of this edition and how it helped you solve the particular design (or career) challenge you've just been handed. I'm always interested in hearing from my readers.

Enough talk, let's get started.

Roger C. Parker

Dover, NH

http://www.rcparker.com

Email: rcpcom@aol.com

Table Of Contents

Chapter 5 The Art Of Illustration 91

Chapter 6 Working With Photographs 121

PART II Putting Your Knowledge To Work

Chapter 13 Redesign 243

Appendix Prepress Tips And Techniques 269

Index 279

LOOKING GOOD IN PRINT

Looking Good In Print

INTRODUCTION

Before the advent of desktop publishing, graphic design was the exclusive domain of art directors and design professionals. The knowledge and equipment needed to produce printed publications were in the hands of a select few; if you needed design work done, the only logical option was to hire a professional.

Nowadays, the equipment needed for successful design—a personal computer and some layout software—is available to everyone. You don't need to hire someone to create your business cards, advertisements, newsletters and full-color brochures; you can create them yourself, right on your own desktop. Fantastic, eh?

Well, maybe and maybe not. It's certainly convenient that do-it-yourself design is *possible*, but the necessary expertise is not as easily acquired as the necessary equipment. Layout software does not magically transform you into a designer, any more than the acquisition of a whip and a chair would turn you into a lion tamer. It's just a tool of the trade, not the trade itself. If you don't have some design sense to go with your tools, you're not saving any money by "doing it yourself"—where's the triumph in avoiding the professional's fee, if you don't end up with professional-looking results?

Looking Good In Print is a design guide for computer users—particularly for those with little or no design experience—who want to make the most of their desktop publishing investment.

LOOKING GOOD IN PRINT

Cultivating Your Design Sense

Regardless of your level of experience, you already may have more design skills than you suspect. In fact, you probably have an inherent, but as yet undeveloped, sense of good design—often referred to as "good taste."

Your experiences as a reader and consumer probably reflect this. See if any of these scenarios sound familiar:

- You find your community newsletter difficult to slog through, even though you're interested in the information.
- While shopping for wine, you get a sense that one brand is better than another just by looking at the labels.
- At some restaurants, you browse the full menu even if you're pretty sure what you want; at others, you simply order the first entrée that looks good.

- You're able to recall meeting a certain businessman because he gave you a full-color business card.

In such instances, your inherent sense of design is screening the messages you receive: effective designs are getting noticed and appreciated, while ineffective ones are being suffered or ignored. This book will teach you how to hone your innate sense into a useful skill—you'll learn to consciously analyze your preferences, and apply these findings to your own designs.

Who Should Read *Looking Good In Print*?

Looking Good In Print is a practical design guide for anyone discovering the challenges of desktop publishing. If you want to improve the appearance and effectiveness of your desktop-published projects, you should find this book to be a lasting reference tool.

Looking Good In Print is intended for users of all skill levels, from beginners to seasoned pros. Although many of the techniques described within will be familiar to experienced desktop publishers, the book is not intended solely as a teaching aid: it also functions as a methodical, fully-illustrated compendium of design possibilities. The next time your creative well runs dry, try browsing the pages of *Looking Good In Print*; find a chapter that discusses the type of document or page element you're working with, or just flip through randomly, looking at examples. You're bound to stumble upon something useful—a neat design trick you haven't used in years, perhaps, or an unusual layout structure you hadn't considered.

How To Use This Book

Looking Good In Print is organized into three parts:

- Part One, "Elements Of Design," outlines the underlying principles of design and the common tools available in desktop publishing software. You'll learn how to work with text, graphic accents, illustrations, photographs, and color.
- Part Two, "Putting Your Knowledge To Work," applies the principles and techniques of graphic design to specific projects you're likely to undertake. You'll delve into the minutiae of designing newsletters, advertisements, sales brochures, business cards, and much more.
- The Do It In Color section, the full color pages in the middle of the book, features a "before-and-after" gallery of documents which addresses a wide variety of design concerns.

Readers who are new to desktop publishing should read the book from beginning to end, with special emphasis on Section One. Intermediate and advanced users can probably skim lightly through Section One—except when fishing for ideas—but will gain valuable insights from the other two sections.

Please note that throughout this book, the terms *publication* and *document* are used to refer to any desktop publishing project, regardless of its size or content. Referring to a business card as a publication is admittedly a trifle silly, but since most design concepts are not document-specific, the general terms are very appropriate. A good technique presented in the chapter on newsletters might be just the thing for your sales brochure. Take good ideas wherever you can find them!

How Well Should You Know Desktop Publishing?

This book assumes you're already comfortable with your desktop publishing hardware and software. It assumes your computer and printer are up and running, and that you've gone through the tutorials or read the manuals included with your software—enough, anyway, to be familiar with the basic commands.

While not a substitute for your software's documentation, *Looking Good In Print* will help you get the most from your program. You may find that techniques you once found intimidating—drop shadows, perhaps, or runarounds—are less formidable if you know when and how to use them.

Hardware/Software Requirements

Looking Good In Print is a generic guide, independent of any particular hardware or software. It will serve as a valuable resource regardless of whether you're using a dedicated page layout program such as PageMaker or QuarkXPress, or an advanced word processing program such as Microsoft Word or WordPerfect. Likewise, your platform can be Macintosh or PC; it doesn't matter. The elements of good design are constant and achievable in any system.

I've included occasional references—particularly in Chapters 5 and 6, which discuss the use of illustrations and photographs—to effects that can be achieved with the use of an illustration- or photo-manipulation program. Although readers of this book are not required or expected to have these sorts of programs, it seemed remiss to leave them out of the discussion entirely—those who *do* have them deserve to know their full potential, and those who don't might benefit from knowing what's possible. (Who knows, perhaps the possibilities will prove tempting enough to spur a trip to the local software shop!)

What's New In The Fourth Edition?

For starters, most of the examples are new. In general, they're a little more complex than the examples from past editions—this is intentional, and meant to reflect the improvements in hardware and software since the third edition of this book was published. Techniques and tricks that formerly required separate software packages and considerable expertise have become standard, easy-to-use features in today's layout programs; it's appropriate that the illustrations in this book take full advantage of them.

In addition, I've weeded out some of the design suggestions and recommendations which were beginning to show their age. Graphic design is a lot like fashion; what was "in" a few years ago can seem tired or stale today. Whenever possible, I've tried to replace the omissions with new material reflecting current styles and trends.

Last but not least, the color portion of the book is almost wholly new, with discussions of topics not explored in previous editions, and plenty of new examples to feast your eyes on. (The Renaissance Festival poster and the menu cover for the CyberCafé were created by designer Lisa Gill—although they go well beyond the average desktop publisher's abilities to reproduce, they certainly represent something to strive for, n'est-ce pas?)

All Set?

You can't loiter in the introduction forever, you know—the world of graphic design awaits! If you're ready to get your feet wet, simply turn the page.

PART I

ELEMENTS OF DESIGN

1 Getting Started

Part of the challenge of graphic design is that it has no "universal rules." Everything is relative; it can't be reduced to a series of "if...then" statements. Tools and techniques you use effectively in one situation will not necessarily work in another.

For example, framing an advertisement in a generous amount of white space can be an effective way to draw attention to the message. A large border of white space on a newsletter page, however, can make the text look like an afterthought, creating a sparse, uninviting look.

Or, consider typeface choices. A combination of Palatino for text and Helvetica for headlines may look great for an instruction manual, but it's probably too bland for a flyer announcing a jazz concert in the park.

If design were governed by a set of hard-and-fast rules, computer programs would replace graphic artists, and every advertisement, book, brochure, newsletter, and poster would look the same. The resulting uniformity would rob the world of the diversity and visual excitement that add so much to magazines, newspapers, and even our daily mail!

Ultimately, designers should think in terms of *tools*, not rules. There are many guidelines, conventions, and time-honored techniques in the field of graphic layout. These are the tools of design, and a good designer should have a thorough knowledge of them. Equally important, however, is the ability to decide which tools are appropriate for a particular project. A good carpenter doesn't use every tool in his kit on a single task; neither should you.

Understanding Your Message

The design process is simply an extension of the organizing process that began as you developed the concept for your project.

Good design is project-specific. The purpose of your project and the relative importance of each point you wish to make are important factors in determining the most effective layout. If you're unclear about the purpose of your project or unable to prioritize the different parts of your message, you'll find the design process difficult and the results ineffective.

For example, let's say you're designing a layout for a newsletter article that includes a series of photographs. Unless you've considered the roles of the photographs in the article, you won't know how to position them. You'll be forced to make strictly subjective decisions: "I think this photograph looks good here," and so on. But if you know how the pictures relate to the story—and to each other—you'll have an objective basis for deciding the proper size and placement of each one.

Every aspect of a printed document—its size, the typefaces, the amount of text, the relative size and position of each element—conveys a message to its reader. If the document's intended message was not a factor in your design decisions, then your finished product will probably send the wrong message. Before starting a project, ask yourself these questions:

- Who is the intended audience?
- What is the basic message I'm trying to communicate?
- In what format will readers encounter my message?
- What similar messages have my readers encountered from other sources or competitors?
- How does this publication relate to my other publications?

The more clearly you define your project's purpose and environment, the stronger your design will be.

Planning And Experimenting

Turn off your computer during the initial planning stage.

Design solutions are rarely the result of a sudden creative flash, like a light bulb appearing over a cartoon character's head. Successful graphic design usually emerges from trial and error. Solutions are the result of a willingness to try various design options until one looks right.

Although desktop publishing lets you produce graphics on your computer, it's best to sketch initial ideas and trial layouts with pencil and paper. The most powerful computer system won't teach you how to make effective design decisions.

Why Not Plan On The Computer?

You may be thinking to yourself: Why should I bother drawing squiggly lines to represent text and happy faces for photos when I've got the *real* text and photos just waiting to be laid out on my computer? A fair question, but take it from someone who's been there—it's a bad idea. Planning on the computer is counter intuitive. There's a tendency to allot space to page elements based on their original sizes. You'll find yourself doing a lot of repositioning and not enough resizing. Also, it's much slower. You can create five hand-drawn sketches for a newsletter nameplate in the time it takes to create one draft on the computer. The computer nameplate might look a little better in the end, but the extra detail is unnecessary. At this point, you're only trying to determine if the basic idea is good. Most ideas from the initial brainstorming session get pitched anyway, so it's unwise to spend a long time on each one. In the worst case scenario, you might find yourself adopting a bad idea in order to justify the time spent on it.

Try out a variety of ideas. When you finish one sketch, begin another. Let speed become a stimulant. Don't bother with excessive detail—use thin lines for text, thick lines or block lettering for headlines, and happy faces for art or photographs. Even simple representations such as these will give you a sense of which arrangements work, and which don't.

Seek Inspiration

Train yourself to analyze the work of others.

Sensitize yourself to examples of effective and ineffective design. If a certain restaurant's menu catches your eye, take a moment to determine why it appeals to you. If you see an advertisement in the newspaper that seems confusing or cluttered, dissect it, and identify why it doesn't work.

Clip File

Most experienced graphic artists maintain a clip file containing samples they like.

Keep copies of documents that strike you as attractive or eye-catching. Always be on the lookout for new additions, even if they have no bearing on your current project.

When you get stuck on a project, spend a few moments reviewing your favorite designs on file. Chances are, they'll serve as catalysts for your design decisions.

If your projects will be printed in two-, three-, or four-color, you may want to collect samples of color projects that you feel are particularly effective.

Look Beyond Desktop Publishing

It's easy to forget that desktop publishing software is only a tool for implementing your designs. All too often, desktop publishers will unconsciously bend their designs to fit the built-in features of their favorite software. Don't fall into this trap. Keep the creative process separate. There's always a way to implement a great idea.

To focus on design without the technological trappings, skim professional design publications that showcase elegant design examples. Try joining a local advertising group, art directors club, or communications forum. It doesn't matter if you're not involved in the advertising or public relations fields. Desktop publishers share a common goal of informing, motivating, and persuading others. You're likely to return from these meetings with a fresh perspective on your communication and design efforts.

Design Concepts

There are certain qualities that every printed document should have, regardless of its form or purpose. Think of this list as a safety check, similar to a car inspection. If your document falls flat in any category, it's probably a good idea to go back to the repair shop:

- Relevance
- Proportion
- Direction
- Consistency
- Contrast
- The "total picture"
- Restraint
- Attention to detail

Relevance

Each graphic element should fulfill a specific function.

In music, there's nothing right or wrong about notes such as middle C or B-flat. Similarly, there are no good or bad design elements—only appropriate or inappropriate ones.

Successful graphic design is relevant. Design choices convey a message. It's your job to ensure that the message is appropriate for its intended audience.

A letterhead for a prestigious law firm should be easily distinguishable from a letterhead for a music studio.

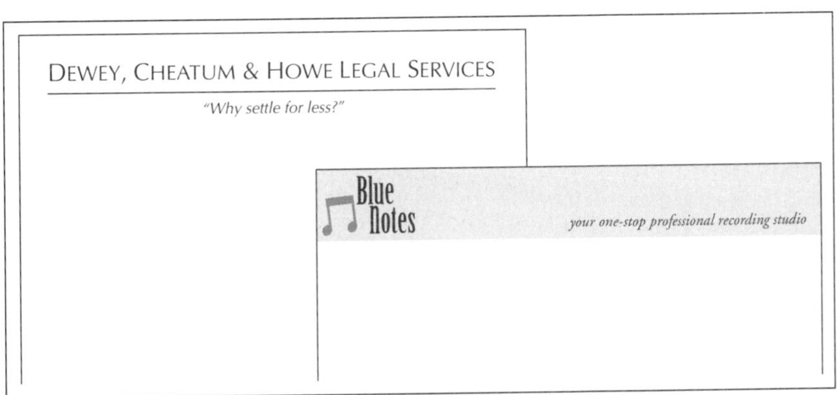

The conservative design used in a financial newsletter would not be appropriate in a gardening newsletter.

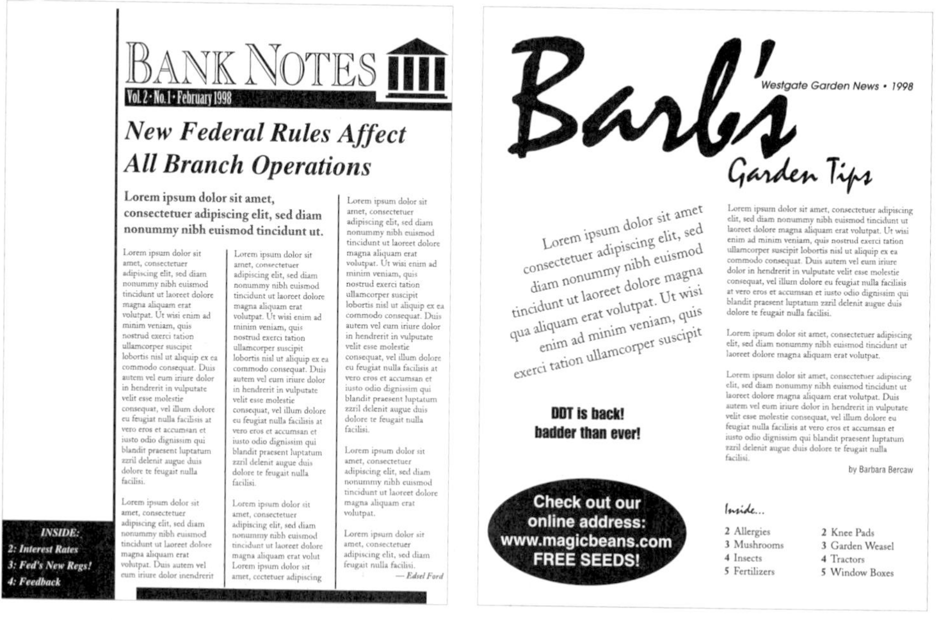

An image-building magazine ad requires a different design approach than a price-based newspaper ad.

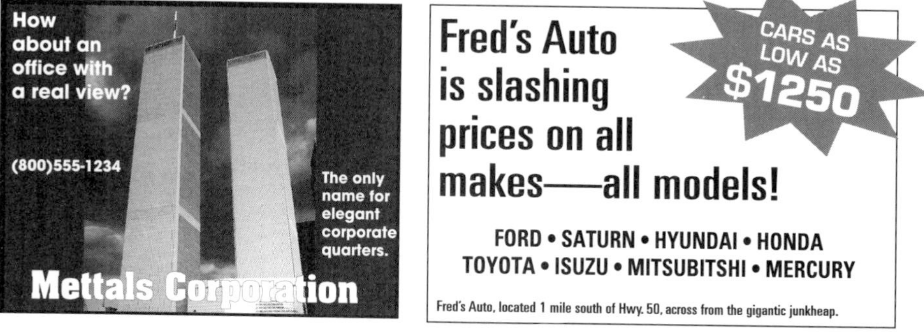

Each design element should be judged on its ability to help the reader understand your message. Don't be afraid to nix an attractive-looking graphic that doesn't really fit into your publication. The world is full of gorgeous graphics that don't belong in your publication. Similarly, don't let your desktop publishing system's capabilities get in the way of clear communication. The ability to create a gradient fill instantly is not a good reason to use a gradient fill. The availability of a decorative typeface doesn't make it appropriate for your task. You shouldn't be asking yourself what you *can* do—the answer to that question doesn't change from project to project. Instead, ask yourself what you *should* do.

Quite often, the correct design solution will be very simple, utilizing few or none of your software's bells and whistles. Clarity, organization, and simplicity are as critical to design as they are to writing.

Proportion

The size of a graphic element should be determined by its relative importance and its environment.

Because there are no absolutes in graphic design, success is determined by how well each piece of the puzzle relates to the pieces around it.

For example, the proper size for a headline is determined partly by its importance and partly by the amount of space that separates it from adjacent borders, text, and artwork. A large headline in a small space looks cramped.

Mighty Big Headline

Lorem ipsum dolor sit amet, adipiscing elit, sed diam nonummy nibh euismod tincidunt ut laoreet dolore magna aliquam erat volutpat. Ut wisi enim ad minim veniam, quis nostrud exerci tation ullamcorper suscipit lobortis nisl ut aliquip ex ea commodo consequat.

Duis autem vel eum iriure dolor in hendrerit in vulputate velit esse molestie consequat, vel illum ut wisi enim ad minim veniam, quis nostrud exerci tation ullamcorper suscipit lobortis nisl ut aliquip ex ea commodo consequat. Duis autem vel eum iriure dolor in hendrerit in vulputate velit esse molestie consequat, vel illum dolore eu feugiat nulla facilisis at vero eros et accumsan et iusto odio dignissim qui blandit praesent luptatum zzril delenit augue duis dolore te feugait nulla facilisi.

Likewise, a small headline in a large space looks lost.

Awfully Small Headline

Lorem ipsum dolor sit amet, adipiscing elit, sed diam nonummy nibh euismod tincidunt ut laoreet dolore magna aliquam erat volutpat. Ut wisi enim ad minim veniam, quis nostrud exerci tation ullamcorper suscipit lobortis nisl ut aliquip ex ea commodo consequat.

Duis autem vel eum iriure dolor in hendrerit in vulputate velit esse molestie consequat, vel illum ut wisi enim ad minim veniam, quis nostrud exerci tation ullamcorper suscipit lobortis nisl ut aliquip ex ea commodo consequat. Duis autem vel eum iriure dolor in hendrerit in vulputate velit esse molestie consequat, vel illum dolore eu feugiat nulla facilisis at vero eros et accumsan et iusto odio dignissim qui blandit praesent luptatum zzril delenit augue duis dolore te feugait nulla facilisi.

The proper thickness of lines—*rules*, in desktop publisher lingo—is determined by the size of the type and the surrounding white space. Rules that are too thick can interfere with legibility.

Who's important here?

Rules that are too thin can lack effectiveness.

FREE TICKETS

Also, consider proportion when working with groups of photographs or illustrations on a page. When one photograph is larger, the reader perceives it as being more important. Crop or resize your photos so that their sizes reflect their relative importance.

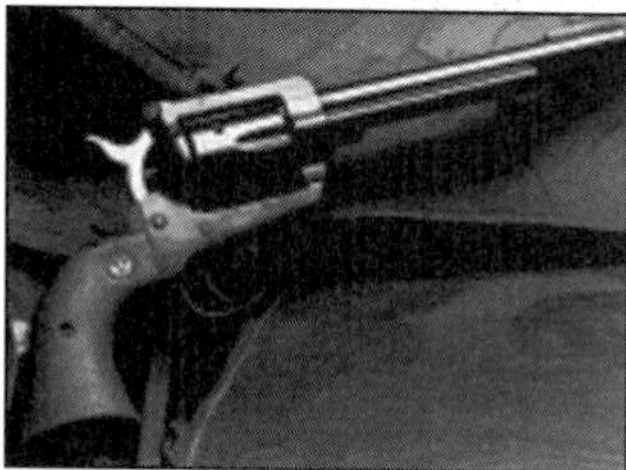

Type size and the distance between lines should relate to the column widths that organize the type. As you'll see later, wide columns are generally preferable for large type, and narrow columns are appropriate for small type.

Direction

Effective graphic design guides the reader through your publication.

Readers should encounter a logical sequence of events as they read through your publication. Graphic design is the road map that steers them from point to point.

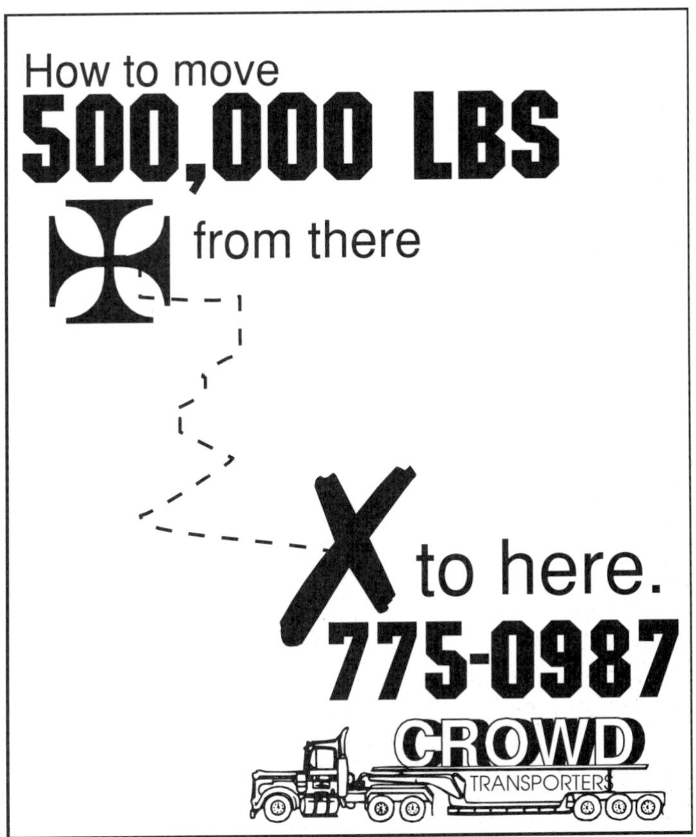

The design of that map generally follows the readers' natural tendency to read from upper left to lower right.

Consistency

Consistency leads to an integrated style.

Style reflects the way you handle elements that come up again and again. Part of a document's style is decided from the beginning. The rest emerges as the document develops visually.

Consistency is a matter of detail. It involves using restraint in choosing typefaces and type sizes, and using the same spacing throughout your document.

Your publications need to be consistent within themselves and with your organization's other print communications. If you use one-inch margins in the first chapter of a book, you need to use one-inch margins in all chapters.

You can provide page-to-page consistency in any of the following ways:

- Consistent top, bottom, and side margins.

- Consistent typeface, type size, and spacing specifications for text, headlines, subheads, and captions.
- Uniform paragraph indents and spaces between columns and around photographs.
- Repeating graphic elements, such as vertical lines, columns, or borders on each page.

For example, you can create an "artificial horizon" by repeating a strong line or graphic on each page in your publication.

TUT'S TOMB DECOR

SIDDOWN

Lorem ipsum dolor sit amet, consectetuer adipiscing elit, sed diam nonummy nibh euismod tincidunt ut laoreet dolore magna aliquam erat volutpat. Ut wisi enim ad minim veniam, quis nostrud exerci tation ullamcorper suscipit lobortis nisl ut aliquip ex ea commodo consequat. Duis autem vel eum iriure dolor in hendrerit in vulputate velit esse molestie consequat, vel illum dolore eu feugiat nulla facilisis at vero eros et accumsan et iusto odio dignissim qui blandit praesent luptatum zzril delenit augue duis dolore te feugait nulla facilisi. Lorem ipsum dolor sit amet, consec tetuer adipiscing elit, diam nonummy nibh euismod tincidunt ut laoreet dolore magna aliquam erat volutpat. Utwisi enim ad minim veniam, quis nostrud exerci tation ullamcorper suscipit

BIG BIRD

Ut wisi enim ad minim veniam, quis nostrud exerci tation ullamcorper suscipit lobortis nisl ut aliquip ex ea commodo consequat. Duis autem vel eum iriure dolor in hendrerit in vulputate velit esse molestie consequat, vel illum dolore eu feugiat nulla facilisis at vero eros et accumsan et iusto odio dignissim qui blandit praesent luptatum zzril delenit augue duis dolore te feugait nulla facilisi. Nam liber tempor cum soluta nobis eleifend option congue nihil imperdiet doming id quod mazim placerat facer possim assum. Lorem ipsum dolor sit amet, consectetuer adipiscing elit, sed diam nonummy nibh euismod tincidunt ut laoreet dolore magna aliquam erat volutpat.

FLOWERS

Lobortis nisl ut aliquip ex ea commodo duis autem vel eum iriure dolor in hendrerit in vulputate velit esse molestie consequat, vel illum dolore eu feugiat nulla facilisis, suscipit lobortis nisl ut aliquip ex ea commodo consequat. Duis autem vel eum iriure dolor in hendrerit in vulputate velit esse molestie consequat, vel illum dolore eu feugiat nulla facilisis at vero eros et accumsan et iusto odio dignissim qui blandit praesent luptatum zzril delenit augue duis dolore te feugait nulla facilisi. Nam liber tempor cum soluta nobis eleifend option congue nihil imperdiet doming id quod mazim placerat facer possim assum.

SQUIGGLIES

Lorem ipsum dolor sit amet, consectetuer adipiscing elit, sed diam nonummy nibh euismod tincidunt ut laoreet dolore magna aliquam erat volutpat. Ut wisi enim ad minim veniam, quis nostrud exerci tation ullamcorper suscipit. ea commodo consequat. Duis autem vel eum iriure dolor in hendrerit in vulputate velit esse molestie consequat, vel illum dolore eu feugiat nulla facilisis at vero eros et accumsan et iusto odio dignissim facilisis at vero eros et accumsan et iusto odio dignissim qui blandit praesent luptatum zzril delenit augue duis dolore te feugait nulla facilisi facer possim assum facilisis at vero eros et accumsan et iusto odio dignissim qui blandit praesent luptatum zzril delenit augue duis dolore te feugait nulla facilisi.

CLICKER

Odio dignissim blandit praesent luptatum zzril delenit augue duis bortis nisl ut aliquip commodo duis autem vel eum iriure dolor in hendrerit in vulputate velit esse molestie consequat, vel illum dolore eu feugiat nulla facilisis, suscipit lobortis nisl ut aliquip ex ea commodo consequat. Duis autem vel eum iriure dolor in hendrerit in vulputate velit esse molestie consequat, vel illum dolore eu feugiat nulla facilisis at vero eros et accumsan et iusto odio dignissim qui blandit praesent luptatum zzril delenit augue duis dolore te feugait nulla facilisi. Nam liber tempor cum soluta nobis eleifend option congue nihil imperdiet doming id quod mazim placerat facer possim assum.

One of your biggest challenges as a designer is to reconcile the continuing conflict between consistency and variety. Your goal is to create documents that remain consistent without becoming boring. Boredom occurs when predictability and symmetry dominate a document.

Contrast

Contrast provides dynamic interest.

Contrast gives "color" to your publication by balancing the space devoted to text, artwork, and white space. When analyzing an attractive publication, compare dark areas—such as large, bold headlines, dark photographs, or blocks of text—and notice how they're offset by lighter areas with less type.

High-impact publications tend to have a lot of contrast. Each page or two-page spread has definite light and dark areas, with lots of white space and illustrations.

Printed by the Society for Political Correctness

September 1998

In Session & In Trouble

Lorem ipsum dolor sit amet, consectetuer adipiscing elit, sed diam nonummy nibh euismod tincidunt ut laoreet dolore magna aliquam erat volutpat. Ut wisi enim ad minim veniam, quis nostrud exerci tation ullamcorper suscipit lobortis nisl ut aliquip ex ea commodo consequat.

Duis autem vel eum iriure dolor in hendrerit in vulputate velit esse molestie consequat, vel illum dolore eu feugiat nulla facilisis at vero eros et accumsan et iusto odio dignissim qui blandit praesent luptatum zzril delenit augue duis dolore te feugait nulla facilisi. Lorem ipsum sit amet,

consectetuer adipiscing elit, diam nibh euismod tincidunt ut laoreet dolore magna autem vel iriure dolor in hendrerit in vulputate dolore eu feugiat nulla facilisis at vero.

Republicans on the Move

Ut wisi enim ad minim veniam, quis nostrud exercitation ullam corper suscipit lobortis nisl ut aliquip commodo conseq. Duis autem vel eum dolor in hendrerit in vulputate velit esse molestie consequat, vel illum dolore eu feugiat nulla facilisis at vero eros et accumsan et odio dignissim qui blandit praesent luptatum zzril delenit augue duis dolore te feugait nulla facilisi option congue nihil imperdiet.

Duis autem vel eum iriure dolor in hendrerit in vulputate velit esse molestie consequat, vel illum dolore eu feugiat nulla facilisis at vero eros et accumsan et iusto odio dignissim qui blandit praesent luptatum zzril delenit augue duis dolore te feugait nulla facilisi. Lorem ipsum sit amet, consectetuer adipiscing elit, diam nonummy nibh euismod tincidunt ut laoreet dolore magna.Lorem dolor sit amet, consectetuer adipiscing, sedl diam nonummy euismod tincidunt ut laoreet dolore magna aliquam erat volutpat. Ut wisi enim minim veniam,

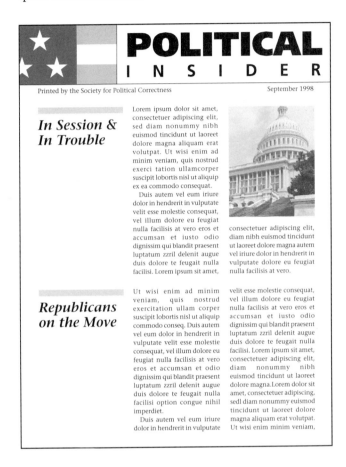

Text-rich documents tend to be rather low in contrast—every page is a uniform shade of gray. This low-impact approach is appropriate for publications such as formal reports, policy statements, and press releases.

A good way to observe contrast is to turn the publication upside down. Viewed from that perspective, your eyes aren't misled by the tendency to read individual words. Instead, you concentrate on the overall color of the publication.

Contrasting sizes can create visual tension, which helps keep the reader interested. For example, you might have a headline set in a large size above a subhead set in the same typeface at a much smaller size.

CHAPTER EIGHT

❧

The Plot Thickens

Lorem ipsum dolor sit amet, adipiscing elit, sed diam nonummy nibh euismod tincidunt ut laoreet dolore magna aliquam erat volutpat. Ut wisi enim ad minim veniam, quis nostrud exerci tation ullamcorper suscipit lobortis nisl ut aliquip ex ea commodo consequat.

Duis autem vel eum iriure dolor in hendrerit in vulputate velit esse molestie consequat, vel illum dolore eu feugiat nulla facilisis at vero eros et accumsan et iusto odio dignissim qui blandit praesent luptatum zzril delenit augue duis dolore te feugait nulla facilisi. Lorem ipsum dum dolor sit amet, consectetuer adipiscing elit, sed diam nonummy nibh euismod tincidunt ut laoreet dolore magna aliquam ut wisi enim ad minim veniam, quis nostrud exerci tation ullamcorper suscipit lobortis nisl ut aliquip ex ea commodo consequat. Duis autem vel eum iriure dolor in hendrerit in vulputate velit esse molestie consequat, vel illum dolore eu feugiat nulla facilisis at vero eros et accumsan et iusto odio dignissim qui blandit praesent luptatum zzril delenit augue duis dolore te feugait nulla facilisi.

Nam liber tempor cum soluta nobis eleifend option congue nihil imperdiet doming id quod mazim placerat facer possim assum. Lorem ipsum dolor sit amet, consectetuer adipiscing elit, sed diam nonummy nibh euismod tincidunt ut laoreet dolore magna aliquam erat volutpat. Ut wisi enim ad minim. Lorem ipsum dolor sit amet, adipiscing elit, sed diam nonummy nibh euismod tincidunt ut laoreet dolore magna aliquam erat volutpat. Ut wisi enim ad minim veniam, quis nostrud exerci tation ullamcorper suscipit lobortis nisl ut aliquip ex ea commodo consequat.

Duis autem vel eum iriure dolor in hendrerit in vulputate velit esse molestie consequat, vel illum dolore eu feugiat nulla facilisis at vero eros et accumsan et iusto odio dignissim qui blandit praesent luptatum zzril delenit augue duis dolore te feugait nulla facilisi. Lorem ipsum dum dolor sit amet, consectetuer adipiscing elit, sed diam nonummy nibh euismod tincidunt ut laoreet dolore magna aliquam ut wisi enim ad minim veniam,

Lorem ipsum dolor sit amet, adipiscing elit, sed diam nonummy nibh euismod tincidunt ut laoreet dolore magna aliquam erat volutpat. Ut wisi enim ad minim veniam, quis nostrud exerci tation ullamcorper suscipit lobortis nisl ut aliquip ex ea commodo consequat.

VISUAL TENSION

THE CAUSE AND THE CURE

Duis autem vel eum iriure dolor in hendrerit in vulputate velit esse molestie consequat, vel illum dolore eu feugiat nulla facilisis at vero eros et accumsan et iusto odio dignissim qui blandit praesent luptatum zzril delenit augue duis dolore te

Effective graphic design is based on balancing contrast and consistency. Your designs must be dynamic enough to keep the reader interested, yet consistent enough so that your publication emerges with a strong identity.

The Total Picture

Think of graphic design as the visual equivalent of a jigsaw puzzle.

Your job is to assemble a total picture from a series of parts. No piece of the puzzle should be isolated from the others. The various parts need to fit together harmoniously.

The "total picture" includes consideration of the environment in which your advertisement or publication will be distributed. For example, when designing a newspaper advertisement, consider how it will look when surrounded by news items and other ads. When planning a newsletter or direct-mail piece, imagine how it will look when it arrives in the recipient's mailbox. When creating product literature, visualize it displayed in a brochure rack.

Inside a publication, the most important part of the total picture is the two-page spread. When designing multipage publications such as newsletters, brochures, or books, focus on two-page spreads instead of individual pages. If you design each page as a self-contained entity, you might end up creating two pages that look good individually but don't work side by side.

This left-hand page is visually attractive and self-contained.

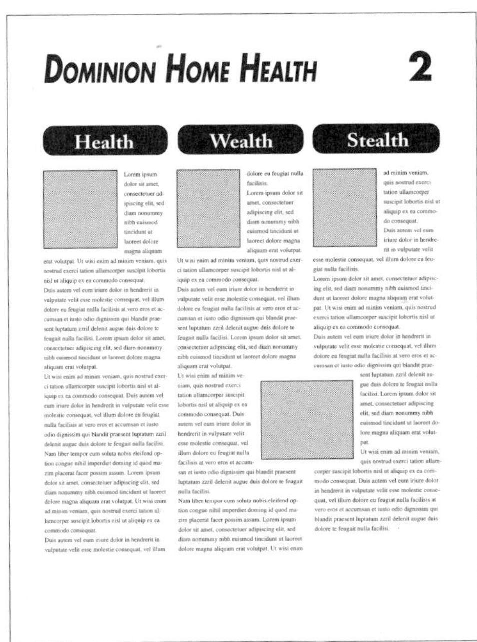

This right-hand page also works well on its own.

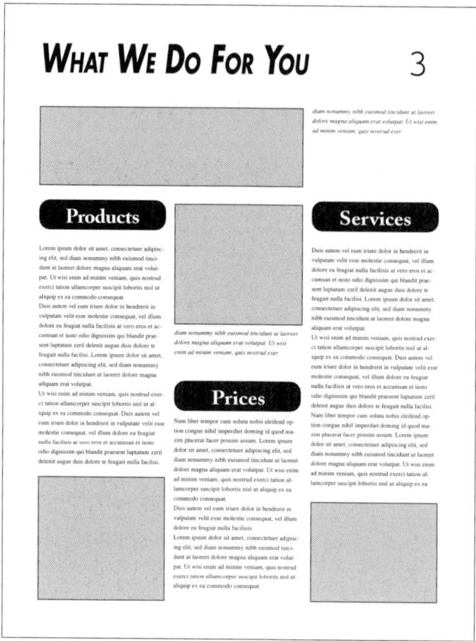

When viewed side by side, however, they fight each other and present a disorganized, difficult-to-read image.

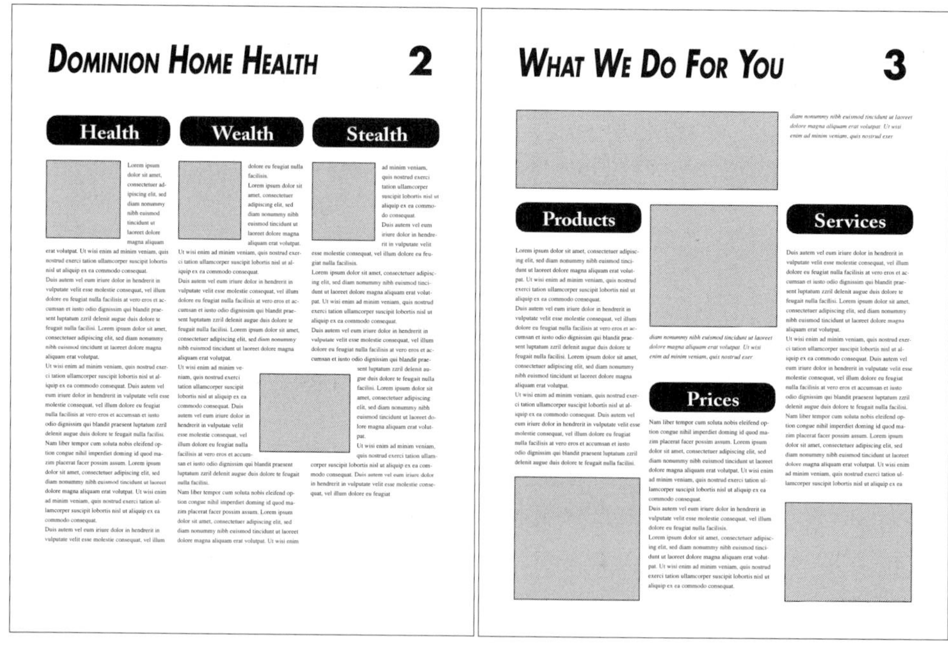

Remember that readers see left- and right-hand pages together as one large piece.

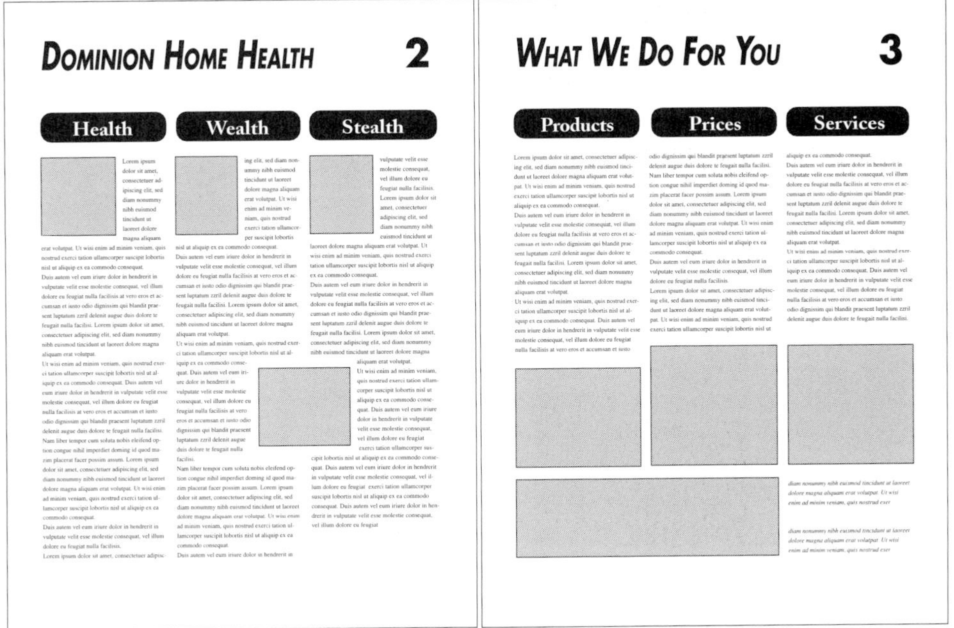

Restraint

Strive for simplicity in design.

Restraint is probably the most difficult design principle to apply in a consistent manner. That's because desktop publishing presents you with tremendous design power—power which used to be limited to those who had years of training and thousands of dollars worth of equipment.

With so much power at your fingertips, it's easy to forget that straightforwardness is a virtue and graphic design should be invisible to the reader. Overuse of graphic gimmickry results in a cluttered look.

Restraint is exemplified by sticking to a few carefully chosen typefaces, styles, and sizes.

Remember that emphasis can be effective only within a stable framework. If every item on the page is clamoring for the reader's attention, the result will be that nothing really stands out. Excessive use of emphasis weakens your publication to the point of losing all impact.

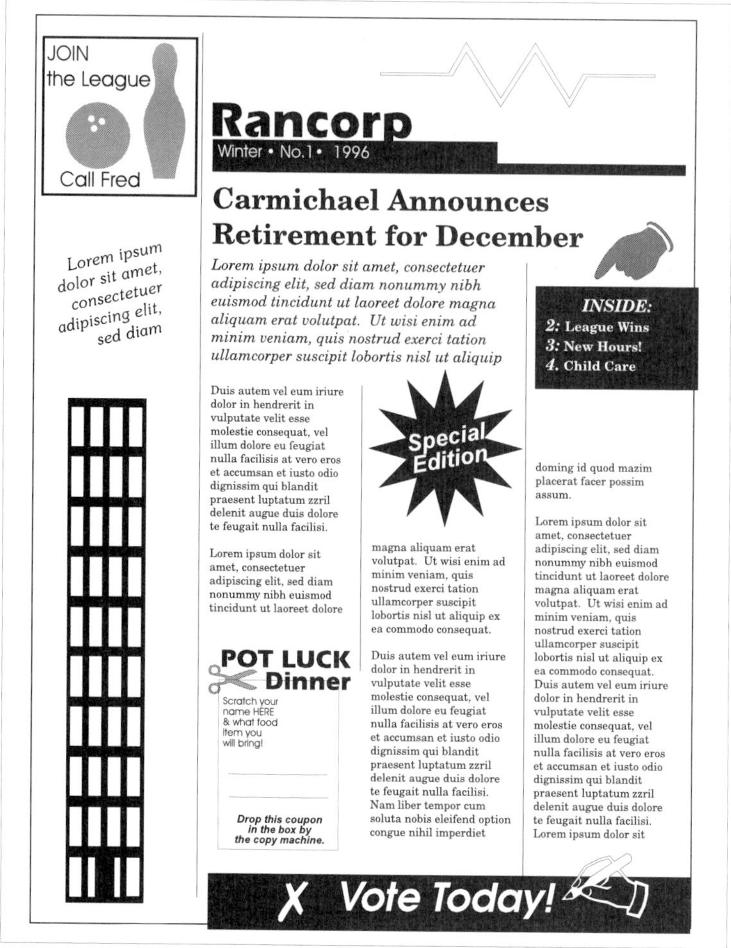

JOIN
the League
Call Fred

Lorem ipsum dolor sit amet, consectetuer adipiscing elit, sed diam

Rancorp
Winter • No.1• 1996

Carmichael Announces Retirement for December

Lorem ipsum dolor sit amet, consectetuer adipiscing elit, sed diam nonummy nibh euismod tincidunt ut laoreet dolore magna aliquam erat volutpat. Ut wisi enim ad minim veniam, quis nostrud exerci tation ullamcorper suscipit lobortis nisl ut aliquip

INSIDE:
2: League Wins
3: New Hours!
4. Child Care

Duis autem vel eum iriure dolor in hendrerit in vulputate velit esse molestie consequat, vel illum dolore eu feugiat nulla facilisis at vero eros et accumsan et iusto odio dignissim qui blandit praesent luptatum zzril delenit augue duis dolore te feugait nulla facilisi.

Lorem ipsum dolor sit amet, consectetuer adipiscing elit, sed diam nonummy nibh euismod tincidunt ut laoreet dolore

Special Edition

magna aliquam erat volutpat. Ut wisi enim ad minim veniam, quis nostrud exerci tation ullamcorper suscipit lobortis nisl ut aliquip ex ea commodo consequat.

Duis autem vel eum iriure dolor in hendrerit in vulputate velit esse molestie consequat, vel illum dolore eu feugiat nulla facilisis at vero eros et accumsan et iusto odio dignissim qui blandit praesent luptatum zzril delenit augue duis dolore te feugait nulla facilisi. Nam liber tempor cum soluta nobis eleifend option congue nihil imperdiet

doming id quod mazim placerat facer possim assum.

Lorem ipsum dolor sit amet, consectetuer adipiscing elit, sed diam nonummy nibh euismod tincidunt ut laoreet dolore magna aliquam erat volutpat. Ut wisi enim ad minim veniam, quis nostrud exerci tation ullamcorper suscipit lobortis nisl ut aliquip ex ea commodo consequat. Duis autem vel eum iriure dolor in hendrerit in vulputate velit esse molestie consequat, vel illum dolore eu feugiat nulla facilisis at vero eros et accumsan et iusto odio dignissim qui blandit praesent luptatum zzril delenit augue duis dolore te feugait nulla facilisi. Lorem ipsum dolor sit

POT LUCK Dinner
Scratch your name HERE & what food item you will bring!

Drop this coupon in the box by the copy machine.

X Vote Today!

Attention To Detail

Successful design is based on attention to detail.

The old maxim holds true: The devil is in the details. The smallest offending detail can sabotage the appearance of an otherwise attractive project.

Double-spacing after periods, for example, can create annoying rivers of white space in a text block. This can also be true of columns of text with full justification—that is, columns in which all lines are the same length. Some lines can get very sparse, creating huge gaps between words. The reader's eyes end up following the gaps instead of the text.

Headlines and subheads placed at the bottom of columns or pages set the readers up for disappointment, because the promised topic doesn't appear until the start of the next column or page.

Rivers of white space...

Lorem ipsum dolor sit amet, consectetuer adipis cing elit, sed diam nonum nibh euismod tinc idunt laoreet ut dolore magna aliquam erat volutpat. Ut wisi enim minim veniam, quis nostrud exerci tation ullamcorper suscipit lob ortis nisl ut aliquip ex ea commodo consequat.

Duis autem vel eum iriure dolor in hendrerit vulputate velit esse molestie conseq vel illum dolore eu feugiat nulla facilisis at vero eros et accumsan et iusto odio dignissim qui blandit praesent luptatum zzril delenit augue duisdolore feugait nulla facilisi. Lor ipsum dolor sit amet, conse ctetuer adipiselit, sed diam nonum mynibh euism tincidunt ut laoreet dolore magna aliquam erat volutpat.

Ut wisi enim ad minim veniam, quis nostrud exerci tation ullam corper susci pit lobortis nisl ut aliquip ex ea commodo conse quat. Duis autem vel eum iriure dolor hendrerit in vulputate velit es molestie consequat, vel illum dolore eu feugiat nulla facilisis at vero amet.

Eros et accumsan et iusto odio dignissim qui blandit praesent luptatum zzril delenit augue duis dolore te feugait nulla facilisi.

Nam liber tempor cum soluta nobis eleifend option congue nihil imperdiet doming id quod mazim placerat facer possim assum. Lorem ipsum dolor sit amet, consectetuer adipiscing elit, sed diam nonummy nibh euismod tincidunt laoreet dolore magna aliquam erat volutpat. Ut wisi enim ad minim veniam, quis nostrud exerci tation ullamcorper suscipit lobortis nisl ut aliquip ex ea com modo consequat.

Duis autem vel eum iriure dolor in hendrerit in vulp utate velit molestie con sequat, vel illum dolore eu feugiat nulla facilisis.

Ut wisi enim ad minim veniam, quis nostrud exerci tation ullamcorper suscipit

Pay Attention to Detail

Lorem ipsum dolor sit amet, adipiscing elit, sed diam nonummy nibh euismod tincidunt ut laoreet dolore magna aliquam erat volutpat. Ut wisi enim ad minim veniam, quis nostrud exerci tation ullamcorper suscipit lobortis nisl ut aliquip ex ea commodo consequat.

Duis autem vel eum iriure dolor in hendrerit in vulputate velit esse molestie consequat, vel illum dolore eu feugiat nulla facilisis at vero eros et accumsan et iusto odio dignissim qui blandit praesent luptatum zzril delenit augue duis dolore te feugait nulla facilisi. Lorem ipsum dum dolor sit amet, consectetuer adipiscing elit, sed diam nonummy nibh euismod tincidunt ut laoreet dolore magna aliquam ut wisi enim ad minim veniam, quis nostrud exerci tation ullamcorper suscipit lobortis nisl ut aliquip ex ea commodo consequat. Duis autem vel eum iriure dolor in hendrerit in vulputate velit esse molestie consequat, vel illum dolore eu feugiat nulla facilisis at vero eros et accumsan et iusto odio dignissim qui blandit praesent luptatum zzril delenit augue duis dolore te feugait nulla facilisi.

Nam liber tempor cum soluta nobis eleifend option congue nihil imperdiet doming id quod mazim placerat facer possim assum. Lorem ipsum dolor sit amet, consectetuer adipiscing elit, sed diam nonummy nibh euismod tincidunt ut laoreet dolore magna aliquam erat volutpat. Ut wisi enim ad minim. Lorem ipsum dolor sit amet, adipiscing elit, sed diam nonummy nibh euismod tincidunt ut laoreet dolore magna aliquam erat volutpat. Ut wisi enim ad minim veniam, quis nostrud exerci tation ullamcorper suscipit lobortis.

Not Good!

Duis autem vel eum iriure dolor in hendrerit in vulputate velit esse molestie consequat, vel illum

Text placed in boxes should be indented on both sides. Otherwise, it may bump into the borders of the boxes.

Lorem ipsum dolor sit amet, adipiscing elit, sed diam nonummy nibh euismod tincidunt ut laoreet dolore magna aliquam erat volutpat. Ut wisi enim ad minim veniam, quis nostrud exerci tation ullamcorper suscipit lobortis nisl ut aliquip ex ea commodo consequat.

Duis autem vel eum iriure dolor in hendrerit in vulputate velit esse molestie consequat, vel illum dolore eu feugiat nulla facilisis at vero eros et accumsan et iusto odio dignissim qui blandit praesent luptatum zzril delenit augue duis dolore te feugait nulla facilisi.

Lorem ipsum dum dolor sit amet, consectetuer adipiscing elit, sed diam nonummy nibh euismod tincidunt ut laoreet dolore magna aliquam ut wisi enim ad minim veniam, quis nostrud exerci tation ullamcorper suscipit lobortis nisl ut aliquip ex ea commodo consequat.

Editorial tasks such as proofreading also require a lot of attention to detail. Correctly spelled yet misused words can sneak by spell-checking programs, which can't differentiate spelling from usage.

The inns and outs of hotel management.

Have several people proofread your document before you send it to press. Although most printers supply their clients with *galleys* (mock-ups of the finished product, suitable for making last-minute corrections), you shouldn't expect to make major changes to galley prints. Galleys are designed to flag printer-related problems, like spots and scratches on the film or overly-dark photos. Editorial errors should be weeded out long before the galley stage.

Examining Proofs

Analyze reduced-size copies of your pages.

Most desktop publishing programs let you print out *thumbnail proofs*—smaller copies of your pages arranged so that multiple pages fit on a single sheet of paper. Facing pages are typically printed side by side, so you can preview the spreads.

Thumbnail proofs let you see where good design has been sacrificed for expediency. Overuse of symmetry or contrast also becomes obvious.

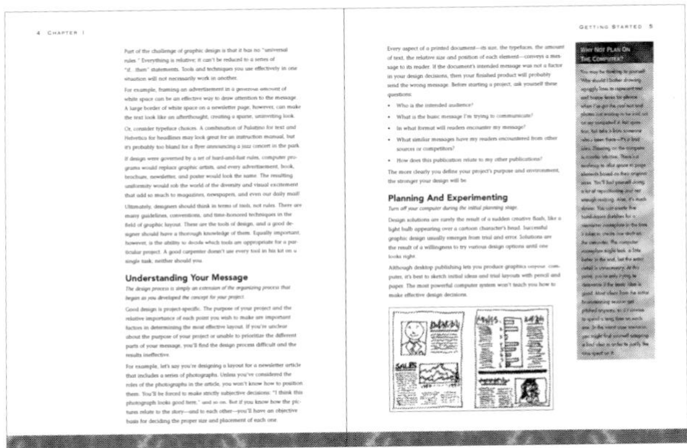

Understanding Your Message

Planning And Experimenting

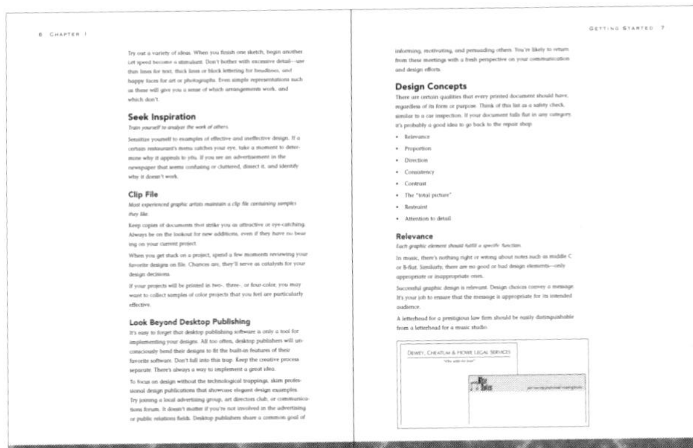

Seek Inspiration

Clip File

Look Beyond Desktop Publishing

Design Concepts

Relevance

Moving On

All of these lofty design concepts probably seem like a lot to remember, but don't panic. If you keep the purpose of your project firmly in mind while developing the design, you'll find that most of these concerns take care of themselves. Still, it's a good idea to run the drafts of your designs through the concept checklist, to see if any particular qualities are lacking.

The next chapter explores the organizational tools you'll use in creating your published projects.

2 Tools Of Organization

Once you've prepared a few pencil-and-paper sketches of the basic layout, it's tempting to leap in with both feet. Bring on the text and graphics! Hey, you can tweak the margins later, right?

Well, I suppose you *can*, but it's certainly not the easiest way. A little organization at this point will save you hours of work later on. It's like a 10-minute warmup prior to strenuous exercise; yes, it's a slight nuisance, but you're ultimately spared a lot of pain.

Why is organization so important? A well-organized document has several tangible benefits:

- *It's easier to produce.* Establishing a grid for your pages will help you determine workable sizes and placements for page elements. You'll have a logical basis for design decisions, rather than be forced to play arbitrary guessing games.
- *It's easier to edit.* Tagging your page elements with styles will make editing a snap. You say you want more space before those subheads? Italic type rather than bold for the captions? Using styles, these sorts of changes can be made in seconds, regardless of the length of your document. Without styles, you'll have to track down and tweak each individual case.
- *It's easier to read.* Organization steers the reader's eyes. It shows them what's of primary importance, and what's supplemental. Best of all, it shows them where to find the information they want. If you've ever spent an hour flipping through a poorly organized instruction manual, looking for some specific tidbit of information, you know how frustrating a lack of organization can be.

Your desktop publishing program is brimming with tools that will help you produce well-organized documents. Learn to use them. Your readers will thank you.

Page Organizers

Page organizing tools—grids, columns, gutters, and margins—define the usable space on a page and provide a framework for placing page elements. All desktop publishing software contains these tools, though the implementation will vary slightly from program to program.

Grids

Grids establish the overall structure of a page by specifying the placement of text, display type, and artwork.

Grids consist of nonprinted lines that show up on your computer screen but not on the finished publication. Grids determine the number of columns, margin size, placement of headlines, subheads, pull quotes, and other page elements.

They're valuable for a number of reasons. They set page-to-page or project-to-project consistency, and they help you avoid reinventing the wheel each time you create another ad or newsletter issue. Layout can be determined once and reused with only slight variations.

Desktop publishing programs differ in their ability to create grids. Some programs provide you with ready-made grids that you can modify.

Many programs use a series of horizontal and vertical lines that define columns and page margins.

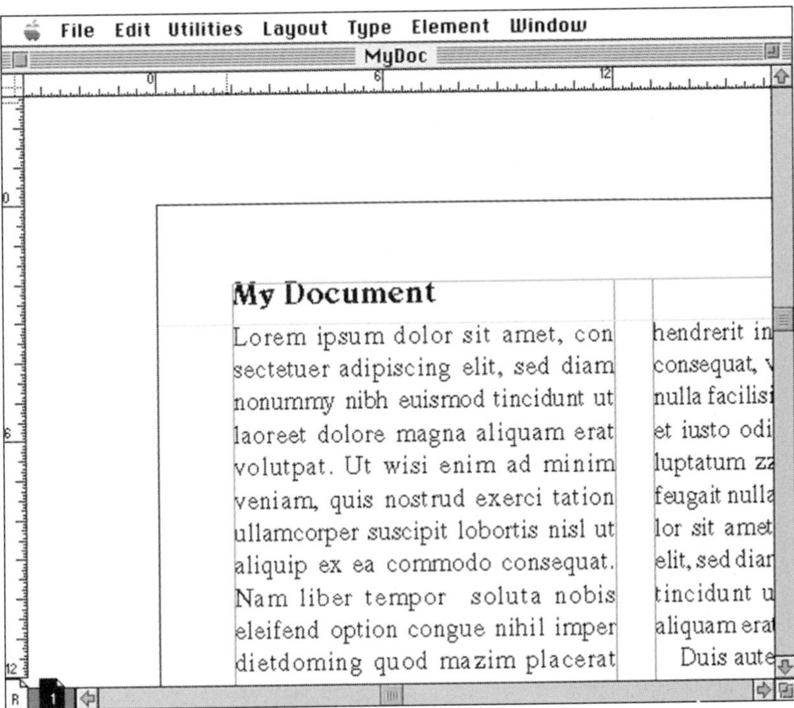

Other page-layout programs are based on setting text into boxes or frames.

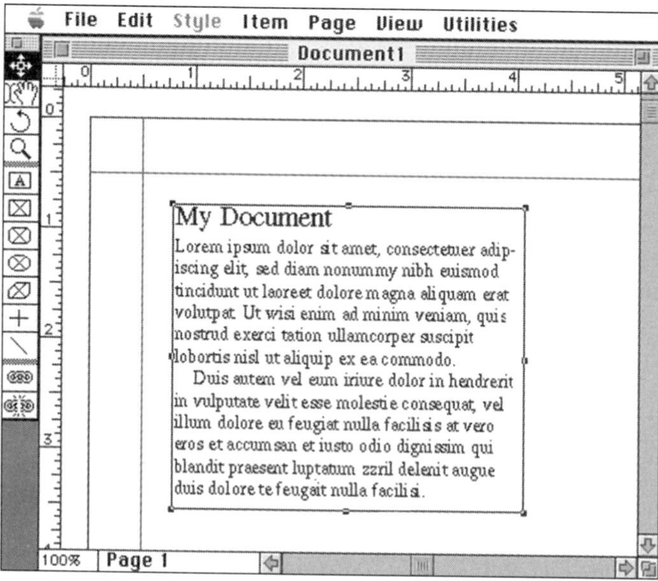

Many word processing programs also let you format pages by setting parameters that define column placement and margins, even though the column boundaries aren't always visible on screen.

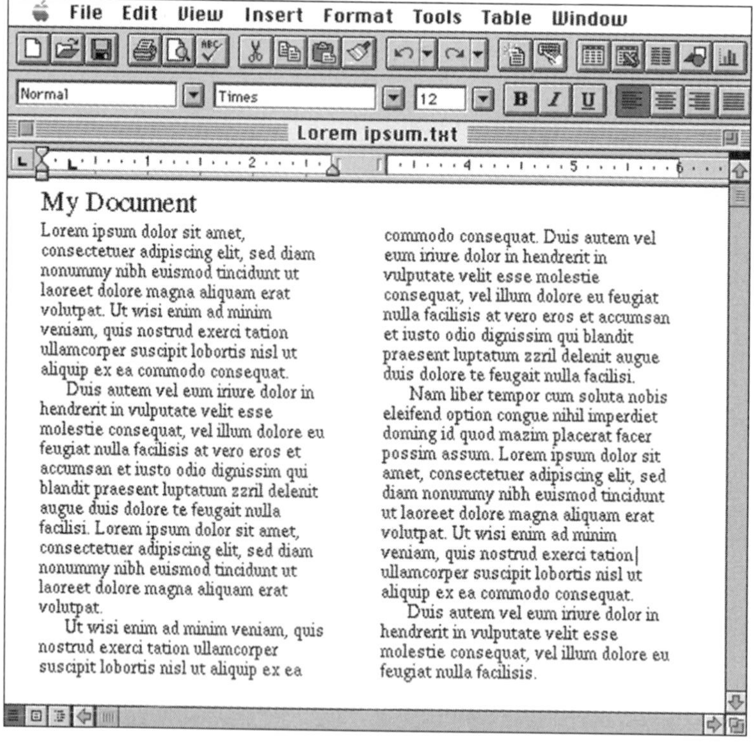

One way or another, all programs let you establish formats that are automatically maintained from page to page or throughout a series of documents. The virtue of consistency becomes relatively easy to achieve.

Text, photos, and illustrations can be sized and shaped to work within the invisible guidelines of a grid. You can position elements to fit within your structure by:

- Centering between two column guides.
- Justifying between two column guides.
- Applying flush right or left against a guideline.
- Aligning against a horizontal guideline at the top or bottom of a page.

A lot of guesswork is eliminated by using grids. For example, suppose you're trying to figure out the correct size and placement for a photo. If you're not using a grid, you'll probably come up with a pretty vague answer, "Upper-right part of the page, pretty big." If you're using a grid, the answer is much clearer, "The right edge of the photo will be socked up against the top-right page margin, and the left edge will be stretched to fit one of the central guidelines." You still have a choice to make—namely, which guideline?—but because there is a finite number of options, the decision will be much simpler.

The sense of order established by grids is also useful for emphasis. Page elements placed at angles that break the grid's neat confines will draw more attention than neatly aligned elements.

A Kinder, Gentler Nation

Lorem ipsum dolor sit amet, consectetuer adipiscing elit, sed diam nonummy nibh euismod tincidunt ut laoreet dolore magna aliquam erat volutpat. Ut wisi enim ad minim veniam, quis nostrud exerci tation ullamcorper suscipit lobortis nisl ut aliquip ex ea commodo consequat.

Duis autem vel eum iriure dolor in hendrerit in vulputate velit esse molestie consequat, vel illum dolore eu feugiat nulla facilisis at vero eros et accumsan et iusto odio dignissim qui blandit praesent luptatum zzril delenit augue duis dolore te feugait nulla facilisi. Lorem ipsum dolor sit amet, consectetuer adipiscing elit, sed diam nonummy nibh euismod tincidunt ut laoreet dolore magna aliquam erat volutpat.

Ut wisi enim ad minim veniam, quis nostrud exerci tation ullamcorper suscipit lobortis nisl ut aliquip ex ea commodo consequat. Duis autem vel eum iriure dolor in hendrerit in vulputate velit esse molestie consequat, vel illum dolore eu feugiat nulla facilisis at vero eros et accumsan et iusto odio dignissim qui blandit praesent luptatum zzril delenit augue duis dolore te feugait nulla facilisi et iusto.

Nam liber tempor cum soluta nobis eleifend option congue nihil imperdiet doming id quod mazim placerat facer possim assum. Lorem ipsum dolor sit amet, consectetuer adipiscing elit, sed diam nonummy nibh euismod tincidunt ut laoreet dolore magna aliquam erat volutpat. Ut wisi enim ad minim veniam, quis nostrud exerci tation ullamcorper suscipit lobortis nisl ut aliquip ex ea commodo consequat.

Duis autem vel eum iriure dolor in hendrerit in vulputate velit esse molestie consequat, vel illum dolore eu feugiat nulla facilisis. Ut wisi enim ad minim veniam, quis nostrud exerci tation ullamcorper suscipit lobortis.

Remember, though, it's the uniqueness of the unaligned element that gives it emphasis. A page full of unaligned elements doesn't emphasize anything—and besides, it looks messy.

Columns

Columns are fundamental parts of a grid—they organize text and visuals on a page.

Text and visuals rarely extend in an unbroken line from the left side of the page to the right. They're usually arranged in columns or vertical blocks. For most documents, column formats range from single-column to seven-column page layout. As the number of columns increases, so do the possibilities for creative layout.

There's not a lot of flexibility in a one-column format. Lorem ipsum dolor sit amet, con sectetuer adipiscing elit, sed diam nonummy nibh euismod tincidunt ut laoreet dolore magna aliquam erat volutpat. Ut wisi enim ad minim veniam, quis nostrud exerci tation ullamcorper suscipit lobortis nisl ut aliquip ex ea commodo consequat. Nam liber tempor soluta nobis eleifend option congue nihil imper dietdoming quod mazim placerat possim assum. Lorem ipsum dolor sit amet, consec tetuer elit, sed diam nonummy nibh euismod.

Duis autem vel eum dolor in hendrerit in vulputate velit molestie consequat, vel illum dolore eu feugiat nulla facilisis at vero eros et accumsan et iusto odio dignissim qui praesent luptatum zzril augue duis dolore te feugait nulla facilisi. Lorem ipsum dolor sit amet, consectetuer adipiscing elit, sed diam nonummy nibh euismod tincidunt ut laoreet dolore magna aliquam erat volutpat.

Cuismod tincidunt ut laoreet dolore magna aliquam erat volutpat. Ut wisi enim ad minim veniam, quis nostrud exerci tation ullamcorper suscipit lobortis nisl ut aliquip ex ea commodo conse. Nam liber tempor soluta nobis eleifend option congue nihil imper dietdoming quod mazim placerat possim assum. Lorem ipsum dolor sit amet, consec tetuer elit, sed diam nonummy nibh euismod tincidunt ut laor dolore magna aliquam erat volutpat. Ut wisi enim ad minim veniam, nostrud exerci tation ullamcorper suscipit lobortis nisl ut aliquip ex ea commodo consequat ex ea commodo. Duis autem vel eum dolor in hendrerit in vulputate velit molestie consequat, vel illum dolore eu feugiat nulla facilisis at vero eros et accumsan et iusto odio dignissim qui praesent luptatum zzril augue duis dolore te feugait nulla facilisi. Lorem ipsum dolor sit amet, consectetuer adipiscing elit, sed diam nonummy nibh euismod tincidunt ut laoreet dolore magna aliquam erat volutpat.

Duis autem vel eum iriure dolor in hendrerit in vulputate velit esse molestie consequat, vel illum dolore eu feugiat nulla facilisis. Nam liber tempor soluta nobis eleifend option congue nihil imper. Lorem ipsum dolor sit amet, con sectetuer adipiscing elit, sed diam nonummy nibh euismod tincidunt ut laoreet dolore magna aliquam erat volutpat. Ut wisi enim ad minim veniam, quis nostrud exerci tation ullamcorper suscipit lobortis nisl ut aliquip ex ea commodo consequat. ❧

As the number of columns on a page increases, the columns get narrower and the lines get shorter. Column width has a profound influence on a publication's readability. Because readers tend to scan groups of words, rather than individual letters, narrow columns can be difficult to read. The readers' eyes have to shift to the next line more often.

On the other hand, wider columns make it more difficult for a reader's eyes to make a smooth transition from the end of one line to the beginning of the next without getting lost.

Column width should be a factor in your choice of type size. Narrow columns work best with small type sizes, while wider columns usually require larger type sizes.

Put small text in small columns. Lorem ipsum dolor sit amet, consectetuer adipiscing elit, sed diam nonummy nibh euismod tincidunt ut laoreet dolore magna aliquam erat volutpat. Ut wisi enim ad minim veniam, quis nostrud exerci tation ullamcorper suscipit lobortis nisl ut aliquip.

Duis autem vel eum iriure dolor in hendrerit in vulputate velit esse molestie consequat, vel illum dolore eu feugiat nulla facilisis at vero eros et accumsan et iusto odio dignissim qui blandit praesent luptatum zzril delenit augue duis dolore te feugait nulla facilisi. Lorem ipsum dolor sit amet, consectetuer adipiscing elit, sed diam nonummy nibh euismod tincidunt ut laoreet dolore magna aliquam erat volutpat.

Ut wisi enim ad minim veniam, quis nostrud exerci tation ullamcorper suscipit lobortis nisl ut aliquip ex ea commodo consequat. Duis autem vel eum iriure dolor in hendrerit in vulputate velit esse molestie consequat, vel illum dolore eu feugiat nulla facilisis at vero eros et accumsan et iusto odio dignissim qui blandit praesent luptatum zzril delenit augue duis dolore te feugait nulla facilisi.

Nam liber tempor cum soluta nobis eleifend option congue nihil imperdiet doming id quod mazim placerat facer possim assum. Lorem ipsum dolor sit amet, consectetuer adipiscing elit, sed diam nonummy nibh euismod tincidunt ut laoreet dolore magna aliquam erat volutpat. Ut wisi enim ad minim veniam, quis nostrud exerci tation ullamcorper suscipit lobortis nisl ut aliquip ex ea commodo consequat.

Duis autem vel eum iriure dolor in hendrerit in vulputate velit esse molestie consequat, vel illum

Put large text in large columns. Lorem ipsum dolor sit amet, consectetuer adipiscing elit, sed diam nonummy nibh euismod tincidunt ut laoreet dolore magna aliquam erat volutpat. Ut wisi enim ad minim veniam, quis nostrud exerci tation ullamcorper suscipit lobortis nisl ut aliquip.

Duis autem vel eum iriure dolor in hendrerit in vulputate velit esse molestie consequat, vel illum dolore eu feugiat nulla facilisis at vero eros et accumsan et iusto odio dignissim qui blandit praesent luptatum zzril delenit augue duis dolore

The number of columns on the page doesn't have to be the same as the number of columns in your grid. Good-looking publications can be cre-ated by varying column widths based on an established multi-column grid.

For example, the five-column grid lends itself to a variety of arrangements.

An extremely popular technique is to leave one or two of the leftmost columns empty of text. Sidebars and illustrations can be placed in these empty columns, alongside the text they accompany.

Planning the Wedding

Lorem ipsum dolor sit amet, consectetuer adipiscing elit, sed diam nonummy nibh euismod tincidunt ut laoreet dolore magna aliquam erat volutpat. Ut wisi enim ad minim veniam, quis nostrud exerci tation ullamcorper suscipit lobortis nisl ut aliquip ex ea commodo consequat.

Duis autem vel eum iriure dolor in hendrerit in vulputate velit esse molestie consequat, vel illum dolore eu feugiat nulla feugait nulla facilisi. Lorem ipsum dolor sit amet, consectetuer adipiscing elit, sed diam nonummy nibh euismod tincidunt ut laoreet dolore magna aliquam erat volutpat.

Ut wisi enim ad minim veniam, quis nostrud exerci tation ullamcorper suscipit lobortis nisl ut aliquip ex ea commodo consequat. Duis autem vel eum iriure dolor in hendrerit in vulputate velit esse molestie consequat, vel illum dolo eu feugiat nulla facilisis at vero eros et accumsan et iusto odio dignissim qui blandit praesent luptatum zzril delenit augue duis dolore te feugait nulla facilisi.

Nam liber tempor cum soluta nobis eleifend option congue nihil imperdiet doming id quod mazim placerat facer possim assum. Lorem ipsum dolor sit amet, consectetuer adipiscing elit, sed diam nonummy.Duis autem vel eum iriure dolor in hendrerit in vulputate velit esse molestie consequat, vel illum dolore eu feugiat nulla facilisis.

Lorem ipsum dolor sit amet, consectetuer adipiscing elit, sed aliquam erat volutpat. Ut wisi enim ad minim veniam, nostrud exerci tation ullamcorper suscipit lobortis nisl ut aliquip ex ea commodo consequat.

The Flower Girl

Nibh euismod tincidunt ut laoreet dolore magna aliquam erat volutpat. Ut wisi enim ad minim veniam, quis nostrud exerci tation ullamcorper suscipit lobortis nisl ut aliquip consequat.

Duis autem vel eum iriure dolor in hendrerit in vulputate velit esse molestie consequat, vel illum dolore eu feugiat nulla facilisis at vero eros et accumsan et iusto odio dignissim qui blandit praesent luptatum zzril delenit augue duis dolore te feugait nulla facilisi. Lorem ipsum dolor sit amet, consectetuer adipiscing elit, sed diam nonummy nibh euismod tincidunt ut laoreet dolore magna aliquam erat volutpat.

Placement of page items should conform to the overall column scheme. A two-column photo, "A," in the illustration, on a five-column grid looks good when its edges are aligned with column guides.

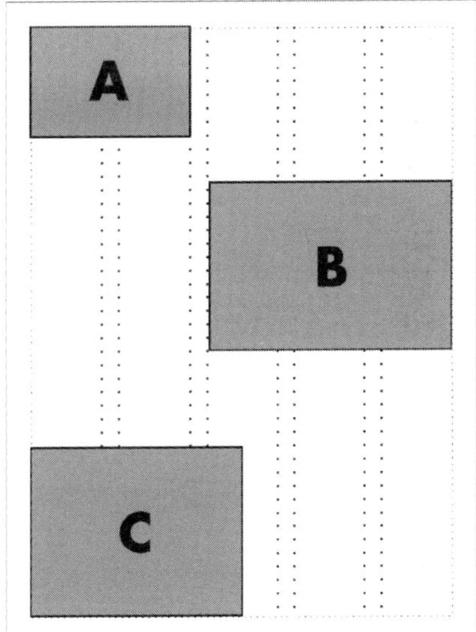

Likewise, a three-column photograph, "B," on a five-column grid works well when the edges of the photograph are lined up with the column guides.

However, a two-and-a-half-column photograph, "C," on a five-column grid creates unsightly half-columns of white space or short columns of type.

Just as establishing the number of columns influences the color and feel of a publication, so does the space between columns. Closely spaced columns darken a document and often make it more difficult to read—the reader's eye tends to jump the gap between columns. Extra space between columns lightens, or opens up, a page, and clearly separates one column from another.

2

Eyes Jump the Gap

2

Eyes Stay in Line

Gutters

In designing multipage documents, pay particular attention to the gutter—the inner space of facing pages.

Gutter size depends primarily on the type of binding you plan to use. Most books (including this one) use perfect binding, a method in which all pages are glued together. It's usually a safe bet to leave a traditional gutter margin of ½-inch to accommodate this type of binding.

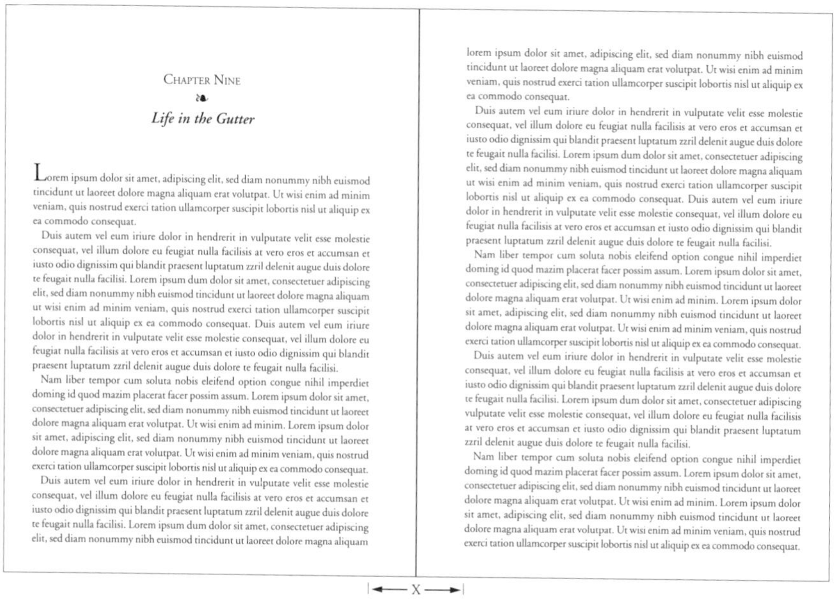

CHAPTER NINE

Life in the Gutter

Lorem ipsum dolor sit amet, adipiscing elit, sed diam nonummy nibh euismod tincidunt ut laoreet dolore magna aliquam erat volutpat. Ut wisi enim ad minim veniam, quis nostrud exerci tation ullamcorper suscipit lobortis nisl ut aliquip ex ea commodo consequat.

Duis autem vel eum iriure dolor in hendrerit in vulputate velit esse molestie consequat, vel illum dolore eu feugiat nulla facilisis at vero eros et accumsan et iusto odio dignissim qui blandit praesent luptatum zzril delenit augue duis dolore te feugait nulla facilisi. Lorem ipsum dum dolor sit amet, consectetuer adipiscing elit, sed diam nonummy nibh euismod tincidunt ut laoreet dolore magna aliquam ut wisi enim ad minim veniam, quis nostrud exerci tation ullamcorper suscipit lobortis nisl ut aliquip ex ea commodo consequat. Duis autem vel eum iriure dolor in hendrerit in vulputate velit esse molestie consequat, vel illum dolore eu feugiat nulla facilisis at vero eros et accumsan et iusto odio dignissim qui blandit praesent luptatum zzril delenit augue duis dolore te feugait nulla facilisi.

Nam liber tempor cum soluta nobis eleifend option congue nihil imperdiet doming id quod mazim placerat facer possim assum. Lorem ipsum dolor sit amet, consectetuer adipiscing elit, sed diam nonummy nibh euismod tincidunt ut laoreet dolore magna aliquam erat volutpat. Ut wisi enim ad minim. Lorem ipsum dolor sit amet, adipiscing elit, sed diam nonummy nibh euismod tincidunt ut laoreet dolore magna aliquam erat volutpat. Ut wisi enim ad minim veniam, quis nostrud exerci tation ullamcorper suscipit lobortis nisl ut aliquip ex ea commodo consequat.

Duis autem vel eum iriure dolor in hendrerit in vulputate velit esse molestie consequat, vel illum dolore eu feugiat nulla facilisis at vero eros et accumsan et iusto odio dignissim qui blandit praesent luptatum zzril delenit augue duis dolore te feugait nulla facilisi. Lorem ipsum dum dolor sit amet, consectetuer adipiscing elit, sed diam nonummy nibh euismod tincidunt ut laoreet dolore magna aliquam

lorem ipsum dolor sit amet, adipiscing elit, sed diam nonummy nibh euismod tincidunt ut laoreet dolore magna aliquam erat volutpat. Ut wisi enim ad minim veniam, quis nostrud exerci tation ullamcorper suscipit lobortis nisl ut aliquip ex ea commodo consequat.

Duis autem vel eum iriure dolor in hendrerit in vulputate velit esse molestie consequat, vel illum dolore eu feugiat nulla facilisis at vero eros et accumsan et iusto odio dignissim qui blandit praesent luptatum zzril delenit augue duis dolore te feugait nulla facilisi. Lorem ipsum dum dolor sit amet, consectetuer adipiscing elit, sed diam nonummy nibh euismod tincidunt ut laoreet dolore magna aliquam ut wisi enim ad minim veniam, quis nostrud exerci tation ullamcorper suscipit lobortis nisl ut aliquip ex ea commodo consequat. Duis autem vel eum iriure dolor in hendrerit in vulputate velit esse molestie consequat, vel illum dolore eu feugiat nulla facilisis at vero eros et accumsan et iusto odio dignissim qui blandit praesent luptatum zzril delenit augue duis dolore te feugait nulla facilisi.

Nam liber tempor cum soluta nobis eleifend option congue nihil imperdiet doming id quod mazim placerat facer possim assum. Lorem ipsum dolor sit amet, consectetuer adipiscing elit, sed diam nonummy nibh euismod tincidunt ut laoreet dolore magna aliquam erat volutpat. Ut wisi enim ad minim. Lorem ipsum dolor sit amet, adipiscing elit, sed diam nonummy nibh euismod tincidunt ut laoreet dolore magna aliquam erat volutpat. Ut wisi enim ad minim veniam, quis nostrud exerci tation ullamcorper suscipit lobortis nisl ut aliquip ex ea commodo consequat.

Duis autem vel eum iriure dolor in hendrerit in vulputate velit esse molestie consequat, vel illum dolore eu feugiat nulla facilisis at vero eros et accumsan et iusto odio dignissim qui blandit praesent luptatum zzril delenit augue duis dolore te feugait nulla facilisi. Lorem ipsum dum dolor sit amet, consectetuer adipiscing vulputate velit esse molestie consequat, vel illum dolore eu feugiat nulla facilisis at vero eros et accumsan et iusto odio dignissim qui blandit praesent luptatum zzril delenit augue duis dolore te feugait nulla facilisi.

Nam liber tempor cum soluta nobis eleifend option congue nihil imperdiet doming id quod mazim placerat facer possim assum. Lorem ipsum dolor sit amet, consectetuer adipiscing elit, sed diam nonummy nibh euismod tincidunt ut laoreet dolore magna aliquam erat volutpat. Ut wisi enim ad minim. Lorem ipsum dolor sit amet, adipiscing elit, sed diam nonummy nibh euismod tincidunt ut laoreet dolore magna aliquam erat volutpat. Ut wisi enim ad minim veniam, quis nostrud exerci tation ullamcorper suscipit lobortis nisl ut aliquip ex ea commodo consequat.

|←— X —→|

For ring binding, reserve a ⅝- to ¾-inch gutter. Most plastic spiral bindings don't require such wide gutters. The best plan is to choose a particular binding first, then design your gutter width around it.

Margins

Margins determine the space between columns and the edges of a page.

Effective design allows breathing room between the live area and the physical boundaries of a page, referred to as *trim size.*

A document with wide margins is generally more inviting to the reader. Narrow margins indicate that space is precious, and they're generally reserved for reference works and other information-rich documents.

Text Organizers

Imagine if a newspaper used only one typeface and all the text was set at the same size. How many pages would you be able to read before getting tired of it? Probably not too many.

Keep in mind that large expanses of text are daunting for a reader—they look like hard work. You're less likely to scare off your reader if your text is divided into manageable-looking pieces. Using text organizers like headlines, subheads, captions, and pull quotes will make your text look more inviting.

Headlines

Use headlines to invite readers to become involved.

Headlines, the most basic text-organizing tool, help a reader decide whether to read a document. They're meant to be perused quickly, so it's best to keep them concise.

Your headlines will be more effective if they're clearly differentiated from the text. A larger type size is a good start. You can also add emphasis to headlines by setting them in a different typeface. For example, headlines set in sans serif type are often used with text set in a serif typeface—a popular font combination for documents such as advertisements, books, brochures, and newsletters.

SERIF VS. SANS SERIF

The letters in a serif typeface have flared-out tops and bases. The body text of this book is set in a serif typeface. Type that lacks these embellishments, like the text within this sidebar, is called sans serif.

Advance, and Be Recognized!

Consectetuer adipiscing elit, sed diam nonummy nibh euismod tincidunt ut laoreet dolore magna aliquam erat volutpat. Ut wisi enim ad minim veniam, quis nostrud exerci tation ullamcorper suscipit lobortis nisl ut aliquip ex ea commodo consequat.

Duis autem vel eum iriure dolor in hendrerit in vulputate velit esse molestie consequat, vel illum dolore eu feugiat nulla facilisis. Lorem ipsum dolor sit amet, consectetuer adipiscing elit, sed diam nonummy nibh euismod tincidunt ut laoreet dolore magna aliquam erat volutpat. Ut wisi enim ad minim veniam, quis nostrud exerci tation ullamcorper suscipit commodo consequat.

Duis autem vel eum iriure dolor in hendrerit in vulputate velit esse molestie consequat, vel illum dolore eu feugiat nulla facilisis at vero eros et accumsan et iusto odio dignissim qui blandit praesent luptatum zzril delenit augue duis dolore te feugait nulla facilisi. Lorem ipsum dolor sit amet, consectetuer adipiscing elit, sed diam nonummy nibh euismod tincidunt ut laoreet dolore magna aliquam erat.

Ut wisi enim ad minim veniam, quis nostrud exerci tation ullamcorper suscipit lobortis nisl ut aliquip ex ea commodo consequat. Duis autem vel eum iriure dolor in hendrerit in vulputate velit esse molestie consequat, vel illum dolore eu feugiat nulla facilisis at vero eros et accumsan et iusto odio dignissim qui blandit praesent luptatum zzril delenit augue

Lorem ipsum dolor sit amet, consectetuer adipiscing elit, sed diam nonummy nibh euismod tincidunt ut laoreet dolore magna aliquam erat volutpat. Ut wisi enim ad minim veniam, quis nostrud exerci tation ullamcorper suscipit lobortis nisl ut aliquip ex ea commodo consequat.

Duis autem vel eum iriure dolor in hendrerit in vulputate velit esse molestie consequat, vel illum dolore eu feugiat nulla facilisis at vero eros et accumsan et iusto odio dignissim qui blandit praesent luptatum zzril delenit augue duis dolore te feugait nulla facilisi. Lorem ipsum dolor sit amet, consectetuer adipiscing elit, sed diam nonummy nibh euismod tincidunt ut laoreet dolore magna aliquam erat volutpat.

Ut wisi enim ad minim veniam, quis nostrud exerci tation ullamcorper suscipit lobortis nisl ut aliquip ex ea commodo consequat. Duis autem vel eum iriure dolor in hendrerit in vulputate velit esse molestie consequat, vel illum dolore eu feugiat nulla facilisis at vero eros et accumsan et iusto odio dignissim qui blandit praesent luptatum zzril delenit augue duis dolore te feugait nulla facilisi.

Nam liber tempor cum soluta nobis eleifend option congue nihil imperdiet doming id quod mazim placerat facer possim assum. Lorem ipsum dolor sit amet,

Greater Contrast Makes Reading Easier

Lorem ipsum dolor sit amet, adipiscing elit, sed diam nonummy nibh euismod tincidunt ut laoreet dolore magna aliquam erat volutpat. Ut wisi enim ad minim veniam, quis nostrud exerci tation ullamcorper suscipit lobortis nisl ut aliquip ex ea commodo consequat.

Duis autem vel eum iriure dolor in hendrerit in vulputate velit esse molestie consequat, vel illum dolore eu feugiat nulla facilisis at vero eros et accumsan et iusto odio dignissim qui blandit praesent luptatum zzril delenit augue duis dolore te feugait nulla facilisi. Lorem ipsum dum dolor sit amet, vel eum iriure dolor in hendrerit in vulputate velit esse molestie consequat, vel illum dolore eu feugiat nulla facilisis at vero eros et accumsan et iusto odio dignissim qui blandit praesent luptatum zzril delenit augue duis dolore te feugait nulla facilisi.

Nam liber tempor cum soluta nobis eleifend option congue nihil imperdiet doming id quod mazim placerat facer possim assum. Lorem ipsum dolor sit amet, consectetuer adipiscing elit, sed diam nonummy nibh euismod tincidunt ut laoreet dolore magna aliquam erat volutpat. Ut wisi enim ad minim lorem ipsum dum dolor sit amet, consectetuer adipiscing elit,

You don't have to switch typefaces for your headlines. Setting the text typeface in a larger size and/or heavier weight will often provide sufficient contrast.

The greater the size difference between headline and text, the easier it is for readers to identify and read your headline.

Greater Contrast Makes Reading Easier

Lorem ipsum dolor sit amet, adipiscing elit, sed diam nonummy nibh euismod tincidunt ut laoreet dolore magna aliquam erat volutpat. Ut wisi enim ad minim veniam, quis nostrud exerci tation ullamcorper suscipit lobortis nisl ut aliquip ex ea commodo consequat.

Duis autem vel eum iriure dolor in hendrerit in vulputate velit esse molestie consequat, vel illum dolore eu feugiat nulla facilisis at vero eros et accumsan et iusto odio dignissim qui blandit praesent luptatum zzril delenit augue duis dolore te feugait nulla facilisi. Lorem ipsum dum dolor sit amet, vel eum iriure dolor in hendrerit in vulputate velit esse molestie consequat, vel illum dolore eu feugiat nulla facilisis at vero eros et accumsan et iusto odio dignissim qui blandit praesent luptatum zzril delenit augue duis dolore te feugait nulla facilisi.

Nam liber tempor cum soluta nobis eleifend option congue nihil imperdiet doming id quod mazim placerat facer possim assum. Lorem ipsum dolor sit amet, consectetuer adipiscing elit, sed diam nonummy nibh euismod tincidunt ut laoreet dolore magna aliquam erat volutpat. Ut wisi enim ad minim lorem ipsum dum dolor sit amet, consectetuer adipiscing elit,

Headlines are designed for impact, so make them as readable as possible. Avoid setting long headlines in uppercase type. Not only do long uppercase headlines occupy more space, but they slow readers down because they're difficult to read.

READERS QUICKLY BECOME FED UP WITH LONG UPPERCASE HEADLINES

Lorem ipsum dolor sit amet, adipiscing elit, sed diam nonummy nibh euismod tincidunt ut laoreet dolore magna aliquam erat volutpat. Ut wisi enim ad minim veniam, quis nostrud exerci tation ullamcorper suscipit lobortis nisl ut aliquip ex ea commodo consequat.

Duis autem vel eum iriure dolor in hendrerit in vulputate velit esse molestie consequat, vel illum dolore eu feugiat nulla facilisis at vero eros et accumsan et iusto odio dignissim qui blandit praesent luptatum zzril delenit augue duis dolore te feugait nulla facilisi. Lorem ipsum dum dolor sit amet, vel eum iriure dolor in hendrerit in vulputate velit esse molestie consequat, vel illum dolore eu feugiat nulla facilisis at vero eros et accumsan et iusto odio dignissim qui blandit praesent luptatum zzril delenit augue duis dolore te feugait nulla facilisi.

Nam liber tempor cum soluta nobis eleifend option congue nihil imperdiet doming id quod mazim placerat facer possim assum. Lorem ipsum dolor sit amet, consectetuer adipiscing elit, sed diam nonummy nibh euismod tincidunt ut laoreet dolore magna aliquam erat volutpat. Ut wisi enim ad minim lorem ipsum dum dolor sit amet, consectetuer adipiscing elit,

It's best to limit uppercase headlines to a few words. This adds impact without slowing the reader down.

MUCH BETTER

Lorem ipsum dolor sit amet, adipiscing elit, sed diam nonummy nibh euismod tincidunt ut laoreet dolore magna aliquam erat volutpat. Ut wisi enim ad minim veniam, quis nostrud exerci tation ullamcorper suscipit lobortis nisl ut aliquip ex ea commodo consequat.

Duis autem vel eum iriure dolor in hendrerit in vulputate velit esse molestie consequat, vel illum dolore eu feugiat nulla facilisis at vero eros et accumsan et iusto odio dignissim qui blandit praesent luptatum zzril delenit augue duis dolore te feugait nulla facilisi. Lorem ipsum dum dolor sit amet, vel eum iriure dolor in hendrerit in vulputate velit esse molestie consequat, vel illum dolore eu feugiat nulla facilisis at vero eros et accumsan et iusto odio dignissim qui blandit praesent luptatum zzril delenit augue duis dolore te feugait nulla facilisi.

Nam liber tempor cum soluta nobis eleifend option congue nihil imperdiet doming id quod mazim placerat facer possim assum. Lorem ipsum dolor sit amet, consectetuer adipiscing elit, sed diam nonummy nibh euismod tincidunt ut laoreet dolore magna aliquam erat volutpat. Ut wisi enim ad minim lorem ipsum dum dolor sit amet, consectetuer adipiscing elit,

The most readable type scheme for headlines is to use uppercase for the first letter of each word (except articles and short prepositions, which should be left uncapitalized).

Set Headlines With Initial Caps For Maximum Readability

Lorem ipsum dolor sit amet, adipiscing elit, sed diam nonummy nibh euismod tincidunt ut laoreet dolore magna aliquam erat volutpat. Ut wisi enim ad minim veniam, quis nostrud exerci tation ullamcorper suscipit lobortis nisl ut aliquip ex ea commodo consequat.

Duis autem vel eum iriure dolor in hendrerit in vulputate velit esse molestie consequat, vel illum dolore eu feugiat nulla lobortis nisl ut aliquip ex ea commodo consequat. Duis autem vel eum iriure dolor in hendrerit in vulputate velit esse molestie consequat, vel illum dolore eu feugiat nulla facilisis at vero eros et accumsan et iusto odio dignissim qui blandit praesent luptatum zzril delenit augue duis dolore te feugait nulla facilisi.

Nam liber tempor cum soluta nobis eleifend option congue nihil imperdiet doming id quod mazim placerat facer possim

Try to limit headlines to three lines. Headlines of four or more lines can look too wordy and complex to read at a glance. Also, avoid centering headlines that contain more than two lines. Long centered headlines slow readers down because they have to search for the beginning of each line.

Long Centered Headlines Cause Readers to Give Up in Frustration; Editor-in-Chief Advises Shortening Them For the Sake of Clarity

Lorem ipsum dolor sit amet, adipiscing elit, sed diam nonummy nibh euismod tincidunt ut laoreet dolore magna aliquam erat volutpat. Ut wisi enim ad minim veniam, quis nostrud exerci tation ullamcorper suscipit lobortis nisl ut aliquip ex ea commodo consequat.

Duis autem vel eum iriure dolor in hendrerit in vulputate velit esse molestie consequat, vel illum dolore eu feugiat nulla tincidunt ut laoreet dolore magna aliquam ut wisi enim ad minim veniam, quis nostrud exerci tation ullamcorper suscipit lobortis nisl ut aliquip ex ea commodo consequat. Duis autem vel eum iriure dolor in hendrerit in vulputate velit esse molestie consequat, vel illum dolore eu feugiat nulla facilisis at vero eros et accumsan et iusto odio dignissim qui blandit praesent luptatum zzril delenit augue duis dolore te feugait nulla facilisi.

Flush-left headlines, on the other hand, let readers move directly down to the first words of the following paragraph.

Left-Aligned Headlines Start Readers Off Right

Lorem ipsum dolor sit amet, adipiscing elit, sed diam nonummy nibh euismod tincidunt ut laoreet dolore magna aliquam erat volutpat. Ut wisi enim ad minim veniam, quis nostrud exerci tation ullamcorper suscipit lobortis nisl ut aliquip ex ea commodo consequat.

Duis autem vel eum iriure dolor in hendrerit in vulputate velit esse molestie consequat, vel illum dolore eu feugiat nulla lobortis nisl ut aliquip ex ea commodo consequat. Duis autem vel eum iriure dolor in hendrerit in vulputate velit esse molestie consequat, vel illum dolore eu feugiat nulla facilisis at vero eros et accumsan et iusto odio dignissim qui blandit praesent luptatum zzril delenit augue duis dolore te feugait nulla facilisi.

Nam liber tempor cum soluta nobis eleifend option congue nihil imperdiet doming id quod mazim placerat facer possim

Kickers

Lead into your headline with a kicker—a short summary phrase.

Kickers are used to introduce headlines. Quite often, they're used to add meaning to headlines that don't stand well on their own—headlines involving plays on words, for example. Kickers also can be used to categorize an article.

Profile of a Modern Hero:

Fireman Saves Cat Caught in Tree

Lorem ipsum dolor sit amet, adipiscing elit, sed diam nonummy nibh euismod tincidunt ut laoreet dolore magna aliquam erat volutpat. Ut wisi enim ad minim veniam, quis nostrud exerci tation ullamcorper suscipit lobortis nisl ut aliquip ex ea commodo consequat.

Duis autem vel eum iriure dolor in hendrerit in vulputate velit esse molestie consequat, vel illum dolore eu feugiat nulla facilisis at vero eros et accumsan et iusto odio dignissim qui blandit praesent luptatum zzril delenit augue duis dolore te minim veniam, quis nostrud exerci tation ullamcorper suscipit lobortis nisl ut aliquip ex ea commodo consequat. Duis autem vel eum iriure dolor in hendrerit in vulputate velit esse molestie consequat, vel illum dolore eu feugiat nulla facilisis at vero eros et accumsan et iusto odio dignissim qui blandit praesent luptatum zzril delenit augue duis dolore te feugait nulla facilisi.

Nam liber tempor cum soluta nobis eleifend option congue nihil imperdiet doming id quod mazim placerat facer possim assum. Lorem ipsum dolor sit amet, consectetuer adipiscing elit, sed diam nonummy nibh euismod tincidunt ut laoreet dolore magna aliquam erat volutpat. Ut wisi enim ad minim lorem ipsum dum dolor sit amet, consectetuer adipiscing elit, sed diam nonummy nibh euismod tincidunt ut laoreet dolore magna aliquam ut wisi enim ad minim veniam, quis nostrud exerci tation ullamcorper suscipit lobortis nisl ut aliquip ex ea commodo consequat. Duis autem vel eum iriure dolor in hendrerit in vulputate velit esse molestie consequat duis autem

Subheads

Subheads indicate how information within a document is organized.

Subheads serve many functions. Placed immediately after headlines, they provide a smooth transition from headlines to text. This type of layout is convenient when the content divides neatly into comparable subtopics.

IT'S A BIRD

Lorem ipsum dolor sit amet, adipiscing elit, sed diam nonummy nibh euismod tincidunt ut laoreet dolore magna aliquam volutpat. Ut wisi enim ad minim veniam, quis nostrud exerci tation ullamcorper suscipit lobortis nisl ut aliquip ex ea commodo consequat.

Duis autem vel eum iriure dolor in hendrerit in vulputate velit esse molestie consequat, vel illum dolore eu feugiat nulla facilisis at vero eros et

IT'S A PLANE

Aliquam ut wisi enim ad minim veniam, quis nostrud exerci tation ullamcorper suscipit lobortis nisl ut aliquip ex ea commodo consequat. Duis autem vel eum iriure dolor in hendrerit in vulputate velit esse molestie consequat, vel illum dolore eu feugiat nulla facilisis at vero eros et accumsan et iusto odio dignissim qui blandit praesent luptatum zzril delenit augue duis dolore te feugait nulla facilisi.

IT'S SUPERMAN

Ut wisi enim ad minim autem vel eum iriure dolor in hendrerit in vulputate velit esse molestie consequat, vel illum dolore eu feugiat nulla facilisis at vero eros et accumsan et iusto odio dignissim qui blandit praesent luptatum zzril delenit augue duis dolore te feugait nulla facilisi. Lorem ipsum dum dolor sit amet, consectetuer adipiscing elit, sed diam nonummy nibh euismod tincidunt ut laoreet dolore magna.

Subheads can also be placed within the text, to break it into manageable segments. The left-hand example below is cumbersome to read. The page is depressingly gray, and there's no way to get an immediate sense of the content.

The right-hand example is more inviting. The white space preceding each subhead breaks up the expanse of gray, and hurried readers can skim the subheads to decide whether the text relates to their interests.

Don't Make Reading a Chore

Don't Make Reading a Chore

Add Subheads Frequently

Open Up Your Pages

Use Various Subhead Techniques

You'll need to position subheads so that they are closely associated with the text they introduce. Leaving more space above a subhead than below it will link it with the correct text.

Subheads clue readers into the content organization within an article. Subheads break text into manageable segments, improve the appearance of a page and enhance readership by providing a transition between headlines and text.

Subhead Linked to Text Mystery

Subheads can be set apart from text by using various techniques. For example, they can be placed inside or next to the text. Subheads should always be closely associ-

Incorrect

Subheads clue readers into the content organization within an article. Subheads break text into manageable segments, improve the appearance of a page and enhance readership by providing a transition between headlines and text.

Subhead Linked to Text Mystery

Subheads can be set apart from text by using various techniques. For example, they can be placed inside or next to the text. Subheads should always be closely associ-

Correct

Like headlines, subheads tend to stand out when set in a larger type size and a different typeface than the text.

Subheads clue readers into the content organization within an article. Subheads break text into manageable segments, improve the appearance of a page and enhance readership by providing a transition between headlines and text.

Missing Contrast Is Suspected

Subheads can be set apart from text by using various techniques. For example, they can be placed inside or next to the text. Subheads should always be closely associated with the text they introduce. There should contrast between the subhead

Subheads clue readers into the content organization within an article. Subheads break text into manageable segments, improve the appearance of a page and enhance readership by providing a transition between headlines and text.

Correct Contrast Has Been Located

Subheads can be set apart from text by using various techniques. For example, they can be placed inside or next to the text. Subheads should always be closely associated with the text they introduce. There

Subheads can be set centered or flush left.

Subheads clue readers into the content organization within an article. Subheads break text into manageable segments, improve the appearance of a page and enhance readership by providing a transition between headlines and text.

Subheads Offer Great Variety

Subheads can be set apart from text by using various techniques. For example, they can be placed inside or next to the text. Subheads should always be closely associated with the

Subheads clue readers into the content organization within an article. Subheads break text into manageable segments, improve the appearance of a page and enhance readership by providing a transition between headlines and text.

Subheads Offer Great Variety

Subheads can be set apart from text by using various techniques. For example, they can be placed inside or next to the text. Subheads should always be closely associated with the

Horizontal rules above or below subheads can add emphasis.

Lorem ipsum dolor sit amet, adipiscing elit, sed diam nonummy nibh euismod tincidunt ut laoreet dolore magna aliquam erat volutpat. Ut wisi enim ad minim veniam, quis nostrud exerci tation ullamcorper suscipit lobortis nisl ut aliquip ex ea commodo consequat.

The Rules of Subheads

Duis autem vel eum iriure dolor in hendrerit in vulputate velit esse molestie consequat, vel illum dolore eu feugiat nulla facilisis at vero eros et accumsan et iusto odio dignissim qui blandit praesent luptatum zzril delenit augue duis dolore te feugait nulla facilisi. Lorem ipsum dum dolor sit amet, consectetuer adipiscing elit, sed diam nonummy nibh euismod tincidunt ut laoreet dolore magna aliquam ut wisi enim ad minim veniam, quis nostrud exerci tation ullamcorper suscipit lobortis nisl ut aliquip ex ea commodo consequat. Ut wisi enim ad minim veniam, quis nostrud exerci tation ullamcorper suscipit lobortis nisl ut aliquip ex consequat. Lorem ipsum dum dolor sit amet, consectetuer

Subheads don't have to be positioned above the accompanying text. Placing them to the side, for example, is often quite effective.

As with other organizing tools, uniformity is important. Remember to treat subheads consistently throughout your desktop-published document.

Put Subheads on the Side

They Look Good Here!

Lorem ipsum dolor sit amet, adipiscing elit, sed diam nonummy nibh euismod tincidunt ut laoreet dolore magna aliquam erat volutpat. Ut wisi enim ad minim veniam, quis nostrud exerci tation ullamcorper suscipit lobortis nisl ut aliquip ex ea commodo consequat.

Duis autem vel eum iriure dolor in hendrerit in vulputate velit esse molestie consequat, vel illum dolore eu feugiat nulla facilisis at vero eros et accumsan et iusto odio dignissim qui blandit praesent luptatum zzril delenit augue duis dolore te feugait nulla facilisi. Lorem ipsum dum dolor sit amet, consectetuer adipiscing elit, sed diam nonummy nibh euismod tincidunt ut laoreet dolore magna aliquam ut wisi enim ad minim veniam, quis nostrud exerci tation ullamcorper suscipit lobortis nisl ut aliquip ex ea commodo consequat.

You'll Be Pleasantly Surprised

Duis autem vel eum iriure dolor in hendrerit in vulputate velit esse molestie consequat, vel illum dolore eu feugiat nulla facilisis at vero eros et accumsan et iusto odio dignissim qui blandit praesent luptatum zzril delenit augue duis dolore te feugait nulla facilisi. Lorem ipsum dum dolor sit amet, consectetuer adipiscing elit, sed diam nonummy nibh euismod tincidunt ut laoreet dolore magna aliquam ut wisi enim ad minim veniam, quis nostrud exerci tation ullamcorper suscipit lobortis nisl ut aliquip ex ea commodo consequat. Duis autem vel eum iriure dolor in hendrerit in vulputate velit esse molestie

Captions

Use captions to tie photographs and illustrations into the rest of your publication.

Headlines and captions are more likely to be read than any other part of a publication. You can take advantage of this by using captions to summarize important points.

Captions can be placed in a variety of ways. Most often, captions are placed above or below the artwork. It's a good idea to either center your captions or align them to one of the visual's edges.

Lorem ipsum dolor sit amet, consec tetuer adipiscing elit, diam nonummy nibh euismod tincidunt ut laoreet dolore magna aliquam erat volutpat. Ut wisi enim ad minim veniam, quis nostrud exerci tation ullamcorper suscipit lobortis nisl ut aliquip ex ea commodo consequat.

Duis autem vel eum iriure dolor in hendrerit in vulputate velit esse molestie consequat, vel illum dolore eu feugiat nulla facilisis at vero eros et facilisi. Lorem ipsum dolor sit amet, consectetuer adipiscing elit, sed diam nonummy nibh euismod tincidunt ut laoreet dolore magna aliquam erat volutpat.

Ut wisi enim ad minim veniam, nostrud exerci tation ullamcorper suscipit lobortis nisl ut aliquip ex ea commodo consequat. Duis autem vel eum iriure dolor in hendrerit in vulputate velit molestie consequat, illum dolore eu feugiat nulla facilisis

Persistence is the key to rock climbing—that, and not falling off.

accumsan et iusto odio dignissim qui blandit praesent luptatum zzril delenit augue duis dolore te feugait nulla at vero eros et accumsan et iusto odiodignissim qui blandit praesent luptatum zzril delenit augue duis possim assum. Lorem ipsum dolor sit amet, consectetuer adipiscing elit, sed diam nonummy nibh euismod tincidunt ut laoreet dolore magna aliquam erat volutpat. Ut wisi enim ad minim veniam, quis nostrud exerci tation ullamcorper suscipit lobortis nisl ut ex ea commodo consequat.

Duis autem vel eum iriure dolor in hendrerit in vulputate velit esse molestie consequat, vel illum dolore eu feugiat nulla facilisis. Ut wisi enim ad minim veniam, nostrud exerci tation ullamcorper suscipit lobortis nisl ut aliquip ex ea commodo consequat. Duis autem vel eum iriure dolor in hendrerit in vulputate velit molestie consequat, illum dolore eu feugiat nulla facilisis at vero eros et accumsan et iusto odiodignissim qui blandit praesent ipsum dolor sit amet, consec tetuer adipiscing elit, diam nonummy nibh euismod tincidunt ut laoreet dolore magna aliquam erat volutpat. Ut wisi enim ad minim veniam, quis nostrud exerci tation ullamcorper suscipit lobortis nisl ut aliquip ex ea commodo consequat. Lorem ipsum dolor sit amet, consectetuer adipiscing elit, sed diam nonummy nibh euismod tincidunt ut laoreet dolore magna aliquam erat volutpat. Lorem ipsum dolor sit amet, consectetuer wisi enim ad minim veniam, quis nostrud exerci tation ullamcorper suscipit lobortis nisl ut aliquip ex ea quis nostrud exerci commodo consequat.

Another possibility is to place the caption alongside the artwork. Generally, the caption is aligned to fit flush against the visual.

Lorem ipsum dolor sit amet, consec tetuer adipiscing elit, diam nonummy nibh euismod tincidunt ut laoreet dolore magna aliquam erat volutpat. Ut wisi enim ad minim veniam, quis nostrud exerci tation ullamcorper suscipit lobortis nisl ut aliquip ex ea commodo consequat.

Duis autem vel eum iriure dolor in hendrerit in vulputate velit esse molestie consequat, vel illum dolore eu feugiat nulla facilisis at vero eros et nonummy nibh euismod tincidunt ut laoreet dolore magna aliquam erat volutpat.

Ut wisi enim ad minim veniam, nostrud exerci tation ullamcorper suscipit lobortis nisl ut aliquip ex ea commodo consequat. Duis autem vel eum iriure dolor in hendrerit in vulputate velit molestie consequat, illum dolore eu feugiat nulla facilisis at vero eros et accumsan et iusto odiodignissim qui blandit praesent

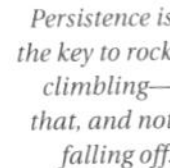

Persistence is the key to rock climbing—that, and not falling off.

accumsan et iusto odio dignissim qui blandit praesent luptatum zzril delenit augue duis dolore te feugait nulla facilisi. Lorem ipsum dolor sit amet, consectetuer adipiscing elit, sed diam luptatum zzril delenit augue duis dolore te feugait nulla facilisi.

Nam liber tempor cum soluta nobis eleifend option congue nihil imperdiet doming id quod mazim placerat facer

If part of your picture is relatively empty, you can place the caption inside the artwork.

Lorem ipsum dolor sit amet, consec tetuer adipiscing elit, diam nonummy nibh euismod tincidunt ut laoreet dolore magna aliquam erat volutpat. Ut wisi enim ad minim veniam, quis nostrud exerci tation ullamcorper suscipit lobortis nisl ut aliquip ex ea commodo consequat.

Duis autem vel eum iriure dolor in hendrerit in vulputate velit esse molestie consequat, vel illum dolore eu feugiat nulla facilisis at vero eros et

nonummy nibh euismod tincidunt ut laoreet dolore magna aliquam erat volutpat.

Ut wisi enim ad minim veniam, nostrud exerci tation ullamcorper suscipit lobortis nisl ut aliquip ex ea commodo consequat. Duis autem vel eum iriure dolor in hendrerit in vulputate velit molestie consequat, illum dolore eu feugiat nulla facilisis at vero eros et accumsan et iusto odiodignissim qui blandit praesent

Persistence is the key to rock climbing—that, and not falling off.

accumsan et iusto odio dignissim qui blandit praesent luptatum zzril delenit augue duis dolore te feugait nulla facilisi. Lorem ipsum dolor sit amet, consectetuer adipiscing elit, sed diam

luptatum zzril delenit augue duis accumsan et iusto odio dignissim qui blandit praesent luptatum zzril delenit augue duis dolore te feugait nulla facilisi. Lorem ipsum dolor sit amet,

possim assum. Lorem ipsum dolor sit amet, consectetuer adipiscing elit, sed diam nonummy nibh euismod tincidunt ut laoreet dolore magna aliquam erat volutpat. Ut wisi enim ad minim veniam, quis nostrud exerci tation ullamcorper suscipit lobortis nisl ut ex ea commodo consequat.

Duis autem vel eum iriure dolor in hendrerit in vulputate velit esse molestie consequat, vel illum dolore eu feugiat nulla facilisis. Ut wisi enim ad minim veniam, nostrud exerci tation ullamcorper suscipit lobortis nisl ut aliquip ex ea commodo consequat. Duis autem vel eum iriure dolor in hendrerit in vulputate velit molestie consequat, illum dolore eu feugiat nulla facilisis at vero eros et accumsan et iusto odiodignissim qui blandit praesent ipsum dolor sit amet, consec tetuer adipiscing elit, diam nonummy nibh euismod tincidunt ut laoreet dolore magna aliquam erat volutpat. Ut wisi enim ad minim veniam, quis nostrud exerci tation ullamcorper suscipit lobortis nisl ut aliquip ex ea commodo consequat. Lorem ipsum dolor sit amet, consectetuer adipiscing elit, sed diam nonummy nibh euismod tincidunt ut laoreet dolore magna aliquam erat volutpat. Lorem ipsum dolor sit amet, consectetuer wisi enim ad minim veniam, quis nostrud exerci tation ullamcorper suscipit lobortis nisl ut aliquip ex ea quis nostrud exerci commodo consequat.

Whatever your choice, be consistent throughout your publication. Captions are high-profile items, and your readers will notice any inconsistencies.

Headers And Footers

Information at the top or bottom of each page in a newsletter, book, or training manual can reinforce the publication's identity and help readers locate information.

Information repeated at the top of every page is known as a *header*, or, if it's located at the bottom of every page, it's called a *footer*. Typically, headers and footers include such information as the publication's title, section and chapter titles, chapter number, and page number.

You might choose to have both a header *and* a footer, and divide the necessary information between them.

Reference works often include page-specific information in each header, to help readers locate information quickly. Looking up a word in a dictionary, for instance, would take much longer without the aid of headers.

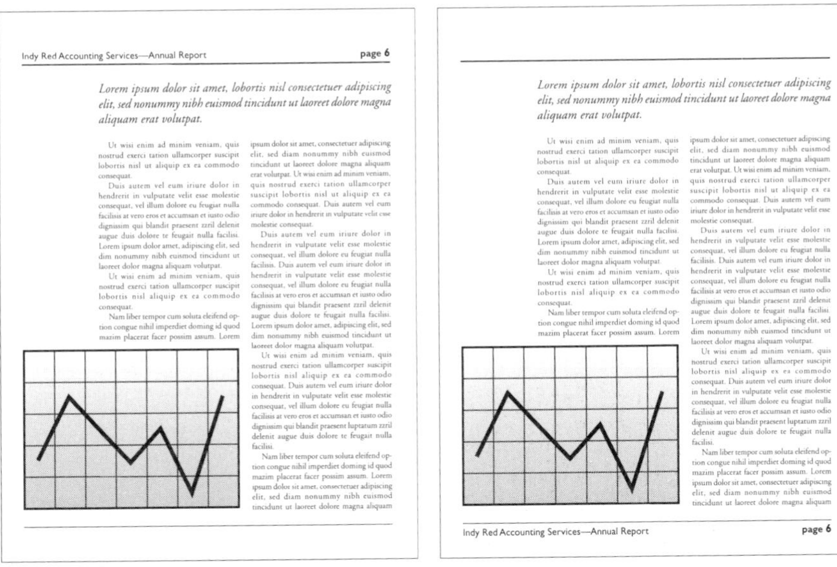

Pull Quotes And Sidebars

Pull quotes and sidebars give your pages editorial diversity and add visual interest to your layouts.

In addition to subheads, you can add graphic interest to your page by using *pull quotes*—a sentence or two extracted from the text and set in display type within the text column or in a side margin.

Pull quotes should only occupy a few short lines, so readers can take them in at a glance. You might choose to paraphrase the text rather than quote it verbatim, to keep the pull quote pithy.

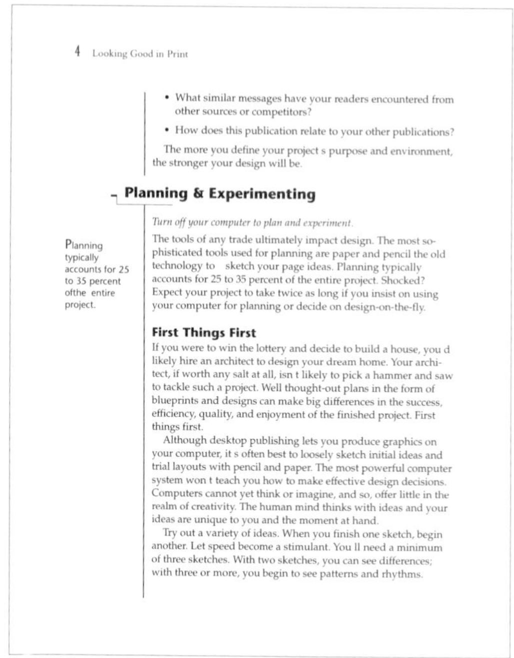

4 Looking Good in Print

- What similar messages have your readers encountered from other sources or competitors?
- How does this publication relate to your other publications?

The more you define your project s purpose and environment, the stronger your design will be.

Planning & Experimenting

Turn off your computer to plan and experiment.

Planning typically accounts for 25 to 35 percent ofthe entire project.

The tools of any trade ultimately impact design. The most sophisticated tools used for planning are paper and pencil the old technology to sketch your page ideas. Planning typically accounts for 25 to 35 percent of the entire project. Shocked? Expect your project to take twice as long if you insist on using your computer for planning or decide on design-on-the-fly.

First Things First

If you were to win the lottery and decide to build a house, you d likely hire an architect to design your dream home. Your architect, if worth any salt at all, isn t likely to pick a hammer and saw to tackle such a project. Well thought-out plans in the form of blueprints and designs can make big differences in the success, efficiency, quality, and enjoyment of the finished project. First things first.

Although desktop publishing lets you produce graphics on your computer, it s often best to loosely sketch initial ideas and trial layouts with pencil and paper. The most powerful computer system won t teach you how to make effective design decisions. Computers cannot yet think or imagine, and so, offer little in the realm of creativity. The human mind thinks with ideas and your ideas are unique to you and the moment at hand.

Try out a variety of ideas. When you finish one sketch, begin another. Let speed become a stimulant. You ll need a minimum of three sketches. With two sketches, you can see differences; with three or more, you begin to see patterns and rhythms.

Another page element you may want to use is the *sidebar*—a block of copy set apart from but related to the rest of the text on a page. This is an ideal format for supplemental information, such as a biographical sketch of an individual important to a major article.

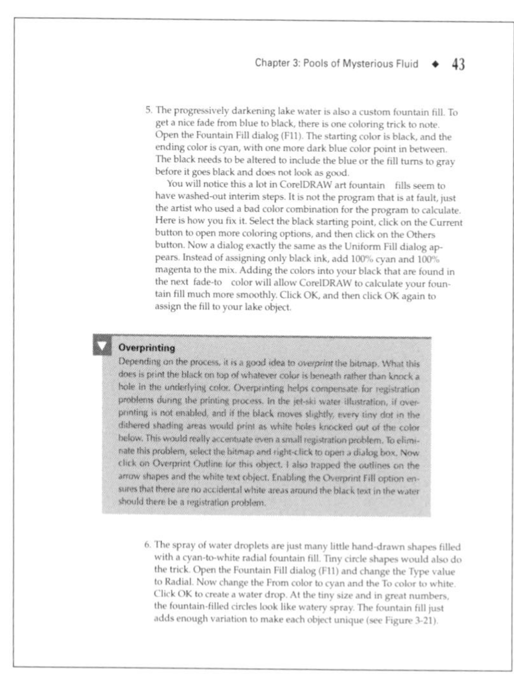

Chapter 3: Pools of Mysterious Fluid ◆ 43

5. The progressively darkening lake water is also a custom fountain fill. To get a nice fade from blue to black, there is one coloring trick to note. Open the Fountain Fill dialog (F11). The starting color is black, and the ending color is cyan, with one more dark blue color point in between. The black needs to be altered to include the blue or the fill turns to gray before it goes black and does not look as good.

   You will notice this a lot in CorelDRAW art fountain fills seem to have washed-out interim steps. It is not the program that is at fault, just the artist who used a bad color combination for the program to calculate. Here is how you fix it. Select the black starting point, click on the Current button to open more coloring options, and then click on the Others button. Now a dialog exactly the same as the Uniform Fill dialog appears. Instead of assigning only black ink, add 100% cyan and 100% magenta to the mix. Adding the colors into your black that are found in the next fade-to color will allow CorelDRAW to calculate your fountain fill much more smoothly. Click OK, and then click OK again to assign the fill to your lake object.

Overprinting

Depending on the process, it is a good idea to *overprint* the bitmap. What this does is print the black on top of whatever color is beneath rather than knock a hole in the underlying color. Overprinting helps compensate for registration problems during the printing process. In the jet-ski water illustration, if overprinting is not enabled, and if the black moves slightly, every tiny dot in the dithered shading areas would print as white holes knocked out of the color below. This would really accentuate even a small registration problem. To eliminate this problem, select the bitmap and right-click to open a dialog box. Now click on Overprint Outline for this object. I also trapped the outlines on the arrow shapes and the white text object. Enabling the Overprint Fill option ensures that there are no accidental white areas around the black text in the water should there be a registration problem.

6. The spray of water droplets are just many little hand-drawn shapes filled with a cyan-to-white radial fountain fill. Tiny circle shapes would also do the trick. Open the Fountain Fill dialog (F11) and change the Type value to Radial. Now change the From color to cyan and the To color to white. Click OK to create a water drop. At the tiny size and in great numbers, the fountain-filled circles look like watery spray. The fountain fill just adds enough variation to make each object unique (see Figure 3-21).

Bullet Lists

To add emphasis to a list, use bullets or icons to mark each item.

Often, you'll want to list items in a long column instead of running them in with the text. By inserting a bullet (usually a boldface dot or square) or other icon, the list takes on a new importance and invites readership. This technique is particularly effective in advertising.

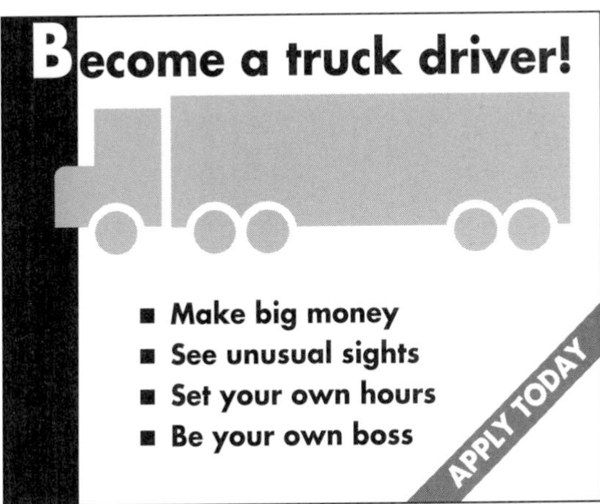

Jumplines

Use jumplines to inform readers when articles are continued from one page to another.

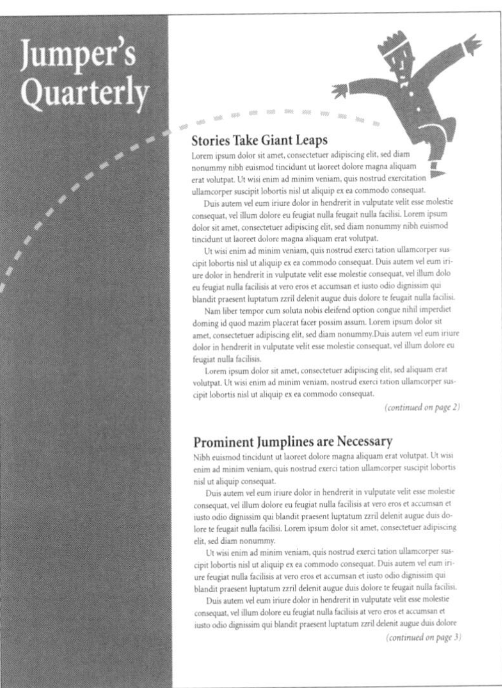

Jumper's Quarterly

Stories Take Giant Leaps

Lorem ipsum dolor sit amet, consectetuer adipiscing elit, sed diam nonummy nibh euismod tincidunt ut laoreet dolore magna aliquam erat volutpat. Ut wisi enim ad minim veniam, quis nostrud exercitation ullamcorper suscipit lobortis nisl ut aliquip ex ea commodo consequat.

Duis autem vel eum iriure dolor in hendrerit in vulputate velit esse molestie consequat, vel illum dolore eu feugiat nulla feugait nulla facilisi. Lorem ipsum dolor sit amet, consectetuer adipiscing elit, sed diam nonummy nibh euismod tincidunt ut laoreet dolore magna aliquam erat volutpat.

Ut wisi enim ad minim veniam, quis nostrud exerci tation ullamcorper suscipit lobortis nisl ut aliquip ex ea commodo consequat. Duis autem vel eum iriure dolor in hendrerit in vulputate velit esse molestie consequat, vel illum dolo eu feugiat nulla facilisis at vero eros et accumsan et iusto odio dignissim qui blandit praesent luptatum zzril delenit augue duis dolore te feugait nulla facilisi.

Nam liber tempor cum soluta nobis eleifend option congue nihil imperdiet doming id quod mazim placerat facer possim assum. Lorem ipsum dolor sit amet, consectetuer adipiscing elit, sed diam nonummy.Duis autem vel eum iriure dolor in hendrerit in vulputate velit esse molestie consequat, vel illum dolore eu feugiat nulla facilisis.

Lorem ipsum dolor sit amet, consectetuer adipiscing elit, sed aliquam erat volutpat. Ut wisi enim ad minim veniam, nostrud exerci tation ullamcorper suscipit lobortis nisl ut aliquip ex ea commodo consequat.

(continued on page 2)

Prominent Jumplines are Necessary

Nibh euismod tincidunt ut laoreet dolore magna aliquam erat volutpat. Ut wisi enim ad minim veniam, quis nostrud exerci tation ullamcorper suscipit lobortis nisl ut aliquip consequat.

Duis autem vel eum iriure dolor in hendrerit in vulputate velit esse molestie consequat, vel illum dolore eu feugiat nulla facilisis at vero eros et accumsan et iusto odio dignissim qui blandit praesent luptatum zzril delenit augue duis dolore te feugait nulla facilisi. Lorem ipsum dolor sit amet, consectetuer adipiscing elit, sed diam nonummy.

Ut wisi enim ad minim veniam, quis nostrud exerci tation ullamcorper suscipit lobortis nisl ut aliquip ex ea commodo consequat. Duis autem vel eum iriure feugiat nulla facilisis at vero eros et accumsan et iusto odio dignissim qui blandit praesent luptatum zzril delenit augue duis dolore te feugait nulla facilisi.

Duis autem vel eum iriure dolor in hendrerit in vulputate velit esse molestie consequat, vel illum dolore eu feugiat nulla facilisis at vero eros et accumsan et iusto odio dignissim qui blandit praesent luptatum zzril delenit augue duis dolore

(continued on page 3)

By continuing articles on inside pages, you can offer readers a wider variety of editorial material on the front page of your publication. As the number of articles included on page 1 increases, so does the likelihood that you'll interest the reader.

Continuing articles on other pages also allows for more flexibility in laying out a long story that won't fit on a single page. The jumpline eliminates any confusion readers may have about where to read next.

Nameplates And Logos

Establish the identity of your publication with a distinctive and prominent nameplate.

A nameplate is a distinctive type treatment of your publication's title. As the first item on the first page, it should be prominent enough to establish a lasting visual identity, and it should remain the same from issue to issue.

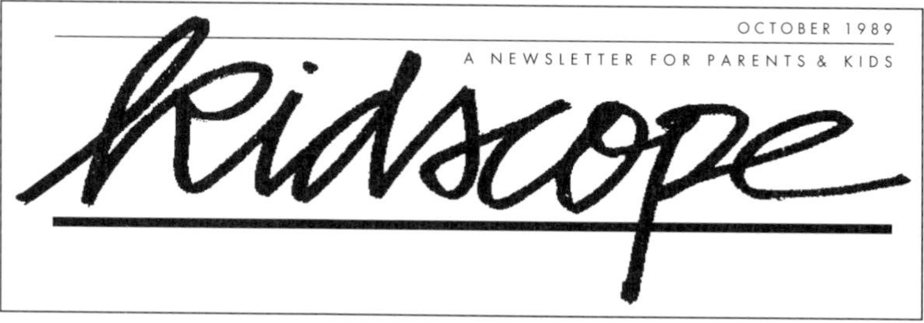

A logo is a graphic device that symbolizes your firm. The best logos reflect the nature of the business they symbolize yet are simple enough to retain legibility over a wide variety of reproductions—business cards, letterheads, merchandise, and so forth. An overly detailed logo can become an unrecognizable mess when sent through a fax machine or shrunk down to fit on the side of a pen. (Okay, maybe you weren't planning on having pens engraved with your logo—but who knows what the future holds?)

Many logos are based on a simple but effective illustration.

Logos don't have to be graphical. Often, setting the company's name in a distinctive typeface will form a memorable logo.

Sometimes the letters are modified to create a unique effect. For example, spacing can be altered to make the letters touch or overlap.

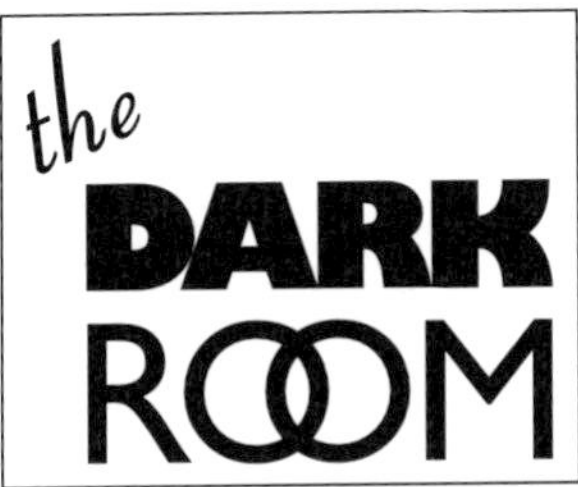

In other cases, portions of the letters are omitted or exaggerated.

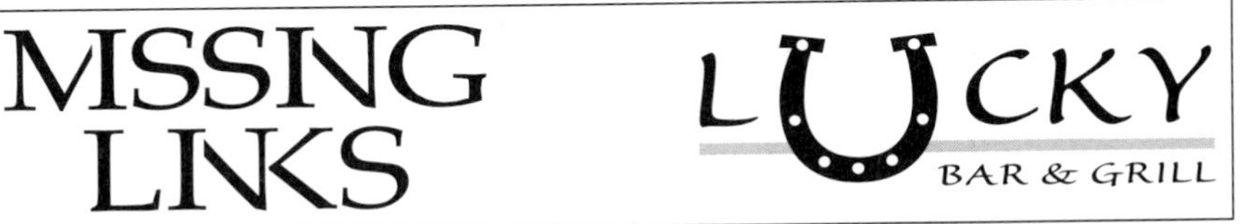

Logos are particularly important in magazine and newspaper advertisements. They provide a visual shorthand for immediate identification and ad-to-ad consistency. They also give the ad a strong finish.

MAKE STYLES A HABIT

Some desktop publishers refuse to put unstyled text in their documents—every paragraph gets tagged with a style. That probably sounds extreme, but the idea is sound. The extra time spent applying styles is a pittance, compared to the time that editing an unstyled document could take. Fully styled documents have an additional benefit—they can be used as templates if you're ever asked to create a similar document in the future. Don't be too quick to write off a given project as a "one-shot-deal"—more often than not, time will prove you wrong.

Styles

Styles provide the memory bank for desktop publishing, giving you instant access to the design specifications on a project.

Keeping track of all these organizers—column specifications, headline font and size, caption placement and size, picas between a subhead and the text—is too daunting for those of us not blessed with a photographic memory. Fortunately, desktop publishing programs offer the ultimate organizer—styles.

Each specification concerning type or format in your document can be defined as part of your document's styles. Once defined, the styles can be conveniently applied as you create your document.

Styles are critical if you're creating a multipage document or a standard format that will be repeated frequently on future projects. Styles ensure consistency. They're also useful for making document-wide changes—a blessing for freelance desktop publishers with fickle clients.

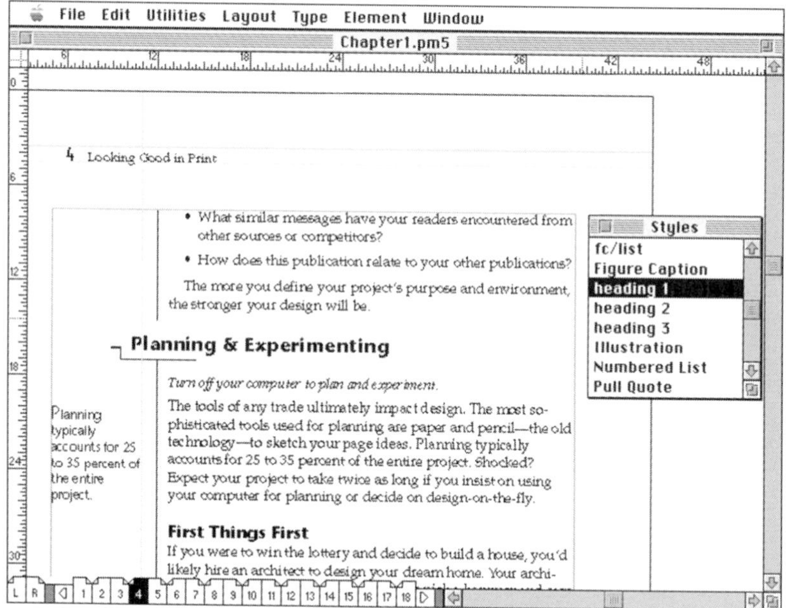

Moving On

This concludes our discussion of graphic design's organizing tools. Consider yourself organized! It's time, at long last, to put some words on the page—and the next chapter shows you the most effective approach.

3 The Architecture of Type

Typography—the design of the characters that make up text and display type (headlines, subheads, captions) and the way they're presented on a page—influences your print communications more than any other single visual element.

The typeface you choose sends an important message about your message. It conveys mood and communicates attitude. If the tone of the typeface doesn't match the message you're trying to convey, you risk confusing your readers.

There are other factors besides the "character" of a given font that must be considered when choosing type. Some fonts require more space between lines than others for optimum readability, some lose readability at small sizes, and some lose impact at large sizes. Many desktop publishing systems offer additional options that must be considered, such as rotation and distortion of type, and the ability to wrap text around a visual.

There *are* rules to follow when selecting and arranging type—this chapter describes them in some detail—but, as with many rules, you're bound to stumble upon an exception sooner or later. Develop faith in your aesthetic judgment. If something "just looks right" to you, it's probably worth keeping, even if the rules don't support you. Likewise, if you've followed the rules but still have nagging doubts, keep experimenting.

Examining Type And Type Decisions

The finer characteristics of letter shapes create an overall distinct mood.

One way to begin working with type is to dissect it architecturally. Become familiar with the basic parts of letters, and notice how they vary in detail from one typeface to another.

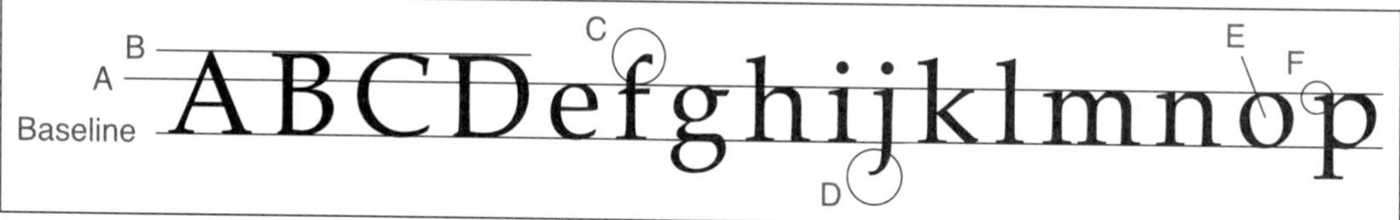

A. *X-height*—The height of the main body of the lowercase letterforms in a font, ignoring ascenders and descenders (see items D and E). The term literally refers to the height of a lowercase x.

B. *Cap height*—The height of the uppercase letterforms in a font.

C. *Ascender*—The part of a lowercase letter that extends above the x-height, as in the characters *b*, *d*, and *h*.

D. *Descender*—The part of a lowercase letter that extends below the baseline, as in the characters *g*, *p*, and *y*.

E. *Bowl (counter)*—The space found within some letters, as in the characters *b* and *Q*.

F. *Serif*—The short cross-strokes at the top and bottom ends of a letter. This term is also a classification for typefaces that feature serifs. Typefaces without serifs are called *sans serif* fonts.

Fluctuations in these variables influence the overall tone of a typeface. As you become more familiar with typefaces, you'll spot general stylistic patterns. For example:

- *Conventional*—Serif, small x-height, tall ascenders and descenders.
- *Contemporary*—Sans serif, high x-height, short ascenders and descenders.
- *Dignified*—Serif with slightly pinched bowls and vertical letterforms.
- *Friendly*—Rounded bowls and letterforms.

Typefaces with rounded serifs tend to be friendly (Caslon244):

Many hands make light work.

Typefaces with squared serifs look official or architectural (Officina Serif):

Tax Form Enclosed

The simplicity and elegance of sans serif typefaces make them ideal for large headlines and other display treatments.

A TOUCH OF CLASS

Serif type, on the other hand, works well in smaller sizes, particularly for a text face, but can lack authority when set in large sizes for display purposes.

Serifs help the reader recognize the shapes of the letters. Take away the serifs and there's less letter-to-letter differentiation.

Distinct letters

A RATHER CONFUSING LEXICON

Unfortunately, the terms used in typography have very unclear meanings. Technically, the term *typeface* refers to a complete set of characters of a given font, in a given weight—so for example, Helvetica Bold is an example of a typeface. A *font family* is a collection of related typefaces: Helvetica, Helvetica Oblique, Helvetical Bold, and Helvetical Bold Oblique are four *typefaces* within the Helvetica *font family*.

Helvetica	AaBbCcDdEeFf
Helvetica Oblique	*AaBbCcDdEeFf*
Helvetica Bold	**AaBbCcDdEeFf**
Helvetica Bold Oblique	***AaBbCcDdEeFf***

The problem is, the word *font* can refer to a typeface *or* a font family. It's completely dependent upon context. If all of this arcana has your head spinning, remember this simple rule: When in doubt, say "font."

Indistinct letters

Using Font Families

Working with a font family allows you to assign roles to each variation.

Novice typographers tend to use too many fonts. They want each text element within their document to be distinct from the others, so they assign each one a different font. Unfortunately, this technique usually results in typographic overload.

You can avoid this problem by choosing fonts with large families. Each font family generally includes several different styles such as normal, italic, bold, and bold italic. These variations can be used to add contrast without resorting to entirely new typefaces. For example, you could use the regular weight of a font for body text, bold for headlines, bold italic for pull quotes or subheads, and medium italic for captions. The resulting document is rich in contrast, even though a single font is used throughout.

Type Style

Type style refers to variations in weight and stroke that lend flexibility in contrast and emphasis to each type family.

Characters set in bold type have thicker strokes and add authority or emphasis to a typeface. Bold type is also frequently used for subheads to break up long expanses of text.

Lend **Contrast** to Your Publication

Lorem ipsum dolor sit amet, consectetuer adipiscing elit, sed diam nonummy nibh euismod tincidunt ut laoreet dolore magna aliquam erat volutpat. Ut wisi enim ad minim veniam, quis nostrud exerci tation ullamcorper suscipit lobortis nisl ut aliquip ex ea commodo consequat.

Duis autem vel eum iriure dolor in hendrerit in vulputate velit esse molestie consequat, vel illum dolore eu feugiat nulla facilisis at vero eros et accumsan et iusto odio dignissim qui blandit praesent luptatum zzril delenit augue duis dolore te feugait nulla facilisi. Lorem ipsum dolor sit amet, consectetuer adipiscing elit, sed diam nonummy nibh euismod tincidunt ut laoreet dolore magna aliquam erat volutpat.

Lorem ipsum dolor sit amet consecteteur

Ut wisi enim ad minim veniam, quis nostrud exerci tation ullamcorper suscipit lobortis nisl ut aliquip ex ea commodo consequat. Duis autem vel eum iriure dolor in hendrerit in vulputate velit esse molestie consequat, vel illum dolo eu feugiat nulla facilisis at vero eros et iusto odio dignissim qui blandit praesent luptatum zzril delenit augue duis dolore te feugait nulla facilisi.

Nam liber tempor cum soluta nobis eleifend option congue nihil imperdiet doming id quod mazim placerat facer possim assum. Lorem ipsum dolor sit amet, consectetuer adipiscing elit, sed diam nonummy.

Ut wisi enim ad minim veniam

Nibh euismod tincidunt ut laoreet dolore magna aliquam erat volutpat. Ut wisi enim ad minim veniam, quis nostrud exerci tation ullamcorper suscipit lobortis nisl ut aliquip ex ea consequat.

Duis autem vel eum iriure dolor in hendrerit in vulputate velit esse molestie consequat, vel illum dolore eu feugiat nulla facilisis.

Lorem ipsum dolor sit amet, consectetuer adipiscing elit, sed diam nonummy nibh euismod tincidunt ut laoreet dolore magna aliquam erat volutpat. Ut wisi enim ad minim veniam, quis nostrud exerci tation ullamcorper suscipit lobortis nisl ut aliquip ex ea commodo consequat.

tate velit esse molestie consequat, vel illum dolore eu feugiat nulla facilisis at vero eros et accumsan et iusto odio dignissim qui blandit praesent luptatum zzril delenit augue duis dolore te feugait nulla facilisi. Lorem ipsum dolor sit amet, consectetuer adipiscing elit, sed diam nonummy nibh euismod tincidunt ut laoreet dolore magna aliquam erat volutpat.

Ut wisi enim ad minim veniam, quis nostrud exerci tation ullamcorper suscipit lobortis nisl ut aliquip ex ea commodo consequat. Duis autem vel eum iriure dolor in hendrerit in vulputate velit esse molestie consequat, vel illum dolo eu feugiat nulla facilisis at vero eros et accumsan et iusto odio dignissim qui blandit praesent luptatum zzril delenit augue duis dolore te feugait nulla facilisi.

Duis autem veleum iriure dolor henderit

Nam liber tempor cum soluta nobis eleifend option congue nihil imperdiet doming id quod mazim placerat facer possim assum. Lorem ipsum dolor sit amet, consectetuer adipiscing elit, sed diam nonummy nibh euis-

Use bold type carefully and sparingly. Too much bold type darkens a page, making it look dense and uninviting.

Bold Not Always Better

Characters set in boldface type have thicker strokes and add authority or emphasis to a typeface. Bold type is frequently used for subheads that break up long expanses of text.

Close-Up of Typefaces

Boldface type must be used carefully. In small sizes, the counters-enclosed spaces within letters like e and o – often become filled in on laser printed output. A lot of boldface type also darkens a page.

Setting isolated words in boldface type in the middle of a block of text can draw more attention to a word than it warrants and can also create a "checkerboard" appearance on the page. Characters set in boldface type have thicker strokes and add authority or emphasis to a typeface. Bold type is frequently used for.

Letters Move In

Setting isolated words in boldface type in the middle of a block of text can draw more attention to a word than it warrants and can also create a "checkerboard" appearance on the page.

Characters set in boldface type have thicker strokes and add authority or emphasis to a typeface. Bold type is frequently used for subheads that break up long expanses of text.

Boldface type must be used carefully. In small sizes, the counters - enclosed spaces within letters like e and o - often become filled in on laser printed output. A lot of boldface type also darkens a page.

Setting isolated words in boldface type in the middle of a block of text can draw more attention to a word than it warrants and can also create a "checkerboard" appearance on the page. Characters set in boldface type have thicker strokes and add authority or emphasis to a typeface. Bold type is frequently used for subheads that break up long expanses of text. Boldface type must be used carefully. In small sizes, the counters often fill in on laser printed output. Characters set in boldface type have thicker strokes and add authority or emphasis to a typeface. Bold type is frequently used for subheads that break up long expanses of text.

Boldface type must be used carefully. In small sizes, the counters – enclosed spaces within letters like e and o – often become filled in on laser printed output. A lot of boldface type also darkens a page.

Setting isolated words in boldface type in the middle of a block of text can draw more attention to a word than it warrants and can also create a "checkerboard" appearance on the page.

Avoid using boldface type to emphasize isolated words in the middle of a block of text. The bold type can draw more attention to a word than it warrants and create a checkerboard look to the page.

You can use italic type for emphasis or when irony or humor is intended. Italic text implies a conversational tone. It's sometimes used to indicate a quote where no quote exists—as if someone were speaking.

Using **bold** as a means of emphasis can create a **checkerboard look** to your page. It's **much** better to use **italic type** for emphasis. Words in italic type are perceived as **spoken words**.	Using *bold* as a means of emphasis can create a *checkerboard look* to your page. It's *much* better to use *italic type* for emphasis. Words in italic type are perceived as *spoken words*.

Shadow, outline, and underline are also offered as styles for some typefaces. Exercise restraint when using these kinds of styles, because they're generally more difficult to read. In the following example, shadow and outline seriously hinder legibility.

Outline and shadow text
should be used sparingly.

Likewise, underlining interferes with the reader's ability to recognize letterforms by obscuring descenders.

Lines of emphasis quickly
become lines of annoyance.

Small caps refers to a type style in which the lowercase letters are replaced with smaller versions of the uppercase letters. Small caps can provide emphasis without darkening the page with bold type.

Small caps can also be used to replace uppercase letters in acronyms. Because all-caps text is occasionally used for emphasis, acronyms can unintentionally draw too much attention. Using small caps avoids this snare.

He's a VIP in the CIA.
He's a VIP in the CIA.

Most software packages allow you to set the size ratio between small caps and large caps. Generally, small caps look best from 80 through 90 percent of the large cap size. Be careful: the default value in some programs is closer to 70 percent. The resulting text can look jarring, because the large caps have noticeably thicker strokes.

SMALL CAPS
SMALL CAPS

Type Weight

Type weight—the letter width and stroke thickness—offers further flexibility in lightening or darkening your page.

But what about those ultra-quirky display faces? It may seem harsh to say, but there are a great many fonts you'll never have occasion to use. Fonts that look like overstylized calligraphy, rubber stamps, or cattle brands from the Old West may look kind of intriguing, but they carry too many associations to be used in any general sort of way. Likewise, script fonts don't have too many uses; they're extremely fancy, but not all that readable. You see them on wedding invitations and the occasional gourmet menu. It may seem like an entire branch of typography is being ignored, but don't let it concern you. It's not your job to find a use for these weirdo fonts. Stick with fonts that fit your project, and you'll never go wrong.

THE POINT/PICA SCHEME

6 picas = 1 inch

12 points = 1 pica

72 points = 1 inch

Presenting Type Effectively

Typography doesn't end with the choosing of a typeface—the presentation is equally important.

Once you've made your typeface choices, it's time to determine how to present them effectively in your layout environment. Your attention must shift to type sizes, word and line spacing, line endings, and column widths. Many of these concerns involve measurement, so we'd better start by defining the units of the trade: *points* and *picas*.

If you're not already familiar with points and picas, you're probably wondering why you should go through the trouble of learning a whole new measurement scheme—especially since your desktop-publishing program will let you use inches. Truthfully, though, the point/pica scheme is better. The units are smaller, so you don't spend so much time talking in fractions. Besides, points and picas are part of the vocabulary of typesetting. Type size is measured in points. Most programs let you adjust font size in 0.1-point increments. Line spacing and rule thickness (discussed in Chapter 4) are also on the point standard—even if you've set the rulers in your program to inches. You can't escape points, so why fight them? Make them your new standard.

Type Size

Type size is determined by the importance of the message and the available space.

When choosing type size, consider the amount of white space available. Remember that the width of the text column should be a factor in choosing font sizes (see Chapter 2 for a review).

Ultimately, you're trying to strike a balance. The idea is not to fill every square inch of white space with type—that only clutters your document. On the other hand, you don't want your publication to have gaping holes, as if something dropped out when the pages went to press. Somewhere between these two extremes is the ideal: properly-sized type with a good amount of breathing room. The definition of *a good amount* is dependent upon type size. Display text requires more breathing room than body text. For instance, don't feel you have to extend a headline across the entire length of the text columns. It will attract more attention if it's framed in white space.

White Space Comes in Handy

Lorem ipsum dolor sit amet, consec tetuer adipiscing elit, sed nonummy nibh euismod tincidunt ut laoreet dolore magna aliquam erat volutpat. Ut wisi enim ad minim veniam, quis nostrud exerci tation ullamcorper suscipit lobortis nisl ut aliquip ex ea commodo consequat.

Duis autem vel eum iriure dolor in hendrerit in vulputate velit esse laoreet dolore magna aliquam erat volutpat.

Ut wisi enim ad minim veniam, quis nostrud exerci tation ullamcorper suscipit lobortis nisl ut aliquip ex ea commodo consequat. Duis autem vel eum iriure dolor in hendrerit in vulputate velit esse molestie consequat, vel illum dolore eu feugiat nulla facilisis at vero eros et accumsan et

Large type squeezed into a small area produces a claustrophobic effect.

White Space Is Sorely Needed

Lorem ipsum dolor sit amet, consec tetuer adipiscing elit, sed nonummy nibh euismod tincidunt ut laoreet dolore magna aliquam erat volutpat. Ut wisi enim ad minim veniam, quis nostrud exerci tation ullamcorper suscipit lobortis nisl ut aliquip ex ea commodo consequat.

Duis autem vel eum iriure dolor in hendrerit in vulputate velit esse laoreet dolore magna aliquam erat volutpat.

Ut wisi enim ad minim veniam, quis nostrud exerci tation ullamcorper suscipit lobortis nisl ut aliquip ex ea commodo consequat. Duis autem vel eum iriure dolor in hendrerit in vulputate velit esse molestie consequat, vel illum dolore eu feugiat nulla facilisis at vero eros et accumsan et

Your software won't stop you from setting a given font at any size, so you've got to use common sense to decide what works. Serif fonts with extreme variation in stroke width, like Bodoni don't work well at small sizes (the thin strokes all but disappear). Fonts will small x-heights lose readability at small sizes, and so do many condensed faces.

This text is not very easy to read.

Unbolded serif fonts, while great for body text, can look out of place when set at large sizes. They're too thin and spidery to command attention. And if you're working with a font that's extremely detailed or decorative, be prepared to set it big. Some fonts were never meant to be used for anything but headlines. Remember, if you can't read it, nobody else can either.

Alignment

Alignment can affect the readability of your publication.

There are four basic options for aligning type:

- Justified (flush left/flush right)
- Flush left with a ragged right margin
- Flush right with a ragged left margin
- Centered

Readability studies tend to favor flush-left/ragged-right alignment, meaning that the first letters of each line are lined up with each other, but the lines themselves are of irregular length. The irregular line endings create a ragged margin of white space, giving publications a lighter look. In addition, the even word spacing enables readers to easily recognize word groups. Flush-left text has an informal, contemporary feeling to it.

> "This country, with its institutions, belongs to the people who inhabit it. Whenever they shall grow weary of the existing government, they can exercise their constitutional right of amending it, or their constitutional right to dismember or overthrow it."
>
> *Abraham Lincoln*

Justified type produces lines of equal length. The type aligns to both the left and right margins. Word spacing is adjusted automatically to create the even line endings.

Because of the uniform line length, justified columns lack the white space created with ragged alignment, and thus tend to "darken" a publication. In addition, justified type is sometimes considered more difficult to read, because more words are hyphenated and large gaps often appear between words.

Nevertheless, many magazines, newspapers, and books use justified alignment because the word density is higher. Less space is needed to communicate the same amount of information, which can reduce the number of pages in a document and result in cost savings.

"This country, with its institutions, belongs to the people who inhabit it. Whenever they shall grow weary of the existing government, they can exercise their constitutional right of amending it, or their constitutional right to dismember or overthrow it."

Abraham Lincoln

Centered alignment is often used for display type, particularly for short headlines that span more than one text column. Centering text can lend a formal tone to a document. It's frequently used for wedding invitations and official announcements.

Ozzie & Harriet
invite you to join them
in the celebration of
their marriage

Saturday, April 12, 1998

The Harcourt Gardens

However, avoid centering long blocks of type, particularly for a three- or four-line headline. Because readers have to search for the beginning of each line, centered type is more difficult to read.

In lengthy center-justified headlines, readers must search for the beginning of each line.

Type also can be set flush right/ragged left. Like centered type, flush-right alignment forces the reader to slow down to find the beginning of the next line, and, therefore, you'll need to limit its use to concise headings and headlines.

Try not to be too wordy when setting subheads flush right	**Be concise instead**
Lorem ipsum dolor sit amet, consec tetuer adipiscing elit, sed nonummy nibh euismod tincidunt ut laoreet dolore magna aliquam erat volutpat. Ut wisi enim ad minim veniam, quis nostrud exerci tation ullamcorper suscipit lobortis nisl ut aliquip ex ea commodo consequat. Duis autem vel eum iriure dolor in hendrerit in vulputate velit esse	Lorem ipsum dolor sit amet, consec tetuer adipiscing elit, sed nonummy nibh euismod tincidunt ut laoreet dolore magna aliquam erat volutpat. Ut wisi enim ad minim veniam, quis nostrud exerci tation ullamcorper suscipit lobortis nisl ut aliquip ex ea commodo consequat. Duis autem vel eum iriure dolor in hendrerit in vulputate velit esse dignissim qui blandit praesent veleum iriure dolor in hendrerit in vulputate velit esse dignissim qui blandit

Kerning And Tracking

Most page layout programs provide you with multiple tools to adjust spacing.

Kerning is the adjustment of space between selected pairs of letters. *Tracking* automatically governs the amount of space placed between each character throughout a block of text.

Certain pairs of letters sometimes appear to be separated by too much space. This effect is particularly apparent in a headline with an uppercase T next to a lowercase o, or an uppercase W next to a lowercase a, and so on.

WA	Want	Today	any.
WA	Want	Today	any.

Kerning reduces the space between individual pairs of letters to improve readability. It can also be used to add space between certain letter pairs. This is often done to improve legibility when setting white type against a black background.

USING FORCE

Some programs offer the option of *force justification* (also known as *justify last line*), which stretches the available text to fill the entire line. It's only really good for the occasional special effect. For best results, use a sans serif face and set it in all caps—you don't want too much differentiation between letterforms.

L o o k i n g
B a d

LOOKING
GOOD

Well-constructed fonts include *kerning pairs*, which automatically determine the amount of space needed between any two characters. Even so, type set at large sizes will probably require some manual kerning on your part.

Desktop publishing software also uses tracking to determine the amount of space between each character. Different programs allow you to adjust tracking in different ways. Some use numerical values, while others use general terms like *loose* and *tight*. By tightening tracking, you increase the density of your text, fitting more words into the same amount of space. This tends to darken a publication.

Conversely, loose tracking lightens a page.

Usually, if you've set reasonable parameters for justification in your program, the very worst offenders in hyphenation will be lines with bad breaks, caused by long single-syllable words or words with	**Usually, if you've set reasonable parameters for justification in your program, the very worst offenders in hyphenation will be lines with bad breaks, caused by long**

Word Spacing

The amount of space between words affects the density—and consequently, the readability—of a publication.

When word spacing is tight, more words can be included on each line. In certain situations, this reduces the number of hyphenated words.

When word spacing is tight, more words can be included on each line. In certain situations, this reduces the number of hyphenated words. You ll need to be careful with word spacing. If you reduce word spacing too much, the text becomes difficult to read and the publication looks too dark. Tracking and word spacing are often adjusted simultaneously. One common	When word spacing is tight, more words can be included on each line. In certain situations, this reduces the number of hyphenated words. You ll need to be careful with word spacing. If you reduce word spacing too much, the text becomes difficult to read and the publication looks too dark. Tracking and word spacing are often adjusted simultaneously. One common

You'll need to be careful with word spacing. If you reduce word spacing too much, the text becomes difficult to read and the publication looks too dark.

Tracking and word spacing are often adjusted simultaneously. One common technique, especially with high x-height typefaces, is to slightly reduce letter spacing and increase word spacing.

When experimenting with tracking and word spacing, be sure to review proofs to ensure you've achieved the right balance.

Paragraph Spacing, Tabs, And Indents

Use tabs, indents, or extra space between paragraphs to enhance readability. Tabs and indents also can be used to effectively set off lists and quotations.

The space associated with the beginning of a paragraph should be consistent throughout your document. Generally, two types of spacing schemes are used: a two- to five-space indent at the beginning of the first line of each paragraph, or extra spacing between paragraphs with the first line set flush-left.

If you decide to use indents, don't use the system defaults. Set the tabs yourself. The standard tab default in most programs is half an inch (three picas), which is way too large for most body text.

Adding space between paragraphs makes each paragraph look like a self-contained unit. It also adds an openness to a publication by breaking up the grayness of large expanses of text.

Goods & Services

Headline

Your job is to assemble a total picture from a series of individual parts. No piece of the puzzle should be isolated from the others. The parts must fit together harmoniously.

The total picture includes consideration of the environment in which your advertisement or publication will be distributed.

For example, when designing a newspaper advertisement, consider how it will look when surrounded by news items and other advertisements.

Your job is to assemble a total picture from a series of individual parts. No piece of thepuzzle should be isolated from the others. The various parts must

Software

The total picture includes consideration of the environment in which your advertisement or publication is going to be distributed.

For example, when designing a newspaper advertisement, consider how it will look when surrounded by news.

Your job is to assemble a total picture from a series of individual parts. No piece of the puzzle should be isolated from the others. The parts must fit together harmoniously.

The total picture includes consideration of the environment in which your publication will be distributed.

Typesetting

For example, when designing a newspaper advertisement, consider how it will look when surrounded by news.

Your job is to assemble a total picture from a series of individual parts. No piece of the puzzle should be isolated from the others. The various parts must fit together.

The total picture includes consideration of the environment in which your advertisement or publication will be distributed.

For example, when designing a newspaper advertisement, consider how it will look when surrounded by news.

Your job is to assemble a total picture from a series of individual parts. No piece of the puzzle should be isolated from the others. The various parts must fit together.

For example, when designing a newspaper advertisement, consider how it will look when surrounded by news.

Your job is to assemble a total picture from a series of individual parts. No piece of the

To increase paragraph spacing, use your desktop publishing program's paragraph-spacing command, rather than inserting two carriage returns, which usually results in far too much space between paragraphs. The paragraph-spacing command lets you add just

WHO'S IN CHARGE HERE?

So, what's really determining the amount of space between letters—kerning or tracking? Both, actually.

Think of kerning as a set of proportions. The average two characters need x amount of space between them, but certain combinations need either some fraction of x or some multiple of x. Once you've defined all the combinations in terms of x, changing x's value will change the letter spacing while still maintaining the spatial proportions established by kerning.

When you adjust tracking, you're essentially changing the value of x. It gets smaller when tracking is tightened, and larger when tracking is loosened. (I've simplified the matter greatly for the sake of explanation, but this gives you a rough idea of how the two methods interact.)

enough space between paragraphs to add interest, without creating a page filled with distracting parallel bands of white space.

also adds an openess to a publication by breaking up the "grayness" of large expanses of text.

To increase spacing between paragraphs, always use your desktop publishing program's paragraph-spacing command, rather than using two carriage returns, which can result in too much space between paragraphs.

The paragraph-spacing command lets you add just enough white space between paragraphs to add interest without creating a page filled with distracting parallel bands of white space.

Extra space between paragraphs enhances readability. Adding additional space between paragraphs makes each paragraph appear

also adds an openess to a publication by breaking up the "grayness" of large expanses of text.

To increase spacing between paragraphs, always use your desktop publishing program's paragraph-spacing command, rather than using two carriage returns, which can result in too much space between paragraphs.

The paragraph-spacing command lets you add just enough white space between paragraphs to add interest without creating a page filled with distracting parallel bands of white space.

Extra space between paragraphs enhances readability. Adding additional space between paragraphs makes each paragraph appear more like a self-contained unit. It

Tabs can be used in conjunction with extra space to further open up a publication.

Goods & Services

Headline

Your job is to assemble a total picture from a series of individual parts. No piece of the puzzle should be isolated from the others. The parts must fit together harmoniously.

The total picture includes consideration of the environment in which your advertisement or publication will be distributed.

For example, when designing a newspaper advertisement, consider how it will look when surrounded by news items and other advertisements.

Your job is to assemble a total picture from a series of individual parts. No piece of

Software

The total picture includes consideration of the environment in which your advertisement or publication is going to be distributed.

For example, when designing a newspaper advertisement, consider how it will look when surrounded by news.

Your job is to assemble a total picture from a series of individual parts. No piece of the puzzle should be isolated from the others. The parts must fit together harmoniously.

The total picture includes consideration of the environment in which your publication will be distributed.

Typesetting

For example, when designing a newspaper advertisement, consider how it will look when surrounded by news.

Your job is to assemble a total picture from a series of individual parts. No piece of the puzzle should be isolated from the others. The various parts must fit together.

The total picture includes consideration of the environment in which your advertisement or publication will be distributed.

For example, when designing a newspaper advertisement, consider how it will look when surrounded by news.

Your job is to assemble a total picture from a series of individual parts. No piece of the puzzle should be isolated from the others. The various parts must fit together.

For example, when designing a newspaper advertisement, consider how it will look when surrounded by news.

Your job is to assemble a total picture from a series of individual parts. No piece of the

If you want your text to align vertically across adjacent columns, you're probably better off sticking with indents. Otherwise, you'll need a full line space between paragraphs to keep things even—and that's probably too much space.

Indents can be used to call attention to quotations in a publication by moving a text block in from the left- and right-hand margins. Indents can also set off a list from the body copy.

Lorem ipsum dolor sit amet, consec tetuer adipiscing elit, diam nonummy nibh euismod tincidunt ut laoreet dolore magna aliquam erat volutpat. Ut wisi enim ad minim veniam, quis nostrud exerci tation ullamcorper suscipit lobortis nisl ut aliquip ex ea commodo consequat.

> **"It's easy to grin when your ship comes in, and you've got the stock market beat..."**

Duis autem vel eum iriure dolor in hendrerit in vulputate velit esse molestie consequat, vel illum dolore eu feugiat nulla facilisis at vero eros et accumsan et iusto odio dignissim qui blandit praesent luptatum zzril delenit augue duis dolore te feugait nulla facilisi. Lorem ipsum dolor sit amet, consectetuer adipiscing elit, sed diam nonummy nibh euismod tincidunt ut laoreet dolore magna aliquam

Line Spacing

Leading (pronounced "ledding") is the amount of vertical space allotted for a line of type. It's a critical factor in determining legibility. Like type size, it's measured in points.

The default (or automatic) line spacing found on most desktop publishing systems is approximately 120 percent of the type size being used. Thus, the default leading for 10-point type is 12 points—written as 10/12.

Headlines usually read better when leading is tighter. The words form a distinct visual unit, instead of looking like a series of unrelated lines.

Latest Business Research Provides Explanation for Increase in Log Home Sales

The most recent issue of *Log Home Digest* published a survey which indicated that more people are buying log homes because "they like the way they look." Industry sources say a drop in log

Latest Business Research Provides Explanation for Increase in Log Home Sales

The most recent issue of *Log Home Digest* published a survey which indicated that more people are buying log homes because "they like the way they look." Industry sources say a drop in log prices may also be contributing to the trend.

Junking The Auto

Ultimately, you're better off using a fixed value for leading when setting type, rather than relying on your program's automatic leading. Common designer tricks, like using a large, decorative capital letter to begin a paragraph, will cause auto leading to go awry, because it uses the largest character in a line to determine the proper amount of vertical space. You shouldn't want your body text's leading fluctuating for any reason, so why give it the opportunity? If you want your leading to be 120 percent of the font size, do the math, and get a value that won't change.

On the other hand, extra leading often improves the appearance of body text. It opens up the page, making it seem less gray.

Extra leading is usually called for when sans serif typefaces are used for body text.

People are created equal, that they are endowed by their Creator with certain unalienable rights, that among these are Life, Liberty, and the Pursuit of Happiness.

Women in Multimedia

That to secure these rights, governments are instituted among Men and Women. We hold these truths to be self-evident, that all People are created equal, that they are

People are created equal, that they are endowed by their Creator with certain unalienable rights, that among these are Life, Liberty, and the Pursuit of Happiness.

Women in Multimedia

That to secure these rights, governments are instituted among Men and Women. We hold these truths to be self-evident, that all People are created equal, that they are

Leading should be proportional to line length. In general, use minimal leading for short lines of type. Increase leading as line length increases.

Leading also can be used as a design tool for special effects. You may sometimes want to tighten leading so that descenders from one line of type touch the ascenders from the line below. This special effect is often seen in logos and nameplates.

One of the advantages of using uppercase letters for headlines is that you can substantially reduce leading, because capitals lack descenders.

Happy Birthday to
All Employees

HAPPY BIRTHDAY TO
ALL EMPLOYEES

Special Type Effects

Computers offer limitless ways to transform type into a graphic element.

The possibilities for shaping, altering, and manipulating type have increased dramatically with the advent of desktop publishing. As tempting as a creative type treatment may be, though, it's not an end unto itself. Make sure there's a good reason for it. And never sacrifice legibility for the sake of an effect—if your type can't be read, your message isn't getting across.

Reversing And Screening Type

By reversing and screening type, you can achieve the effect of color without the expense.

Two simple but powerful type effects are created by reversing type out of a black background or screening it in a lighter shade of gray.

Using these techniques, you can add enough visual contrast to your pages to achieve a "color" effect with only black ink and white paper.

When screening type against a background, make sure there's enough contrast to keep the words legible.

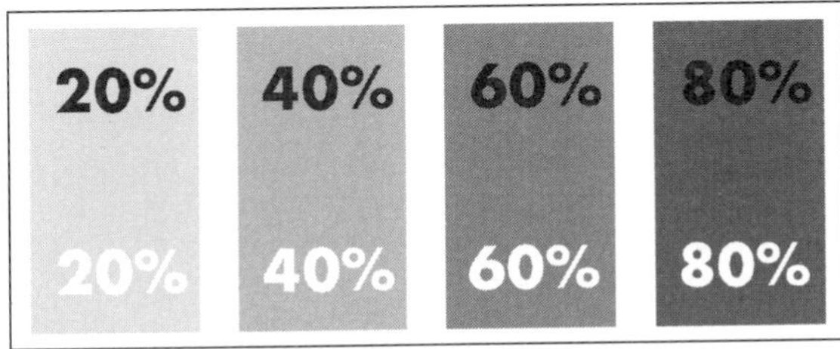

Use light type against dark-gray backgrounds and dark type against light-gray backgrounds; otherwise, the type might be obscured.

Screening type can be used as an attention-getting device, useful for sidebars or logos.

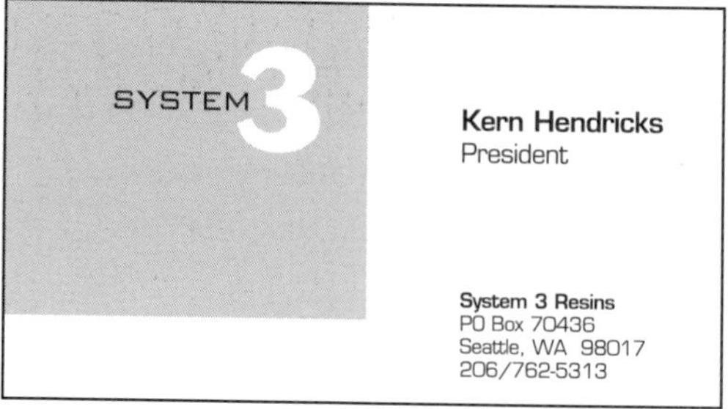

When using screens, consider the limitations of your output device. A 300 dpi laser printer produces a coarse, grainy screen. It may be better to use other design techniques if you're limited to 300 dpi. Another option is to send documents that contain screens to a service bureau, to be output on a high-resolution imagesetter. The results will be much more professional-looking.

Reversing type—setting white type on a black background—is a great way to draw attention to headlines, subheads, and other important display copy.

Lorem ipsum dolor sit amet, consec tetuer adipiscing elit, diam nonummy nibh euismod tincidunt ut laoreet dolore magna aliquam erat volutpat. Ut wisi enim ad minim veniam, quis nostrud exerci tation ullamcorper suscipit lobortis nisl ut aliquip ex ea commodo consequat, dignissim qui blandit praesent luptatum zzril delenit augue duis dolore te feugait nulla facilisi

THRILLS

Duis autem vel eum iriure dolor in hendrerit in vulputate velit esse molestie consequat, vel illum dolore eu feugiat nulla facilisis at vero eros et accumsan et iusto odio. Lorem ipsum dolor sit amet, consectetuer adipiscing elit, sed diam nonummy nibh euismod tincidunt ut laoreet dolore magna aliquam erat volutpat.

Ut wisi enim ad minim veniam, nostrud exerci tation ullamcorper suscipit lobortis nisl ut aliquip ex ea commodo consequat. Duis autem vel eum iriure dolor in hendrerit in vulputate velit molestie consequat, illum dolore eu feugiat nulla facilisis at vero eros et accumsan et iusto odiodignissim qui blandit praesent luptatum zzril delenit augue duis possim assum. Lorem ipsum dolor sit amet, consectetuer adipiscing elit, sed diam nonummy nibh euismod tincidunt ut laoreet dolore magna aliquam.

CHILLS

Erat volutpat. Ut wisi enim ad minim veniam, quis nostrud exerci tation ullamcorper suscipit lobortis nisl ut ex ea commodo consequat.

Duis autem vel eum iriure dolor in hendrerit in vulputate velit esse molestie consequat, vel illum dolore eu feugiat nulla facilisis. Ut wisi enim ad minim veniam, nostrud exerci tation ullamcorper suscipit lobortis nisl ut aliquip ex ea commodo consequat. Duis autem vel eum iriure dolor in hendrerit in vulputate velit molestie consequat, illum dolore eu feugiat nulla facilisis at vero.

SPILLS

Eros et accumsan et iusto odiodignissim qui blandit praesent ipsum dolor sit amet, consec tetuer adipiscing elit, diam nonummy nibh euismod tincidunt ut laoreet dolore magna aliquam erat volutpat. Ut wisi enim ad minim

Reversing works best with large-sized single words or small phrases—lots of small reversed copy is difficult to read.

Keep it Simple

Don't get too wordy when working with reversed type

It's also best to use clean, bold, sans serif typefaces when reversing type. Serif faces, particularly ornate scripts, tend to break up when reversed.

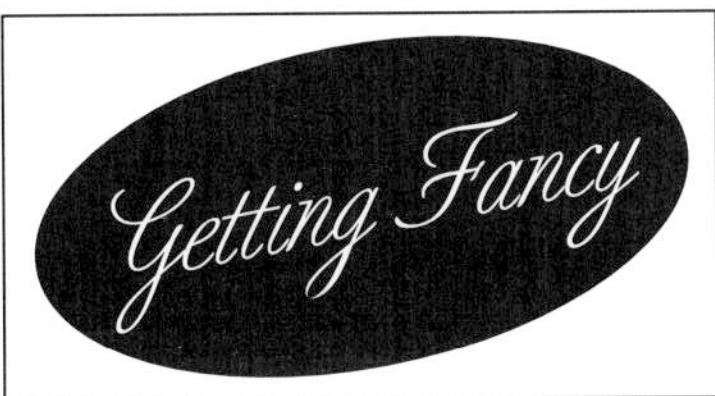

More effects can be achieved by screening and reversing colored type. For more details, see the Do It In Color section of this book.

Stretching And Compressing Type

Interesting effects can be created by changing a typeface's character width.

Most desktop publishing and graphics software packages let you stretch or compress individual letters, words, and sentences to create interesting designs.

STRETCH **COMPRESS**

As with other special effects, use stretched or compressed type sparingly—it's easy to overdo.

Rotating Type

Rotated type can be a real attention-grabber when used strategically.

Most desktop publishing software packages offer some degree of type rotation capabilities. For example, a program may allow rotation in 45- and 90-degree increments, which comes in handy for setting photo credits or copyright notices.

Other programs let you rotate type across all 360 degrees. You can achieve some interesting effects with this feature.

Leland Shutterbug

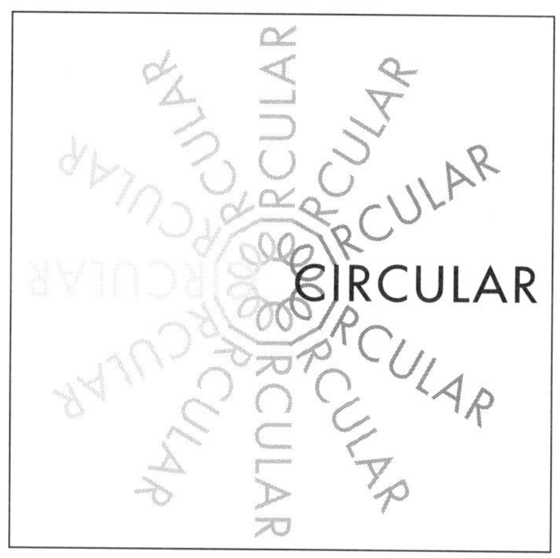

Setting Type Along A Path

Setting type to follow a path offers several design options.

By flowing type along a path, whether it's a geometric shape or a custom-drawn line, you can achieve quick results that would take traditional typesetters hours to create. Often, path-set text can be combined with simple illustrations to create attractive logos.

Filling Type

Filling letters changes their tone, shape, and impact.

Another eye-popping effect involves filling letters with a pattern or image. Limit this technique to one or two easily recognized words. Complex messages are not legible under this treatment. Bold sans serif typefaces work best.

Other Effects

You can achieve a variety of special type effects with most desktop publishing programs.

You can apply dozens of other custom treatments to type, depending on the software you're using.

As always, though, make sure the effect is appropriate to the subject and content at hand. Legibility is more important than novelty.

Fine Tuning

Often, the slightest details will determine whether a document looks professional or amateurish.

Many conventions common to the typewriter are not acceptable in the desktop publishing world. Double-spacing after periods, for instance, is an anachronism. Desktop publishing software automatically beefs up the space placed after periods, so using two spaces will create unsightly gaps. Also, you shouldn't be using two hyphens to represent a dash. A single character known as an em dash will do the job. (You won't see it on your keyboard, but there's some combination of keys that'll access it. Consult the manual of the software you're using if you can't find it.)

"I am in earnest--I will not equivocate--I will not excuse--I will not retreat a single inch--and I will be heard!"

Salutatory Address of
The Liberator

"I am in earnest—I will not equivocate—I will not excuse—I will not retreat a single inch—and I will be heard!"

Salutatory Address of
The Liberator

Also, be sure to use open and closed quotation marks (often called smart quotes or typographer's quotes) instead of vertical ones (straight quotes). Most programs will make the substitution automatically, if you set your software's preferences accordingly.

Moving On

Typography is a time-honored craft and an important one for desktop publishers. There are a great many typefaces at your disposal and an impressive range of spacing controls. Learn to use them appropriately. The knowledge will improve the readability and attractiveness of your publications.

In the next chapter, we'll explore graphic page elements that are used in conjunction with type, to highlight and enhance the printed word.

Building Blocks Of Graphic Design

4

Compared to text and graphics—the content of a document—page features such as lines, boxes, and white space probably don't strike you as very interesting. Just because they're less noticeable, though, doesn't mean they're less important. The role they serve is similar to that of a picture frame. When you look at a picture, you never focus on the frame (unless you're just contrary by nature). But, you'd never consider hanging the picture up without a frame, and you'd certainly notice if the frame was gone.

The page elements discussed in this chapter are your building blocks. They aren't supplied by a copywriter, drawn by an artist, or plucked out of a photo catalog—you make them and unmake them as you see fit. Knowing how and when to use them is the difference between designing a document and just shoving stuff onto a page.

White Space

White space—page space that is free of text or artwork—is one of the most undervalued tools of graphic design.

Designers divide page space into three classifications: black space, gray space, and white space. *Black space* is a photo or illustration, *gray space* is text, and *white space* is the empty space left over. It probably comes as no surprise that black space draws the eye first, but you might be surprised to learn that white space comes next. There's a logical reason for this. Readers' eyes are drawn by contrast, and white space contrasts more sharply with neighboring elements than gray space does, on the average. White space also provides a place for the reader's eyes to rest. Unbroken expanses of gray space, like those found in stock-market listings and reference books, send a grim message to the reader: "Expect to spend lots of time here."

White space can take many forms as illustrated in our diagram:

A. *The open area surrounding a headline*—Adding white space around a headline is usually a better way to attract attention to it than increasing the type size.

B. *The page margins of an advertisement or publication*—Wide margins direct the readers' attention toward the center of the page.

C. *The vertical space between columns of type*—As columns get wider, more space is needed between them.

D. *The space created by ragged line endings of unjustified type*—Justified text is considered more formal than flush-left text, simply because it lacks these gaps.

E. *Paragraph indents and extra line space between paragraphs*—These small but effective increments of space make text look more inviting by breaking it into discrete chunks.

F. *The space associated with subheads*—Larger breaks in the gray space indicate more dramatic changes in topic.

G. *Leading between lines of type*—Tightly-packed lines of type darken a publication page.

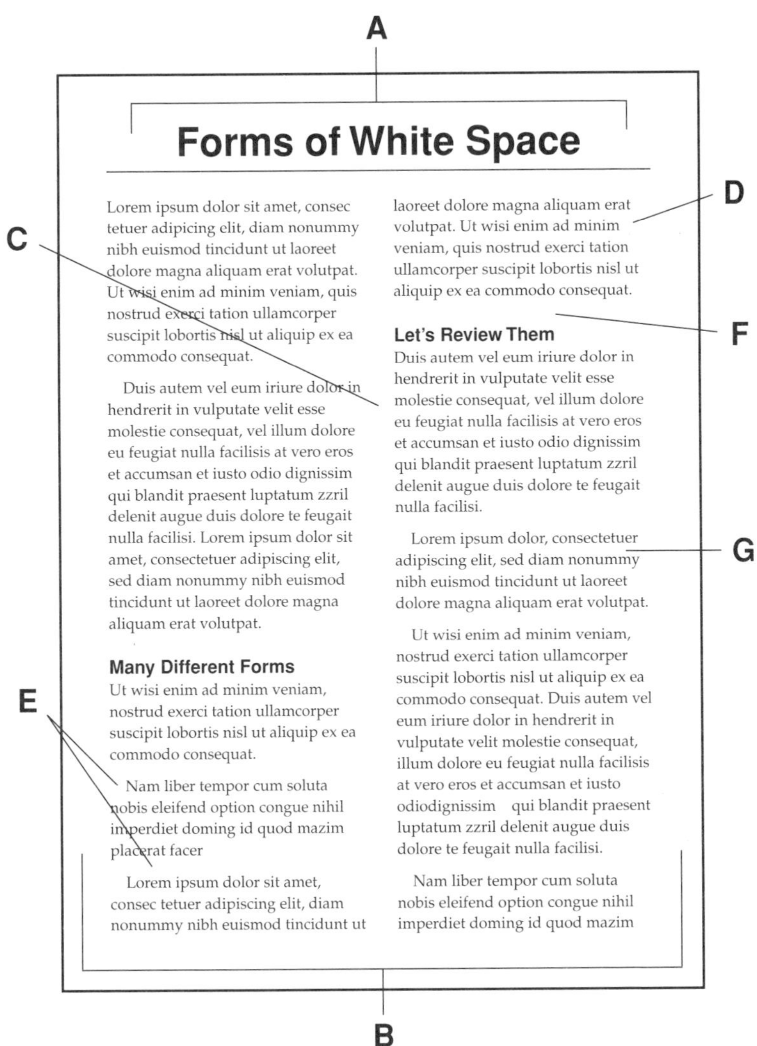

JUST IN CASE...

This is probably too obvious to mention, but white space merely means space devoid of text or graphics. If you're printing on tan paper, your white space will be tan. (Feel free to say "duh" if you felt that was beneath you.)

Sinks

One of the easiest ways to enliven your publication is to include a sink—a band of white space, also called a drop*—at the top of each page.*

A sink draws attention to the page elements below it by adding contrast. It can greatly dramatize headlines.

That Sinking Feeling

Lorem ipsum dolor sit amet, consectetuer adipiscing elit, sed diam nonummy nibh euismod tincidunt ut laoreet dolore magna aliquam erat volutpat. Ut wisi enim ad minim veniam, quis nostrud exerci tation ullamcorper suscipit lobortis nisl ut aliquip ex ea commodo consequat.

Duis autem vel eum iriure dolor in hendrerit in vulputate velit esse molestie consequat, vel illum dolore eu feugiat nulla facilisis at vero eros accumsan et iusto odio dignissim qui blandit praesent luptatum zzril delenit augue duis dolore te feugait nulla facilisi. Lorem ipsum dolor sit amet, consectetuer adipiscing elit, sed nonummy nibh euismod tincidunt ut laoreet dolore magna aliquam erat volutpat.

Ut wisi enim ad minim veniam, quis nostrud exerci tation ullamcorper suscipit lobortis nisl ut aliquip ex ea commodo consequat. Duis autem vel eum iriure dolor in hendrerit in vulputate velit esse molestie consequat, vel illum dolore eu feugiat nulla facilisis at vero eros et accumsan iusto odio dignissim qui blandit praesent luptatum zzril delenit augue duis dolore te feugait nulla facilisi.

Nam liber tempor cum soluta nobis eleifend option congue imperdiet doming id quod mazim placerat facer possim. Lorem ipsum dolor sit amet, consectetuer elit, sed diam nonummy nibh euismod tincidunt ut laoreet dolore magna aliquam erat volutpat.

Ut wisi enim ad minim veniam, nostrud exerci tation ullamcorper suscipit lobortis nisl ut aliquip ex ea commodo consequat.

Duis autem vel eum iriure dolor in hendrerit in vulputate velit esse molestie, vel illum dolore eu feugiat nulla facilisis. Lorem ipsum dolor sit amet, consectetuer adipiscing elit, sed diam nonummy nibh euismod tincidunt ut laoreet dolore magna aliquam erat volutpat. Ut wisi enim ad minim veniam, quis nostrud exerci tation ullamcorper suscipit lobortis nisl ut aliquip ex ea commodo consequat.

Duis autem vel eum iriure dolor in hendrerit in vulputate velit esse molestie consequat, vel illum dolore eu feugiat nulla facilisis at vero eros accumsan et iusto odio dignissim qui blandit praesent luptatum zzril delenit augue duis dolore te feugait nulla facilisi. Lorem ipsum dolor sit amet, consectetuer adipiscing elit, sed diam nonummy nibh euismod tincidunt ut laoreet dolore magna aliquam erat volutpat.

Ut wisi enim ad minim veniam, quis nostrud exerci tation ullamcorper suscipit lobortis nisl ut aliquip ex ea commodo consequat. Duis autem vel eum iriure dolor in hendrerit in vulputate velit esse molestie consequat, vel illum dolore eu feugiat nulla facilisis at vero eros et accumsan iusto odio dignissim qui blandit praesent luptatum zzril delenit augue duis dolore te feugait nulla facilisi.

You can place photographs to slightly extend into the sink, rather than align with the top text margin.

Rising High

Lorem ipsum dolor sit amet, consec tetuer adipiscing elit, diam nonummy nibh euismod tincidunt ut laoreet dolore magna aliquam erat volutpat. Ut wisi enim ad minim veniam, quis nostrud exerci tation ullamcorper suscipit lobortis nisl ut aliquip ex ea commodo consequat.

Duis autem vel eum iriure dolor in hendrerit in vulputate velit esse molestie consequat, vel illum dolore eu feugiat nulla facilisis at vero eros et accumsan et iusto odio dignissim qui blandit praesent luptatum zzril delenit augue duis dolore te feugait nulla facilisi. Lorem ipsum dolor sit amet, consectetuer adipiscing elit, sed diam nonummy nibh euismod tincidunt ut laoreet dolore magna aliquam erat volutpat.

Ut wisi enim ad minim veniam, nostrud exerci tation ullamcorper suscipit lobortis nisl ut aliquip ex ea commodo consequat.

Nam liber tempor cum soluta nobis eleifend option congue nihil imperdiet doming id quod mazim placerat facer

Lorem ipsum dolor sit amet, consec tetuer adipiscing elit, diam nonummy nibh euismod tincidunt ut laoreet dolore magna aliquam erat volutpat. Ut wisi enim ad minim veniam, quis nostrud exerci tation ullamcorper suscipit lobortis nisl ut aliquip ex ea commodo consequat.

Duis autem vel eum iriure dolor in hendrerit in vulputate velit esse molestie consequat, vel illum dolore eu feugiat nulla facilisis at vero eros et accumsan et iusto odio dignissim qui blandit praesent luptatum zzril delenit augue duis dolore te feugait nulla facilisi. Lorem ipsum dolor sit amet, consectetuer adipiscing elit, sed diam nonummy nibh euismod tincidunt ut laoreet dolore magna aliquam erat volutpat.

Ut wisi enim ad minim veniam, nostrud exerci tation ullamcorper suscipit lobortis nisl ut aliquip ex ea commodo consequat. Duis autem vel eum iriure dolor in hendrerit in vulputate velit molestie consequat, illum dolore eu feugiat nulla facilisis at vero eros et accumsan et iusto odiodignissim qui blandit praesent luptatum zzril delenit augue duis dolore te feugait nulla facilisi.

Nam liber tempor cum soluta nobis eleifend option congue nihil imperdiet doming id quod mazim placerat facer duis autem vel eum iriure dolor in hendrerit in vulputate velit molestie consequat, illum dolore eu feugiat nulla facilisis at vero eros et accumsan et iusto odiodignissim qui blandit praesent luptatum zzril delenit augue duis dolore te feugait nulla facilisi. Ut wisi enim ad minim veniam, quis nostrud exerci tation ullamcorper liber tempor cum soluta nobis eleifend option congue nihil imperdiet doming id quod mazim placerat facer duis

A consistent sink provides important page-to-page continuity throughout your publication. The publication loses unity if the text begins at a different level on each page.

Lorem ipsum dolor sit amet, consec tetuer adipiscing elit, diam nonummy nibh euismod tincidunt ut laoreet dolore magna aliquam erat volutpat. Ut wisi enim ad minim veniam, quis nostrud exerci tation ullamcorper suscipit lobortis nisl ut aliquip ex ea commodo consequat.

Duis autem vel eum iriure dolor in hendrerit in vulputate velit esse molestie consequat, vel illum dolore eu feugiat nulla facilisis at vero eros et accumsan et iusto odio dignissim qui blandit praesent luptatum zzril delenit augue duis dolore te feugait nulla facilisi. Lorem ipsum dolor sit amet, consectetuer adipiscing elit, sed diam nonummy nibh euismod tincidunt ut laoreet dolore magna aliquam erat volutpat.

Ut wisi enim ad minim veniam, nostrud exerci tation ullamcorper suscipit lobortis nisl ut aliquip ex ea commodo consequat.

Nam liber tempor cum soluta nobis eleifend option congue nihil imperdiet doming id quod mazim placerat facer

Lorem ipsum dolor sit amet, consec tetuer adipiscing elit, diam nonummy nibh euismod tincidunt ut laoreet dolore magna aliquam erat volutpat. Ut wisi enim ad minim veniam, quis nostrud exerci tation ullamcorper suscipit lobortis nisl ut aliquip ex ea commodo consequat.

Duis autem vel eum iriure dolor in hendrerit in vulputate velit esse molestie consequat, vel illum dolore eu feugiat nulla facilisis at vero eros et accumsan et iusto odio dignissim qui blandit praesent luptatum zzril delenit augue duis dolore te feugait nulla facilisi. Lorem ipsum dolor sit amet, consectetuer adipiscing elit, sed diam nonummy nibh euismod tincidunt ut laoreet dolore magna aliquam erat volutpat.

Ut wisi enim ad minim veniam, nostrud exerci tation ullamcorper suscipit lobortis nisl ut aliquip ex ea commodo consequat. Duis autem vel eum iriure dolor in hendrerit in vulputate velit molestie consequat, illum dolore eu feugiat nulla facilisis.

At vero eros et accumsan et iusto odiodignissim qui blandit praesent luptatum zzril delenit augue duis dolore te feugait nulla facilisi.

Nam liber tempor cum soluta nobis eleifend option congue nihil imperdiet doming id quod mazim placerat facer duis autem vel eum iriure dolor in hendrerit in vulputate velit molestie consequat, illum dolore eu feugiat nulla facilisis at vero eros et accumsan et iusto odiodignissim qui blandit praesent

Luptatum zzril delenit augue duis dolore te feugait nulla facilisi. Ut wisi enim ad minim veniam, quis nostrud exerci tation ullamcorper liber.

iDiam nonummy nibh euismod tincidunt ut laoreet dolore magna aliquam erat volutpat. Ut wisi enim ad minim veniam, quis nostrud exerci tation ullamcorper suscipit lobortis nisl ut aliquip ex ea commodo consequat. Duis autem vel eum iriure dolor in hendrerit in vulputate velit esse molestie consequat, vel illum dolore eu feugiat nulla facilisis at vero eros et accumsan et iusto odio dignissim qui blandit praesent luptatum zzril delenit augue duis dolore te feugait nulla facilisi. Lorem ipsum dolor sit amet, consectetuer adipiscing elit, sed diam nonummy nibh euismod tincidunt ut laoreet dolore magna aliquam erat volutpat.

Ut wisi enim ad minim veniam, nostrud exerci tation ullamcorper suscipit lobortis nisl ut aliquip ex ea commodo consequat.

Nam liber tempor cum soluta nobis eleifend option congue nihil imperdiet doming id quod mazim placerat facer

Lorem ipsum dolor sit amet, consec tetuer adipiscing elit, diam nonummy nibh euismod tincidunt ut laoreet dolore magna aliquam erat volutpat. Ut wisi enim ad minim veniam, quis nostrud exerci tation ullamcorper suscipit lobortis nisl ut aliquip ex ea commodo consequat.

Duis autem vel eum iriure dolor in hendrerit in vulputate velit esse molestie consequat, vel illum dolore eu feugiat nulla facilisis at vero eros et accumsan et iusto odio dignissim qui blandit praesent luptatum zzril delenit augue duis dolore te feugait nulla facilisi. Lorem ipsum dolor sit amet, consectetuer adipiscing elit, sed diam nonummy nibh euismod tincidunt ut laoreet dolore magna aliquam erat volutpat.

Ut wisi enim ad minim veniam, nostrud exerci tation ullamcorper suscipit lobortis nisl ut aliquip ex ea commodo consequat. Duis autem vel eum iriure dolor in hendrerit in vulputate velit molestie consequat, illum dolore eu feugiat nulla facilisis at vero eros et accumsan et iusto odiodignissim qui blandit praesent luptatum zzril delenit augue duis dolore te feugait nulla facilisi.

Nam liber tempor cum soluta nobis eleifend option congue nihil imperdiet doming id quod mazim placerat facer duis autem vel eum iriure

How to Decipher Latin Gibberish

Diam nonummy nibh euismod tincidunt ut laoreet dolore magna aliquam erat volutpat. Ut wisi enim ad minim veniam, quis nostrud exerci tation ullamcorper suscipit lobortis nisl ut aliquip ex ea commodo consequat. Duis autem vel eum iriure dolor in hendrerit in vulputate velit esse molestie consequat, vel illum dolore eu feugiat nulla facilisis at vero eros et accumsan et iusto odio dignissim qui blandit praesent luptatum zzril delenit augue duis dolore te feugait nulla facilisi. Lorem ipsum dolor sit amet, consectetuer adipiscing elit, sed diam nonummy nibh euismod tincidunt ut laoreet dolore magna aliquam erat volutpat.

Ut wisi enim ad minim veniam, nostrud exerci tation ullamcorper suscipit lobortis nisl ut aliquip ex ea commodo consequat. Nam liber tempor cum soluta nobis eleifend option congue nihil imperdiet doming id quod mazim placerat facer.

Lorem ipsum dolor sit amet, consec tetuer adipiscing elit, diam nonummy nibh euismod tincidunt ut laoreet dolore magna aliquam erat volutpat. Ut wisi enim ad minim veniam.

Vertical White Space

A good way to make your text more approachable is to build a significant amount of vertical white space into each page—perhaps by omitting a column of text.

Be Dashing, Yet Diabolical

Diam nonummy nibh euismod tincidunt ut laoreet dolore magna aliquam erat volutpat. Ut wisi enim ad minim veniam, quis nostrud exerci tation ullamcorper suscipit lobortis nisl ut aliquip ex ea commodo consequat. Duis autem vel eum iriure dolor in hendrerit in vulputate velit esse molestie consequat, vel illum dolore eu feugiat nulla facilisis at vero eros et accumsan et iusto odio dignissim qui blandit praesent luptatum zzril delenit augue duis dolore te feugait nulla facilisi. Lorem ipsum dolor sit amet, consectetuer adipiscing elit, sed diam nonummy nibh euismod tincidunt ut laoreet dolore magna aliquam erat volutpat.

Ut wisi enim ad minim veniam, nostrud exerci tation ullamcorper suscipit lobortis nisl ut aliquip ex ea commodo consequat.

Nam liber tempor cum soluta nobis eleifend option congue nihil imperdiet doming id quod mazim placerat facer.

Parleying With James Bond

Lorem ipsum dolor sit amet, consec tetuer adipiscing elit, diam nonummy nibh euismod tincidunt ut laoreet dolore magna aliquam erat volutpat. Ut wisi enim ad minim veniam, quis nostrud exerci tation ullamcorper suscipit lobortis nisl ut aliquip ex ea commodo consequat.

"Mr. Bond will leave you shaken, but not stirred," claims Dr. No

Duis autem vel eum iriure dolor in hendrerit in vulputate velit esse molestie consequat, vel illum dolore eu feugiat nulla facilisis at vero eros et accumsan et iusto odio dignissim qui blandit praesent luptatum zzril delenit augue duis dolore te feugait nulla facilisi. Lorem ipsum dolor sit amet, consectetuer adipiscing elit,

A vertical column of white space on your page can improve the readability of your text and open up your page. If you're planning on setting your text in a single column, vertical white space is practically a necessity—otherwise, your column width will be excessively large.

Vertical white space also provides a good place for elements like sidebars, illustrations, and pull quotes—you can align them horizontally with the text they're meant to enhance.

Don't get carried away with this technique, though. If you fill your empty column to bursting, it no longer serves the function of white space.

Rules

Rules are lines used to emphasize or frame page elements (headlines, pull quotes, captions, and so on). They're also used to separate page elements from one another.

Many varieties of rules, from the simple to the ornate, are available. They can be horizontal, vertical, or angled; thick, or thin; or solid, dotted, dashed, patterned, or graphical.

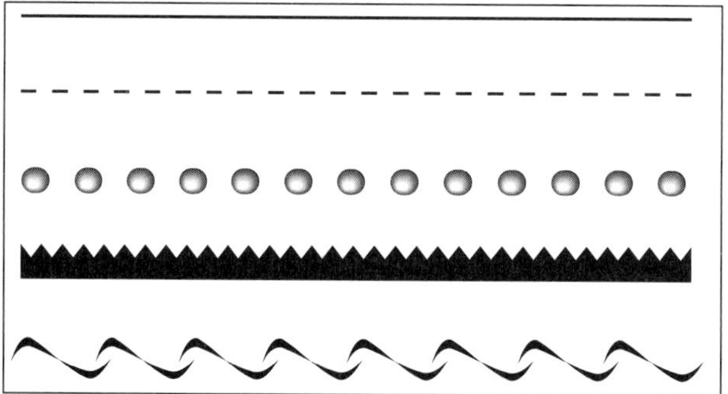

Vertical rules, called *downrules*, are often used to separate columns—particularly when type isn't justified.

Lorem ipsum dolor sit amet, consectetuer adipiscing elit, sed diam nonummy nibh euismod tincidunt ut laoreet dolore magna aliquam erat volutpat. Ut wisi enim ad minim veniam, quis nostrud exerci tation ullamcorper suscipit lobortis nisl ut aliquip ex ea commodo consequat.

Duis autem vel eum iriure dolor in hendrerit in vulputate velit esse molestie consequat, vel illum dolore eu feugiat nulla facilisis at vero eros et accumsan et iusto odio dignissim qui blandit praesent luptatum zzril hendrerit in vulputate velit esse molestie consequat, vel illum dolore eu feugiat nulla facilisis at vero eros et accumsan et iusto odio dignissim qui blandit praesent luptatum zzril delenit augue duis dolore te feugait nulla facilisi.

Nam liber tempor cum soluta nobis eleifend option congue nihil imperdiet doming id quod mazim placerat facer possim assum. Lorem ipsum dolor sit amet,sed diam nonummy nibh euismod tincidunt ut laoreet dolore magna aliquam erat

Dolor sit amet, consectetuer adipiscing elit, sed diam nonummy nibh euismod tincidunt ut laoreet dolore magna aliquam erat volutpat. Ut wisi enim ad minim veniam, quis nostrud exerci tation ullamcorper suscipit lobortis nisl ut aliquip ex ea commodo consequat.Lorem ipsum dolor sit amet, consectetuer adipiscing elit, sed diam nonummy.

Duis autem vel eum iriure dolor in hendrerit in vulputate velit esse molestie consequat, vel illum dolore eu feugiat nulla facilisis at vero eros

Horizontal rules can be used to separate topics within a column or to draw attention to subheads.

Be Dashing, Yet Diabolical

Diam nonummy nibh euismod tincidunt ut laoreet dolore magna aliquam erat volutpat. Ut wisi enim ad minim veniam, quis nostrud exerci tation ullamcorper suscipit lobortis nisl ut aliquip ex ea commodo consequat. Duis autem vel eum iriure dolor in hendrerit in vulputate velit esse molestie consequat, vel illum dolore eu feugiat nulla facilisis at vero eros et accumsan et iusto odio dignissim qui blandit praesent luptatum zzril delenit augue duis dolore te feugait nulla facilisi. Lorem ipsum dolor sit amet, consectetuer adipiscing elit, sed diam nonummy nibh euismod tincidunt ut laoreet dolore magna aliquam erat volutpat.

Ut wisi enim ad minim veniam, nostrud exerci tation ullamcorper suscipit lobortis nisl ut aliquip ex ea commodo consequat.

Nam liber tempor cum soluta nobis eleifend option congue nihil imperdiet doming id quod mazim placerat facer.

Parleying With James Bond

Lorem ipsum dolor sit amet, consec tetuer adipiscing elit, diam nonummy nibh euismod tincidunt ut laoreet dolore magna aliquam erat volutpat. Ut wisi enim ad minim veniam, quis nostrud exerci tation ullamcorper suscipit lobortis nisl ut aliquip ex ea commodo consequat.

Duis autem vel eum iriure dolor in hendrerit in vulputate velit esse molestie consequat, vel illum dolore eu feugiat nulla facilisis at vero eros et accumsan et iusto odio dignissim qui blandit praesent luptatum zzril delenit augue duis dolore te feugait nulla facilisi. Lorem ipsum dolor sit amet, consectetuer adipiscing elit, sed diam nonummy nibh euismod tincidunt ut laoreet dolore magna aliquam erat volutpat.

Horizontal rules are also used to draw attention to pull quotes.

Be Dashing, Yet Diabolical

Diam nonummy nibh euismod tincidunt ut laoreet dolore magna aliquam erat volutpat. Ut wisi enim ad minim veniam, quis nostrud exerci tation ullam corper suscipit lobortis nisl ut aliquip ex commodo consequat. Duis autem vel eum iriure dolor in hendrerit in vulputate velit esse molestie consequat, vel illum dolore eu feugiat nulla facilisis at vero eros et accumsan et iusto odio dignissim qui blandit praesent luptatum zzril delenit augue duis dolore te feugait nulla facilisi. Lorem ipsum dolor sit amet, consectetuer adipiscing elit, sed diam nonummy nibh euismod tincidunt ut laoreet dolore magna aliquam erat volutpat.

Ut wisi enim ad minim veniam, nostrud exerci tation ullamcorper suscipit lobortis nisl ut aliquip ex ea commodo.

Nam liber tempor cum soluta nobis eleifend option congue nihil imperdiet doming id quod mazim placerat facer.

Diam nonummy euismod tincidunt ut laoreet dolore magna aliquam erat volutpat. Ut wisi enim ad minim veniam, quis nostrud exerci tation ullam corper suscipit lobortis nisl ut aliquip ex commodo consequat. Duis autem vel eum iriure dolori in hendrerit in vulputate velit esse molestie consequat, vel illum dolore eu feugiat nulla facilisis at vero eros et accumsan et iusto odio dignissim qui blandit praesent luptatum zzril delenit augue duis dolore te feugait nulla facilisi. Lorem ipsum dolor sit amet, consectetuer adipiscing elit, sed diam nonummy nibh euismod tincidunt ut laoreet dolore magna aliquam erat volutpat.

Maniacal laughter is a poor substitute for a snappy one-liner.

Ut wisi enim ad minim veniam, nostrud exerci tation ullamcorper suscipit lobortis nisl ut aliquip ex ea commodo consequat.

Nam liber tempor cum soluta nobis eleifend option congue nihil imperdiet doming id quod mazim placerat facer.

Lorem ipsum dolor sit amet, consec tetuer adipiscing elit, diam nonummy nibh euismod tincidunt ut laoreet dolore magna aliquam erat volutpat. Ut wisi enim ad minim veniam, quis nostrud tation ullamcorper suscipit lobortis nisl ut aliquip ex ea commodo consequat.

Duis autem vel eum iriure dolor in hendrerit in vulputate velit esse molestie consequat, vel illum dolore eu feugiat nulla facilisis at vero eros et accumsan et iusto

Choose rules that fit the tone of your document. Thick rules are attention-getters. Use them in high-contrast documents like ads and newsletters.

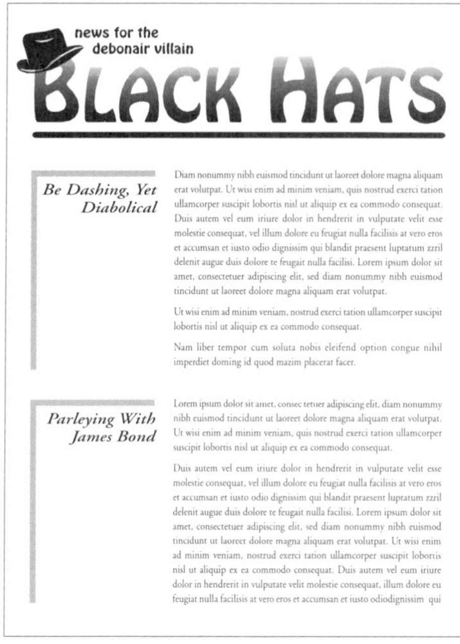

news for the debonair villain

BLACK HATS

Be Dashing, Yet Diabolical

Diam nonummy nibh euismod tincidunt ut laoreet dolore magna aliquam erat volutpat. Ut wisi enim ad minim veniam, quis nostrud exerci tation ullamcorper suscipit lobortis nisl ut aliquip ex ea commodo consequat. Duis autem vel eum iriure dolor in hendrerit in vulputate velit esse molestie consequat, vel illum dolore eu feugiat nulla facilisis at vero eros et accumsan et iusto odio dignissim qui blandit praesent luptatum zzril delenit augue duis dolore te feugait nulla facilisi. Lorem ipsum dolor sit amet, consectetuer adipiscing elit, sed diam nonummy nibh euismod tincidunt ut laoreet dolore magna aliquam erat volutpat.

Ut wisi enim ad minim veniam, nostrud exerci tation ullamcorper suscipit lobortis nisl ut aliquip ex ea commodo consequat.

Nam liber tempor cum soluta nobis eleifend option congue nihil imperdiet doming id quod mazim placerat facer.

Parleying With James Bond

Lorem ipsum dolor sit amet, consec tetuer adipiscing elit, diam nonummy nibh euismod tincidunt ut laoreet dolore magna aliquam erat volutpat. Ut wisi enim ad minim veniam, quis nostrud exerci tation ullamcorper suscipit lobortis nisl ut aliquip ex ea commodo consequat.

Duis autem vel eum iriure dolor in hendrerit in vulputate velit esse molestie consequat, vel illum dolore eu feugiat nulla facilisis at vero eros et accumsan et iusto odio dignissim qui blandit praesent luptatum zzril delenit augue duis dolore te feugait nulla facilisi. Lorem ipsum dolor sit amet, consectetuer adipiscing elit, sed diam nonummy nibh euismod tincidunt ut laoreet dolore magna aliquam erat volutpat. Ut wisi enim ad minim veniam, nostrud exerci tation ullamcorper suscipit lobortis nisl ut aliquip ex ea commodo consequat. Duis autem vel eum iriure dolor in hendrerit in vulputate velit molestie consequat, illum dolore eu feugiat nulla facilisis at vero eros et accumsan et iusto odiodignissim qui

Thin rules are more businesslike, appropriate for documents with a lot of copy.

DICTIONARY OF LATIN TERMS

aliquam Lorem ipsum dolor sit amet, consectetuer adipiscing elit, sed diam nonummy nibh euismod tincidunt ut laoreet dolore magna erat volutpat

aliquip Ut wisi enim ad minim veniam, quis nostrud exerci tation ullamcorper suscipit lobortis nisl ut ex ea commodo consequat. Duis autem vel eum iriure dolor in hendrerit in vulputate velit esse molestie consequat, vel illum dolore eu feugiat nulla facilisis at vero eros accumsan et iusto odio dignissim qui blandit praesent luptatum zzril delenit augue duis dolore te feugait nulla facilisi.

amet Lorem ipsum dolor sit amet, consectetuer adipiscing elit, sed nonummy nibh euismod tincidunt ut laoreet dolore magna aliquam erat volutpat. Ut wisi enim ad minim veniam, quis nostrud exerci tation ullamcorper suscipit lobortis nisl ut aliquip ex ea commodo consequat.

augue Duis autem vel eum iriure dolor in hendrerit in vulputate velit esse molestie consequat, vel illum dolore eu feugiat nulla facilisis at vero eros et accumsan iusto odio dignissim qui blandit praesent luptatum zzril delenit augue duis dolore te feugait nulla facilisi.

avogadro Nam liber tempor cum soluta nobis eleifend option congue imperdiet doming id quod mazim placerat facer possim. Lorem ipsum dolor sit amet, consectetuer elit, sed diam nonummy nibh euismod tincidunt ut laoreet dolore magna aliquam erat volutpat. Ut wisi enim ad minim veniam, nostrud exerci tation ullamcorper suscipit lobortis nisl ut aliquip ex ea commodo consequat. Duis autem vel eum iriure dolor in hendrerit in vulputate velit esse molestie, vel illum dolore eu feugiat nulla facilisis. Lorem ipsum dolor sit amet, consectetuer adipiscing elit, sed diam nonummy nibh euismod tincidunt ut laoreet dolore magna aliquam erat volutpat. Ut wisi enim ad minim veniam, nostrud exerci tation ullamcorper suscipit lobortis nisl ut aliquip ex ea commodo consequat.

axum Duis autem vel eum iriure dolor in hendrerit in vulputate velit esse molestie consequat, vel illum dolore eu feugiat nulla facilisis at vero eros accumsan et iusto odio dignissim qui blandit praesent luptatum zzril delenit augue duis dolore te feugait nulla facilisi. Lorem ipsum dolor sit, consectetuer adipiscing elit, sed diam nonummy nibh euismod tincidunt ut laoreet dolore magna aliquam erat volutpat.

aztecum Ut wisi enim ad minim veniam, quis nostrud exerci tation ullamcorper suscipit lobortis nisl ut aliquip ex ea commodo consequat. Duis autem vel eum iriure dolor in hendrerit in vulputate velit esse molestie consequat, vel illum dolore eu feugiat nulla facilisis at vero eros et accumsan iusto odio dignissim qui blandit praesent luptatum zzril delenit augue duis dolore te feugait nulla facilisi. Nam liber tempor cum soluta nobis eleifend option congue imperdiet doming id quod mazim placerat facer possim.

baabaa Lorem ipsum sit amet, consectetuer euismod tincidunt ut laoreet dolore magna aliquam erat volutpat.

baobab Ut wisi enim ad minim veniam, suscipit lobortis nisl ut aliquip ex ea quis commodo consequat. Duis autem vel eum iriure dolor in hendrerit in vulputate velit esse molestie consequat, vel illum dolore eu feugiat nulla facilisis. Lorem ipsum dolor sit amet, consectetuer adipiscing elit, sed diam nonummy nibh euismod tincidunt ut laoreet dolore magna aliquam erat volutpat.

8

DICTIONARY OF LATIN TERMS

Ut wisi enim ad minim veniam, nostrud exerci tation ullamcorper suscipit lobortis nisl ut aliquip ex ea commodo. Duis autem veleum iriure dolor in hendrerit vulputate velit esse molestie consequat, vel illum dolo eu feugiat facilisis at vero eros accumsan et iusto odio dignissim qui blandit praesent luptatum zzril delenit augue duis dolore te feugait nulla facilisi. Lorem ipsum dolor sit amet, consectetuer adipiscing, nonummy nibh euismod tincidunt ut laoreet dolore magna aliquam erat volutpat.

bembo Ut wisi enim ad minim veniam, quis nostrud exerci tation ullamcorper suscipit lobortis nisl ut aliquip ex ea commodo consequat. Duis autem vel eum iriure dolor in hendrerit in vulputate velit esse molestie consequat, vel illum dolore eu feugiat nulla facilisis at vero eros et accumsan iusto odio dignissim qui blandit praesent luptatum zzril delenit augue duis dolore te feugait nulla facilisi. Nam liber tempor cum soluta nobis eleifend option congue imperdiet doming id quod mazim placerat facer possim.

bezique Lorem ipsum dolor sit amet, consectetuer elit, sed diam nonummy nibh euismod tincidunt ut laoreet dolore magna aliquam erat volutpat. Ut wisi enim ad minim veniam, nostrud exerci tation ullamcorper suscipit lobortis nisl ut aliquip ex ea commodo consequat. Duis autem vel eum iriure dolor in hendrerit in vulputate velit esse molestie, vel illum dolore eu feugiat nulla facilisis. Lorem ipsum dolor sit amet, consectetuer adipiscing elit, sed diam nonummy nibh euismod tincidunt ut laoreet dolore magna aliquam erat volutpat. Ut wisi enim ad minim veniam, quis nostrud exerci tation ullamcorper suscipit lobortis nisl ut aliquip ex ea commodo consequat. Duis autem vel eum iriure dolor in hendrerit in vulputate velit esse molestie consequat, vel illum dolore eu feugiat nulla facilisis at vero eros accumsan et iusto odio dignissim qui blandit praesent luptatum zzril delenit augue duis dolore te feugait nulla facilisi. Lorem ipsum dolor sit amet, consectetuer adipiscing elit, sed diam nonummy nibh euismod tincidunt ut laoreet dolore magna aliquam erat volutpat.

billabong Ut wisi enim ad minim veniam, quis nostrud exerci tation ullamcorper suscipit lobortis nisl ut aliquip ex ea commodo consequat. Duis autem vel eum iriure dolor in hendrerit in vulputate velit esse molestie consequat, vel illum dolore eu feugiat nulla facilisis at vero eros et accumsan iusto odio dignissim qui blandit praesent luptatum zzril delenit augue duis dolore te feugait nulla facilisi. Nam liber tempor cum soluta nobis eleifend option congue imperdiet doming id quod mazim placerat facer possim. Lorem ipsum dolor sit amet, consectetuer adipiscing elit, sed diam nonummy nibh euismod tincidunt ut laoreet dolore magna aliquam erat volutpat. Ut wisi enim ad minim veniam, quis nostrud exerci tation ullamcorper suscipit lobortis nisl ut aliquip ex ea commodo consequat.

blandit Duis autem vel eum iriure dolor in hendrerit in vulputate velit esse molestie consequat, vel illum dolore eu feugiat nulla facilisis. Lorem ipsum dolor sit amet, consectetuer adipiscing elit, sed diam nonummy nibh euismod tincidunt ut laoreet dolore magna aliquam erat volutpat. Ut wisi enim ad minim veniam, quis nostrud exerci tation ullamcorper suscipit lobortis nisl ut aliquip ex ea commodo consequat. Duis autem vel eum iriure dolor in hendrerit in vulputate velit esse molestie consequat, vel illum dolore eu feugiat nulla

9

When using rules to embellish display text, try varying the length of the rule to fit the text length. Most desktop publishing programs offer the option of doing this automatically.

Who Is Fireside Distributors?

We are best known as the largest fireplace accessory distributor in the U.S. But did you know Fireside Distributors offers one of the largest selections of sweep products anywhere?

Our products include: Merry Sweep, Webster, Dicon, Metalbestos, Flitz, Chimfex, Chamber-Aid, Adapt-A-Place, American Stove Products, Mirror, Lyemance, Air-Jet, Worcester, Homesaver, Kemstone, Dura-Vent, Versagrid, O.D. Funk, Condar, Chimline, Schaefer and Flam-X.

Our experienced staff is looking forward to talking with you and welcomes the opportunity to answer your product and installation questions.

Besides stocking over 2,000 sweep and specialty fireplace products, Fireside Sweep Service includes:

- 800 toll-free information
- Extra 5% check-with-order discount
- VISA and MasterCard welcomed
- No minimum order
- 24-hour order processing
- $3.50 U.P.S. per carton
- Prepaid flight available
- Credit for qualified sweeps

We make working with us easy! Give us a call today and we'll send you your free catalog, "Products for the Sweep."

US 1-800-334-3210
NC 1-800-662-7025

Fireside Distributors, 4013 Winton Road, Raleigh, NC 27604

Borders

Use borders to frame the live area*—the space in which text and artwork appear.*

Tangible borders are rules, boxes, or other graphic boundaries that surround the contents of the page. You can use the rectangle-drawing tool in your desktop publishing software to draw simple borders.

You can also use the straight-line tool to create partial borders or borders with different styles of rules for the vertical and horizontal sides.

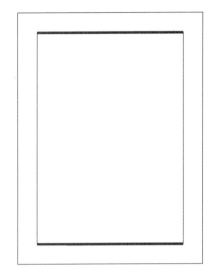

More complex borders can be drawn in an illustration program or borrowed from a clip art gallery. There are numerous clip art packages that focus on borders exclusively.

Even if you don't choose to box off your live area, your publication will probably have *assumed* borders if you're using a grid to aid with layout. The edges of artwork and text columns will delineate the edge of the live area, forming a border subconsciously perceived by the reader.

Gorilla Goes Ape, Attacks Grocery Store

"He seemed particularly interested in the bananas," recalls store manager

When Good Gorillas Turn Bad

Boxes

Boxes can be used to separate or isolate elements on the page.

Conceptually, boxes are easy to understand—they're just smaller versions of borders. Instead of framing the entire page, they frame some portion of it—an article, a chart or graph, an advertisement. Simple, no?

Well, frankly, no. Layout novices probably misuse boxes more than any other design element. (They also tend to overuse them, which doesn't help matters.) The most common mistake is to use a box purely for emphasis. For instance, a novice might place a box around the headline of an important story to draw attention to it.

The trouble is, boxes aren't really emphasis tools. They *can* emphasize, but their primary function is separation. Placing something in a box isolates it from the rest of the page. By boxing a headline, you're isolating it from its corresponding story, which isn't advisable.

Boxes are usually used to isolate supplementary information, so the reader isn't interrupted or distracted while reading primary information. Sidebars, for instance, are often set in boxes.

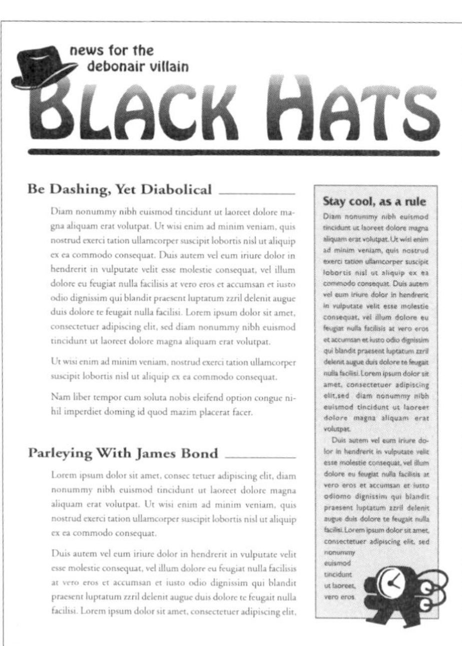

Boxes are also used for repeated features in a periodical, like the table of contents or the publication's masthead. This not only separates them from the primary content but makes them easy to find.

But Why?

If it seems odd to you that boxes should be considered containers for secondary information, consider a familiar analogy—computer file directories.

Suppose there's a folder on your hard drive that contains two items, a file and a subfolder. Which is more important: the file or whatever's in the subfolder? The file, of course. You place the most important item "highest" in the hierarchy so you can get to it easily.

The same logic applies to pages. Unboxed elements are perceived as top-level items. You won't see the lead story of a newspaper stuffed inside a box; it's always loose within the live area.

IN THIS ISSUE

2 Obscure nomenclature

4 The real meaning of "Lorem ipsum"

6 Latin—Is It All Greek to You?

7 Vernacular Sins, & How to Avoid Them

commodo consequat.

Duis autem vel eum iriure dolor in hendrerit in vulputate velit esse molestie consequat, vel illum dolore eu feugiat nulla facilisis at vero eros et accumsan et iusto odio dignissim qui blandit praesent luptatum zzril delenit augue duis dolore te feugait nulla facilisi. Lorem ipsum dolor sit amet, consectetuer adipiscing elit, sed diam nonummy nibh euismod tincidunt ut laoreet dolore magna aliquam erat volutpat.

Ut wisi enim ad minim veniam, nostrud exerci tation ullamcorper suscipit lobortis nisl ut aliquip ex ea commodo consequat. Duis

ea commodo consequat.

Duis autem vel eum iriure dolor in hendrerit in vulputate velit esse molestie consequat, vel illum dolore eu feugiat nulla facilisis. Ut wisi enim ad minim veniam, nostrud exerci tation ullamcorper suscipit lobortis nisl ut aliquip ex ea commodo consequat. Duis autem vel eum iriure dolor in hendrerit in vulputate velit molestie consequat, illum dolore eu feugiat nulla facilisis at vero eros et accumsan et iusto odiodignissim qui blandit

Information from an article that a reader might want at a glance is often placed inside a box. For instance, an article about a rock band might include a box containing the location, date, and time of their next concert.

The "Head Cases" Rock the Civic Arena

Lorem ipsum dolor sit amet, consec tetuer adipiscing elit, diam nonummy nibh euismod tincidunt ut laoreet dolore magna aliquam erat volutpat. Ut wisi enim ad minim veniam, quis nostrud exerci tation ullamcorper suscipit lobortis nisl ut aliquip ex ea commodo consequat.

Duis autem vel eum iriure dolor in hendrerit in vulputate velit esse molestie consequat, vel illum dolore eu feugiat nulla facilisis at vero eros et accumsan et iusto odio dignissim qui blandit praesent luptatum zzril delenit augue duis dolore dolor sit amet, consectetuer adipiscing elit, sed diam nonummy nibh euismod tincidunt ut laoreet dolore magna aliquam erat volutpat.

Ut wisi enim ad minim veniam, nostrud exerci tation ullamcorper suscipit lobortis nisl ut aliquip ex ea commodo consequat. Duis autem vel eum iriure dolor in hendrerit in vulputate velit molestie consequat, illum dolore eu feugiat nulla facilisis at vero eros et accumsan et iusto odiodignissim qui blandit praesent luptatum zzril delenit

Nam liber tempor cum soluta nobis eleifend option congue nihil imperdiet doming id quod mazim placerat facer possim assum. Lorem ipsum dolor sit amet, consectetuer adipiscing elit, sed diam nonummy nibh euismod tincidunt ut laoreet dolore magna aliquam erat volutpat. Ut wisi enim ad minim veniam, quis nostrud exerci tation ullamcorper suscipit lobortis nisl ut ex ea commodo

Head Cases Concert

Where: Civic Arena
When: Tues, Apr 9, 8 PM
Why: No earthly idea
Cost: $25

A common mistake made by design novices is to use overly decorative boxes or boxes with extremely thick lines. Remember, boxed text is usually supplementary information. Overly prominent boxes draw an undue amount of attention. This is especially true for small boxes.

tincidunt ut laoreet dolore magna aliquam erat volutpat.

Ut wisi enim ad minim veniam, nostrud exerci tation ullamcorper suscipit lobortis nisl ut aliquip ex ea commodo consequat. Duis autem vel eum iriure dolor in hendrerit in vulputate velit molestie consequat, illum dolore eu feugiat nulla facilisis at vero eros et accumsan et iusto odiodignissim qui blandit praesent luptatum zzril delenit augue duis dolore te feugait nulla facilisi.

quis nostrud exerci tation ullamcorper suscipit lobortis nisl ut ex ea commodo consequat.

Head Cases Concert
Where: Civic Arena
When: Tues, Apr 9, 8 PM
Why: No earthly idea
Cost: $25

tincidunt ut laoreet dolore magna aliquam erat volutpat.

Ut wisi enim ad minim veniam, nostrud exerci tation ullamcorper suscipit lobortis nisl ut aliquip ex ea commodo consequat. Duis autem vel eum iriure dolor in hendrerit in vulputate velit molestie consequat, illum dolore eu feugiat nulla facilisis at vero eros et accumsan et iusto odiodignissim qui blandit praesent luptatum zzril delenit augue duis dolore te feugait nulla facilisi.

quis nostrud exerci tation ullamcorper suscipit lobortis nisl ut ex ea commodo consequat.

Head Cases Concert

Where: Civic Arena
When: Tues, Apr 9, 8 PM
Why: No earthly idea
Cost: $25

Boxes are also used to define the boundaries of a visual. They're especially useful for photographs with light-colored or indistinct edges; otherwise, the photo blends into the background, creating a vague, unfinished look.

Drop Shadows

Drop shadows create an attention-getting three-dimensional effect.

Drop shadows can draw attention to boxes or visuals. They can help emphasize a photo, illustration, or checkbox by isolating it from its background.

Use drop shadows with discretion. They tend to be overused, in part because they're so easy to create.

Gorilla Regains Composure, Apologizes

"He still seemed rather interested in the bananas," recalls store manager

Diam nonummy nibh euismod tincidunt ut laoreet dolore magna aliquam erat volutpat. Ut wisi enim ad minim veniam, quis nostrud exerci tation ullamcorper suscipit lobortis nisl ut aliquip ex ea commodo consequat. Duis autem vel eum iriure dolor in hendrerit in vulputate velit esse molestie consequat, vel illum dolore eu feugiat nulla facilisis at vero eros et accumsan et iusto odio dignissim qui blandit praesent luptatum zzril delenit augue duis dolore te feugait nulla facilisi. Lorem ipsum dolor sit amet, consectetuer adipiscing elit, sed diam nonummy nibh euismod tincidunt ut laoreet dolore magna aliquam erat volutpat.

Ut wisi enim ad minim veniam, nostrud exerci tation ullamcorper suscipit lobortis nisl ut aliquip ex ea commodo consequat.

Nam liber tempor cum soluta nobis eleifend option congue nihil imperdiet doming id quod mazim placerat facer.

Lorem ipsum dolor sit amet, consectetuer adipiscing elit, diam nonummy nibh euismod tincidunt ut laoreet dolore magna aliquam erat volutpat. Ut wisi enim ad minim veniam, quis nostrud exerci tation ullamcorper suscipit lobortis nisl ut aliquip ex ea commodo consequat. Ut wisi enim ad minim veniam, quis nostrud exerci tation ullamcorper suscipit lobortis nisl ut aliquip ex ea commodo consequat.

Duis autem vel eum iriure dolor in hendrerit in vulputate velit esse molestie consequat, vel illum dolore eu feugiat nulla facilisis at vero eros et accumsan et iusto odio dignissim qui

When Bad Gorillas Turn Good Again

Diam nonummy nibh euismod tincidunt ut laoreet dolore magna aliquam erat volutpat. Ut wisi enim ad minim veniam, quis nostrud exerci tation ullamcorper suscipit lobortis nisl ut aliquip ex ea commodo consequat. Duis autem vel eum iriure dolor in hendrerit in vulputate velit esse molestie

Gradient Fills

A special type of screen is the *gradient fill*—a gradual transition between two shades. Many desktop publishing programs will let you create linear and radial gradient fills automatically.

linear gradient fills

radial gradient fill

Like drop shadows, however, gradients sometimes suffer from being too easy to use—designers apply them because they can and not because they should. It's better to save them for moments when the effect is truly warranted—which is to say, the gradient fill you place on page 6 will be much more effective if your reader hasn't been tripping over gradients on pages 1 through 5.

Screens

Screens add color and contrast to a document.

Screens make a document look more inviting. They break up the monotony of black and white. Adding a screened rule to a subhead, for instance, can add color to a text block. Notice how much heavier the same rule seems when set in black.

Lorem ipsum dolor sit amet, consectetuer adipiscing elit, sed diam nonummy nibh euismod tincidunt ut enim veniam, quis nostrud exercitation ullamcorper suscipit lobortis nisl ut aliquip ex ea commodo consequat.

USING SCREENS
Duis autem vel eum iriure dolor in hendrerit in vulputate velit esse molestie consequat, illum

Lorem ipsum dolor sit amet, consectetuer adipiscing elit, sed diam nonummy nibh euismod tincidunt ut enim veniam, quis nostrud exercitation ullamcorper suscipit lobortis nisl ut aliquip ex ea commodo consequat.

USING SCREENS
Duis autem vel eum iriure dolor in hendrerit in vulputate velit esse molestie consequat, illum

Screening boxed text can help set it apart from the rest of the page. It also allows a designer to dispense with the box's border, if desired. The screen itself delineates the edges.

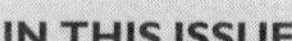

IN THIS ISSUE

2 Obscure nomenclature

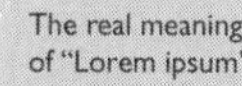

4 The real meaning of "Lorem ipsum"

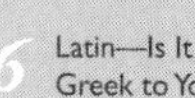

6 Latin—Is It All Greek to You?

7 Vernacular Sins, & How to Avoid Them

Lorem ipsum dolor sit amet, consec tetuer adipiscing elit, diam nonummy nibh euismod tincidunt ut laoreet dolore magna aliquam erat volutpat. Ut wisi enim ad minim veniam, quis nostrud exerci tation ullamcorper suscipit lobortis nisl ut aliquip ex ea commodo consequat.

Duis autem vel eum iriure dolor in hendrerit in vulputate velit esse molestie consequat, vel illum dolore eu feugiat nulla facilisis at vero eros et accumsan et iusto odio dignissim qui blandit praesent luptatum zzril delenit augue duis dolore te feugait nulla facilisi. Lorem ipsum dolor sit amet, consectetuer adipiscing elit, sed diam nonummy nibh euismod tincidunt ut laoreet dolore magna aliquam erat volutpat.

possim assum. Lorem ipsum dc consectetuer adipiscing elit nonummy nibh euismod tincidı dolore magna aliquam erat volu enim ad minim veniam, quis n tation ullamcorper suscipit lobo ea commodo consequat.

Duis autem vel eum iriu hendrerit in vulputate velit e consequat, vel illum dolore eu facilisis. Ut wisi enim ad mir nostrud exerci tation ullamco lobortis nisl ut aliquip ex e consequat. Duis autem vel eum in hendrerit in vulputate ve consequat, illum dolore eu f facilisis at vero eros et accum odiodignissim qui blandit

In tables and order forms, screening every other line prevents readers from losing their place.

Feature	Standard	Optional	Not Available
Power windows	•		
Antilock brakes		•	
Driver air bag	•		
Passenger air bag		•	
Sunroof			•
Air conditioning	•		
Ejection seat			•

Bleeds

Some of the most dynamic design results are achieved with bleeds.

A printed image that extends all the way to the edge of a page is called a *bleed*. Bleeds can impart a very artistic look. The reader perceives the page as a window which shows only a portion of the scene, rather than the entire picture.

An oversize initial cap or chapter number can bleed to the top or side edges of a page.

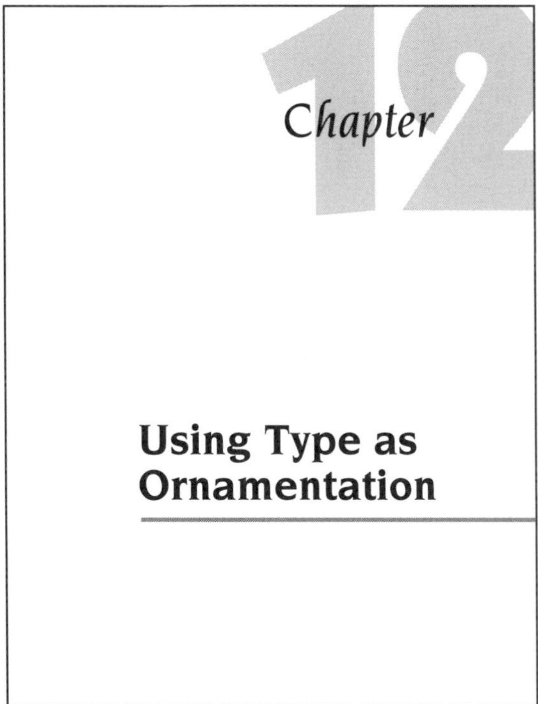

Photographs that bleed to one or more edges of the page lose the sense of isolation imparted by boxes. They tend to look larger and more important.

Rising High

Lorem ipsum dolor sit amet, consec tetuer adipiscing elit, diam nonummy nibh euismod tincidunt ut laoreet dolore magna aliquam erat volutpat. Ut wisi enim ad minim veniam, quis nostrud exerci tation ullamcorper suscipit lobortis nisl ut aliquip ex ea commodo consequat.

Duis autem vel eum iriure dolor in hendrerit in vulputate velit esse molestie consequat, vel illum dolore eu feugiat nulla facilisis at vero eros et accumsan et iusto odio dignissim qui blandit praesent luptatum zzril delenit augue duis dolore te feugait nulla facilisi. Lorem ipsum dolor sit amet, consectetuer adipiscing elit, sed diam nonummy nibh euismod tincidunt ut laoreet dolore magna aliquam erat volutpat.

Ut wisi enim ad minim veniam, nostrud exerci tation ullamcorper suscipit lobortis nisl ut aliquip ex ea commodo consequat.

Nam liber tempor cum soluta nobis eleifend option congue nihil imperdiet doming id quod mazim placerat facer

Lorem ipsum dolor sit amet, consec tetuer adipiscing elit, diam nonummy nibh euismod tincidunt ut laoreet dolore magna aliquam erat volutpat. Ut wisi enim ad minim veniam, quis nostrud exerci tation ullamcorper suscipit lobortis nisl ut aliquip ex ea commodo consequat.

Duis autem vel eum iriure dolor in hendrerit in vulputate velit esse molestie consequat, vel illum dolore eu feugiat nulla facilisis at vero eros et accumsan et iusto odio dignissim qui blandit praesent luptatum zzril delenit augue duis dolore te feugait nulla facilisi. Lorem ipsum dolor sit amet, consectetuer adipiscing elit, sed diam nonummy nibh euismod tincidunt ut laoreet dolore magna aliquam erat volutpat.

Ut wisi enim ad minim veniam, nostrud exerci tation ullamcorper suscipit lobortis nisl ut aliquip ex ea commodo consequat. Duis autem vel eum iriure dolor in hendrerit in vulputate velit molestie consequat, illum dolore eu feugiat nulla facilisis at vero eros et accumsan et iusto odiodignissim qui blandit praesent luptatum zzril delenit augue duis dolore te feugait nulla facilisi.

Nam liber tempor cum soluta nobis eleifend option congue nihil imperdiet doming id quod mazim placerat facer duis autem vel eum iriure dolor in hendrerit in vulputate velit molestie consequat, illum dolore eu feugiat nulla facilisis at vero eros et accumsan et iusto odiodignissim qui blandit praesent luptatum zzril delenit augue duis dolore te feugait nulla facilisi. Ut wisi enim ad minim veniam, quis nostrud exerci tation ullamcorper liber tempor cum soluta nobis eleifend option congue nihil imperdiet doming id quod mazim placerat facer duis

Horizontal rules that bleed to the sides of a page add continuity to a spread.

Newsletter nameplates gain impact when their backgrounds bleed to the top or sides of the page.

Who's Left?

Lorem ipsum dolor sit amet, consectetuer adipiscing elit, sed diam nonummy nibh euismod tincidunt ut laoreet dolor magna aliquam erat volutpat. Ut wisi enim ad minim veniam, quis nostrud exerci tation ullamcorper suscipit lobortis nisl ut aliquip.

Duis autem vel eum iriure dolor in hendrerit in vulputate velit esse molestie consequat, vel illum dolore eu feugiat nulla facilisis at vero eros et accumsan et iusto odio dignissim qui blandit praesent luptatum zzril delenit augue duis dolore te feugait nulla facilisi. Lorem ipsum dolor sit amet, consectetuer adipiscing elit, sed diam nonummy nibh euismod tincidunt ut laoreet dolor magna aliquam erat volutpat.

Ut wisi enim ad minim veniam, quis nostrud exercitation ullamcorper suscipit lobortis nisl ut aliquip ex ea commodo consequat. Duis autem vel eum iriure dolor in hendrerit in vulputate velit esse molestie consequat, vel illum dolo eu feugiat nulla facilisis at vero eros et accumsan et iusto odio dignissim qui blandit praesent luptatum zzril delenit augue duis dolore te feugait nulla facilisi. Nam liber tempor cum soluta nobis eleifend option congue nihil

Cost can be a consideration when using bleeds. Commercial offset printers have to use oversized sheets of paper, and trim it to actual publication size after printing. This increases the cost somewhat. If you want to use bleeds, find out how much extra your service bureau will charge, and check your budget.

Color documents often bleed on all four edges, using a full-page photo or a large block of spot color to cover the page. See the Do It In Color section for examples.

Moving On

We're pretty far along now. Using only the techniques covered so far, you could produce an impressive variety of documents. But if you're itching to create a little black space on the page, the next two chapters are must-reads. Chapter 5 shows you how to choose graphic elements and position them on the page for maximum effect. Chapter 6 addresses those issues and techniques particular to photographic artwork.

5 The Art Of Illustration

Visual images in a document can communicate your message at a glance. A well-placed illustration can make a document more effective, more informative, and more attractive. Illustrations are powerful because they communicate at a glance; associations come instantly, without the pause—however brief—that separates reading and comprehension. It's not merely that readers look at the pictures first, as the conventional wisdom goes. More accurately, the pictures speak to the reader first.

Of course, lofty claims like that one have induced many novices to turn their documents into virtual clip art catalogs. New designers often fall into the trap of using illustrations whenever they want to fill up space, break up copy, or just add a bit of visual spice. Illustrations *do* serve these functions, but if these are the only justifications you have for using a given graphic, you probably shouldn't be using it. *Any* graphic can take up space or give the reader something to look at. That doesn't mean that every graphic belongs in your publication. It's even possible that none do.

Using Illustrations Effectively

Illustrations, like every other page element, are meant to help communicate your document's message. Using inappropriate graphics can be worse than using no graphics at all. This doesn't merely refer to graphics that don't fit contextually, like a clip art jack-o'-lantern on the cover of a Christmas catalog. Even a graphic that seemingly fits the *content* of a document might not fit the *tone*. Every illustration conveys a tone—formality or informality, elegance or earthiness, simplicity or complexity. If this tone is at odds with your document's message and purpose, you shouldn't be using that illustration. For instance, cartoonish graphics—even business-oriented ones—almost certainly don't belong in a company report. Their presence would imply that the report should not be taken seriously.

Illustrations Vs. Photographs

Follow your instincts when choosing between illustrations and photos.

Designers with years of experience can (and often do) disagree over whether a particular layout calls for a photo or an illustration. Like most other aspects of graphic design, there are no hard-and-fast rules, and the issue usually comes down to the individual preference of the designer.

Photos are generally used to report or document an event or realistically portray an individual or group of people. Illustrations are the logical choice to evoke a particular mood or depict a complex object, such as the internal structure of a high-suspension bridge. While recent advances in computer imaging are blurring the line between photos and illustrations, they are treated as separate subjects in this book.

Concepts particular to photographic artwork will be described in Chapter 6. However, there are certain guidelines that apply equally well to both types:

- *Don't crowd your artwork.* Leave generous borders around it, so the eye flows to it naturally.
- *Vary size and shape.* Running lots of illustrations at roughly the same size and shape gets boring. Be creative with the size, shape, and placement of each image.
- *Keep the styles consistent.* Using a vast array of different illustration styles can make your document appear disjointed or poorly planned.
- *Less is more.* Running fewer illustrations at a larger size yields a higher visual impact than running lots of smaller ones. You also get more bang for your illustration buck.

As always, take sweeping statements like these with a grain of salt. You can often achieve a specific and unique effect by disregarding one or more of these rules. In general, though, crowded or repetitive illustrations make for an unattractive document.

Illustrious Possibilities

Illustrations offer far more opportunities for interpretation than photos do. The artist decides which aspects of a drawing to emphasize and how much detail to include. Accuracy may be freely foregone for the sake of aesthetics.

Accurate, detailed illustrations are useful when you want to portray a literal image. When you're more interested in the symbolic meaning of an image, use a highly stylized or exaggerated illustration.

Cutaways (line diagrams) of objects are often used in technical manuals instead of photos. These illustrations can show the internal structure of an object and its components with more clarity than a photograph can.

Copyright Law and the Internet

Today's technology makes it easy to acquire and radically alter images with little respect for copyrights. Just because an image appears on the internet and you're able to save it to your hard drive does not mean that you can use that image without violating copyright laws. Many Web sites will include a list of restrictions from the author/artist concerning image use. Make sure you read them, so you know how far your privileges extend. If you can't find any such list, it's safest to assume that you have no privileges.

Ready-Made Art

Use ready-made art to save yourself time and effort.

You may be relieved to learn that not every professional designer is also a talented artist. Luckily, with today's technology and choices, you don't need to master drawing skills to illustrate your ideas. If you know what sort of image you want, you can probably find it for sale somewhere. Even if you only have a rough idea, a little digging will probably produce a dizzying array of options.

Using ready-made art allows you to try out a number of illustrations in your layout before making a final choice, without having to create each illustration from scratch. And with the wide proliferation and low cost of ready-made art, such as electronic clip art, background textures and patterns, and picture fonts, designers have never had more options to choose from.

There are numerous companies that sell ready-made art. Still more artwork is available on the Internet—much of it for free.

Clip Art

Use clip art to add pizzazz and professionalism to ads, brochures, menus, and newsletters.

Clip art consists of files of existing artwork that can be dropped into your desktop-published documents. Clip art can save you lots of time and money by letting you brighten your publication without having to create your own illustrations.

There are many different styles of clip art. Some of it is strictly functional, such as and anatomical drawings, maps, and computer hardware.

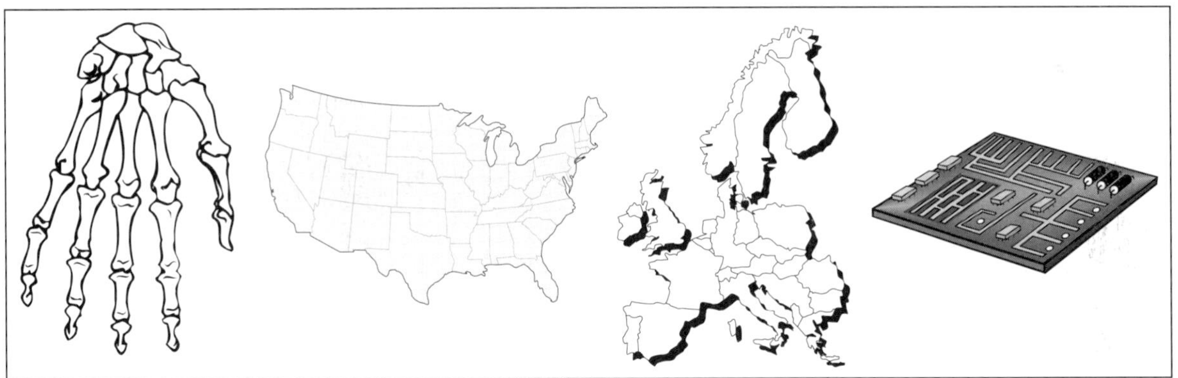

Other clip art is more artistic, mimicking the look of hand-drawn images, watercolors, or woodcuts.

Clip art is often used for borders. There are hundreds of unique and specific clip art border treatments.

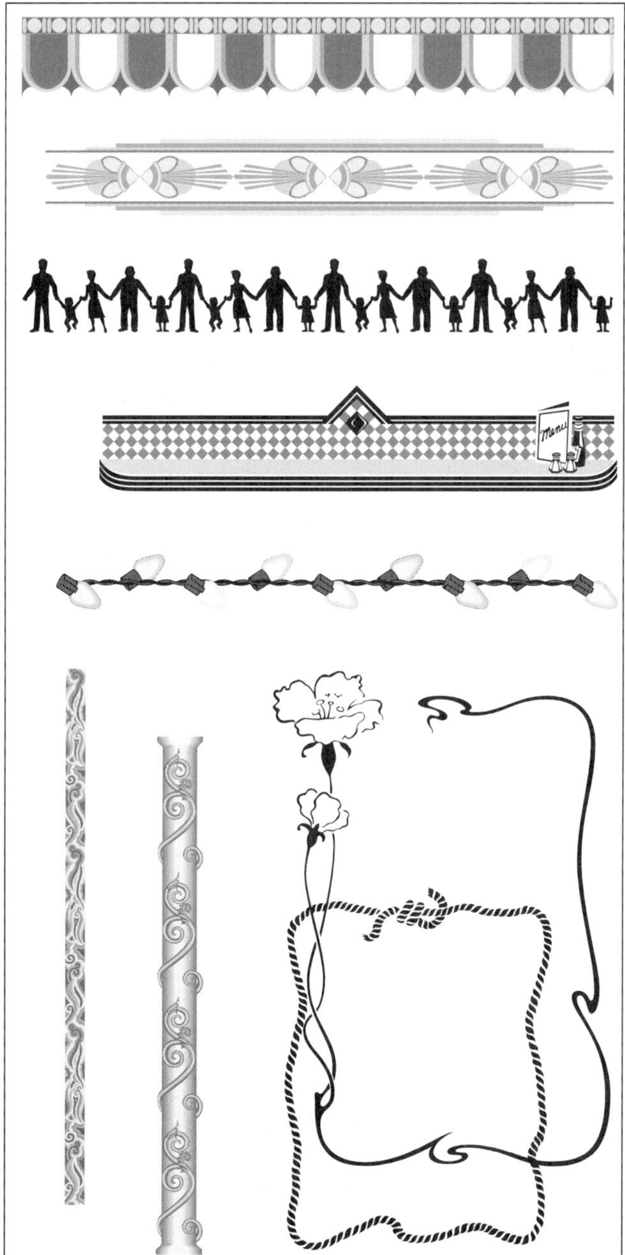

There are thousands of other clip art files available to suit any conceivable subject or interest.

As versatile as clip art is, it has its drawbacks. Charges can add up when you're forced to buy an entire package of art in order to get the one or two images you really wanted. Not all clip art vendors create art of equal quality—some of it is poorly drawn or outdated in style. You also run the risk of seeing your art in someone else's work. None of these drawbacks are meant to deter you from using clip art. You'll want to use it often—just pay attention to its quality and freshness when you do.

Clip art doesn't have to be used "as is." You can often change or customize it relatively easily. For example, you can use just a portion of a clip art image, but greatly increase its size.

Another technique involves combining several clip art images. For example, individual clip art items can be brought together to form a dynamic visual, such as the still life superimposed on the geometric figure in the following example.

For more on manipulating clip art, see the section "Manipulating Illustrations," later in this chapter.

Background Textures And Patterns

You can achieve impressive results with patterns and textures.

Background textures and patterns, which are either created by professional graphic artists or scanned from actual objects like marble or fabric, can be used to lend a touch of elegance or respectability to a layout.

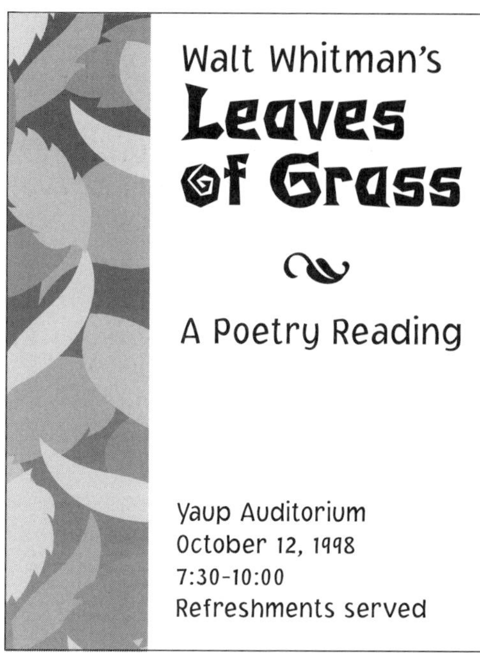

Unlike clip art, background textures and patterns are used more to lend color or weight to a document, not to illustrate a particular part of the text. They are especially effective for ads, brochures, invitations, and flyers. Often, they're used as backdrops for text.

As with clip art, you don't have to use textures or patterns as they originally appear. A little editing and manipulation go a long way toward making commercially created artwork look like a unique graphic.

Dingbat Sets And Picture Fonts

Image fonts are an often overlooked source of illustrations.

Although most designers don't turn to fonts when they're looking for a particular illustration, a host of companies produce non-text fonts that can be used to illustrate everything from books to flyers. Most designers are familiar with dingbat fonts, such as the popular Zapf Dingbats.

Dingbat sets are useful sources of bullets, slugs, icons, and other small pictures. Because they function as fonts, they can be conveniently embedded in lines of text, and you don't have to worry about placing or importing them when using page layout programs. But bullets and slugs are just the beginning. You may be able to solve many of your illustration needs using picture fonts.

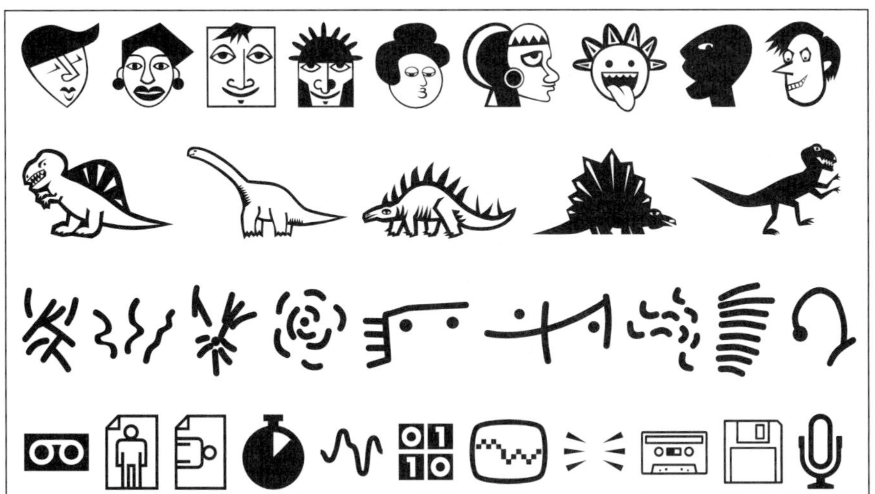

Shopping For Ready-Made Art

Before buying commercial graphics, it's important to know what you need—and what you're capable of using.

There's no shortage of sources for clip art and graphics, and each vendor offers a huge array of products. But to make sure you're buying the right graphic for the job, here are a few guidelines you should follow:

- Graphics are saved in a number of file formats. Images saved in TIFF or EPS formats are usually compatible with any software program.
- Graphics come on floppy disk, CD-ROM, and via online services. Make sure the source medium your graphics vendor uses is compatible with your system.
- Be sure to find out how many images are included in each package purchase—find out how much you're paying per image, so you can comparison shop. Find out if the graphics are provided in color, black and white, or both.
- Some graphics are saved in a form that you can edit with a paint or draw program, while others aren't. If you plan to alter individual objects in an image, make sure your software is capable of working with it. (You should probably try to buy editable clip art even if you don't have any specific plans for editing it. It's best to keep your options open.)

Manipulating Illustrations

Illustrations can be manipulated in a number of dramatic ways.

Most page layout, paint, and draw programs will let you enlarge, reduce, and stretch an image.

There are a number of special techniques (besides the simple cut-and-paste and cropping techniques discussed in the "Clip Art" section of this chapter) that you can use to manipulate or change an illustration to suit the needs of a specific layout. Many software packages allow you to edit images in a variety of dynamic ways. Lightening, lowering the contrast, or fading an image can lend a whole new look and feel to a simple graphic.

Generally, computer-generated illustrations are created using either a paint program or a draw program.

Images in paint formats are bitmaps—a huge collection of tiny squares that make up the larger picture. Enlarging a bitmapped image causes the individual squares to become more clearly visible, yielding jagged or chunky results.

You can't typically manipulate individual objects or single items in a bitmapped graphic, at least not without first "cutting them out" of the picture—a difficult task, ordinarily. You can, however, use special techniques and filters to change the appearance of the entire bitmapped graphic.

On the other hand, images in draw formats are composed of a series of lines, curves, or objects that you can usually edit using a draw program. Because draw programs use equations to define the curves and lines in individual objects, the resulting images have the same quality of smoothness at practically any size.

Using a draw program, you can isolate and edit specific objects in a larger image, while leaving the rest of the graphic unchanged.

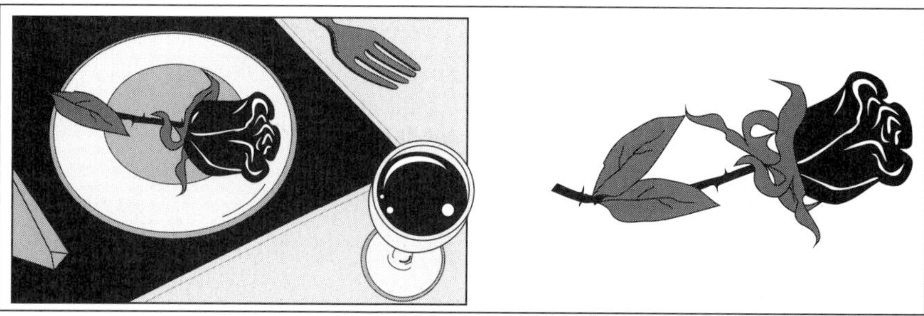

The kind of effects you can create using ready-made art depend largely on the software at your disposal and the format of the image itself, but nearly every program that handles graphics will allow you to stretch, size, and crop an image, regardless of its format.

Information Graphics

Information graphics are used to communicate trends, comparisons, and organizational structures.

Information graphics—charts, graphs, tables, and maps—are often the most efficient way to organize and present an unwieldy set of facts or figures. Statistics can be difficult to grasp in textual form, and they usually bore readers stiff besides. By converting such information into a graphic, relationships and trends become easier to notice, and the reader is more likely to retain interest. Even the simplest graphic has an aesthetic appeal which text lacks.

You can create these kinds of illustrations easily using clip art and the drawing tools available in your page layout program, or by using a separate drawing program. Some software packages, particularly spreadsheet applications, will create information graphics automatically. All you have to do is supply the data and specify how you want it presented. The program does the rest.

The information graphics appearing in publications such as *USA Today* and *Time* show that charts, diagrams, and tables can be presented in visually exciting ways. These shouldn't be considered the standard, though. Not every chart or graph needs to be presented in full color or feature 3D effects. In fact, these sorts of adornments often make graphs more difficult to understand. Ultimately, the purpose of an information graphic should be to inform, not to impress. If decoration starts getting in the way of meaning, simplify.

Actually, perfectly serviceable information graphics can be constructed from nothing more than combinations of circles, straight lines, fill patterns (such as parallel lines or dots), and clip art. Don't be afraid to keep things simple—your charts and graphs will have a clean, organized look.

Charts And Diagrams

Charts and diagrams translate numbers and values into visual images.

Charts communicate comparisons, relationships, and trends. There are many different types of charts. The nature of the data you wish to present will usually determine the appropriate chart to use.

Pie charts display part-to-whole relationships.

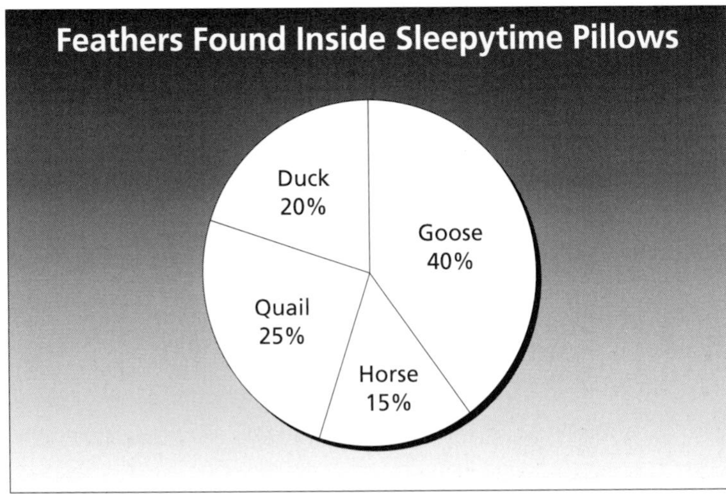

Pie charts work best when the slices are large and few. Dividing a pie chart into too many slices results in confusion.

Bar charts make comparisons.

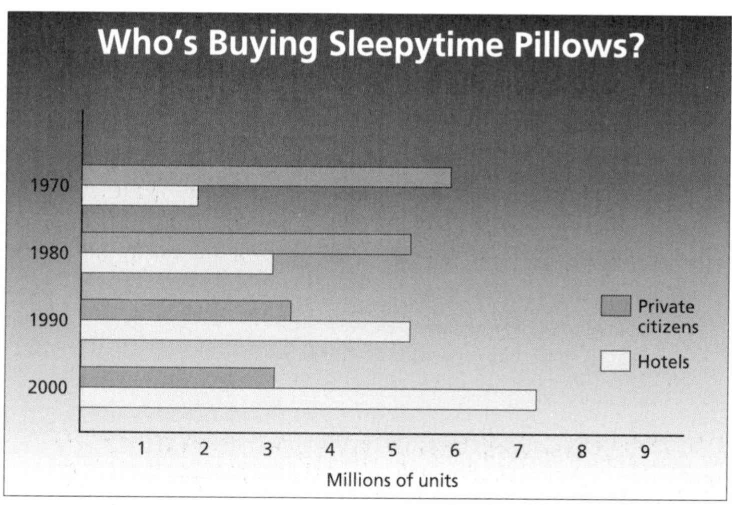

Stacked bar charts display the parts that contribute to the totals.

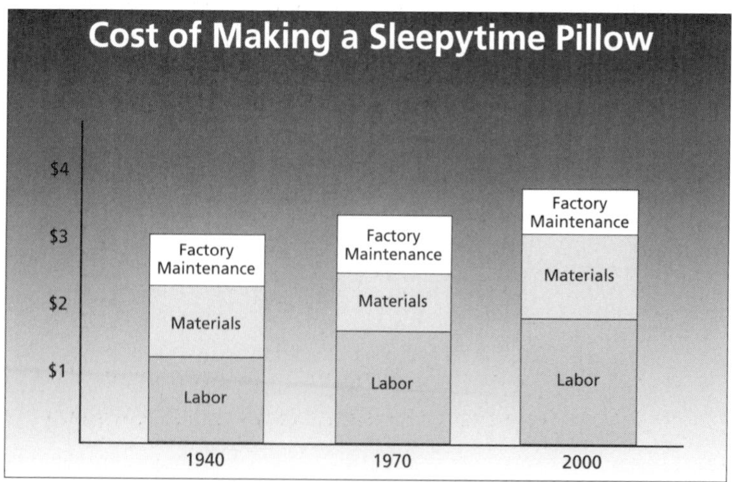

The bars can be drawn vertically or horizontally. Sometimes, objects are used instead of bars. If you decide to use objects in your bar graphs, pick images that can be lengthened or shortened while remaining recognizable—pencils, for example. Scaling objects in both directions can be misleading, because the objects gain volume disproportionately. In the chart below, the apparent difference in volume between the houses is misleading—the only relevant measurement is height.

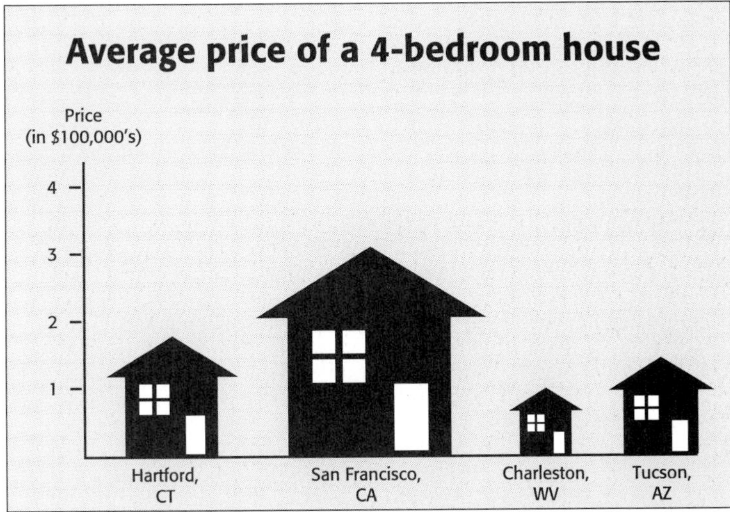

Line charts show trends.

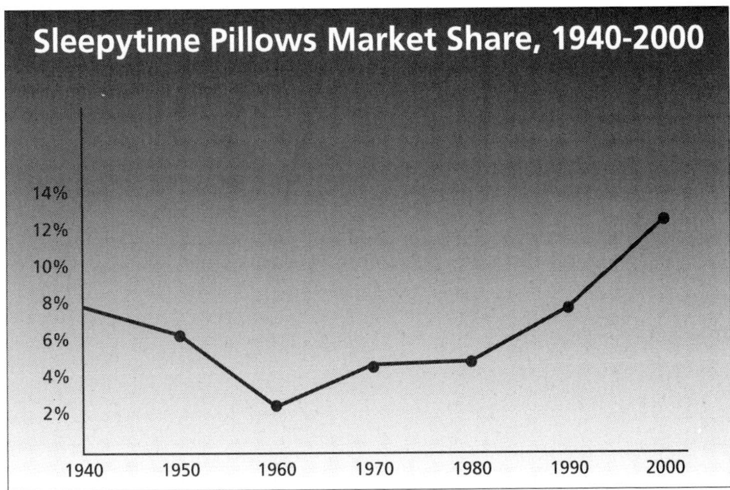

You can also combine chart types. This compound chart shows both total yearly sales and departmental contributions to the total yearly sales.

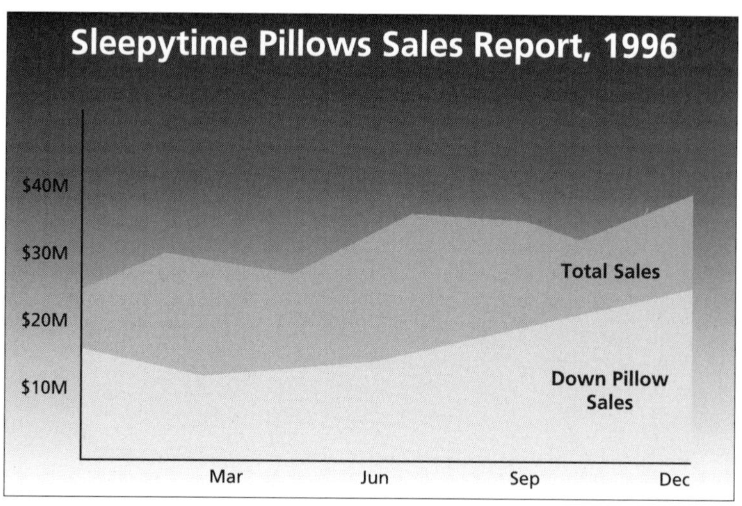

Diagrams

Choose diagrams rather than charts when you want to emphasize relationships and sequences rather than numbers.

Organizational diagrams are one of the most frequently encountered types of diagrams. These display dominant/subordinate relationships—who reports to whom, in other words.

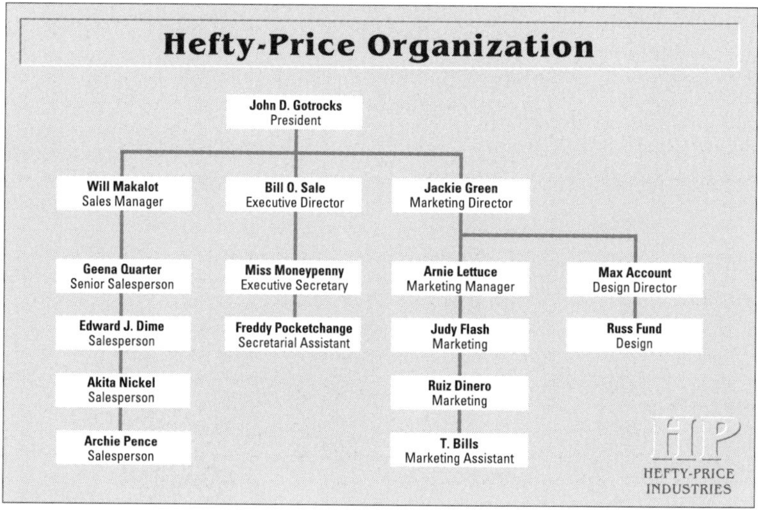

Flow (or *process*) *diagrams* are used to display sequences—what must be done first, what must be done second, and so on.

Timelines help you visually communicate historical perspectives. You can show when certain events occurred and how much time elapsed between them.

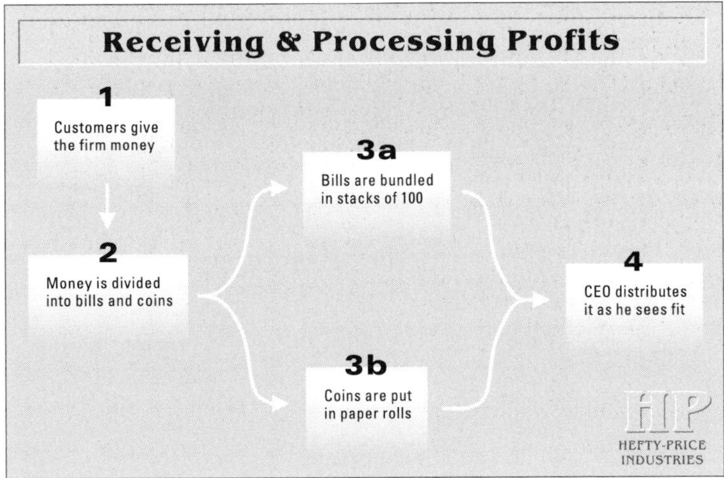

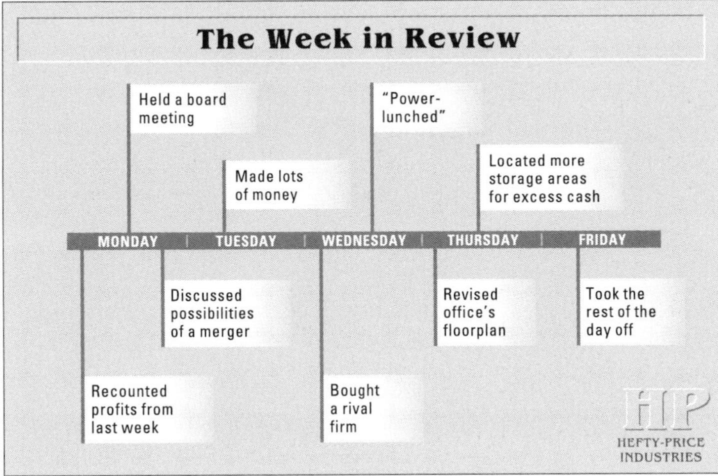

Diagrams can also be used to display spatial relationships, like floor plans or cutaway product drawings.

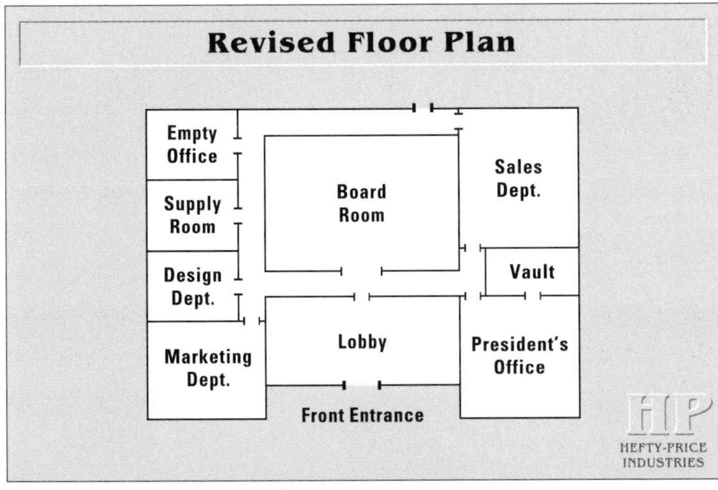

There are numerous ways you can increase the impact and communicating power of your charts and diagrams:

- Include a title that summarizes the purpose or importance of the information being displayed.

This title lacks impact:

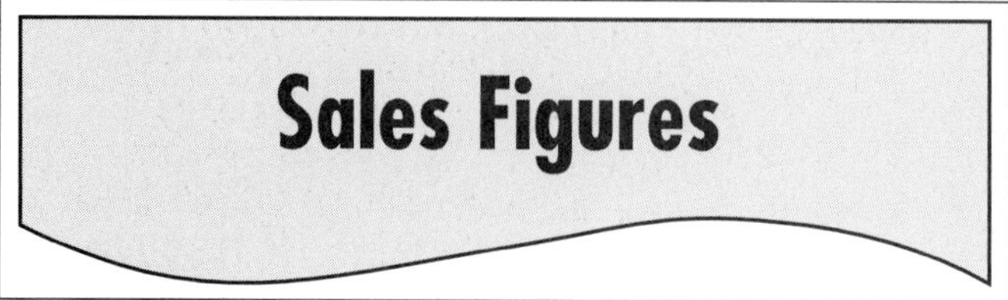

This title commands more attention:

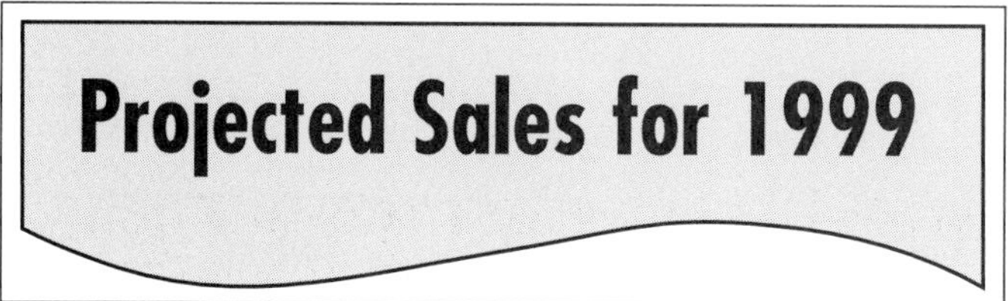

- Use labels to indicate the exact amounts displayed in each chart segment or bar graph column.

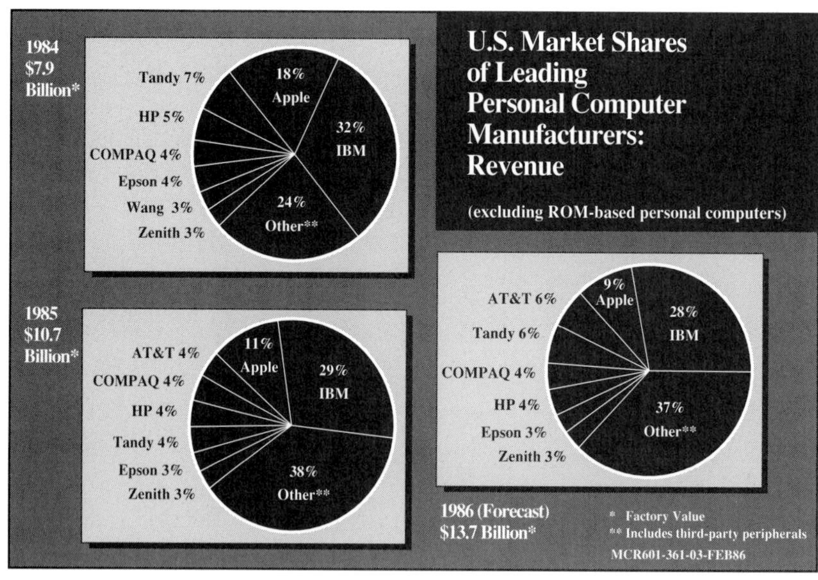

- Include a background grid indicating the major numeric divisions, to provide a frame of reference.

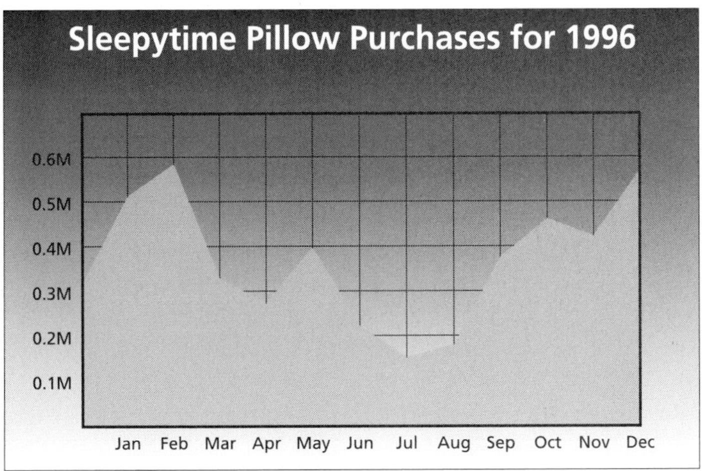

- Include tick marks that define subdivisions.

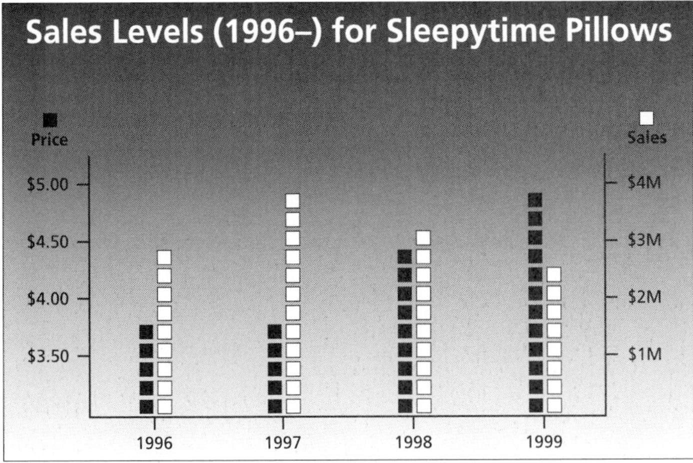

- Use a legend in a chart or diagram to identify symbols and units of measure. Place it near the graph—or inside the graph, if there's room available.
- Use shades, patterns, and colors that complement each other. Avoid adjacent colors that clash or blend together.
- Use a different typeface for chart and diagram labels than the one used for body text. Make sure the labels are large enough to be legible.

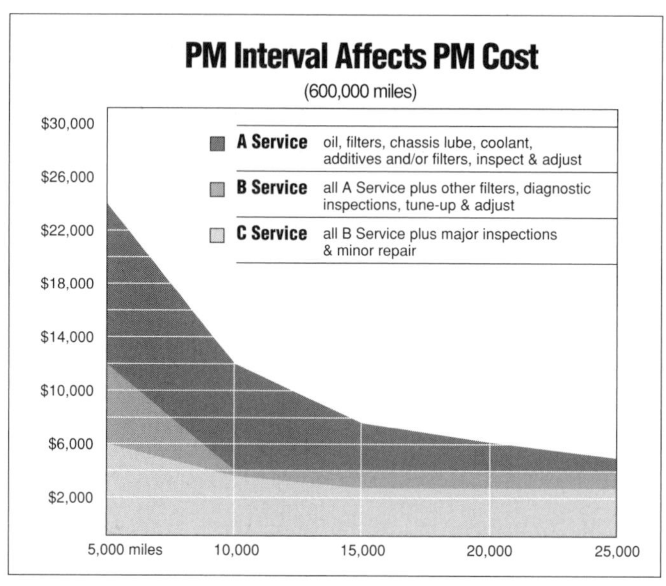

Tables

Tables present a lot of information in a concise and orderly way.

Tables are useful when you want to focus your reader's attention on the data itself, rather than on representations.

Preferred Morning Beverage (1,000s)

COFFEE	1960	1970	1980	1990
Instant	540	562	580	590
Perk	453	444	420	410
Drip	622	690	725	950
TEA				
Black	325	320	315	250
Herbal	105	110	160	200

When readers are less interested in general trends and more interested in finding a specific bit of information, a table will serve better than a graph. Tables are also better if exact values are important, because readers are not required to guesstimate when a graph point lands between two tick marks.

When placing information in tables, be sure to leave enough breathing room around the text or numbers. Row and column headings should be larger or bolder than the information they introduce. Screens can also be used to set off header information.

Preferred Morning Beverage (1,000s)				
COFFEE	**1960**	**1970**	**1980**	**1990**
Instant	540	562	580	590
Perk	453	444	420	410
Drip	622	690	725	950
TEA				
Black	325	320	315	250
Herbal	105	110	160	200

Avoid including more detail than necessary. Instead of including all digits in large numbers, round numbers off to the nearest hundred, thousand, or million. (Be sure you prominently indicate the scale you're using.)

Although column headings are often centered, flush-right alignment can be used for row identifiers. This locks the information together.

Preferred Morning Beverage (1,000s)				
COFFEE	**1960**	**1970**	**1980**	**1990**
Instant	540	562	580	590
Perk	453	444	420	410
Drip	622	690	725	950

When tables contain numbers, decimal alignment ensures that the numbers will line up, regardless of the size of the number or the number of decimal points after it.

1,567.98	1,567.98
257	257.00
3,410.3	3,410.30
957.69	957.69
2,113.54	2,113.54

Avoid using thick rules that darken a table and overwhelm the information presented.

Preferred Morning Beverage (1,000s)				
COFFEE	**1960**	**1970**	**1980**	**1990**
Instant	540	562	580	590
Perk	453	444	420	410
Drip	622	690	725	950
TEA				
Black	325	320	315	250
Herbal	105	110	160	200

Screen Captures

Computer documentation often contains a specialized form of art, called screen captures.

Most computer systems will allow you to take a picture of the computer screen, and save it as an image file. Screen captures are often used as examples in software manuals.

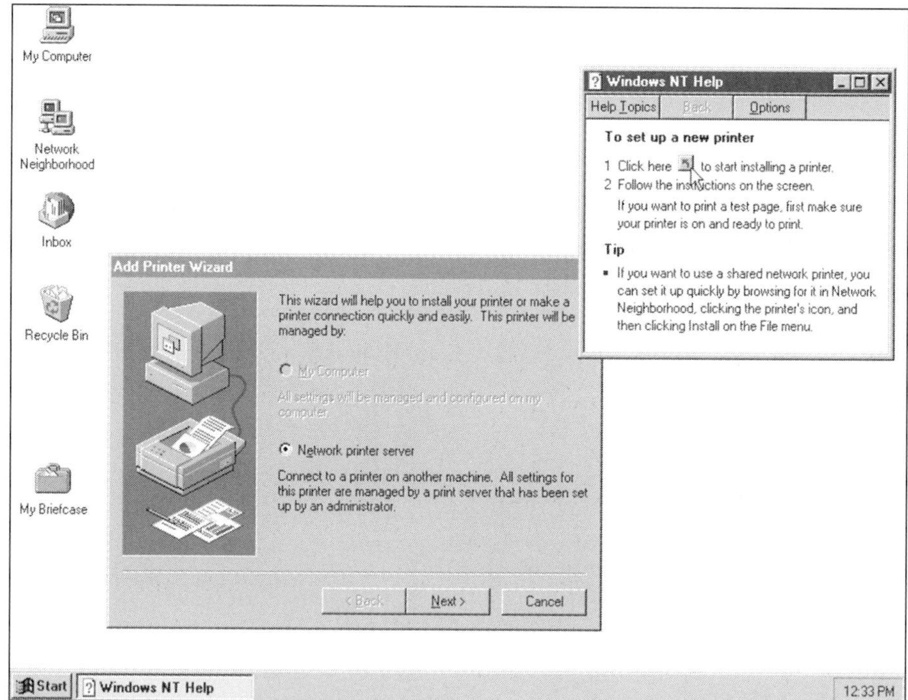

Maps

Maps depict locations (or information about locations) in simplified form.

The simplest map locates a point by relating it to known landmarks.

Maps are also used to compare locations. For instance, a map of the U.S. might use different colors to show the average yearly rainfall of each region.

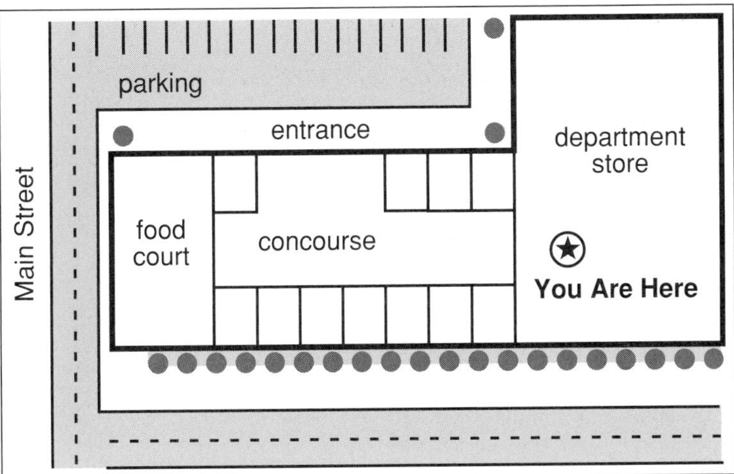

Maps should include only as much detail as is needed for clarity. The more information you can omit without diminishing the map's purpose, the more readable your map will be. Think of the map you might draw when supplying directions to your house. It wouldn't show every street in town. You'd only draw the ones that needed to be traveled, or ones that made useful landmarks.

Presenting And Positioning Illustrations

A illustration can lose impact if it's poorly presented or positioned.

The presentation and placement of an image can affect how it's perceived. Observe the following guidelines:

- When an illustration ties in with the body text, place it near the relevant text. Don't position it to interrupt the text flow, however, unless you want to require the reader to study it before reading further. (Yes, that's right, you're *required* to study the following illustration.)

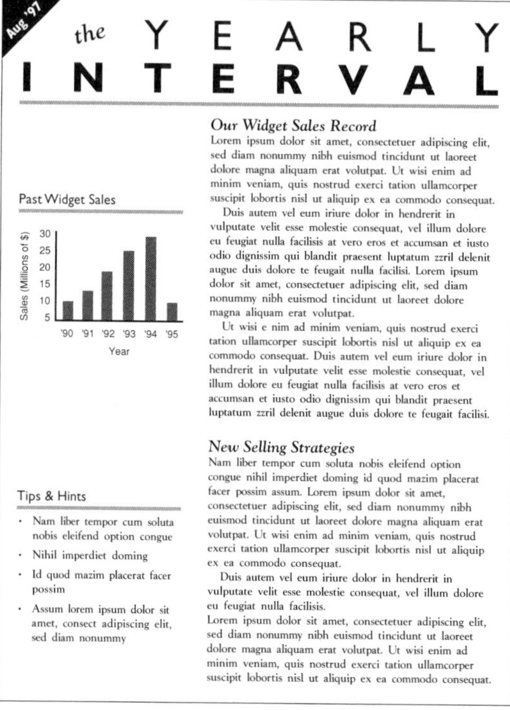

Aug '97

the YEARLY INTERVAL

Past Widget Sales

Our Widget Sales Record

Lorem ipsum dolor sit amet, consectetuer adipiscing elit, sed diam nonummy nibh euismod tincidunt ut laoreet dolore magna aliquam erat volutpat. Ut wisi enim ad minim veniam, quis nostrud exerci tation ullamcorper suscipit lobortis nisl ut aliquip ex ea commodo consequat.

Duis autem vel eum iriure dolor in hendrerit in vulputate velit esse molestie consequat, vel illum dolore eu feugiat nulla facilisis at vero eros et accumsan et iusto odio dignissim qui blandit praesent luptatum zzril delenit augue duis dolore te feugait nulla facilisi. Lorem ipsum dolor sit amet, consectetuer adipiscing elit, sed diam nonummy nibh euismod tincidunt ut laoreet dolore magna aliquam erat volutpat.

Ut wisi e nim ad minim veniam, quis nostrud exerci tation ullamcorper suscipit lobortis nisl ut aliquip ex ea commodo consequat. Duis autem vel eum iriure dolor in hendrerit in vulputate velit esse molestie consequat, vel illum dolore eu feugiat nulla facilisis at vero eros et accumsan et iusto odio dignissim qui blandit praesent luptatum zzril delenit augue duis dolore te feugait facilisi.

Tips & Hints

- Nam liber tempor cum soluta nobis eleifend option congue
- Nihil imperdiet doming
- Id quod mazim placerat facer possim
- Assum lorem ipsum dolor sit amet, consect adipiscing elit, sed diam nonummy

New Selling Strategies

Nam liber tempor cum soluta nobis eleifend option congue nihil imperdiet doming id quod mazim placerat facer possim assum. Lorem ipsum dolor sit amet, consectetuer adipiscing elit, sed diam nonummy nibh euismod tincidunt ut laoreet dolore magna aliquam erat volutpat. Ut wisi enim ad minim veniam, quis nostrud exerci tation ullamcorper suscipit lobortis nisl ut aliquip ex ea commodo consequat.

Duis autem vel eum iriure dolor in hendrerit in vulputate velit esse molestie consequat, vel illum dolore eu feugiat nulla facilisis.

Lorem ipsum dolor sit amet, consectetuer adipiscing elit, sed diam nonummy nibh euismod tincidunt ut laoreet dolore magna aliquam erat volutpat. Ut wisi enim ad minim veniam, quis nostrud exerci tation ullamcorper suscipit lobortis nisl ut aliquip ex ea commodo consequat.

- Balance the black or dark tones of a photograph with other heavy and contrasting elements on the page. In the following layout, the nameplate and bold headline balance the photo at the bottom.

serving the greater metropolitan area • august 1997

Community **News**

New Construction Starts With a Bang

Lorem ipsum dolor sit amet, consectetuer adipiscing elit, sed diam nonummy nibh euismod tincidunt ut laoreet dolore magna aliquam erat volutpat. Ut wisi enim ad minim veniam, quis nostrud exerci tation ullamcorper suscipit lobortis nisl ut aliquip ex ea commodo consequat.

Duis autem vel eum iriure dolor in hendrerit in vulputate velit esse molestie consequat, vel illum dolore eu feugiat nulla facilisis at vero eros et accumsan et iusto odio dignissim qui blandit praesent luptatum zzril delenit augue duis dolore te feugait nulla facilisi. Lorem ipsum dolor sit amet, consectetuer adipiscing elit, sed diam nonummy nibh euismod tincidunt ut laoreet dolore magna aliquam erat volutpat.

Ut wisi e nim ad minim veniam, quis nostrud exerci tation ullamcorper suscipit lobortis nisl ut aliquip ex ea commodo consequat. Duis autem vel eum iriure dolor in hendrerit in vulputate velit esse molestie consequat, vel illum dolore eu feugiat nulla facilisis at vero eros et accumsan et iusto odio dignissim qui blandit praesent luptatum zzril delenit augue duis dolore te feugait nulla facilisi.

Nam liber tempor cum soluta nobis eleifend option congue nihil imperdiet doming id quod mazim placerat facer possim assum. Lorem ipsum dolor sit amet, consectetuer adipiscing elit, sed diam nonummy nibh euismod tincidunt ut laoreet dolore magna aliquam erat volutpat. Ut wisi enim ad minim veniam, quis nostrud exerci tation ullamcorper suscipit lobortis nisl ut aliquip ex ea commodo consequat.

Duis autem vel eum iriure dolor in hendrerit in vulputate velit esse molestie consequat, vel illum dolore eu feugiat nulla facilisis.

Lorem ipsum dolor sit amet, consectetuer adipiscing elit, sed diam nonummy nibh euismod tincidunt ut laoreet dolore magna aliquam erat volutpat. Ut wisi enim ad minim veniam, quis nostrud exerci tation ullamcorper suscipit lobortis nisl ut aliquip ex ea commodo consequat.

Duis autem vel eum iriure dolor in hendrerit in vulputate velit esse molestie consequat, vel illum dolore eu feugiat nulla facilisis at vero eros et accumsan et iusto odio dignissim qui blandit praesent luptatum zzril delenit augue

- Illustrations used similarly throughout a document should be identical in style.

How to Prepare...

Meats

Lorem ipsum dolor sit amet, adipiscing elit, sed diam nonummy nibh euismod tincidunt ut laoreet dolore magna aliquam erat volutpat. Ut wisi enim ad minim veniam, quis nostrud exerci tation ullamcorper suscipit lobortis nisl ut aliquip ex ea commodo consequat.

Duis autem vel eum iriure dolor in hendrerit in vulputate velit esse

Veggies

Nam liber tempor cum soluta nobis eleifend option congue nihil imperdiet doming id quod mazim placerat facer possim assum. Lorem ipsum dolor sit amet, consectetuer adipiscing elit, sed diam nonummy nibh euismod tincidunt ut laoreet dolore magna aliquam erat volutpat. Ut wisi enim ad minim lorem ipsum dum dolor sit amet, consectetuer

Spices

Dolore magna aliquam ut wisi enim ad minim veniam, quis nostrud exerci tation ullamcorper suscipit lobortis nisl ut aliquip ex ea commodo consequat. Duis autem vel eum iriure dolor in consectetuer adipiscing elit, sed diam nonummy nibh euismod tincidunt ut laoreet dolore magna aliquam erat volutpat.

Ut wisi enim ad minim lorem

- When illustrations or photographs are the central focus of your project, keep the typography and design simple.
- Leave even margins of white space when text wraps around an image.
- When grouping illustrations or photographs of different sizes, try not to leave "holes" in your document.

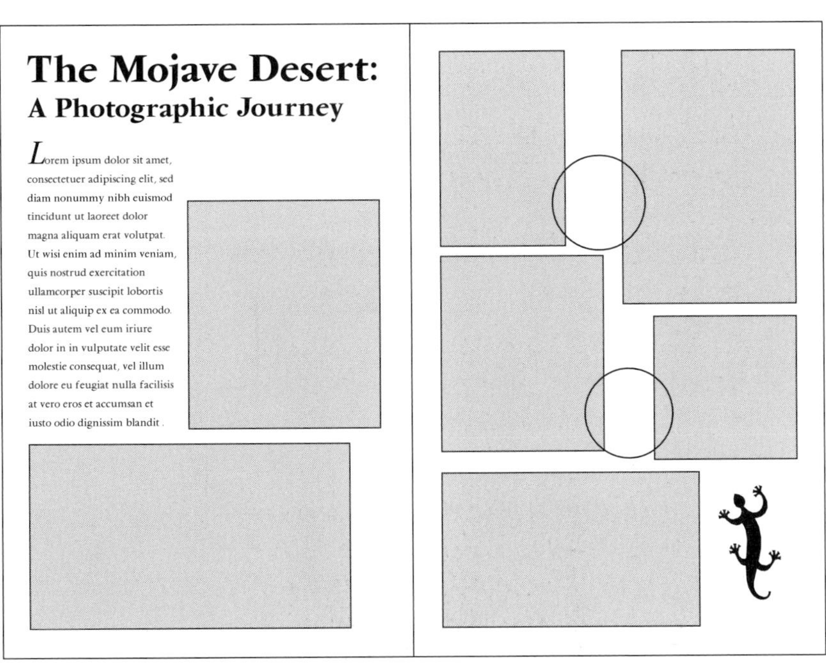

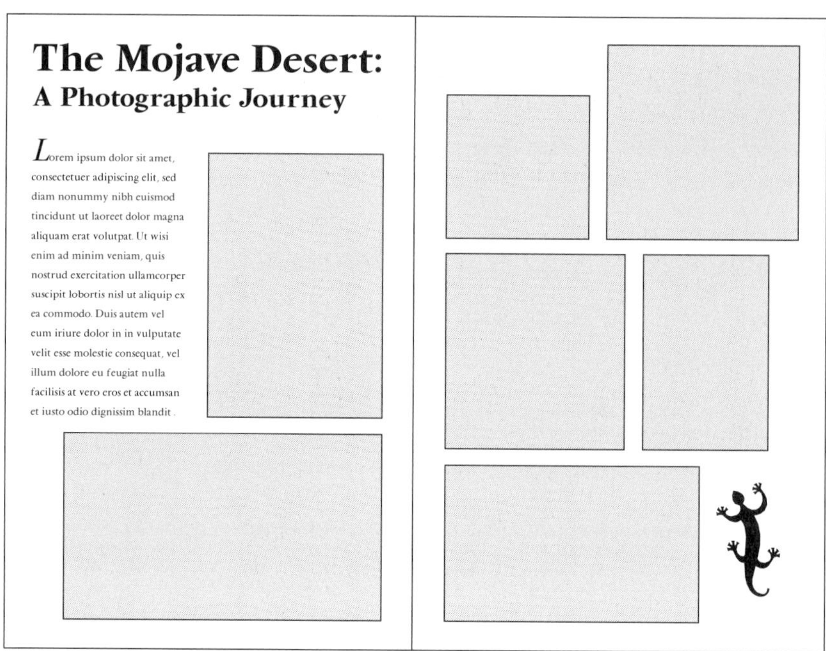

Tips And Tricks

The previous list of guidelines will help you avoid making errors when placing illustrations, and error-free layouts are usually good-looking layouts. Every once in a while, though, you'll follow all the rules and still end up with a blasé result. If a given illustration still doesn't seem like an integrated part of your document—if, in fact, it seems more like a paper cutout that got dropped on *top* of your document—try one of these more exotic techniques:

- Turn your illustration into a screen, and place it partially or fully behind the text. Be careful with this technique—screens of more than 30 percent can hinder legibility. (That's for black ink. You can use higher percentages for colored inks, depending on the brightness of the color. The print quality of your output device is also a factor—low-end printers produce coarser screens.)
- Create a screened backdrop for your illustration. The backdrop doesn't have to be fancy—a simple circle or polygon will usually do the trick.
- For a really fancy look, combine the previous two techniques, and use a large, screened version of your illustration as a backdrop for the real thing. (You won't want to use this trick too often—save it for that really important project.)

Disaster Area:

The Quake of '56

Lorem ipsum dolor amet, consectetuer adipiscing elit, sed dim nonummy nibh euismod tincidunt ut laoreet dolore magna aliquam erat volutpat. Ut wisi enim ad minim veniam, quis nostrud exerci tation ullamcorper lobortis nisl ut aliquip ex ea commodo consequat.

Duis autem vel eum iriure dolor in velit hendrit in vulputate velit esse molestie consequat, vel illum dolore eu feugiat nulla facilisis at vero eros et accumsan et iusto odio dignissim blandit praesent luptatum zzril delenit augue dolore te feugait nulla facilisi. Lorem ipsum dolor sit amet, consectetuer adipiscing elit, sed diam nonummy euismod tincidunt ut laoreet dolore magna aliquam erat volutpat.

Ut wisi enim ad minim veniam, quis nostrud exerci tation ullamcorper suscipit lobortis nisl ut aliquip ex ea commodo consequat. Duis autem vel eum iriure dolor in hendrerit vulputate velit esse molestie consequat, vel illum dolore eu feugiat nulla facilisis at vero eros et accumsan et iusto odio ipsum dolor sit amet, consectetuer dignissim qui blandit praesent luptatum zzril del enit augue sit amet, consectetuer duis dolore te feugait nulla facilisi.

Nam liber tempor cum soluta nobis eleifend option congue nihil imperdiet doming id quod mazim placerat facer possim assum. Lorem ipsum dolor sit amet, consectetuer adipiscing elit, sed diam nonummy nibh euismod ticidunt ut laoreet dolore magna aliquam erat volupat. Ut wisi enim ad minim venim, quis nostrud exerci tation ullamcorper suscipit lobortis nisl ut aliquip ex ea commodo consequat.

Duis autem vel eum iriure dolor in hendrerit in vulputate velit esse molestie consequat, vel illum dolore eu feugiat nulla facilisis. Lorem ipsum dolor sit amet, consectetuer adipiscing elit, sed diam nonummy nibh euismod tincidunt ut laoreet dolore magna aliquam erat volutpat.

I've got a bike, you can ride it if you like...

Duis autem vel eum iriure dolor in velit hendrit in vulputate velit esse molestie consequat, vel illum dolore eu feugiat nulla facilisis at vero eros et accumsan et iusto odio dignissim blandit present luptatum zzril delenit augue dolore te feugait nulla facilisi. Lorem ipsum dolor sit amet, consectetuer adipiscing elit, sed diam nonummy euismod tincidunt ut laoreet dolore magna aliquam erat volutpat. Ut wisi enim ad minim venim, quis nostrud exerci tation ullamcorper suscipit lobortis nisl ut aliquip ex ea commodo consequat. Duis autem vel eum iriure dolor in hendrerit vulputate velit esse molestie consequat, vel illum

Disaster Area:

The Quake of '56

Lorem ipsum dolor amet, consectetuer adipiscing elit, sed dim nonummy nibh euismod tincidunt ut laoreet dolore magna aliquam erat volutpat. Ut wisi enim ad minim veniam, quis nostrud exerci tation ullamcorper lobortis nisl ut aliquip ex ea commodo consequat.

Duis autem vel eum iriure dolor in velit hendrit in vulputate velit esse molestie consequat, vel illum dolore eu feugiat nulla facilisis at vero eros et accumsan et iusto odio dignissim blandit praesent luptatum zzril delenit augue dolore te feugait nulla facilisi. Lorem ipsum dolor sit amet, consectetuer adipiscing elit, sed diam nonummy euismod tincidunt ut laoreet dolore magna aliquam erat volutpat.

Ut wisi enim ad minim veniam, quis nostrud exerci tation ullamcorper suscipit lobortis nisl ut aliquip ex ea commodo consequat. Duis autem vel eum iriure dolor in hendrerit vulputate velit esse molestie consequat, vel illum dolore eu feugiat nulla facilisis at vero eros et accumsan et iusto odio ipsum dolor sit amet, consectetuer dignissim qui blandit praesent luptatum zzril del enit augue sit amet, consectetuer duis dolore te feugait nulla facilisi.

The quake leveled every building in the township of Nowhere Special, Nevada. It was never rebuilt.

Nam liber tempor cum soluta nobis eleifend option congue nihil imperdiet doming id quod mazim placerat facer possim assum. Lorem ipsum dolor sit amet, consectetuer adipiscing elit, sed diam nonummy nibh euismod ticidunt ut laoreet dolore magna aliquam erat volupat. Ut wisi enim ad minim venim, quis nostrud exerci tation ullamcorper suscipit lobortis nisl ut aliquip ex ea commodo consequat.

Duis autem vel eum iriure dolor in hendrerit in vulputate velit esse molestie consequat, vel illum dolore eu feugiat nulla facilisis. Lorem ipsum dolor sit amet, consectetuer adipiscing elit, sed diam nonummy nibh euismod tincidunt ut laoreet dolore magna aliquam erat volutpat.

- Create several duplicates of your illustration, and arrange them dynamically on the page. Try setting them at different sizes or angles. Make it look as if the illustration is growing, shrinking, or moving across the page.

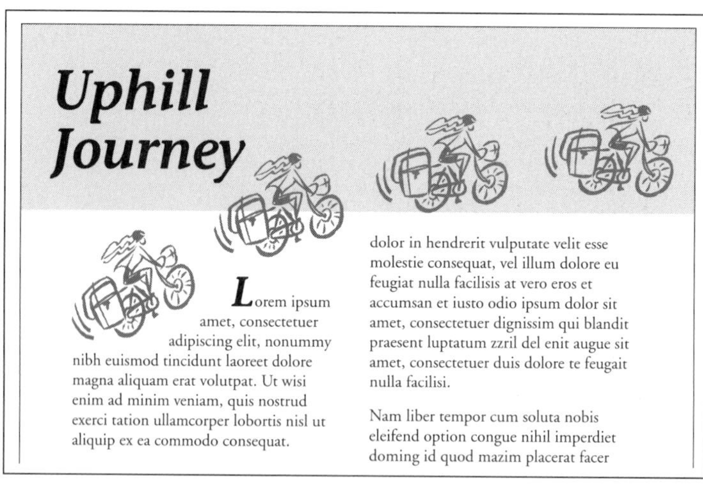

Uphill Journey

Lorem ipsum amet, consectetuer adipiscing elit, nonummy nibh euismod tincidunt laoreet dolore magna aliquam erat volutpat. Ut wisi enim ad minim veniam, quis nostrud exerci tation ullamcorper lobortis nisl ut aliquip ex ea commodo consequat.

dolor in hendrerit vulputate velit esse molestie consequat, vel illum dolore eu feugiat nulla facilisis at vero eros et accumsan et iusto odio ipsum dolor sit amet, consectetuer dignissim qui blandit praesent luptatum zzril del enit augue sit amet, consectetuer duis dolore te feugait nulla facilisi.

Nam liber tempor cum soluta nobis eleifend option congue nihil imperdiet doming id quod mazim placerat facer

- If your illustration is boxed, position it to break its box. The graphic has an illusory tendency to look bigger, because the box is perceived as being too small to contain it.

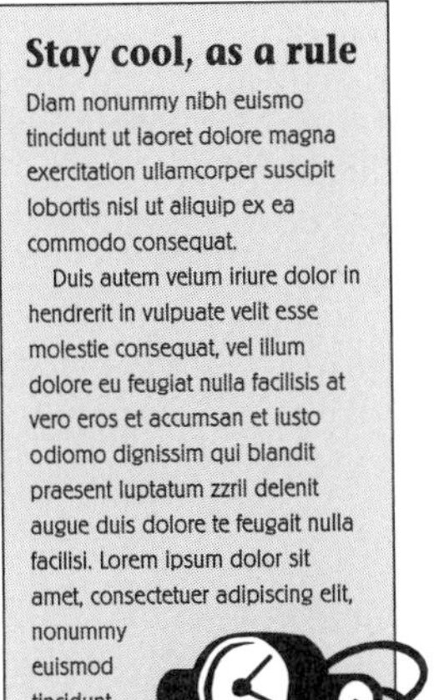

Stay cool, as a rule

Diam nonummy nibh euismo tincidunt ut laoret dolore magna exercitation ullamcorper suscipit lobortis nisl ut aliquip ex ea commodo consequat.

Duis autem velum iriure dolor in hendrerit in vulpuate velit esse molestie consequat, vel illum dolore eu feugiat nulla facilisis at vero eros et accumsan et iusto odiomo dignissim qui blandit praesent luptatum zzril delenit augue duis dolore te feugait nulla facilisi. Lorem ipsum dolor sit amet, consectetuer adipiscing elit, nonummy euismod tincidunt ut laoreet, vero eros.

- Got a photo that's as big as your page? Don't resize it—make the whole page a photo! Using a photo with large empty areas will allow you to include text as well—just print it right on top of the picture. (You may need to lighten the photo in a paint program first, to ensure that the overprinted text will be readable.)

Seventh Heaven

Consectetuer adipiscing elit, sed dim nonummy nibh euismod tincidunt ut laoreet dolore magna aliquam erat volutpat. Ut wisi enim ad minim veniam, quis nostrud exerci tation ullamcorper lobortis nisl ut aliquip ex ea commodo consequat.

Duis autem vel eum iriure dolor in velit hendrit in vulputate velit esse molestie consequat, vel illum dolore eu feugiat nulla facilisis at vero eros et accumsan et iusto odio dignissim blandit praesent luptatum zzril delenit augue dolore te feugait nulla facilisi. Lorem ipsum dolor sit amet, consectetuer adipiscing elit, sed diam nonummy euismod tincidunt ut laoreet dolore magna aliquam erat volutpat.

Ut wisi enim ad minim veniam, quis nostrud exerci tation ullamcorper suscipit lobortis nisl ut aliquip ex ea commodo consequat. Duis autem vel eum iriure dolor in hendrerit vulputate velit esse molestie consequat, vel illum dolore eu feugiat nulla facilisis at vero eros et accumsan et iusto odio ipsum dolor sit amet, consectetuer dignissim qui blandit praesent luptatum zzril del enit augue sit amet, consectetuer duis dolore te feugait nulla facilisi.

Nam liber tempor cum soluta nobis eleifend option congue nihil imperdiet doming id quod mazim placerat facer possim assum. Lorem ipsum dolor sit amet, consectetuer adipiscing elit, sed diam nonummy nibh euismod ticidunt ut laoreet dolore magna aliquam erat volupat. Ut wisi enim ad minim venim, quis nostrud exerci tation ullamcorper suscipit lobortis nisl ut aliquip ex ea commodo consequat.

Duis autem vel eum iriure dolor in hendrerit in vulputate velit esse molestie consequat, vel illum dolore eu feugiat nulla facilisis. Lorem ipsum dolor sit amet, consectetuer adipiscing elit, sed diam nonummy nibh euismod tincidunt ut laoreet.

This is only a brief list of the possibilities—and it's limited to situations when you have *one* illustration to place. With two or more, the number of options grows exponentially. Flip through magazines, newsletters, or other publications and you'll soon stumble upon more neat tricks you'll want to use (remember to keep copies of your favorites in your clip file). Also, don't forget about the building blocks from Chapter 4 of this book—a simple rule, box, or drop shadow might be all that your illustration needs to go from humdrum to eye-popping. Remember, graphics shouldn't require much embellishment to stand out—they're natural focal points by themselves.

Moving On

We've covered a lot of ground in this chapter. You now know how to choose appropriate illustrations for your document and how to position them on the page with relative confidence. (After you've designed a few layouts of your own, upgrade this to "substantial confidence." Instruction is useful, but there's no substitute for experience.)

This chapter also contains a cursory amount of information on arranging photographs, but, believe me, you've only seen the tip of the iceberg. The use of photographic artwork in design is a broad topic, well deserving of further study. If most of the black space in your documents will in fact be photos, you owe it to yourself to read the next chapter.

6 Working With Photographs

Sometimes words alone seem inadequate.

If you watch television news, you've probably seen countless political reporters delivering their spiels while standing in front of the Capitol building. It seems gratuitous, when you think about it—wouldn't it be just as easy to wire the story to the newsroom and deliver it from there? Why show us the Capitol building, which we've all seen a million times anyway?

But all the networks do it, and there's a reason: The story becomes more credible as a result. If only subconsciously, we're more likely to believe reporters when we *see* them near the source of the story. The undeniable reality of the pictures lends credence to the words. A story is just a story, but seeing is believing.

The same holds true for printed publications. Pictures represent the real thing, in a way that words and illustrations cannot. This makes them extremely powerful page elements, if used properly. Advances in scanning, printing, and photo manipulation have made them much easier to work with, but, as always, you'll need a good idea of what you *want* to do in advance. No matter how good your equipment is, it can't make decisions—it can only implement the ones you make. Hopefully, this chapter will help you make the right ones.

Why Use Photographs?

Photographs bring realism and authenticity to a document.

The most obvious reason to use photographs is that they seem real—they offer concrete visual proof to back up your text. This is why newspapers and magazines use photos for hard news stories and illustrations for more abstract articles.

Walking a Political Tightrope

Bill Clinton struggles to balance competing interests

For the past week, the factions have hounded Bill Clinton. They all want a piece of the pie. Five hundred years ago, Christopher Columbus was on his knees in throne rooms throughout Europe, scrambling to finance his first voyage to the New World. Meanwhile, his Venetian countryman Aldus Manutius scholar , printer, and entrepreneur was establishing what would become the greatest publishing house in Europe, the Aldine Press. Like Columbus, Aldus Manutius was driven by force of of intellect and personality to realize a lifelong dream.

Aldus greatest passion was Greek literature, which was rapidly going up in smoke in the

Numerous studies show that readers are more likely to believe a story, statistic, advertising claim, or other assertion if it features a photo. Photos can also evoke a greater sense of urgency and drama from readers than illustrations can. If you try to recall the most important events of the last 50 years, chances are you associate the events you remember with photos you've seen.

Finally, there are some situations where photographs are mandated. This is almost never true of illustrations. A news story about an eggplant in the shape of Elvis's head, for instance, would make no sense without a photograph. A written description of any length would be inadequate, and a clip-art picture of an eggplant would be worse than useless. If your story needs to be *shown* as well as told, photographs are not an option—they're a requirement.

Choosing Good Photographs

Not all photos are created equal.

If you've ever suffered through a relative's lackluster holiday snapshots, you know that not all photos are created equal. A good photograph captures attention, conveys emotion, and tells a story.

Your eye will usually tell you when a photo is "bad" even if you can't immediately diagnose why. The most obvious problems are technical, such as poor exposure might result in dark or grainy photos. More subtle errors arise when a photograph is poorly *framed*—such as when the primary visual element is awkwardly off-center or too small to fill more than a fraction of the available space. Good photographers are not merely handy with a camera; they have an eye for where to point the lens, and when to click the shutter.

While it's much easier to recognize a great photo than it is to take one, every good photograph shares a few common elements:

- *A decisive moment*. Any shot of a person or event should suggest to the reader that the photo was taken at the optimum instant.
- *Emotional context*. Even photos of inanimate objects can convey emotion and imply meaning, if shot correctly. Images devoid of feeling will not evoke strong responses.
- *Powerful visual imagery*. The underlying geometry, tone, and composition of a photo can make the difference between a mediocre shot and a great one.
- *Strong cropping and framing*. Poor framing can nullify a photo's impact. Fortunately, this problem is sometimes correctible using

your layout software. You can crop an image to improve the framing. Of course, if you need *more* photo rather than less, cropping can't help you.

Technical Fine-Tuning

Numerous technical factors influence how a photograph looks.

Desktop publishers must be able to recognize a technically correct photo. It should fulfill a number of common, related requirements:

- *Focus.* Above all, a photo must be in proper focus. Except when striving for a particular effect, fuzzy, vague, or blurry pictures look unprofessional.

- *Clarity.* It's possible for an image to appear grainy and diffuse even when the negative and print appear to be in proper focus.

- *Contrast.* Black-and-white photos must have balanced contrast. Too much contrast makes whites look too light and blacks look too dark. Not enough contrast makes the entire image seem gray and washed out.

- *Brightness.* A photo should be neither too dark nor too light, regardless of its subject matter.

Occasionally, you might wish to intentionally blur, overexpose, or otherwise alter a technical aspect of a photo to create a dramatic effect—but this is rare indeed. Most of the time, breaking the conventions of good photography will look like an error, not an effect. Unless your reasons are impeccable, follow the rules.

Designing With Photographs

The perceived quality of a photo depends heavily upon its presentation.

As with illustrations, the placement of photographs will affect their impact. There are a few important design concepts and conventions that must be heeded.

Use Dominant Photos

Dominant photos tell readers where to look first.

The Road to Recovery

Today's farmers are embracing new methods—and their open-mindedness is paying off

Lorem ipsum dolor amet, consectetuer adipiscing elit, sed diam nonummy nibh euismod tincidunt ut laoreet dolore magna aliquam erat volutpat. Ut wisi enim ad minim veniam, quis nostrud exerci tation ullamcorper suscipit lobortis nisl ut velit aliquip ex ea commodo consequat.

Duis autem vel eum iriure dolor in hendrerit in vulputate velit esse molestie

consequat, vel illum dolore eu feugiat nulla facilisis at vero eros et accumsan et iusto odio dignissim blandit praesent luptatum zzril delenit augue duis dolore te feugait nulla facilisi. Lorem ipsum dolor, consectetuer adipiscing elit, sed diam nonummy nibh euismod tincidunt ut laoreet dolore magna aliquam erat ut volutpat.

Ut wisi enim ad minim veniam, quis nostrud exerci tation ullamcorper suscipit lobortis nisl ut aliquip ex ea commodo consequat. Duis autem vel eum iriure dolor in hendrerit vulputate velit esse molestie consequat, vel illum dolore eu feugiat nulla facilisis at vero eros et accumsan et iusto odio dignissim blandit praesent luptatum zzril delenit augue duis dolore te feugait nulla facilisi.

Nam liber tempor cum soluta nobis eleifend option congue nihil imperdiet doming id quod mazim placerat facer possim assum. Lorem ipsum dolor sit amet, consectetuer adipiscing elit, sed diam nonummy nibh euismod tincidunt ut laoreet dolore magna aliquam volutpat. Ut wisi enim ad mini veniam, quis nostrud exerci tation ullamcorper lobortis nisl ut aliquip ex ea commodo.

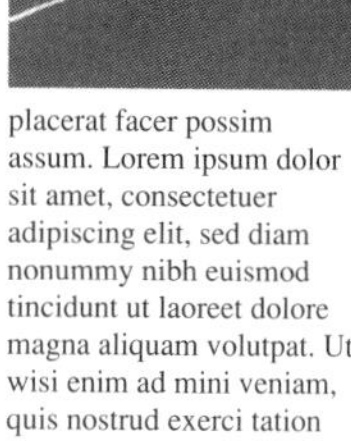

Duis autem vel eum iriure dolor in hendrerit in vulputate velit esse molestie consequat, vel illum dolore eu feugiat nulla facilisis.

Lorem ipsum dolor sit amet, consectetuer adipiscing elit, sed diam nonummy nibh euismod tincidunt ut laoreet dolore magna aliquam erat volpat. Ut wisi enim ad minim veniam, quis nostrud exerci tation ullamcorper suscipit lobortis nisl ut aliquip ex ea commodo consequat.

Duis autem vel eum iriure dolor in hendrerit in vulputate velit esse molestie consequat, vel illum dolore eu feugiat nulla facilisis at vero eros et accumsan et iusto odio dignissim qui blandit praesent luptatum zzril delenit augue dolore te feugait nulla. Consectetuer adipiscing elit, nonummy nibh euismod tincidunt ut laoreet dolore aliquam erat volutpat.

Ut wisi enim ad minim veniam, quis nostrud exerci tation ullamcorper suscipit lobortis nisl ut aliquip ex ea commodo consequat. Duis autem vel eum iriure dolor.

When running several photos on a single page or spread, choose one as the dominant image and position it prominently.

Multiphoto layouts without a dominant image can look uninspired and confusing.

Do It In Color

Color is an extremely powerful design tool. It can be used to attract readers' attention, set a mood, or simply brighten up a page. Numerous marketing studies show that color advertisements generally draw more attention than their black-and-white counterparts. Color can also add beauty, particularly when photographs or artwork are featured prominently.

The first question to ask yourself when considering color is not *how* to use it but *whether* to use it at all. Nearly any document can benefit from the use of color, if it's applied properly. The size of your budget is the primary consideration. Using color bumps up the printing costs, and although it's not as expensive as it used to be, it's still not a decision to be taken lightly.

Some documents require color—for example, a black-and-white clothing store catalog wouldn't be much use to potential customers, but most documents won't have this sort of built-in mandate, so you'll need to ask yourself some questions:

- *Can I afford to use color?* If you can't afford to use color, and you don't have an idea for its use that's earth-shattering enough to prompt a budget rearrangement, forget about it. Don't despair. Black-and-white isn't without its charm. Why do you suppose photographers still use it, with color film available just as cheap?
- *Does my document really require the added impact or beauty provided by color?* This may seem like an odd question, but certain documents are pretty bland by nature, and you probably won't lose much by forgoing color—your readers won't be particularly disappointed by its absence.
- *Will my document have to compete with color documents?* If you're printing black-and-white product brochures while everyone else in the industry is using color, you may be at a distinct disadvantage. When readers expect color, its absence becomes a liability. Of course, a well-designed black-and-white document will still beat a shoddy color document.
- *Which page elements would I set in color?* After determining a set of elements to be "colorized," you might discover that your document would include several pages displaying no color at all or in amounts too negligible to draw much attention. Printing essentially black-and-white pages in full color doesn't give you much bang for your buck.
- *How many different colors would I need?* If you could limit yourself to two colors, for instance, the printing cost would be cheaper than for full-color work. Don't forget to count black, if you're planning on using it.

Choosing Colors

Successful color documents follow a color scheme.

Okay, so you've decided to use color in your document. The next question you must address is which colors to use. This is not merely a question for jobs involving user-chosen ink colors; even if you're printing in full color, you're going to need a color scheme. Two colors that look nice by themselves might look horrid when used together. Appropriateness is also a factor—certain colors evoke moods which might not fit your document's intended message. Finally, like all other design tools, color is susceptible to overuse. If you shove every color of the rainbow onto a single page, your reader is more apt to be nauseated than impressed.

Finding A Color Scheme

Color wheels show relationships between colors and can be a help when devising a color scheme. The color wheel familiar to most people uses red, yellow, and blue as the *primary colors* from which all other colors are mixed. Colors that result from mixing two primary colors are called *secondary colors*—for example, the primary colors red and yellow combine to create the secondary color orange.

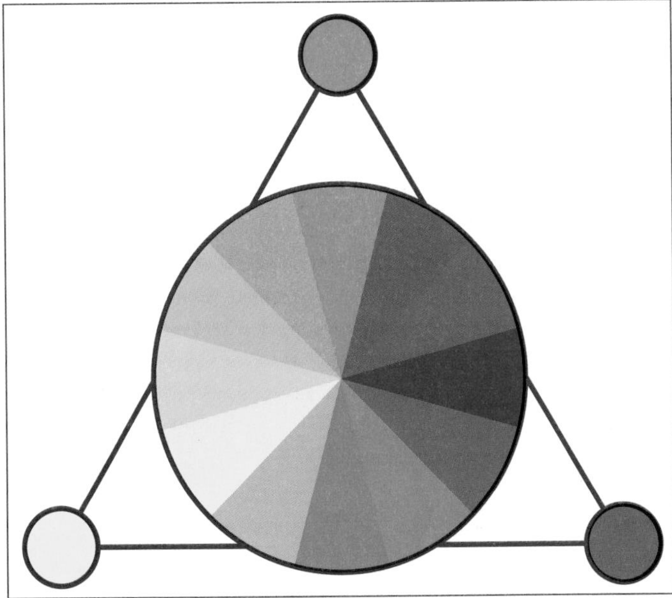

A safe way to generate a color scheme is to pick a set of *analogous colors*—three or four adjacent colors on the wheel. The similarity between analogous colors gives them a good chance of working well together. They tend to create a unified look, albeit one with little color contrast.

If you crave contrast, you *could* choose colors located opposite each other on the color wheel, known as *complementary colors*. (The name is a bit misleading. It's meant to denote two colors that neutralize each other if mixed together. That doesn't necessarily mean they'll complement each other if *used* together—there are certain red-green combinations I wouldn't even use on a Christmas card.) A better scheme for finding high-contrast colors that work together is to use a *triad*—three colors roughly equidistant from each other on the color wheel. Red, yellow, and blue are a triad, and they generally work well together.

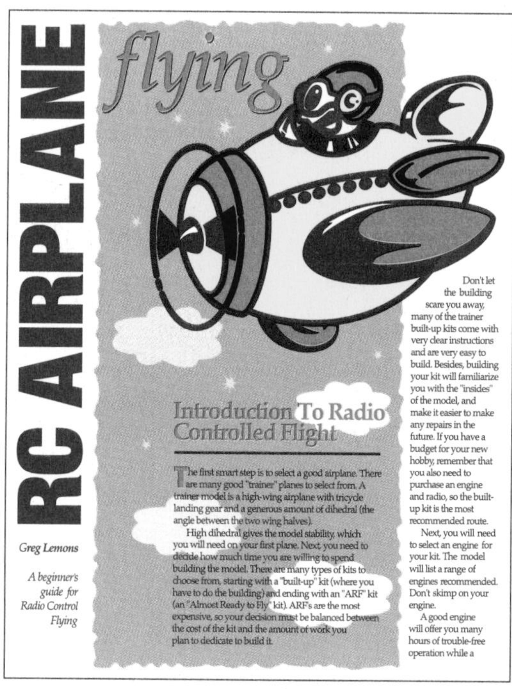

RC AIRPLANE

flying

Greg Lemons

A beginner's guide for Radio Control Flying

Introduction To Radio Controlled Flight

The first smart step is to select a good airplane. There are many good "trainer" planes to select from. A trainer model is a high-wing airplane with tricycle landing gear and a generous amount of dihedral (the angle between the two wing halves).

High dihedral gives the model stability, which you will need on your first plane. Next, you need to decide how much time you are willing to spend building the model. There are many types of kits to choose from, starting with a "built-up" kit (where you have to do the building) and ending with an "ARF" kit (an "Almost Ready to Fly" kit). ARFs are the most expensive, so your decision must be balanced between the cost of the kit and the amount of work you plan to dedicate to build it.

Don't let the building scare you away, many of the trainer built-up kits come with very clear instructions and are very easy to build. Besides, building your kit will familiarize you with the "insides" of the model, and make it easier to make any repairs in the future. If you have a budget for your new hobby, remember that you also need to purchase an engine and radio, so the built-up kit is the most recommended route.

Next, you will need to select an engine for your kit. The model will list a range of engines recommended. Don't skimp on your engine.

A good engine will offer you many hours of trouble-free operation while a

Remember, these are just suggestions on how to get started. They're particularly useful if there's one color you *know* you want to use. You may generate a set of analogous colors or a triad using your color as a starting point and hit upon a workable scheme faster than you would by just picking colors at random.

Color And Mood

Most colors carry emotional and psychological implications that can help or hurt your design. Despite the different reactions people have to various colors, there are some expectations associated with certain colors.

You should consider the differences between *warm* colors (reds, oranges, and yellows) and *cool* colors (greens, blues, and purples). Warm colors are intense and engaging. They're often used to highlight the important elements in a design, because they tend to pop out at the viewer.

Cool colors are more subdued. Documents that use cool colors exclusively tend to have a clean, elegant look. It's also easier for readers to see "cool" documents as a unified whole, because no particular element commands their immediate attention.

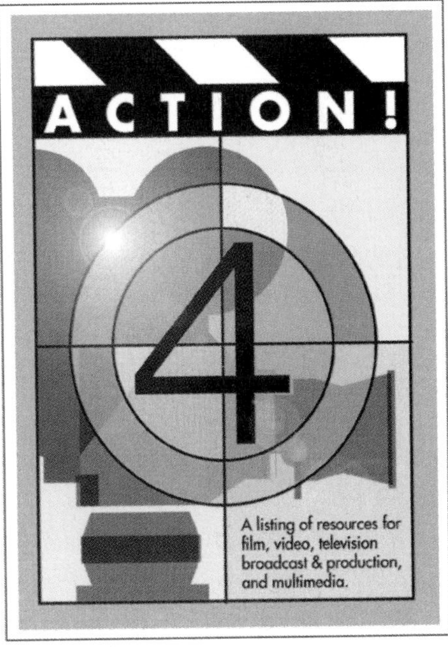

Properties Of Color

The color wheel shown earlier is actually somewhat incomplete. It only shows *hues*—stopping points along the visible color spectrum. Each hue on the wheel actually constitutes a range of possible colors, created by varying the hue's saturation and value.

Saturation is the relative brilliance or vibrancy of a color and is usually expressed as a percentage. The hues on our color wheel are 100 percent saturated. Adding black to a color decreases saturation. The color becomes darker and duller until finally reaching 0 percent saturation—black.

Value is the percentage of hue used. The hues on our color wheel have 100 percent value. Colors lighten as value is decreased. Low value settings produce pastels. At 0 percent value, all color disappears, and you're left with white.

The following chart shows a single hue (the heavily outlined box at the upper left) and some of its possible variations.

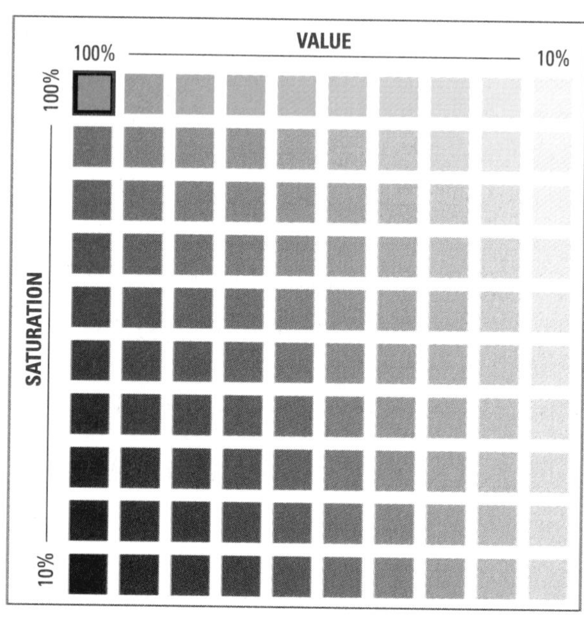

When you *screen* a color, you're essentially tweaking that color's value. For this reason, colors with 100 percent value are good choices for inks. Used in conjunction with screening, they can reproduce the entire value range of a given hue-saturation combination. If your base ink has a lesser value—say, 50 percent—you'll only be able to reproduce values *less* than 50 percent by screening it.

The HSL Color Model

There's a color model known as HSL that describes each shade as a combination of hue, saturation, and *lightness* (the value scale in reverse; 100 percent lightness equals white). Hues are expressed numerically as angles on a predefined color wheel; saturation and lightness are expressed as percentages. The HSL color model isn't used very often—the most useful color models express colors as mixtures of other colors, because that's how printers and computer screens *really* reproduce color—but I thought you might like to know that such a model exists. Incidentally, this model is also known as HSB (*brightness* rather than lightness). Maybe someday the name will be standardized, but I'm not holding my breath.

Working With Spot Color

Two-color printing may be the affordable answer to your color needs.

If you're looking to jazz up your pages but lack the time, money, or expertise to tackle a full-color job, spot color may be the answer. The standard spot color job uses two inks: black and a second color chosen by the designer.

Flyers, letterhead, brochures, and newsletters can undergo a dramatic, eye-catching transformation from a second color.

RECYCLE Weekly

Recognizing environmental contributions

If recognition of a job well done is the top motivator of employee performance in general, then it follows that recognition of employees' environmental contributions should also be a top motivator to encourage increased environmental actions. Personal recognition indicates that someone took the time to notice the achievement, seek out the employee responsible and personally tell the individual that their achievement was impressive.

Book after book on human resource management tells managers to deliver "one-minute praisings", "pats on the back" or "bravo cards" to motivate employees to higher levels of achievement. The principle also applies when encouraging employees to take greater personal responsibility for reducing negative environmental impacts at work.

Thoughtful, personal recognition of an employee's contribution is invaluable both to the employee and to the positive effects it can have on the workplace. The best informal act of recognition is one that creates a story that the person can tell her/his colleagues and family.

It's also important to use the person's name around the office let others know that you're impressed by someone's efforts. The best kind of office gossip is when word gets back to you that your boss has been saying good things about you. Or, if you hear from another employee about someone's environmental efforts, be sure to repeat it back to the individual: let them know that you have heard what they are doing and that you are impressed with their initiative.

Biological diversity

Biological diversity... is the key to the maintenance of the world as we know it... This is the assembly of life that took a billion years to evolve. It ... created the world that creates us. It holds the world steady."

Scientists estimate that 50-100,000 species are made extinct each year. This means that every day on the planet 100-300 species disappear forever...

"...The [Chernobyl] catastrophe caused thousands of deaths....It continues to reach into the future to claim new victims and indeed the spectre of another Chernobyl continues to hang over the region..."

It's always time to recycle

No time to recycle? It doesn't have to be a burden, says Joe Heimlich, waste management specialist with the Ohio Extension Service.

Once a system is set up, recycling should only take about five minutes a week per family member, Heimlich says. The trick is setting up a pattern: "It's hard to get people to that point," Heimlich says. "I tell people to fit recycling into their own kitchen set-up, so it doesn't become a pain."

For example, Heimlich suggests putting a recycling container where the trash bin is now. "Make it easier to recycle than to throw items away--that's what works," he says.

Heimlich also suggests letting glass containers soak in dishwater left over from dirty dishes. Any grease in the warm soapy water helps labels peel off. Just rinse the glass items out later and put them in a recycling container, perhaps under the sink, he says.

Stop Ocean Dumping

As part of a wider campaign against dumping, Greenpeace has maintained from the start that it is wrong in principle to dump oil installations at sea.

To dump structures, such as the Brent Spar, in areas of high marine biodiversity with poorly understood ecology infringes the precautionary principle and presents unknown environmental risks. To do so would set dangerous precedents for future dumping of wastes at sea. It ignores the impact of

RECYCLE Weekly

Recognizing environmental contributions

If recognition of a job well done is the top motivator of employee performance in general, then it follows that recognition of employees' environmental contributions should also be a top motivator to encourage increased environmental actions. Personal recognition indicates that someone took the time to notice the achievement, seek out the employee responsible and personally tell the individual that their achievement was impressive.

Book after book on human resource management tells managers to deliver "one-minute praisings", "pats on the back" or "bravo cards" to motivate employees to higher levels of achievement. The principle also applies when encouraging employees to take greater personal responsibility for reducing negative environmental impacts at work.

Thoughtful, personal recognition of an employee's contribution is invaluable both to the employee and to the positive effects it can have on the workplace. The best informal act of recognition is one that creates a story that the person can tell her/his colleagues and family.

It's also important to use the person's name around the office let others know that you're impressed by someone's efforts. The best kind of office gossip is when word gets back to you that your boss has been saying good things about you. Or, if you hear from another employee about someone's environmental efforts, be sure to repeat it back to the individual: let them know that you have heard what they are doing and that you are impressed with their initiative.

Biological diversity

Biological diversity... is the key to the maintenance of the world as we know it... This is the assembly of life that took a billion years to evolve. It ... created the world that creates us. It holds the world steady."

Scientists estimate that 50-100,000 species are made extinct each year. This means that every day on the planet 100-300 species disappear forever...

"...The [Chernobyl] catastrophe caused thousands of deaths....It continues to reach into the future to claim new victims and indeed the spectre of another Chernobyl continues to hang over the region..."

It's always time to recycle

No time to recycle? It doesn't have to be a burden, says Joe Heimlich, waste management specialist with the Ohio Extension Service.

Once a system is set up, recycling should only take about five minutes a week per family member, Heimlich says. The trick is setting up a pattern: "It's hard to get people to that point," Heimlich says. "I tell people to fit recycling into their own kitchen set-up, so it doesn't become a pain."

For example, Heimlich suggests putting a recycling container where the trash bin is now. "Make it easier to recycle than to throw items away--that's what works," he says.

Heimlich also suggests letting glass containers soak in dishwater left over from dirty dishes. Any grease in the warm soapy water helps labels peel off. Just rinse the glass items out later and put them in a recycling container, perhaps under the sink, he says.

Stop Ocean Dumping

As part of a wider campaign against dumping, Greenpeace has maintained from the start that it is wrong in principle to dump oil installations at sea.

To dump structures, such as the Brent Spar, in areas of high marine biodiversity with poorly understood ecology infringes the precautionary principle and presents unknown environmental risks. To do so would set dangerous precedents for future dumping of wastes at sea. It ignores the impact of

Restraint with spot color keeps your pages tasteful and inviting. It's important to know when *not* to run an item in spot color. The contrast provided by a second color will be nullified if you overuse it—a color can't contrast with itself. The newsletter shown on the right in the above graphic suffers from spot color overkill.

Screening Spot Color

Using screens of spot colors creates the illusion of multiple colors.

Screening—using lower percentages of a color to produce lighter shades—will help you get the most out of spot color. Screens of a color can look surprisingly different from the original shade—a brick red might become more candy-appleish at a 50 percent screen, and fade to a gentle pink at a 10 percent screen.

Don't forget about the black ink, either! Adding shades of gray to your design will increase the multi-color effect.

Have They, At Long Last, No Sense Of Decency?

What's the deal, anyway—why don't printers and monitors get on the same standard and save us all a bunch of headaches?

Unfortunately, they can't.

When you're using light to produce colors, you need a color system that's *additive*—one in which the colors get lighter as more color is added. The color system for ink, on the other hand, has to be *subtractive*, because adding more ink makes colors darker. No way around this, I'm afraid.

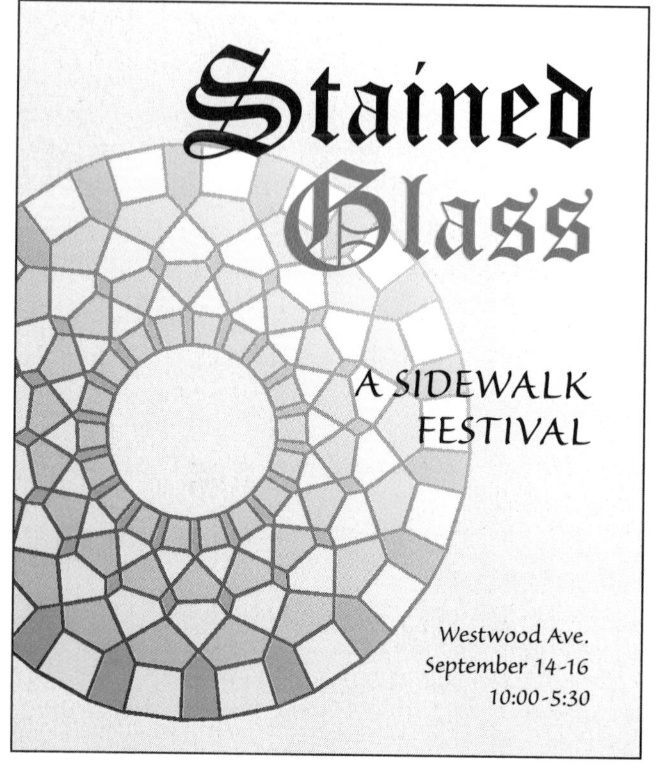

Creating Duotones

Using two different colors of ink when printing black-and-white photographs can add depth and richness.

A duotone is a black-and-white photograph printed using two ink colors. The extra ink increases the range of tones that can be displayed on the page, resulting in a richer photo.

Deciding how much of each color to use and where to use it is the challenge of creating a good duotone. If the nonblack ink is applied liberally in the photo's midtones and highlights, the resulting duotone will be tinted with color.

Sometimes, you want this effect. If your photo is an aerial view of a forest, why not let some green show through in your duotone? Also, it's possible to mimic the amber tint of old photographs by adding yellow or orange to black ink.

More often, though, you're not looking to tint your photo—you just want it to look richer. Using duotones to enhance a photo without adding obvious coloration is a pretty delicate procedure. Unless you're skilled at using image-editing software, you'll probably want to ask your service bureau to do it for you. Check your budget first, because that sort of thing costs extra. Still, the results can be quite impressive.

Varying Spot Color

If you're printing a periodical in two colors, you might consider using a different spot color for each issue. As long as you're consistent about how you *apply* the second color, the publication will retain a unified feel.

A similar technique can be used if you're producing a series of related spot color documents—for instance, product brochures. By retaining the same basic layout throughout the series but varying the spot colors, you can create documents that are strongly unified in style yet very easy to tell apart.

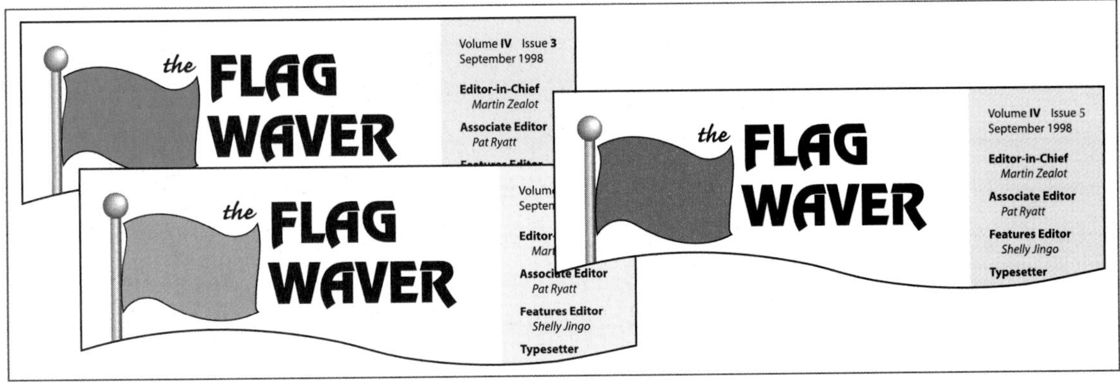

Printing Two-Color Jobs Without Black Ink

Substituting a different color for black in a two-color job can add impact to a publication—but great care is required.

You don't have to use black in your spot color documents—you can hand-choose both of your ink colors, if you wish. This method of printing can be very effective for small projects with eye-catching artwork but not much type—banners, flyers, and bumper stickers, to name a few. Duotones composed of two nonblack inks can produce a startling color range. Your reader might be fooled into thinking it's a full-color job.

It's technically possible to produce text-rich documents like newsletters and company reports without using black, but it's usually a major headache for the designer. All the text in the document must be set either as colored type or reversed type, neither of which is ideal for body text—these treatments are ordinarily reserved for display text, because readers find them distracting in large doses. You can minimize the problem by choosing a nearly-black color as one of your inks—bottle green, navy blue, and so on—and using it for your body text.

Using a different color of paper can also help. Navy ink on tan paper, for instance, might produce a passable imitation of black when printed at full value yet still appear blue when screened.

Working In Full Color

Full-color documents have the most potential to capture and maintain reader interest.

It's possible to print spot color jobs with more than two inks, but it's rarely done. You can print a document in full color for about the same cost using four-color processing.

Four-color processing uses four inks—cyan, magenta, yellow, and black—to reproduce a wide variety of colors.

Cyan

Magenta

Yellow

Black

Cyan, magenta, and yellow act as the primary colors in this scheme. By mixing them in different percentages, the entire color wheel can be re-created (well, mostly). The fourth ink, black, is used to alter the saturations of colors as well as to reproduce "real" black. (Theoretically, mixing 100 percent of cyan, magenta, and yellow will produce black—but in reality, the result is a rather muddy brown.)

You don't need to worry so much about how the inks mix to produce colors, though. That's the printer's concern. A good printer will make sure that the colors in your document are reproduced accurately—but of course, if your document's color scheme is poor to begin with, there's not much a printer can do.

A Brief Color Gallery

Full color is a world unto itself—you could fill an entire book with suggestions and guidelines on using it effectively. Because this is not that book, I'll forego the mammoth list of dos and don'ts and merely present a few examples of effective full-color documents.

Color That Shouts

This menu cover for the CyberCafé uses bright, jarring colors to produce a grungy cyberpunk look, as popularized by *Wired* magazine. This is a good example of how a designer can break the rules and get away with it—the colors in this document were chosen to clash, not to harmonize. While it's not everyone's cup of tea, it's an attention-getter!

Overlapping type adds to the grunge-media effect.

Color That Whispers

Color doesn't have to leap out at the reader—a subtle use of color turns an understatement *into* a statement. Readers who are tired of "loud" documents will appreciate the dignified starkness of this poster, enhanced by the use of cool colors throughout. One has to look closely to appreciate the variations of blue and green in the knight's helmet. Any document that encourages close scrutiny can probably be considered a success!

In a world drowned in catastrophic floods, with an atmosphere of fierce hurricanes and seas of tidal waves only one sanctuary dominates this ruined world: The land of the Dragons.

Pushed to the edge of extinction, man has risen above the planet creating a brave new world powered by the sun and wind. By a marvel of 40th century technology and with the help of the Knight—brave and heroic—a wonderful world exists: earth, where man lives in peace. However, the Flying Dragons must constantly venture to the earth's surface to search for the Amber Crystals that power their world and keep them suspended above the earth—but for how much longer...

Because color attracts attention, you can use it to steer your readers toward important aspects of your document. The thick blue rule in this poster draws the reader's eye to the title, and the colored drop cap highlights the start of the text.

Photo Opportunity

The purpose of this brochure is to get people interested in geology, and what better way than with gorgeous full-color photographs of rocks? To make sure the photos are the "stars" of this piece, color is used sparingly elsewhere. In fact, except for a yellow-orange sink which unifies the pages, there's nothing but black text on white paper.

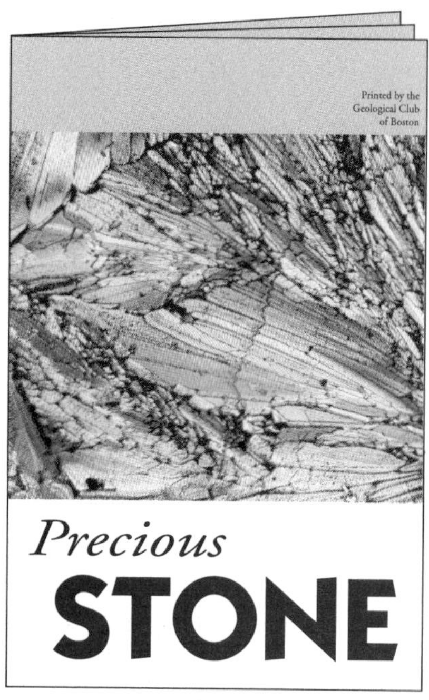

Exaggerated line spacing can add elegance to text—if you've got the space, flaunt it!

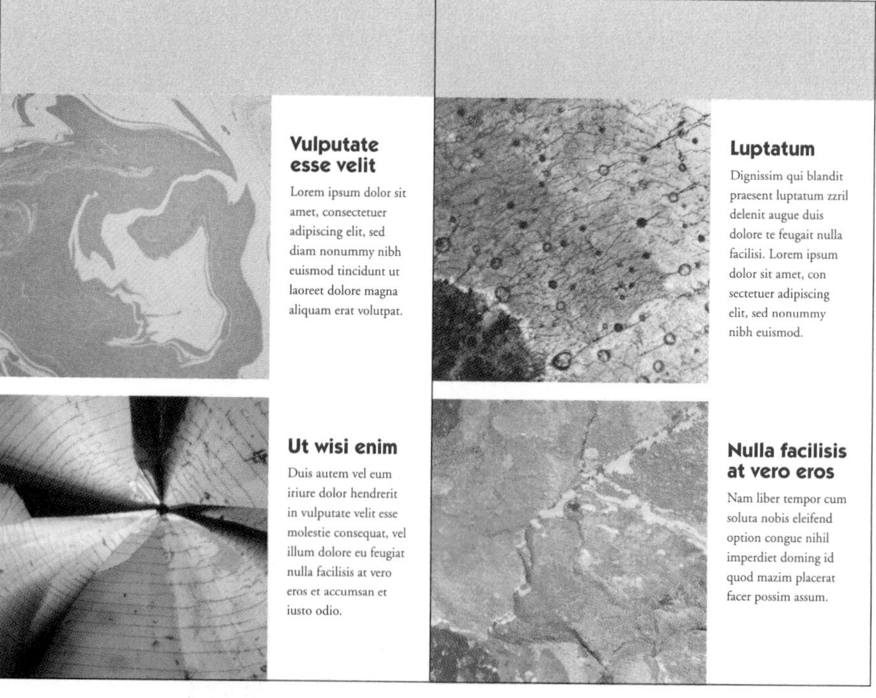

Organizational Color

Sometimes, color is needed to make sense of an information-packed document. The inner spread of this company report shows how color can be used to keep page elements separate and make complex concepts understandable at a glance. The dark blue panel separates the graphical information from the text. The line graphs use screens of different colors to indicate different classifications of graphs, and darker screens of the same colors highlight the graph units. The four colors used for graph lines contrast well with the background screens and with each other.

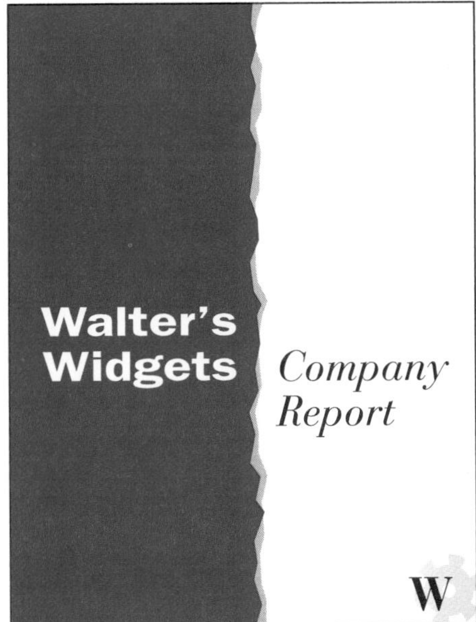

Placing the legend between the two sets of graphs indicates that it is applicable to both sets. Notice how the "Walter's Widgets" label has been colorized and enlarged, to underscore its importance.

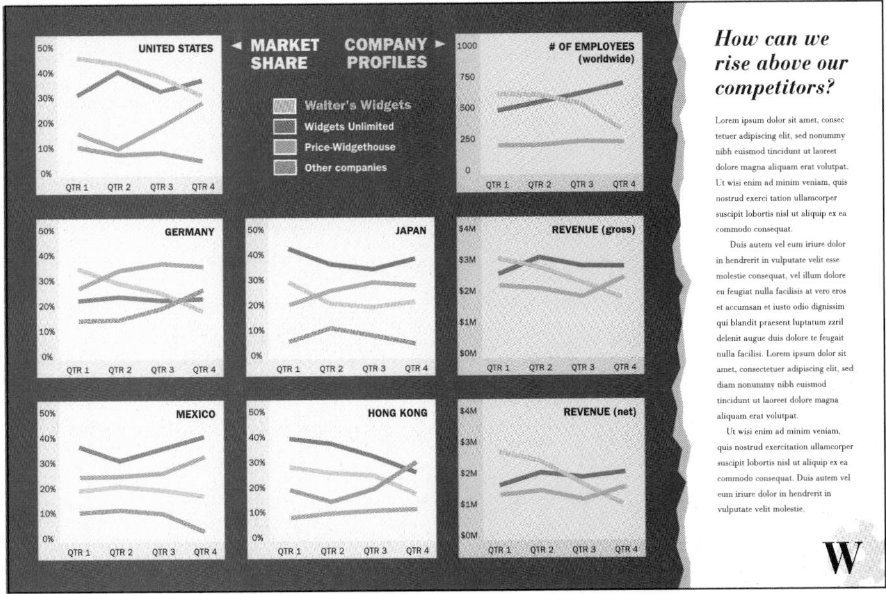

Color Caveats

What you see is not always what you get when working with color.

A major difficulty in working with color documents is the difference between the colors you'll see on screen and the colors that will actually be printed on the page. Unfortunately, computer monitors and printers use different systems to produce colors. Monitors use the RGB model, in which varying amounts of red, green, and blue are mixed together to create a given shade. Printers, as mentioned earlier, generally use the CMYK model. (That stands for cyan, magenta, yellow, and black—K is used to denote black, because B means blue.)

Each color system has a different *gamut*—the total range of colors which can possibly be produced. RGB, for instance, can create bright fluorescent colors that aren't reproducible in CMYK.

So, how can be sure you'll get the colors you want? First, get a *swatch palette*—a booklet of printed color samples. Unfortunately, swatch palettes also use various different systems to describe color—now, *they* should really get standardized!—but the basic idea is always the same. You're choosing your colors based on how they look on paper, instead of on screen. For spot color jobs, always use a swatch palette to choose your inks. (If you don't do enough color work to justify buying a palette, the service bureau handling your project will let you use theirs.)

Second, run a print test. Have a couple of sample pages from your document printed at your service bureau, and see how they look. Tweak your colors based on the test—if a certain shade of blue looks too dull, brighten it up. Don't worry if your document doesn't look as good on screen after it has been corrected—your readers never see the screen version anyway.

One more warning about working in color—it requires a lot of memory. Your computer will need lots of RAM to process your document, and lots of hard drive space to store the finished files. If your computer is pretty slow for plain old black-and-white work, consider upgrading it before taking on color projects. Remember, design is supposed to be a trial-and-error process. If every minor adjustment of a document takes you 10 minutes to implement, you'll find reasons not to make the adjustments—and your designs will suffer accordingly.

Moving On

This completes our summary of the basic design elements—you now have all the tools you need to create any type of document imaginable.

The Health Care Puzzle

Americans come together to create a new set of standards for healing the sick

Lorem ipsum dolor sit amet, consectetuer adipiscing elit, sed diam nonummy nibh euismod tincidunt ut laoreet dolore magna aliquam erat volutpat. Ut wisi enim ad minim veniam, quis nostrud exerci tation ullamcorper suscipit lobortis nisl ut aliquip ex ea commodo consequat.

Duis autem vel eum iriure dolor in hendrerit in vulputate velit esse molestie consequat, vel illum dolore eu feugiat nulla facilisis at vero eros et accumsan et iusto odio dignissim qui blandit praesent luptatum zzril delenit augue duis dolore te feugait nulla facilisi.

Lorem ipsum dolor sit amet, consectetuer adipiscing elit, sed diam nonummy nibh euismod tincidunt ut laoreet dolore magna aliquam erat volutpat.

Lorem ipsum dolor sit amet, consectetuer adipiscing elit, sed diam nonummy nibh euismod tincidunt ut laoreet dolore magna aliquam erat volutpat. Duis autem vel eum iriure dolor in hendrerit in vulputate velit esse molestie consequat, vel illum dolore eu feugiat nulla facilisis at vero eros et accumsan et iusto odio dignissim qui blandit praesent luptatum zzril delenit augue duis dolore te feugait nulla facilisi lorem.

Lorem ipsum dolor sit amet, consectetuer adipiscing elit, sed diam nonummy nibh euismod tincidunt ut laoreet dolore magna aliquam erat volutpat. Ut wisi enim ad minim veniam, quis nostrud exerci tation ullamcorper suscipit lobortis nisl ut aliquip ex ea commodo consequat.

Lorem ipsum dolor sit amet, consectetuer adipiscing elit, sed diam nonummy nibh euismod tincidunt ut laoreet dolore magna aliquam erat volutpat. Duis autem vel eum iriure dolor in hendrerit in vulputate velit esse molestie consequat, vel illum dolore eu feugiat nulla facilisis at vero eros et accumsan et iusto odio dignissim qui blandit praesent luptatum zzril delenit augue duis dolore te feugait nulla facilisi.

Lorem ipsum dolor sit amet, consectetuer adipiscing elit, sed diam nonummy nibh euismod tincidunt ut laoreet dolore magna aliquam erat volutpat. Ut wisi enim ad minim

veniam, quis nostrud exerci tation ullamcorper suscipit lobortis nisl ut aliquip ex ea commodo consequat. Duis autem vel eum iriure dolor in hendrerit in vulputate velit esse molestie consequat, vel illum dolore eu feugiat nulla facilisis at vero eros et accumsan et iusto odio dignissim qui blandit praesent luptatum zzril delenit augue duis dolore te feugait nulla facilisi.

Lorem ipsum dolor sit amet, consectetuer adipiscing elit, sed diam nonummy nibh euismod tincidunt ut laoreet dolore magna aliquam erat volutpat. Ut wisi enim ad minim veniam, quis nostrud exerci tation ullamcorper suscipit lobortis nisl ut aliquip ex ea commodo consequat.

Lorem ipsum dolor sit amet, consectetuer adipiscing elit, sed diam nonummy nibh euismod tincidunt ut laoreet dolore magna aliquam erat volutpat. Duis autem vel eum iriure dolor in hendrerit in vulputate velit esse molestie consequat, vel illum dolore eu feugiat nulla facilisis at vero eros et accumsan et iusto odio dignissim qui blandit praesent luptatum zzril delenit a ugue duis dolore te feugait.

Lines Of Force

Each photo has its own internal geometry, which influences a page's overall design.

Photos have their own underlying lines of force, regardless of how they're arranged on a page. The internal lines and geometry of a photo play an important role in how a page or spread will appear.

For instance, if a person in a photo is pointing or gesturing in a particular direction, the reader's eyes will want to follow that gesture. Be aware of the lines of force in your photos; use them to direct your reader's eyes toward other items of interest on the page.

We've got what it takes to make you look good in print

When it comes to professionals who know how to make your printing work look perfect, nobody beats the Print Haus

the Print Haus
183 Raymond Lane
Barwick, CA 83127
818/555-1894

Follow The Horizon

Be aware of a photo's inherent direction and balance.

Just as people can keep their balance on a pitching ship by watching the horizon, you can get a good idea if a photo in a layout is straight by making sure the horizon is parallel with other horizontal lines on the page, including the caption, headlines, and other lines of type. (Any flat object in your photo can serve as a horizon—desktops, tables, floors, ceilings, and so on.)

Likewise, objects like telephone poles, flagpoles, and tall buildings need to appear at a correct angle to the horizon.

Achieving Motion Through Sequences

You can imply time and motion by using a sequence of still photos.

Running several similar photos taken quickly from the same angle can impart a sense of movement to the reader.

Altering Photographs

Most photos will require editing prior to placement.

Expecting a photo to fit perfectly into a layout without alterations is not generally realistic. Fortunately, desktop publishers have a number of photo-editing tools and techniques at their fingertips.

It's All In The Crop

Cropping is the simplest, most powerful tool for improving photos.

Cropping is one of the most important ways you can improve the quality and impact of photos. Cropping a photo trims away the extraneous elements of the image and lets you present the reader with only the most important part of the photograph. A good crop heightens the message, impact, and attractiveness of any photo.

Mug shots (close-up photos of people's faces) tend to be cropped far too loosely. Since mug shots are usually run at small sizes, crop them tightly to make sure the subject's face is the dominant focus.

While you look for ways to clarify and simplify an image through cropping, don't become so zealous in your efforts that you crop out important details.

Keep an eye out for awkward crops, especially when working with photographs of people. Cutting away entire limbs and heads yields embarrassing results.

Although most desktop publishing software provides cropping tools, it's best to crop the photograph directly if you have photo-editing software. When you crop a photo in a layout program, you're not really deleting any of it; you're just hiding it. The printer is still required to process the entire image, including the cropped parts. This isn't much of a concern when you're merely cropping a few pixels away, but when you're cropping away an entire mountainscape to get a single tree, you're bloating your document with unnecessary information—and guaranteeing yourself long waits beside the ol' laser printer.

Enlarging And Reducing Photographs

Enlarging a photo improperly can cause it to look grainy or fuzzy.

When cropping a photo for maximum impact, designers often enlarge it at the same time. Enlarging a photo can sometimes make the details of a photo look fuzzy or grainy.

When enlarging photographs, work from the largest print available, and be sure the image is digitized at the proper resolution.

Flipping And Flopping Photographs

Reversing photos can improve the impact of a layout.

Designers sometimes reverse an image so that its lines of force lead into the page—drawing the reader's interest inward, rather than outward. This is an effective technique for ensuring that each image on the page guides the reader into the layout.

But flipping (reversing top-to-bottom) and flopping (reversing side-to-side) an image can cause trouble if you don't pay close attention to details. Because reversing a photo creates a mirror-image of the original, any text within the picture will read backwards. Other subtle gaffes can also appear, like soldiers delivering left-handed salutes or watches and rings appearing on the wrong hand. For more on this matter, see "Photographs, Technology, And Ethics" later in this chapter.

Adjusting Contrast And Brightness

You can electronically enhance a photo's contrast and brightness.

Many page layout programs let you change the contrast and relative brightness of a photo you've imported. This can help you optimize a photo for your specific print parameters or correct minor problems in the original photos.

Touching Up Problem Spots

Touch-up work can be done conventionally or on the computer.

Both the conventional airbrush and its electronic counterparts let you eliminate blemishes and minor imperfections from photos.

Touching up a photo should be limited to removing dust, scratches, and small unwanted elements. If a photo needs extensive overhauling, you're probably better off with a different photo.

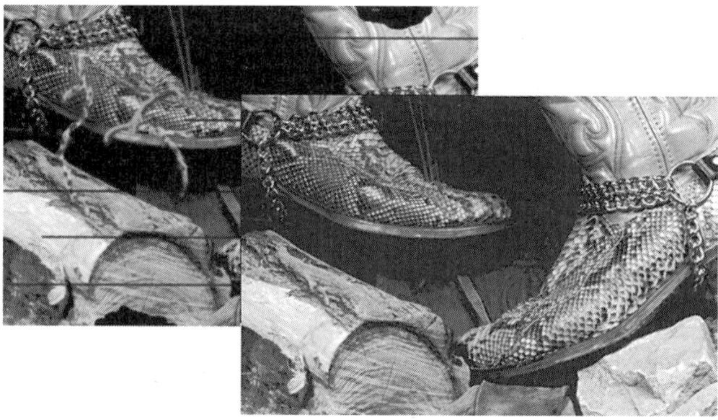

Special Effects With Photographs

When used sparingly, photo effects can have a dramatic impact on a layout.

As with type, you can achieve numerous special effects by manipulating photographs electronically. Digital image editing can now be done with relative ease by most desktop publishers using software bundled with a common flatbed scanner.

Silhouetting an image can achieve eye-popping results for a minimum of time and money.

Several different photos can be combined into a single illustration using photo manipulation software.

Ready-made filters and special add-on modules produce startling effects at the touch of a button.

Remember, though, a special effect will cease to be special if it's used too often. Save your best tricks for occasions that warrant them.

Photographs, Technology, And Ethics

The power of modern imaging technology brings up a number of ethical questions worth considering.

While many designers may never consider the responsibility they face when working with photographs—especially when altering or dramatically changing the context or content of a photo—manipulating photos carries a certain amount of ethical accountability.

You'll need permission from the photographer whose work you're publishing. Written permission is best. In general, you should have the permission of any people who appear in the photos you plan to use, although obtaining permission can be difficult.

Whether you're using stock photos, professionally shot images, or snapshots you took on vacation, use common sense when running or editing photos—especially photos with people in them. Don't portray unsuspecting people in derogatory contexts.

Moving On

Photographs lend authority and realism to a publication. Frequently, a single image can convey more to a reader than a full page of text. Great care is required, though. Page elements that draw the most attention also repel the most attention if used inappropriately.

That warning certainly applies to our next subject—color. In the Do It In Color section we'll take a look at the vitality that color can add to your documents as well as the problems that can result from its misuse. You'll also learn how to achieve professional-looking results on tight schedules and small budgets.

PART II

PUTTING YOUR KNOWLEDGE TO WORK

7 Distribution Media

Let me begin by dispelling an assumption. Just because we're starting our foray into document-specific design with a discussion of the printed news media, that does *not* mean that these sorts of documents are the easiest to design. Actually, they're among the hardest.

So why *are* we starting with them, you ask? Because they provide good experience. Nearly all of the design elements discussed in the first six chapters can find their way into a news document and probably will—columns, grids, subheads, sidebars, boxes, rules, illustrations, and photos. News media usually contain a vast panoply of unrelated information—stories, reports, statistics, reviews, editorials, features, and pictures. The designer must keep all of these elements separate and distinct, while maintaining a consistent look and feel. It's a daunting challenge, I admit, but you'll be ready for anything once you overcome it. Anyway, baby steps are for babies!

Newsletters

Newsletters are major beneficiaries of the desktop publishing revolution. Highly specialized newsletters that once were impractical because of high typesetting and paste-up costs can now be produced using the most basic desktop publishing and word processing software. They've become a very cost-effective advertising medium for businesses and organizations.

One of the most difficult aspects of newsletter layout is devising a design that will work well repeatedly. You don't want to change the layout of each issue to fit the content, for a number of reasons. First of all, it's usually impractical. Good design takes time, which is why you should spend a great deal of time designing your first issue. Once it has been published, you're on a schedule. Coming up with a brand-new design for each successive issue will probably throw you off schedule, and you'll lose your readership. (As you might expect, readers don't think much of periodicals that habitually appear three weeks late or skip the occasional month.)

Besides, if your newsletter looks different every issue, will your readers even recognize it? A consistent design establishes a strong identity for your publication; readers will automatically associate new issues with previous ones they've seen. Some high-profile periodicals—magazines, in particular—are so confident about the strength of their identity, they'll frequently cover up part of their nameplate with artwork or a blurb. Now *that's* recognizability!

Do It With Styles

Styles are a huge help in keeping your design consistent. Don't just set a subhead and move on—create a Subhead style for it. You'll never have to worry about subhead consistency again. You'll just apply your style whenever you need a subhead.

This technique is especially nice if you haven't yet decided what you want your subheads to look like. Define a Subhead style, and don't even bother with the font settings. You can just use the program defaults. Set all of your subheads in this style, *then* go back and tweak the style's font settings. Your subheads will be updated automatically, and you'll be able to choose the right font for the job based on the actual layout. Pretty sweet, huh?

Nameplate

Your nameplate provides immediate visual identification and communicates your newsletter's purpose.

Devote some time and thought to the design of your nameplate. It's the most noticeable feature of a newsletter and is essential for promoting identification and continuity. Successful nameplates are simple in design and easily recognized.

Secure Living

Turn Your House Into a Fortress

Lorem ipsum dolor sit amet, consectetuer adipiscing elit, sed diam nonummy nibh euismod tincidunt ut laoreet dolore magna aliquam erat volutpat. Ut wisi enim ad minim veniam, quis nostrud exerci tation ullamcorper suscipit lobortis nisl ut aliquip ex ea commodo consequat.

Duis autem vel eum iriure dolor in hendrerit in vulputate velit esse molestie consequat, vel illum dolore eu feugiat nulla facilisis at vero eros et accumsan et iusto odio dignissim qui blandit praesent luptatum zzril delenit augue duis dolore te feugait nulla facilisi. Lorem ipsum dolor sit amet, consectetuer adipiscing elit, sed diam nonummy nibh euismod tincidunt ut laoreet dolore magna aliquam erat volutpat.

Ut wisi enim ad minim veniam, quis nostrud exerci tation ullamcorper suscipit lobortis nisl ut aliquip ex ea commodo consequat. Duis autem vel eum iriure dolor in hendrerit in vulputate velit esse molestie consequat, vel illum dolore eu feugiat nulla facilisis at vero eros et accumsan et iusto odio dignissim qui blandit praesent luptatum zzril delenit augue duis dolore te feugait nulla facilisi. eratv olutpat. Ut wisi enim ad minim veniam, nostrud exerci tation ullamcorper suscipit lobortis nisl ut aliquip ex ea commodo consequat.

Duis autem vel eum iriure dolor in hendrerit in vulputate velit esse molestie consequat, vel illum dolore eu feugiat nulla facilisis at vero eros et accumsan et iusto odio dignissim qui blandit praesent luptatum zzril delenit augue duis dolore te feugait nulla facilisi. Lorem ipsum dolor sit amet, consectetuer adipiscing elit, sed diam nonummy nibh euismod tincidunt ut laoreet dolore magna aliquam erat volutpat.

Ut wisi enim ad minim veniam, quis nostrud exerci tation ullamcorper suscipit lobortis nisl ut aliquip ex ea commodo consequat. Duis autem vel eum iriure dolor in hendrerit in vulputate velit esse molestie consequat, vel illum dolore eu feugiat nulla facilisis at vero eros et accumsan et iusto odio dignissim qui blandit praesent luptatum zzril delenit augue duis dolore te feugait nulla facilisi.

Invest in a Chain Bolt

Duis autem vel eum iriure dolor in hendrerit in vulputate velit esse molestie consequat, vel illum dolore eu feugiat nulla facilisis. Ut wisi enim ad minim veniam, quis nostrud exerci tation ullam

Nameplates are generally centered at the top of the first page and sometimes extend across the full width of the page. However, equally effective nameplates can be placed flush left or flush right.

Secure Living

Turn Your House Into a Fortress

Lorem ipsum dolor sit amet, consectetuer adipiscing elit, sed diam nonummy nibh euismod tincidunt ut laoreet dolore magna aliquam erat volutpat. Ut wisi enim ad minim veniam, quis nostrud exerci tation ullamcorper suscipit lobortis nisl ut aliquip ex ea commodo consequat.

Duis autem vel eum iriure dolor in hendrerit in vulputate velit esse molestie consequat, vel illum dolore eu feugiat nulla facilisis at vero eros et accumsan et iusto odio dignissim qui blandit praesent luptatum zzril delenit augue duis dolore te feugait nulla facilisi. Lorem ipsum dolor sit amet, consectetuer adipiscing elit, sed diam nonummy nibh euismod tincidunt ut laoreet dolore magna aliquam erat volutpat.

Nam liber tempor cum soluta nobis eleifend option congue nihil imperdiet doming id quod mazim placerat facer possim assum. Lorem ipsum dolor sit amet, consectetuer adipiscing elit, sed diam

Duis autem vel eum iriure dolor in hendrerit in vulputate velit esse molestie consequat, vel illum dolore eu feugiat nulla facilisis at vero eros et accumsan et iusto odio dignissim qui blandit praesent luptatum zzril delenit augue duis dolore te feugait nulla facilisi. Lorem ipsum dolor sit amet, consectetuer adipiscing elit, sed diam nonummy nibh euismod tincidunt ut laoreet dolore magna aliquam erat volutpat.

Ut wisi enim ad minim veniam, quis nostrud exerci tation ullamcorper suscipit lobortis nisl ut aliquip ex ea commodo consequat. Duis autem vel eum iriure dolor in hendrerit in vulputate velit esse molestie consequat, vel illum dolore eu feugiat nulla facilisis at vero eros et accumsan et iusto odio dignissim qui blandit praesent luptatum zzril delenit augue duis dolore te feugait nulla facilisi.

Invest in a Chain Bolt

Duis autem vel eum iriure dolor in hendrerit in vulputate velit esse molestie consequat, vel illum dolore eu feugiat nulla facilisis. Ut wisi enim ad minim veniam, quis nostrud exerci tation ullam

Secure Living

Turn Your House Into a Fortress

Lorem ipsum dolor sit amet, consectetuer adipiscing elit, sed diam nonummy nibh euismod tincidunt ut laoreet dolore magna aliquam erat volutpat. Ut wisi enim ad minim veniam, quis nostrud exerci tation ullamcorper suscipit lobortis nisl ut aliquip ex ea commodo consequat.

Duis autem vel eum iriure dolor in hendrerit in vulputate velit esse molestie consequat, vel illum dolore eu feugiat nulla facilisis at vero eros et accumsan et iusto odio dignissim qui blandit praesent luptatum zzril delenit augue duis dolore te feugait nulla facilisi. Lorem ipsum dolor sit amet, consectetuer adipiscing elit, sed diam nonummy nibh euismod tincidunt ut laoreet dolore magna aliquam erat volutpat.

Nam liber tempor cum soluta nobis eleifend option congue nihil imperdiet doming id quod mazim placerat facer possim assum. Lorem ipsum dolor sit amet, consectetuer adipiscing elit, sed diam nonummy nibh euismod tincidunt ut laoreet dolore

Duis autem vel eum iriure dolor in hend vulputate velit esse molesti consequat, vel illum dolore eu feugiat nulla facilisis at vero eros accumsan et iusto odio dignissim qui blandit praesent luptatum zzril delenit augue duis dolore te feugait nulla facilisi. Lorem ipsum dolor sit amet, consectetuer adipiscing elit, sed diam nonummy nibh euismod tincidunt ut laoreet dolore magna aliquam erat volutpat.

Ut wisi enim ad minim veniam, quis nostrud exerci tation ullamcorper suscipit lobortis nisl ut aliquip ex ea commodo consequat. Duis autem vel eum iriure dolor in hendrerit in vulputate velit esse molestie consequat, vel illum dolore eu feugiat nulla facilisis at vero eros et accumsan et iusto odio dignissim qui blandit praesent luptatum zzril delenit augue duis dolore te feugait nulla facilisi. aliquip ex ea commodo consequat.

Invest in a Chain Bolt

Duis autem vel eum iriure dolor in hendrerit in vulputate velit esse molestie consequat, vel illum dolore eu feugiat nulla facilisis. Ut wisi enim ad minim veniam, quis nostrud exerci tation ullam

You can also place nameplates approximately one-third of the way down from the top of the page. This location leaves room for a feature headline and article to appear above it.

Turn Your House Into a Fortress

Lorem ipsum dolor sit amet, consectetuer adipiscing elit, sed diam nonummy nibh euismod tincidunt ut laoreet dolore magna aliquam erat volutpat. Ut enim corper suscipit lobortis nisl ut aliquip ex ea commodo consequat et laorbat.

Duis autem vel eum iriure dolor in hendrerit in ad minim veniam, quis nostrud exerci tation ullam vulputate velit esse molestie consequat, vel illum praesent luptatum zzril delenit augue duis dolore te feugait nulla facilisi. Lorem ipsum dolor sit amet, consectetuer adipiscing elit, sed diam nonummy nibh euismod tincidunt ut laoreet dolore magna aliquam erat volutpat ut laoreet dolore magna aliquam nibh

(Continued on page 2)

Secure Living

Bar the Windows

Lorem ipsum dolor sit amet, consectetuer adipiscing elit, sed diam nonummy nibh euismod tincidunt ut laoreet dolore magna aliquam eratv olutpat. Ut wisi enim ad minim veniam, nostrud exerci tation ullamcorper suscipit lobortis nisl ut aliquip ex ea commodo consequat.

Duis autem vel eum iriure dolor in hendrerit in vulputate velit esse molestie consequat, vel illum dolore eu feugiat nulla facilisis at vero eros et accumsan et iusto odio dignissim qui blandit praesent luptatum zzril delenit augue duis dolore te feugait nulla facilisi. Lorem ipsum dolor sit amet, consectetuer adipiscing elit, sed diam nonummy dolore eu feugiat nulla facilisis. Ut wisi enim ad minim veniam, quis nostrud exerci tation ullam corper suscipit lobortis nisl ut aliquip ex ea commodo consequat. Duis autem vel eum iriure dolor hendrerit in vulputate velit esse molestie consequat, vel illum dolore eu feugiat nulla facilisis at vero eros et accumsan et iusto odio dignissim qui blandit praesent luptatum zzril delenit augue duis dolore te feugait nulla facilisi. Nam liber tempor cum soluta nobis eleifend option congue nihil imperdiet doming.

Nail the Doors Shut

Duis autem vel eum iriure dolor in hendrerit in vulputate velit esse molestie consequat, vel illum dolore

There are, of course, other possibilities. Sometimes the logo is incorporated into the nameplate itself. Or, if your logo reproduces well at small sizes, try placing it in the header or footer of each page. You might even choose not to include your logo at all—but at the very least, put the name of your organization in a prominent place.

Secure Living

Published by Ajax Security Systems, Milwaukee, WI

Turn Your House Into a Fortress

Lorem ipsum dolor sit amet, consectetuer adipiscing elit, sed diam nonummy nibh euismod tincidunt ut laoreet dolore magna aliquam erat volutpat. Ut wisi enim ad minim veniam, quis nostrud exerci tation ullamcorper suscipit lobortis nisl ut aliquip ex ea commodo consequat.

Duis autem vel eum iriure dolor in hendrerit in vulputate velit esse molestie consequat, vel illum dolore eu feugiat nulla facilisis at vero eros et accumsan et iusto odio dignissim qui blandit praesent luptatum zzril delenit augue duis dolore te feugait nulla facilisi. Lorem ipsum dolor sit amet, consectetuer adipiscing elit, sed diam nonummy nibh euismod tincidunt ut laoreet dolore magna aliquam erat volutpat.

Ut wisi enim ad minim veniam, quis nostrud exerci tation ullamcorper suscipit lobortis nisl ut aliquip ex ea commodo consequat. Duis autem vel eum iriure dolor in hendrerit in vulputate velit esse molestie consequat, vel illum dolore eu feugiat nulla facilisis at vero eros et accumsan et iusto odio tincidunt ut laoreet dolore magna aliquam dolor in hendrerit in vulputate.

Duis autem vel eum iriure dolor in hendrerit in vulputate velit esse molestie consequat, vel illum dolore eu feugiat nulla facilisis at vero eros et accumsan et iusto odio dignissim qui blandit praesent luptatum zzril delenit augue duis dolore te feugait nulla facilisi. Lorem ipsum dolor sit amet, consectetuer adipiscing elit, sed diam nonummy nibh euismod tincidunt ut laoreet dolore magna aliquam erat volutpat.

Ut wisi enim ad minim veniam, quis nostrud exerci tation ullamcorper suscipit lobortis nisl ut aliquip ex ea commodo consequat. Duis autem vel eum iriure dolor in hendrerit in vulputate velit esse molestie consequat, vel illum dolore eu feugiat nulla facilisis at vero eros et accumsan et iusto odio dignissim qui blandit praesent luptatum zzril delenit augue duis dolore te feugait nulla facilisi.

Invest in a Chain Bolt

Duis autem vel eum iriure dolor in hendrerit in vulputate velit esse molestie consequat, vel illum dolore eu feugiat nulla facilisis. Ut wisi enim ad

Volume numbers, issue numbers, and the date should also be prominently featured. This allows both you and your readers to refer easily to back issues.

Secure Living

Volume II, Issue 9 September 1996

Turn Your House Into a Fortress

Lorem ipsum dolor sit amet, consectetuer adipiscing elit, sed diam nonummy nibh euismod tincidunt ut laoreet dolore magna aliquam erat volutpat. Ut wisi enim ad minim veniam, quis nostrud exerci tation ullamcorper suscipit lobortis nisl ut aliquip ex ea commodo consequat.

Duis autem vel eum iriure dolor in hendrerit in vulputate velit esse molestie consequat, vel illum dolore eu feugiat nulla facilisis at vero eros et accumsan et iusto odio dignissim qui blandit praesent luptatum zzril delenit augue duis dolore te feugait nulla facilisi. Lorem ipsum dolor sit amet, consectetuer adipiscing elit, sed diam nonummy nibh euismod tincidunt ut laoreet dolore magna aliquam erat volutpat.

Ut wisi enim ad minim veniam, quis nostrud exerci tation ullamcorper suscipit lobortis nisl ut aliquip ex ea commodo consequat. Duis autem vel eum iriure dolor in hendrerit in vulputate velit esse molestie consequat, vel illum dolore eu feugiat nulla facilisis at vero eros et accumsan et iusto odio dignissim qui blandit praesent luptatum zzril delenit laoreet dolore magna aliquam eratv olutpat. Ut wisi enim ad minim veniam, nostrud exerci tation ullamcorper suscipit lobortis nisl ut aliquip ex ea commodo consequat.

Duis autem vel eum iriure dolor in hendrerit in vulputate velit esse molestie consequat, vel illum dolore eu feugiat nulla facilisis at vero eros et accumsan et iusto odio dignissim qui blandit praesent luptatum zzril delenit augue duis dolore te feugait nulla facilisi. Lorem ipsum dolor sit amet, consectetuer adipiscing elit, sed diam nonummy nibh euismod tincidunt ut laoreet dolore magna aliquam erat volutpat.

Ut wisi enim ad minim veniam, quis nostrud exerci tation ullamcorper suscipit lobortis nisl ut aliquip ex ea commodo consequat. Duis autem vel eum iriure dolor in hendrerit in vulputate velit esse molestie consequat, vel illum dolore eu feugiat nulla facilisis at vero eros et accumsan et iusto odio dignissim qui blandit praesent luptatum zzril delenit augue duis dolore te feugait nulla facilisi.

Invest in a Chain Bolt

Duis autem vel eum iriure dolor in hendrerit in vulputate velit esse molestie consequat, vel illum

Vertical orientation can draw more attention to an important headline.

Secure Living

Turn Your House Into a Fortress

Lorem ipsum dolor sit amet, consectetuer adipiscing elit, sed diam nonummy nibh euismod tincidunt ut laoreet dolore magna aliquam erat volutpat. Ut wisi enim ad minim veniam, quis nostrud exerci tation ullamcorper suscipit lobortis nisl ut aliquip ex ea commodo consequat.

Duis autem vel eum iriure dolor in hendrerit in vulputate velit esse molestie consequat, vel illum dolore eu feugiat nulla facilisis at vero eros et accumsan et iusto odio dignissim qui blandit praesent luptatum zzril delenit augue duis dolore te feugait nulla facilisi. Lorem ipsum dolor sit amet, consectetuer adipiscing elit, sed diam nonummy nibh euismod tincidunt ut laoreet dolore magna aliquam erat volutpat.

Ut wisi enim ad minim veniam, quis nostrud exerci tation ullamcorper suscipit lobortis nisl ut aliquip ex ea commodo consequat. Duis autem vel eum iriure dolor in hendrerit in vulputate velit esse molestie consequat, vel illum dolore eu feugiat nulla facilisis at vero eros et accumsan et iusto odio dignissim qui blandit praesent luptatum zzril delenit augue duis dolore te feugait nulla facilisi.

Put Bars on the Windows

Lorem ipsum dolor sit amet, consectetuer adipiscing elit, sed diam nonummy nibh euismod tincidunt ut laoreet dolore magna aliquam eratv olutpat. Ut wisi enim ad minim veniam, nostrud exerci tation ullamcorper suscipit lobortis nisl ut aliquip ex ea consequat.

Duis autem vel eum iriure dolor in hend vulputate velit esse molesti consequat, vel illum dolore eu feugiat nulla facilisis at vero eros accumsan et iusto odio dignissim qui blandit praesent luptatum zzril delenit augue duis dolore te feugait nulla facilisi. Lorem ipsum dolor sit amet, consectetuer adipiscing elit, sed diam nonummy nibh euismod tincidunt ut laoreet dolore magna aliquam erat volutpat.

Ut wisi enim ad minim veniam, quis nostrud exerci tation ullamcorper suscipit lobortis nisl ut aliquip ex ea commodo consequat. Duis autem vel eum iriure dolor in hendrerit in vulputate velit esse molestie consequat, vel illum dolore eu feugiat nulla facilisis at vero eros et accumsan et iusto odio dignissim qui blandit praesent luptatum zzril delenit augue duis dolore te feugait nulla facilisi.

Invest in a Chain Bolt

Duis autem vel eum iriure dolor in hendrerit in vulputate velit esse molestie consequat, vel illum dolore eu feugiat nulla facilisis. Ut wisi enim ad minim veniam, quis nostrud exerci tation ullam corper suscipit lobortis nisl ut aliquip ex ea commodo consequat. Duis autem vel eum iriure dolor hendrerit in vulputate velit esse molestie consequat, vel illum dolore eu feugiat nulla facilisis at vero eros et accumsan et iusto odio dignissim qui blandit praesent luptatum zzril delenit augue duis dolore te feugait nulla facilisi. Nam liber tempor cum soluta nobis eleifend option congue nihil imperdiet doming id quod mazim placerat facer possim assum. Lorem ipsum dolor sit amet, consectetuer adipiscing elit, sed diam nonummy nibh euismod tincidunt ut laoreet dolore magna aliquam erat

Publication Information

Your readers should be able to identify the source of the newsletter quickly and easily.

Be sure to tell your readers who you are by leaving space for your organization's logo or name, as well as your address and phone number.

Logically, your logo belongs in a high-profile place. The most logical choices are the front cover or the mailing area. If you choose to place your logo on the front cover, make sure it's large enough to be noticed but small enough to avoid competing with the nameplate. The nameplate deserves higher priority.

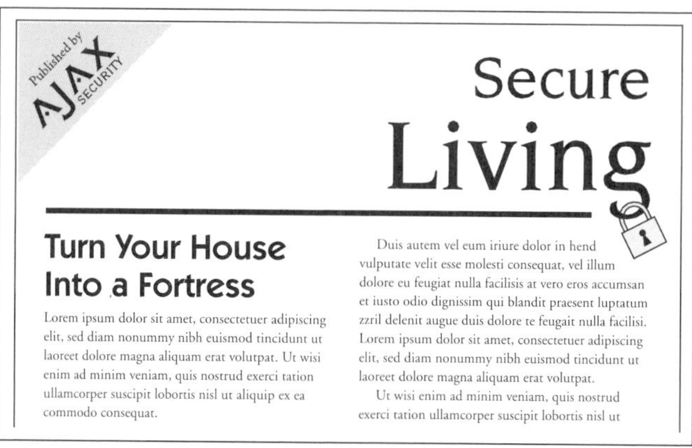

Mailing Information

If your newsletter is a self-mailer, be sure to provide sufficient space for a mailing label and other mailing information.

A newsletter's mailing area normally appears at the bottom of the back page.

Be sure to include your organization's return address next to the mailing label. Sometimes when fulfillment (mailing list maintenance and addressing) is handled by an outside firm, you'll put that firm's return address in the mailing area.

In the mailing area, clearly indicate whether your newsletter is first- or third-class mail. In either case, to avoid licking stamps, include your firm's postal permit number.

Adding *Address Correction Requested* above the mailing label area helps you keep your customer or prospect mailing list up to date. If you include *Address Correction Requested* in the mailing area of your newsletter, you'll be informed of the new address when a recipient moves.

Stockholder Report, 1990's

Such has been the patient sufferance of these created equal, that they are endowed by their Creator with certain inalienable rights, that among these are Life, Liberty, and the Pursuit of Happiness. That to secure these rights, governments are instituted among Men, deriving their just powers from the consent of the governed. That whenever any form of government becomes destructive of these ends, it is the right of the people to alter or to abolish it, and to institute new government, laying its foundation of such principles, and originating its powers in such form, as to them shall seem most likely to effect their safety and happiness. Prudence, indeed, will dictate that governments long established should not be changed for light and transient caused; and accordingly and experience hath shewn, that mankind are more disposed to suffer, while evils are sufferable, than to right themselves by abolishing the forms to which they are accustomed.

But when a long train of abuses and usurpations, pursuing invariably the same object, evinces a design to reduce them under absolute despotism, it is their former systems of government, and to provide new guards for their future security. Such has been the patient sufferance of these colonies; and such is now the necessity which constrains them to alter their former systems of government. The history of the present King of Great Britain is a history of But when a long train of abuses and usurpations, pursuing invariably the same object, evinces a design to reduce them under absolute despotism, it is their former systems of government, and to provide new guards for their future security. Such has been the patient sufferance of these colonies; and such is now the necessity which constrains them to alter their former systems of government. The history of the present King of Great Britain is a history of repeated injuries and usurpations, all having in direct object the established of a absolute tyranny over these States.

That whenever any form of government becomes destructive of these ends, it is the right of the people to alter or to abolish it, and to institute new government, laying its foundation of such principles, and originating its powers in such form, as to them shall seem design to reduce them under absolute despotism, it is their former systems of government, and to provide new guards for their future security. Such has been the patient sufferance of these colonies; and such is now the necessity which constrains them to alter their former systems of government. The history of the present King of Great Britain is a history of repeated injuries and usurpations, all having in direct object the established of a absolute tyranny over these States.

We hold these truths to be self evident, that all People are created equal, that they are endowed by their Creator with certain inalienable rights, that among these are Life, Liberty, and the Pursuit of Happiness.

That to secure these rights, governments are instituted among Men, deriving their just powers from the consent of the governed. That whenever any form of government But when a long train of abuses and usurpations, pursuing invariably the same object, evinces a design to reduce them under absolute despotism, it is their former systems of government, and to provide new guards for their future security.

Subhead Two

Such has been the patient sufferance of these colonies; and such is now the necessity which constrains them to alter their former systems of government. The history of the present King of Great Britain is a history of
But when a long train of abuses and usurpations, pursuing invariably the same object, evinces a design to reduce them under absolute despotism, it is their former systems of government, and to provide new guards for their future security. Such has been the patient sufferance of these colonies; and such is now the necessity which constrains them to alter their former systems of government. The history of the present King of Great Britain is a history of repeated injuries and usurpations, all having in direct object

A C C O U N T I N G
Perspectives

BULK RATE
U.S. POSTAGE
PAID
NEW YORK CITY
PERMIT NO. 1111

Accounting Perspectives
P.O. Box 5432
New York City 12345

Credits

If your newsletter is designed to provide employees or members with opportunities to express themselves, identify the authors by name.

If possible, personalize feature articles by including a photograph or drawing of the author. Photos can become organizers for features.

Secure Living

Volume II, Issue 9 September 1996

Turn Your House Into a Fortress
by John Bolt

Lorem ipsum dolor sit amet, consectetuer adipiscing elit, sed diam nonummy nibh euismod tincidunt ut laoreet dolore magna aliquam erat volutpat. Ut wisi enim ad minim veniam, quis nostrud exerci tation ullamcorper suscipit lobortis nisl ut aliquip ex ea commodo consequat.

Duis autem vel eum iriure dolor in hendrerit in vulputate velit esse molestie consequat, vel illum dolore eu feugiat nulla facilisis at vero eros et accumsan et iusto odio dignissim qui blandit praesent luptatum zzril delenit augue duis dolore te feugait nulla facilisi. Lorem ipsum dolor sit amet, consectetuer adipiscing elit, sed diam nonummy nibh euismod tincidunt ut laoreet dolore magna aliquam erat volutpat.

Ut wisi enim ad minim veniam, quis nostrud exerci tation ullamcorper suscipit lobortis nisl ut aliquip ex ea commodo consequat. Duis autem vel eum iriure dolor in hendrerit indimunso

(Continued on page 2)

So You Want to Install a Portcullis?
by Susan D. Fence

Duis autem vel eum iriure dolor in hendrerit in vulputate velit esse molestie consequat, vel illum dolore eu feugiat nulla facilisis at vero eros et accumsan et iusto odio dignissim qui blandit praesent luptatum zzril delenit augue duis dolore te feugait nulla facilisi. Lorem ipsum dolor sit amet, consec tetuer adipiscing elit, sed nonummy nibh euismod tincidunt ut laoreet dolore magna aliquam erat volutpat.

Ut wisi enim ad minim veniam, quis nostrud exerci tation ullamcorper suscipit lobortis nisl ut aliquip ex ea commodo consequat. Duis autem vel eum iriure dolor in hendrerit in. Lorem ipsum dolor sit amet, consectetuer adipiscing elit, sed diam nonummy nibh euismod tincidunt ut laoreet dolore magna aliquam erat volutpat. Ut wisi enim ad minim veniam, quis nostrud exerci tation ullamcorper suscipit lobortis nisl ut aliquip ex ea commodo consequat, sed nonummy nibh euismod tincidunt ut laoreet dolore magna aliqm erat volutpat, sed nonummy nibh euismod tincidunt ut laoreet. Ut wisi enim ad minim veniam, nostrud exerci tation ullamcorper suscipit nisl, sed nonummy nibh euismod tincidunt ut laoreet dolore magna aliqm erat volutpat

(Continued on page 3)

Headlines

Consider the number of articles included in each issue and the length of each article when designing headlines.

If you plan to feature a single in-depth article plus a few shorter pieces in each issue of your newsletter, you'll use a single, dominant headline.

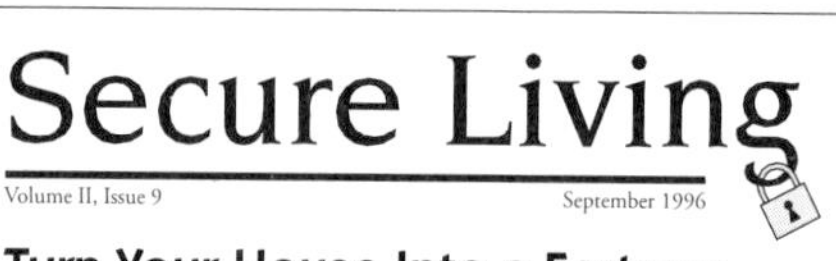

Volume II, Issue 9 September 1996

Turn Your House Into a Fortress

Lorem ipsum dolor sit amet, consectetuer adipiscing elit, sed diam nonummy nibh euismod tincidunt ut laoreet dolore magna aliquam erat volutpat. Ut wisi enim ad minim veniam, quis nostrud exerci tation ullamcorper suscipit lobortis nisl ut aliquip ex ea commodo consequat.

Duis autem vel eum iriure dolor in hendrerit in vulputate velit esse molestie consequat, vel illum dolore eu feugiat nulla facilisis at vero eros et accumsan et iusto odio dignissim qui blandit praesent luptatum zzril delenit augue duis dolore te feugait nulla facilisi. Lorem ipsum dolor sit amet, consectetuer adipiscing elit, sed diam nonummy nibh euismod tincidunt ut laoreet dolore magna aliquam erat volutpat.

Ut wisi enim ad minim veniam, quis nostrud exerci tation ullamcorper suscipit lobortis nisl ut aliquip ex ea commodo consequat. Duis autem vel eum iriure dolor in hendrerit in vulputate velit esse molestie consequat, vel illum dolore eu feugiat nulla facilisis at vero eros et accumsan et iusto odio dignissim qui blandit praesent luptatum zzril delenit augue duis dolore te feugait nulla facilisi.

Nam liber tempor cum soluta nobis eleifend option congue nihil imperdiet doming id quod mazim placerat facer possim assum. Lorem ipsum dolor sit amet, consectetuer adipiscing elit, sed diam nonummy nibh euismod tincidunt ut laoreet dolore magna aliquam erat volutpat.

Put Bars on the Windows

Lorem ipsum dolor sit amet, consectetuer adipiscing elit, sed diam nonummy nibh euismod tincidunt ut laoreet dolore magna aliquam eratv olutpat. Ut wisi enim ad minim veniam, nostrud exerci tation ullamcorper suscipit lobortis nisl ut aliquip ex ea commodo consequat.

Duis autem vel eum iriure dolor in hendrerit in vulputate velit esse molestie consequat, vel illum dolore eu feugiat nulla facilisis at vero eros et accumsan et iusto odio dignissim qui blandit praesent luptatum zzril delenit augue duis dolore te feugait nulla facilisi. Lorem ipsum dolor sit amet, consectetuer adipiscing elit, sed diam nonummy nibh euismod tincidunt ut laoreet dolore magna aliquam erat volutpat.

Ut wisi enim ad minim veniam, quis nostrud exerci tation ullamcorper suscipit lobortis nisl ut aliquip ex ea commodo consequat. Duis autem vel eum iriure dolor in hendrerit in vulputate velit esse molestie consequat, vel illum dolore eu feugiat nulla facilisis at vero eros et accumsan et iusto odio dignissim qui blandit praesent luptatum zzril delenit augue duis dolore te feugait nulla facilisi.

Invest in a Chain Bolt

Duis autem vel eum iriure dolor in hendrerit in vulputate velit esse molestie consequat, vel illum dolore eu feugiat nulla facilisis. Ut wisi enim ad minim veniam, quis nostrud exerci tation ullam corper suscipit lobortis nisl ut aliquip ex ea commodo consequat. Duis autem vel eum iriure dolor hendrerit in vulputate velit esse molestie consequat, vel illum dolore eu feugiat nulla facilisis at vero eros et accumsan et iusto odio dignissim qui blandit praesent luptatum zzril delenit augue duis dolore te feugait nulla facilisi. Nam liber tempor cum soluta nobis eleifend option congue nihil imperdiet doming

On the other hand, if you feature several short articles, the front page can be designed to accommodate more than one significant headline.

Secure Living

Volume II, Issue 9 September 1996

Turn Your House Into a Fortress

Lorem ipsum dolor sit amet, consectetuer adipiscing elit, sed diam nonummy nibh euismod tincidunt ut laoreet dolore magna aliquam erat volutpat. Ut wisi enim ad minim veniam, quis nostrud exerci tation ullamcorper suscipit lobortis nisl ut aliquip ex ea commodo consequat.

Duis autem vel eum iriure dolor in hendrerit in vulputate velit esse molestie consequat, vel illum dolore eu feugiat nulla facilisis at vero eros et accumsan et iusto odio dignissim qui blandit praesent luptatum zzril delenit augue duis dolore te feugait nulla facilisi. Lorem ipsum dolor sit amet, consectetuer adipiscing elit, sed diam nonummy nibh euismod tincidunt ut laoreet dolore magna aliquam erat volutpat.

Ut wisi enim ad minim veniam, quis nostrud exerci tation ullamcorper suscipit lobortis nisl ut aliquip ex ea commodo consequat. Duis autem vel eum iriure dolor in hendrerit in vulputate velit esse molestie consequat, vel illum dolore eu feugiat nulla facilisis at vero eros et accumsan et iusto odio dignissim qui blandit praesent luptatum zzril delenit augue duis dolore te feugait nulla facilisi.

So You Want to Install a Portcullis?

Nam liber tempor cum soluta nobis eleifend option congue nihil imperdiet doming id quod mazim placerat facer possim assum. Lorem ipsum dolor sit amet, consectetuer adipiscing elit, sed diam nonummy nibh euis mod tincidunt ut laoreet dolore magna aliquam erat volutpat. Consectetuer adipiscing elit, sed diam nonummy nibh euismod tincidunt ut laoreet dolore magna aliquam eratv olutpat. Ut wisi enim ad minim veniam, nostrud exerci tation ullamcorper suscipit lobortis nisl ut aliquip ex ea commodo consequat.

Duis autem vel eum iriure dolor in hendrerit in vulputate velit esse molestie consequat, vel illum dolore eu feugiat nulla facilisis at vero eros et accumsan et iusto odio dignissim qui blandit praesent luptatum zzril delenit augue duis dolore te feugait nulla facilisi. Lorem ipsum dolor sit amet, consectetuer adipiscing elit, sed diam nonummy nibh euismod tincidunt ut laoreet dolore magna aliquam erat volutpat.

Ut wisi enim ad minim veniam, quis nostrud exerci tation ullamcorper suscipit lobortis nisl

Typically, headlines are placed above the articles they introduce. However, you might consider placing the headline next to the article instead.

Teasers

Use teasers to invite readers inside your newsletter.

A short table of contents on the front cover can draw attention to articles and features inside. The table of contents should be a focal point. Experiment with different locations and typographic treatments to help it stand out on the page.

Secure Living

Volume II, Issue 9 September 1996

Turn Your House Into a Fortress

Lorem ipsum dolor sit amet, consectetuer adipiscing elit, sed diam nonummy nibh euismod tincidunt ut laoreet dolore magna aliquam erat volutpat. Ut wisi enim ad minim veniam, quis nostrud exerci tation ullamcorper suscipit lobortis nisl ut aliquip ex ea commodo consequat.

Duis autem vel eum iriure dolor in hendrerit in vulputate velit esse molestie consequat, vel illum dolore eu feugiat nulla facilisis at vero eros et accumsan et iusto odio dignissim qui blandit praesent luptatum zzril delenit augue duis dolore te feugait nulla facilisi. Lorem ipsum dolor sit amet, consectetuer adipiscing elit, sed diam nonummy nibh euismod tincidunt ut laoreet dolore magna aliquam erat un volutpat wisi.

Ut wisi enim ad minim veniam, quis nostrud exerci tation ullamcorper suscipit lobortis nisl ut aliquip ex ea commodo consequat. Duis autem vel eum iriure dolor in indimunso exerci tation ullamcorper suscipit lobortis nisl ut aliquip ex ea com consequat

(Continued on page 2)

So You Want to Install a Portcullis?

Duis autem vel eum iriure dolor in hendrerit in vulputate velit esse molestie consequat, vel illum dolore eu feugiat nulla facilisis at vero eros et accumsan et iusto odio dignissim qui blandit praesent luptatum zzril delenit augue duis dolore te feugait nulla facilisi. Lorem ipsum dolor sit amet, consec tetuer adipiscing elit, sed nonummy nibh euismod tincidunt ut laoreet dolore magna aliquam erat volutpat.

Ut wisi enim ad minim veniam, quis nostrud exerci tation ullamcorper suscipit lobortis nisl ut aliquip ex ea commodo consequat. Duis autem vel eum iriure dolor in hendrerit in. Lorem ipsum dolor sit amet, consectetuer adipiscing elit, sed diam nonummy nibh euismod tincidunt ut laoreet dolore magna aliquam erat volutpat. Ut wisi enim ad minim veniam, quis nostrud exerci tation ullamcorper suscipit lobortis nisl ut aliquip ex ea commodo consequat, sed nonummy nibh euismod tincidunt ut laoreet dolore magna aliqm erat volutpat, sed nonummy nibh euismod tincidunt ut laoreet. Ut wisi enim ad minim veniam, nostrud exerci tation ullamcorper suscipit nisl, sed nonummy nibh euismod tincidunt ut laoreet dolore magna aliqm volutpat

(Continued on page 3)

What's Inside

Secure Living

Turn Your House Into a Fortress

Lorem ipsum dolor sit amet, consectetuer adipiscing elit, sed diam nonummy nibh euismod tincidunt ut laoreet dolore magna aliquam erat volutpat. Ut wisi enim ad minim veniam, quis nostrud exerci tation ullamcorper suscipit lobortis nisl ut aliquip ex ea commodo consequat.

Duis autem vel eum iriure dolor in hendrerit in vulputate velit esse molestie consequat, vel illum dolore eu feugiat nulla facilisis at vero eros et accumsan et iusto odio dignissim qui blandit praesent luptatum zzril delenit augue duis dolore te feugait nulla facilisi. Lorem ipsum dolor sit amet, consectetuer adipiscing elit, sed diam nonummy nibh euismod tincidunt ut laoreet dolore magna aliquam erat volutpat.

Nam liber tempor cum soluta nobis eleifend option congue nihil imperdiet doming id quod mazim placerat facer possim assum. Lorem ipsum dolor sit amet, consectetuer adipiscing elit, sed diam nonummy nibh euismod tincidunt ut laoreet dolore magna aliquam erat volutpat. Lorem ipsum dolor sit amet, consectetuer adipiscing elit, tincidunt ut laoreet dolore magna aliquam erat volutpat.

Lorem ipsum dolor sit amet, consectetuer adipiscing elit, sed diam nonummy nibh euismod tincidunt ut laoreet dolore magna aliquam consectetuer adipiscing elit, sed diam nonummy nibh euismod tincidunt ut laoreet dolore magna aliquam eratv olutpat. Ut wisi enim ad minim veniam, nostrud exerci tation ullamcorper suscipit lobortis nisl ut aliquip ex ea commodo consequat.

Duis autem vel eum iriure dolor in hendrerit in vulputate velit esse molestie consequat, vel illum dolore eu feugiat nulla facilisis at vero eros et accumsan et iusto odio dignissim qui blandit praesent luptatum zzril delenit augue duis dolore te feugait nulla facilisi. Lorem ipsum dolor sit amet, consectetuer adipiscing elit, sed diam nonummy nibh euismod tincidunt ut laoreet dolore magna aliquam erat volutpat.

Ut wisi enim ad minim veniam, quis nostrud exerci tation ullamcorper suscipit lobortis nisl ut aliquip ex ea commodo consequat. Duis autem vel eum iriure dolor in hendrerit in vulputate velit esse molestie consequat, vel illum dolore eu feugiat nulla facilisis at vero eros et accumsan et iusto odio dignissim qui blandit praesent luptatum zzril delenit augue duis dolore te feugait nulla facilisi.

Invest in a Chain Bolt

Duis autem vel eum iriure dolor in hendrerit in vulputate velit esse molestie consequat, vel illum dolore eu feugiat nulla facilisis. Ut wisi enim ad minim veniam, quis nostrud exerci tation ullam corper suscipit lobortis nisl ut aliquip ex ea commodo consequat. Duis autem vel eum iriure dolor hendrerit in vulputate velit esse molestie consequat, vel illum dolore eu feugiat nulla facilisis at vero eros et accumsan et iusto odio dignissim qui blandit praesent luptatum zzril delenit augue duis dolore te feugait nulla facilisi. Nam liber tempor cum soluta nobis eleifend option congue nihil imperdiet doming id quod mazim placerat facer possim assum. Lorem ipsum dolor sit amet, consectetuer adipiscing elit, sed diam nonummy nibh euismod tincidunt ut laoreet aliquip ex ea commodo consequat.

Many publications, like newsletters and direct mail pieces, appear in the reader's mailbox with the address label up. You may want to place the table of contents next to the mailing label area where it can't be overlooked.

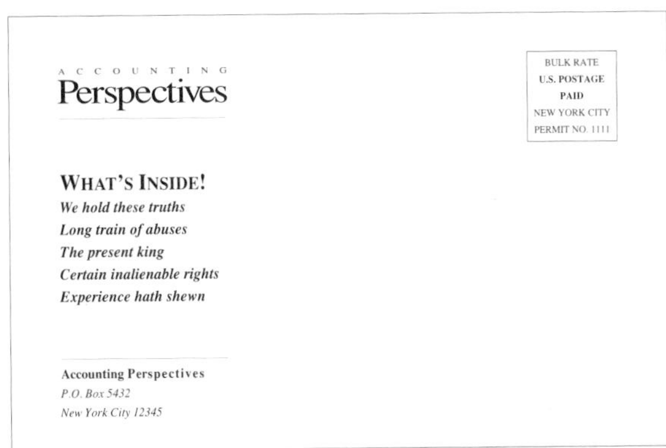

ACCOUNTING
Perspectives

BULK RATE
U.S. POSTAGE
PAID
NEW YORK CITY
PERMIT NO. 1111

WHAT'S INSIDE!

Accounting Perspectives
P.O. Box 5432
New York City 12345

You can also let the entire front cover serve as your table of contents. Include photographs that relate to the articles inside, with photo captions that tease the reader to find out more.

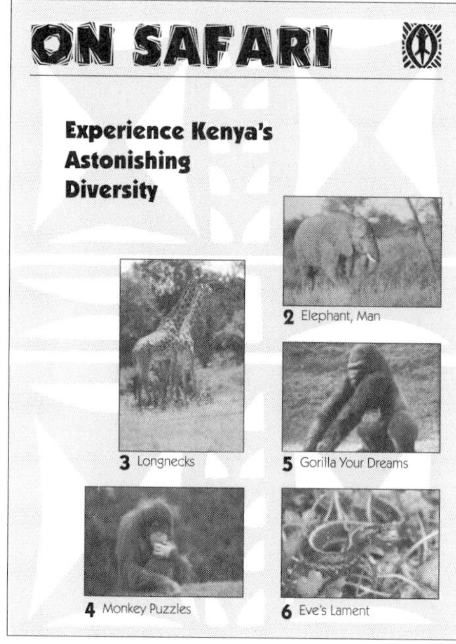

Lead-ins

Use subheads and short summaries to provide transition between headlines and body copy.

Lead-ins can be placed between the headline and text. Frequently, lead-ins span more than one column.

Secure Living

Volume II, Issue 9 September 1996

Turn Your House Into a Fortress

Security is a state of mind. When your house isn't secure, you may also experience feelings of insecurity. But those feelings can be dispelled if you'll just take a few simple precautions.

John Bolt, Security Expert

Lorem ipsum dolor sit amet, consectetuer adipiscing elit, sed diam nonummy nibh euismod tincidunt ut laoreet dolore magna aliquam erat volutpat. Ut wisi enim ad minim veniam, quis nostrud exerci tation ullamcorper suscipit lobortis nisl ut aliquip ex ea commodo consequat.

Duis autem vel eum iriure dolor in hendrerit in vulputate velit esse molestie consequat, vel illum dolore eu feugiat nulla facilisis at vero eros et accumsan et iusto odio dignissim qui blandit praesent luptatum zzril delenit augue duis dolore te feugait nulla facilisi. Lorem ipsum dolor sit amet, consectetuer adipiscing elit, sed diam nonummy nibh euismod tincidunt ut laoreet dolore magna aliquam erat un volutpat wisi.

Ut wisi enim ad minim veniam, quis nostrud exerci tation ullamcorper suscipit lobortis nisl ut aliquip ex ea commodo consequat. Duis autem vel eum iriure dolor in indimunso exerci tation ullamcorper suscipit lobortis nisl ut aliquip ex ea com consequat

Duis autem vel eum iriure dolor in hendrerit in vulputate velit esse molestie consequat, vel illum dolore eu feugiat nulla facilisis at vero eros et accumsan et iusto odio dignissim qui blandit praesent luptatum zzril delenit augue duis dolore te feugait nulla facilisi. Lorem ipsum dolor sit amet, consec tetuer adipiscing elit, sed nonummy nibh euismod tincidunt ut laoreet dolore magna aliquam volupat.

Ut wisi enim ad minim veniam, quis nostrud exerci tation ullamcorper suscipit lobortis nisl ut aliquip ex ea commodo consequat. Duis autem vel eum iriure dolor in hendrerit in. Lorem ipsum dolor sit amet, consectetuer adipiscing elit, sed diam nonummy nibh euismod tincidunt ut laoreet dolore magna aliquam erat volutpat. Ut wisi enim ad minim veniam, quis nostrud exerci tation ullamcorper suscipit lobortis nisl ut aliquip ex ea commodo consequat, sed nonummy nibh euismod tincidunt ut laoreet dolore magna aliqm erat volutpat, sed nonummy nibh euismod tincidunt ut laoreet. Ut wisi enim ad minim veniam, nostrud exerci tation ullamcorper suscipit nisl, sed nonummy nibh euismod tincidunt ut laoreet dolore magna aliqm volutpat

(Continued on page 3)

A lead-in is often placed within the text, set off by horizontal rules or some other device.

Secure Living

Volume II, Issue 9 September 1996

Turn Your House Into a Fortress

Lorem ipsum dolor sit amet, consectetuer adipiscing elit, sed diam nonummy nibh euismod tincidunt ut laoreet dolore magna aliquam erat volutpat. Ut wisi enim ad minim veniam, quis nostrud exerci tation ullamcorper suscipit lobortis nisl ut aliquip ex ea commodo consequat.

Duis autem vel eum iriure dolor in hendrerit in vulputate velit esse molestie consequat, vel illum dolore eu feugiat nulla facilisis at vero eros et accumsan et iusto odio dignissim qui blandit praesent luptatum zzril delenit augue duis dolore te feugait nulla facilisi. Lorem ipsum dolor sit amet, consectetuer adipiscing elit, sed diam nonummy nibh euismod tincidunt ut laoreet dolore magna aliquam erat volutpat.

Ut wisi enim ad minim veniam, quis nostrud exerci tation ullamcorper suscipit lobortis nisl ut aliquip ex ea commodo consequat. Duis autem vel eum iriure dolor in hendrerit in vulputate velit esse molestie consequat, vel illum dolore eu feugiat nulla facilisis at vero eros et accumsan et iusto odio dignissim qui blandit praesent luptatum zzril delenit augue duis dolore te feugait nulla facilisi.

Nam liber tempor cum soluta nobis eleifend option congue nihil imperdiet doming id quod mazim placerat facer possim assum. Lorem ipsum dolor sit amet, consectetuer adipiscing elit, sed diam nonummy nibh euismod tincidunt ut laoreet dolore magna aliquam erat volutpat.

Lorem ipsum dolor sit amet, consectetuer adipiscing elit, sed diam nonummy nibh euismod tincidunt ut laoreet dolore magna aliquam erat volutpat. Ut wisi enim ad minim veniam, nostrud exerci tation ullamcorper suscipit lobortis nisl ut aliquip ex ea commodo consequat. Duis autem vel eum iriure dolor in hendrerit in vulputate velit esse consequat, vel illum dolore feugiat nulla facilisis at vero eros et accumsan et iusto odio dignissim qui blandit praesent luptatum zzril delenit augue duis dolore te fegait nulla facilisi. Lorem ipsum dolor sit amet, consectetuer adipiscing elit, sed diam nonummy nibh euismod tincidunt ut laoreet dolore magna aliquam volutpat.

Security is a state of mind. When your house isn't secure, you may also experience feelings of insecurity.

Ut wisi enim ad minim veniam, quis nostrud exercitation ullam corper suscipit lobortis nisl aliquip ex ea commodo consequat. Duis autem vel eum iriure dolor in hendrerit vulputate velit esse molestie consequat, vel illum dolore eu feugiat nulla facilisis atv ero eros et accumsan et iusto odio dignissim qui blandit praesent luptatum zzril delenit augue duis dolore te feugait nulla facilisi.

Invest in a Chain Bolt

Duis autem vel eum iriure dolor in hendrerit in velit esse molestie consequat, vel illum dolore eu feugiat nulla facilisis. Ut wisi enim ad minim veniam, quis nostrud exerci tation ullam corper suscipit lobortis nisl ut aliquip ex ea comodo consequat. Duis autem vel eum iriure dolor hendrerit in vulputate velit esse molestie consequat, vel illum dolore eu feugiat nulla facilisis at vero eros et accumsan et iusto odio belid

Size

A standard newsletter is created by folding an 11×17-inch sheet of paper, called a signature, into four 8½×11-inch pages. Additional sheets increase the page count in increments of four.

Your newsletter can be any size, of course, but printing costs are generally higher for uncommon sizes. The three most common paper sizes are *letter* (8½×11 inches), *legal* (8½×14 inches), and *tabloid* (11×17 inches); all printers will stock these sizes. If your page size doesn't match one of these, you'll have to pay the additional expense of trimming each page. (Of course, if your newsletter contains bleeds, you have to trim the pages anyway.)

Distribution

How you distribute your publication is a design consideration.

There are two important factors to consider:

- Should the newsletter be folded or sent full size?
- Should the newsletter be enclosed in an envelope or sent as a self-mailer?

Decisions about distribution need to be made early in your planning process. Self-mailers avoid the cost of envelopes, but you lose valuable editorial or selling space because you must leave room for the address area. Additionally, the newsletter's pristine condition off the press might not withstand the rigors of today's automated physical mail delivery system. Often, tears and creases can mar an otherwise good-looking piece. To test the durability of your publication, mail one to yourself.

While a multiple-fold newsletter is easier to mail, the nameplate and headlines aren't visible until the folds are opened. You also lose the advantage of presenting the recipient with the billboard effect of a full-size 8½×11-inch newsletter.

Tabloids

Many of the same principles involved in designing successful newsletters also apply to tabloids, particularly the need to maintain issue-to-issue consistency while accommodating a constantly changing mix of text and visuals. For example, tabloids need high-impact headlines that don't compete with the nameplate or with each other. It's also important to organize photographs of varying size as effectively as possible.

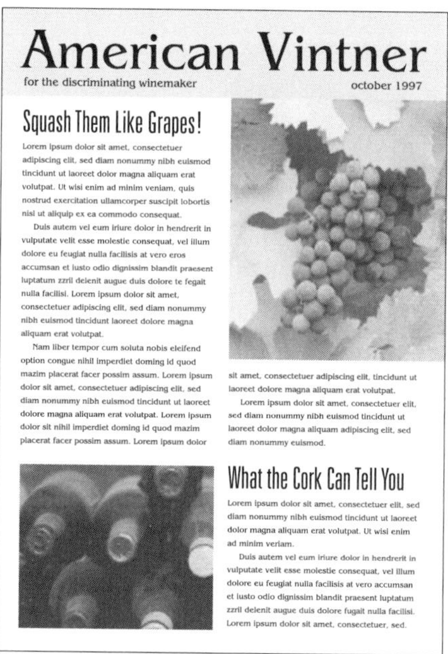

American Vintner

for the discriminating winemaker

october 1997

Squash Them Like Grapes!

Lorem ipsum dolor sit amet, consectetuer adipiscing elit, sed diam nonummy nibh euismod tincidunt ut laoreet dolor magna aliquam erat volutpat. Ut wisi enim ad minim veniam, quis nostrud exercitation ullamcorper suscipit lobortis nisl ut aliquip ex ea commodo consequat.

Duis autem vel eum iriure dolor in hendrerit in vulputate velit esse molestie consequat, vel illum dolore eu feugiat nulla facilisis at vero eros accumsan et iusto odio dignissim blandit praesent luptatum zzril delenit augue duis dolore te fegait nulla facilisi. Lorem ipsum dolor sit amet, consectetuer adipiscing elit, sed diam nonummy nibh euismod tincidunt laoreet dolore magna aliquam erat volutpat.

Nam liber tempor cum soluta nobis eleifend option congue nihil imperdiet doming id quod mazim placerat facer possim assum. Lorem ipsum dolor sit amet, consectetuer adipiscing elit, sed diam nonummy nibh euismod tincidunt ut laoreet dolore magna aliquam erat volutpat. Lorem ipsum dolor sit nihil imperdiet doming id quod mazim placerat facer possim assum. Lorem ipsum dolor sit amet, consectetuer adipiscing elit, tincidunt ut laoreet dolore magna aliquam erat volutpat.

Lorem ipsum dolor sit amet, consectetuer elit, sed diam nonummy nibh euismod tincidunt ut laoreet dolor magna aliquam adipiscing elit, sed diam nonummy euismod.

What the Cork Can Tell You

Lorem ipsum dolor sit amet, consectetuer elit, sed diam nonummy nibh euismod tincidunt ut laoreet dolor magna aliquam erat volutpat. Ut wisi enim ad minim veriam.

Duis autem vel eum iriure dolor in hendrerit in vulputate velit esse molestie consequat, vel illum dolore eu feugiat nulla facilisis at vero accumsan et iusto odio dignissim blandit praesent luptatum zzril delenit augue duis dolore fugait nulla facilisi. Lorem ipsum dolor sit amet, consectetuer, sed.

The typical tabloid page is 11×17 inches, although those dimensions vary from newspaper to newspaper and printer to printer. Tabloids are often printed on a web press, which feeds the paper to the press from a large roll. As a result, the actual image area of the tabloid is slightly smaller than the page size of 11×17 inches.

Laser printers can be used to prepare tabloids, although the coarse paper used for most tabloids absorbs ink and consequently, reduces the high-resolution sharpness normally achieved in phototypeset images. Most laser printers, however, are not designed to handle paper sizes larger than 8½×11 inches. (Tabloid-sized laser printers are available, although uncommon.) To get around that limitation, desktop publishing programs offer a tiling feature that automatically overlaps, or tiles, a series of 8½×11-inch pages that can be pasted together to create one large tabloid page.

Front Cover

Larger page sizes can accommodate large, bold headlines and large photographs.

The most effective tabloid covers contain a dominant visual element. For important or urgent news stories, the headline should probably be the primary focus.

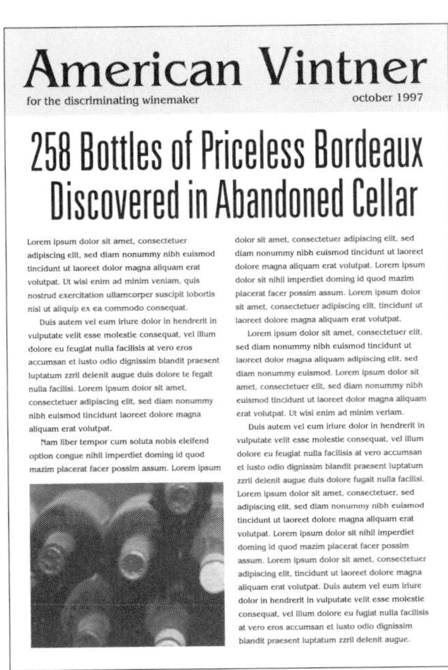

American Vintner

for the discriminating winemaker october 1997

258 Bottles of Priceless Bordeaux Discovered in Abandoned Cellar

Lorem ipsum dolor sit amet, consectetuer adipiscing elit, sed diam nonummy nibh euismod tincidunt ut laoreet dolor magna aliquam erat volutpat. Ut wisi enim ad minim veniam, quis nostrud exercitation ullamcorper suscipit lobortis nisl ut aliquip ex ea commodo consequat.

Duis autem vel eum iriure dolor in hendrerit in vulputate velit esse molestie consequat, vel illum dolore eu feugiat nulla facilisis at vero eros accumsan et iusto odio dignissim blandit praesent luptatum zzril delenit augue duis dolore te fegait nulla facilisi. Lorem ipsum dolor sit amet, consectetuer adipiscing elit, sed diam nonummy nibh euismod tincidunt laoreet dolore magna aliquam erat volutpat.

Nam liber tempor cum soluta nobis eleifend option congue nihil imperdiet doming id quod mazim placerat facer possim assum. Lorem ipsum dolor sit amet, consectetuer adipiscing elit, sed diam nonummy nibh euismod tincidunt ut laoreet dolore magna aliquam erat volutpat. Lorem ipsum dolor sit nihil imperdiet doming id quod mazim placerat facer possim assum. Lorem ipsum dolor sit amet, consectetuer adipiscing elit, tincidunt ut laoreet dolore magna aliquam erat volutpat.

Lorem ipsum dolor sit amet, consectetuer elit, sed diam nonummy nibh euismod tincidunt ut laoreet dolor magna aliquam adipiscing elit, sed diam nonummy euismod. Lorem ipsum dolor sit amet, consectetuer elit, sed diam nonummy nibh euismod tincidunt ut laoreet dolor magna aliquam erat volutpat. Ut wisi enim ad minim veriam.

Duis autem vel eum iriure dolor in hendrerit in vulputate velit esse molestie consequat, vel illum dolore eu feugiat nulla facilisis at vero accumsan et iusto odio dignissim blandit praesent luptatum zzril delenit augue duis dolore fugait nulla facilisi. Lorem ipsum dolor sit amet, consectetuer, sed adipiscing elit, sed diam nonummy nibh euismod tincidunt ut laoreet dolore magna aliquam erat volutpat. Lorem ipsum dolor sit nihil imperdiet doming id quod mazim placerat facer possim assum. Lorem ipsum dolor sit amet, consectetuer adipiscing elit, tincidunt ut laoreet dolore magna aliquam erat volutpat. Duis autem vel eum iriure dolor in hendrerit in vulputate velit esse molestie consequat, vel illum dolore eu fugiat nulla facilisis at vero eros accumsan et iusto odio dignissim blandit praesent luptatum zzril delenit augue.

If your headline is more evocative than informative, you might wish to let a photograph or an illustration dominate the page.

For an extravagant look, you can mimic a magazine cover by using a full-page photo.

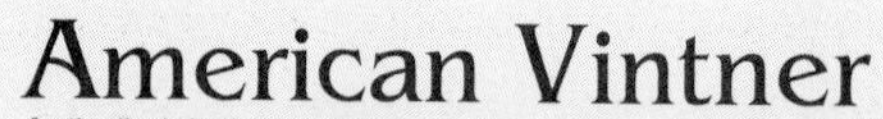

GRAPES
OF WRATH

Lorem ipsum dolor sit amet, consectetuer adipiscing elit, sed diam nonummy nibh euismod tincidunt ut laoreet dolor magna aliquam erat volutpat. Ut wisi enim ad minim veniam, quis nostrud exercitation ullamcorper suscipit lobortis nisl ut aliquip ex ea commodo consequat.

Duis autem vel eum iriure dolor in hendrerit in vulputate velit esse molestie consequat, vel illum dolore eu feugiat nulla facilisis at vero eros accumsan et iusto odio dignissim blandit praesent luptatum zzril delenit augue duis dolore te fegait nulla facilisi. Lorem ipsum dolor sit amet, consectetuer adipiscing elit, sed diam nonummy nibh euismod tincidunt laoreet dolore magna aliquam erat volutpat.

Nam liber tempor cum soluta nobis eleifend option congue nihil imperdiet doming id quod mazim placerat facer possim assum. Lorem ipsum dolor sit amet, consectetuer adipiscing elit, sed diam nonummy nibh euismod tincidunt ut laoreet dolore magna aliquam erat volutpat. Lorem ipsum dolor sit nihil imperdiet doming id quod mazim placerat facer possim assum. Lorem ipsum dolor sit amet, consectetuer adipiscing elit, tincidunt ut laoreet dolore magna aliquam erat volutpat.

Lorem ipsum dolor sit amet, consectetuer adipiscing elit, sed diam nonummy nibh euismod tincidunt ut laoreet dolor magna aliquam adipiscing elit, sed diam nonummy euismod tincidunt ut laoreet dolore magna aliquam eratvolutpat. Ut wis enim minim veniam, nostrud exercitation ullamcorper suscipit lobortis nisl ut aliquip ex ea codo consequat.

Duis autem vel eum iriure dolor in hendrerit in vulputate velit esse molestie consequat, vel illum dolore eu feugiat nulla facilisis at vero eros accumsan et iusto odio dignissim blandit praesent luptatum zzril delenit augue duis dolore te fugait nulla facilisi. Lorem ipsum dolor sit! amet, consectetuer adipiscing elit, sed diam nonummy nibh

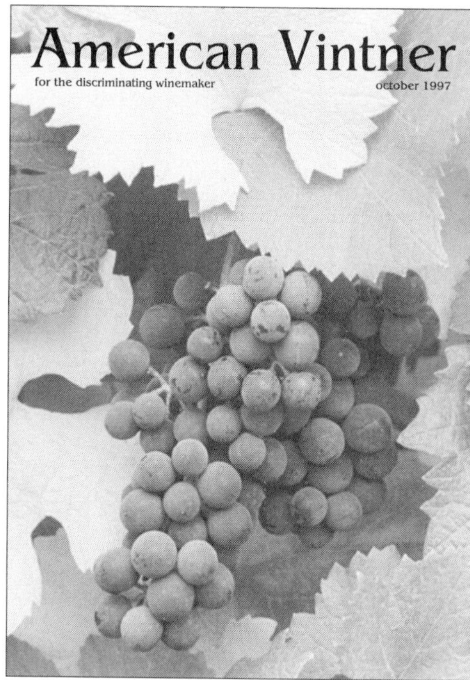

Inside Pages

Choose a consistent format for the inside pages of your tabloid.

Design your tabloid as a series of two-page spreads. Include your organization's logo or publication title at least once on every spread, typically in a running footer. Another ideal place for such items is in a *sink*, a deep top border.

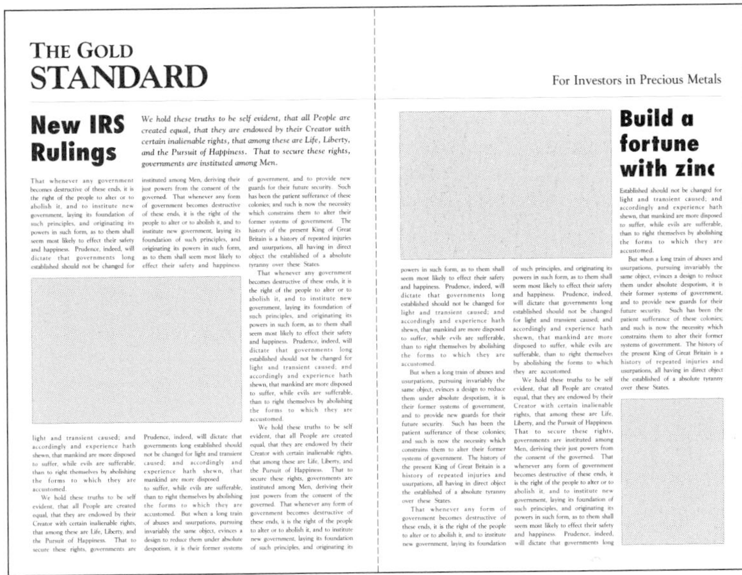

Generally, the more columns you use in your grid, the more design flexibility you have. A five-column grid is extremely flexible.

Back Cover

Don't neglect the back cover. It's almost as high-profile as the front cover. Back-cover information should be immediately accessible to the casual browser and should encourage readers to peruse the rest of the tabloid. Try placing summaries of the front-cover articles in this space or repeating your best ads and promotions.

Planning For Ads

Because of their size, tabloids let you creatively mix editorial and selling space.

Mixing information and advertising is a good way to ensure that readers see everything your tabloid has to offer. It's also a good way to expand the market for your products. The editorial content can answer basic questions that first-time buyers might have.

Experiment with different placements for the editorial information on your pages:

- On the top half of each page.

- At the bottom of each page.

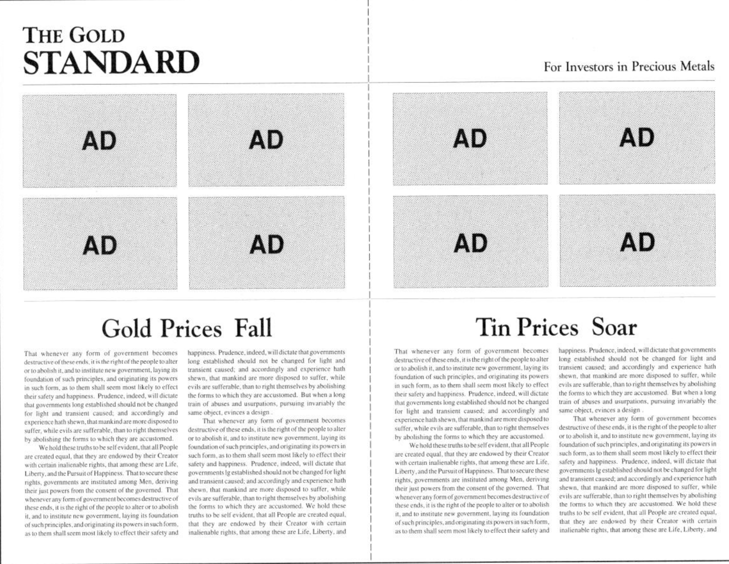

- In vertical columns adjacent to the selling area.

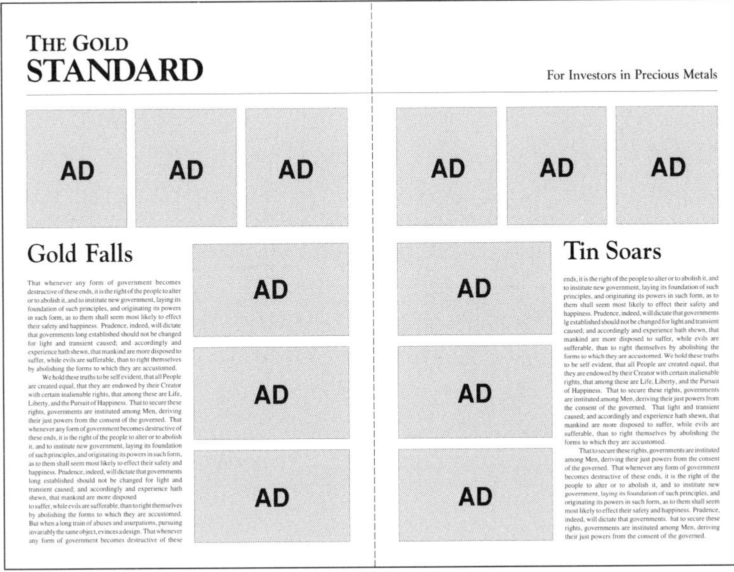

- Between the selling areas.

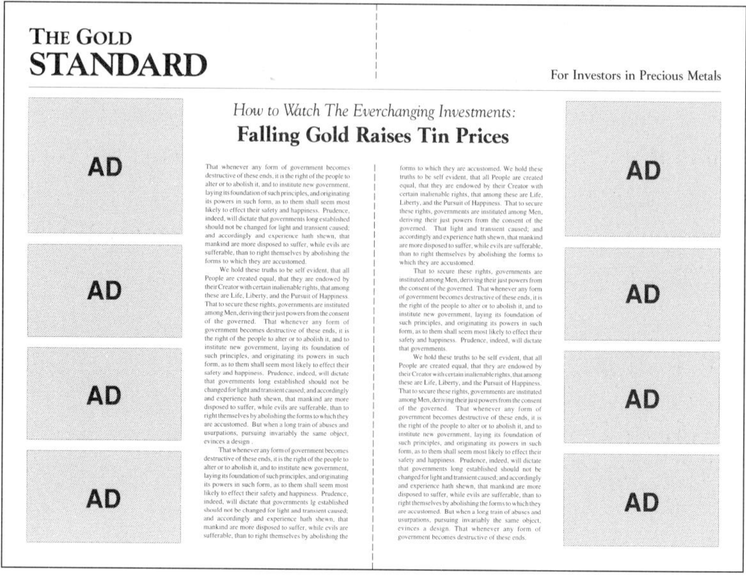

- With a screen to integrate editorial material into one unit.

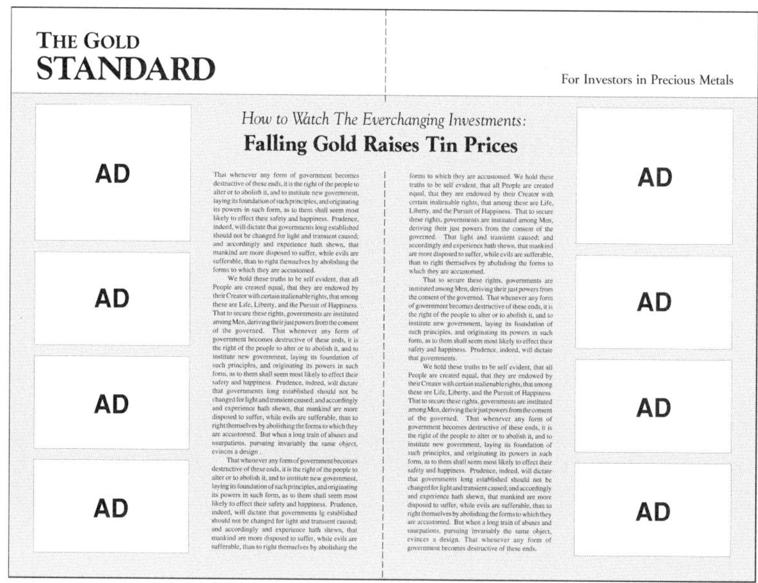

Newspapers

Once you're comfortable producing tabloid-size newsletters, you'll find it easy to step up to newspaper design.

The primary difference between a tabloid and a newspaper is the number of columns. Tabloid pages generally hold two or three wide text columns. Newspaper pages, on the other hand, are divided into narrow text columns—often six or more per page. The shorter line lengths require smaller type sizes, and more attention must be paid to hyphenation, letter spacing, and word spacing.

Our movie critic rates "Jaws 6"—see page 12

THE BIG NEWS

Dow Jones dips again—see the Financial Section

THE BIG NEWS GETS BIGGER!

More of what you like

Exhausted paperboy gasps "It's as heavy as a brick!"

Price gets bigger too

Headlines

When several newspaper headlines appear on the same page, the size and prominence of each should reflect its relative importance.

The type size of a headline should reflect the importance of the story. Make sure there's some variation. Confusion will reign if all articles are introduced by the same size headline.

Let the top of the page carry most of the weight. Your layout will look unbalanced if you place your larger headlines near the bottom.

Our movie critic rates "Jaws 6"—see page 12

THE BIG NEWS

Dow Jones dips again—see the Financial Section

An extremely important story

Lorem ipsum dolor sit amet, consect adipiscing elit, sed diam nonummy nibh euismod tincidunt ut laoreet dolore magna aliquam erat volutpat. Ut wisi enim ad minim veniam, quis nostrud exerci tation ullamcorper suscipit lobortis nisl ut aliquip ex ea commodo consequat.

Duis autem vel eum iriure dolor in hendrerit in vulputate velit esse molestie consequat, vel illum dolore eu feugiat nulla facilisis at vero eros et accumsan et iusto odio dignissim qui blandit praesent luptatum zzril delenit augue duis dolore te feugait nulla facilisi.

Lorem ipsum dolor sit amet, consectetuer adipiscing elit, sed diam nonummy nibh euismod tincidunt ut laoreet dolore magna aliquam erat volutpat.

Ut wisi enim ad minim veniam, quis nostrud exerci tation ullamcorper suscipit lobortis nisl ut aliquip ex ea commodo consequat. Duis autem vel eum iriure dolor in hendrerit in vulputate velit esse molestie consequat, vel illum dolore eu feugiat nulla facilisis at vero eros et accumsan et iusto odio dignissim qui blandit praesent luptatum zzril delenit augue duis dolore te feugait nulla facilisi.

This story is also important

Nam liber tempor cum soluta nobis eleifend option congue nihil imperdiet doming id quod mazim placerat facer possim assum. Lorem ipsum dolor sit amet, consectetuer adipiscing elit, sed diam nonummy nibh euismod tincidunt ut laoreet dolore magna aliquam erat volutpat. Ut wisi enim ad minim veniam, quis nostrud exerci tation ullamcorper suscipit lobortis nisl ut aliquip ex ea commodo consequat.

Duis autem vel eum iriure dolor in hendrerit in vulputate velit esse molestie consequat, vel illum dolore eu feugiat nulla facilisis.

Lorem ipsum dolor sit amet, consect adipiscing elit, sed diam nonummy nibh euismod tincidunt ut laoreet dolore magna aliquam erat volutpat. Ut wisi enim ad minim veniam, quis nostrud exerci tation ullamcorper suscipit lobortis nisl ut aliquip ex ea commodo consequat.

Duis autem vel eum iriure dolor in hendrerit in vulputate velit esse molestie consequat, vel illum dolore eu feugiat nulla facilisis at vero eros et accumsan et iusto odio dignissim qui blandit praesent luptatum zzril delenit augue duis dolore te feugait nulla facilisi. Lorem ipsum dolor sit amet, consectetuer adipiscing elit, sed diam nonummy nibh euismod tincidunt ut laoreet dolore magna aliquam erat volutpat.

Ut wisi enim ad minim veniam, quis nostrud exerci tation ullamcorper suscipit lobortis nisl ut aliquip ex ea commodo.

And so is this one

Lorem ipsum dolor sit amet, consect adipiscing elit, sed diam nonummy nibh euismod tincidunt ut laoreet dolore magna aliquam erat volutpat. Ut wisi enim ad minim veniam, quis nostrud exerci tation ullamcorper suscipit lobortis nisl ut aliquip ex ea commodo consequat.

Duis autem vel eum iriure dolor in hendrerit in vulputate velit esse molestie consequat, vel illum dolore eu feugiat nulla facilisis at vero eros et accumsan et iusto odio dignissim qui blandit praesent luptatum zzril delenit augue duis dolore te feugait nulla facilisi. Lorem ipsum dolor sit amet, consectetuer adipiscing elit, sed diam nonummy nibh euismod tincidunt ut laoreet dolore magna aliquam erat volutpat.

Ut wisi enim ad minim veniam, quis nostrud exerci tation ullamcorper.

Every story's as important as every other story

Lorem ipsum dolor sit amet, consect adipiscing elit, sed diam nonummy nibh euismod tincidunt ut laoreet dolore magna aliquam erat volutpat. Ut wisi enim ad minim veniam, quis nostrud exerci tation ullamcorper suscipit lobortis nisl ut aliquip ex ea commodo consequat.

Lorem ipsum dolor sit amet, consect adipiscing elit, sed diam nonummy nibh euismod tincidunt ut laoreet dolore magna aliquam erat volutpat. Ut wisi enim ad minim veniam, quis nostrud exerci tation ullamcorper suscipit lobortis nisl ut aliquip ex ea commodo consequat.

Duis autem vel eum iriure dolor in hendrerit in vulputate velit esse molestie consequat, vel illum dolore eu feugiat nulla facilisis at vero eros et accumsan et iusto odio dignissim qui blandit praesent luptatum zzril delenit augue duis dolore te feugait nulla facilisi. Lorem ipsum dolor sit amet, consectetuer adipiscing elit, sed diam nonummy nibh euismod tincidunt ut laoreet dolore magna aliquam erat volutpat.

Ut wisi enim ad minim veniam, quis nostrud exerci tation ullamcorper suscipit lobortis nisl ut aliquip ex ea commodo consequat. Duis autem vel eum iriure dolor in hendrerit in vulputate velit esse molestie consequat, vel illum dolore eu feugiat nulla facilisis at vero eros et accumsan et iusto odio dignissim qui blandit praesent luptatum zzril delenit augue duis dolore te feugait facilisi.Duis autem vel eum iriure dolor in hendrerit in vulputate velit esse molestie consequat, vel illum dolore eu feugiat nulla facilisis at vero eros et accumsan et iusto odio dignissim qui blandit luptatum zzril delenit augue duis dolore te feugait nulla facilisi. Lorem ipsum dolor amet, consectetuer adipiscing elit, sed diam nonummy nibh euismod tincidunt ut laoreet dolore magna aliquam erat volutpat.

Ut wisi enim ad minim veniam, quis nostrud exerci tation ullamcorper suscipit lobortis nisl ut aliquip ex ea commodo consequat. Duis autem vel eum iriure dolor in hendrerit in vulputate velit esse molestie consequat, vel illum dolore eu feugiat nulla facilisis

No distinctions

Ut wisi enim ad minim veniam, quis nostrud exerci tation ullamcorper suscipit lobortis nisl ut aliquip ex ea commodo consequat. Duis autem vel eum iriure dolor in hendrerit in vulputate velit esse molestie consequat, at vero eros et accumsan et iusto odio dignissim qui praesent luptatum zzril delenit augue duis dolore te feugait nulla facilisi.

Nam liber tempor cum soluta nobis eleifend option congue nihil imperdiet doming id quod mazim placerat facer possim assum. Lorem ipsum dolor sit amet, consectetuer adipiscing elit, sed diam nonummy nibh euismod tincidunt nisl ut aliquip ex ea commodo consequat.vel illum dolore eu feugiat nulla facilisis at vero eros et accumsan et iusto odio dignissim qui blandit praesent luptatum zzril delenit augue duis dolore te feugait nulla facilisi nam liber tempor soluta.

Nam liber tempor cum soluta nobis eleifend option congue nihil imperdiet domin.

Our movie critic rates "Jaws 6"—see page 12

THE BIG NEWS

Dow Jones dips again—see the Financial Section

A story of minor interest

Lorem ipsum dolor sit amet, consect adipiscing elit, sed diam nonummy nibh euismod tincidunt ut laoreet dolore magna aliquam erat volutpat. Ut wisi enim ad minim veniam, quis nostrud exerci tation ullamcorper suscipit lobortis nisl ut aliquip ex ea commodo consequat.

Duis autem vel eum iriure dolor in hendrerit in vulputate velit esse molestie consequat, vel illum dolore eu feugiat nulla facilisis at vero eros et accumsan et iusto odio dignissim qui blandit luptatum zzril delenit augue duis dolore te feugait nulla facilisi. Lorem ipsum dolor sit amet, consectet adipiscing elit, sed diam nonummy nibh euismod tincidunt ut laoreet dolore magna aliquam erat volutpat.

Ut wisi enim ad minim veniam, quis nostrud exerci tation ullamcorper suscipit lobortis nisl ut aliquip ex ea commodo consequat. Duis autem vel eum iriure dolor in hendrerit in vulputate velit esse molestie consequat, vel illum dolore eu feugiat nulla facilisis at vero eros et accumsan et iusto odio dignissim qui blandit praesent luptatum zzril delenit augue duis dolore te feugait nulla facilisi.

Duis autem vel eum iriure dolor in hendrerit in vulputate velit esse molestie consequat, vel illum dolore eu feugiat nulla facilisis.

Pressed for time? Then skip this story

Nam liber tempor cum soluta nobis eleifend option congue nihil imperdiet doming id quod mazim placerat facer possim assum. Lorem ipsum dolor sit amet, consectetuer adipiscing elit, sed diam nonummy nibh euismod tincidunt ut laoreet dolore magna aliquam erat volutpat. Ut wisi enim ad minim veniam, quis nostrud exerci tation ullamcorper suscipit lobortis nisl ut aliquip ex ea commodo consequat.

Duis autem vel eum iriure dolor in hendrerit in vulputate velit esse molestie consequat, vel illum dolore eu feugiat nulla facilisis quis nostrud exerci.

Lorem ipsum dolor sit amet, consect adipiscing elit, sed diam nonummy nibh euismod tincidunt ut laoreet dolore magna aliquam erat volutpat. Ut wisi enim ad minim veniam, quis nostrud exerci tation ullamcorper suscipit lobortis nisl ut aliquip ex ea commodo consequat.

Duis autem vel eum iriure dolor in hendrerit in vulputate velit esse molestie consequat, vel illum dolore eu feugiat nulla facilisis at vero eros et accumsan et iusto odio dignissim qui blandit luptatum zzril delenit augue duis dolore te feugait nulla facilisi. Lorem ipsum dolor sit amet, consecte adipiscing elit, sed diam nonummy nibh euismod ut laoreet dolore magna aliquam erat volutpat dolore eu feugiat nulla facilisis.

Important stories get pushed down inexplicably

Lorem ipsum dolor sit amet, consect adipiscing elit, sed diam nonummy nibh euismod tincidunt ut laoreet dolore magna aliquam erat volutpat. Ut wisi enim ad minim veniam, quis nostrud exerci tation ullamcorper suscipit lobortis nisl ut aliquip ex ea commodo consequat.

Duis autem vel eum iriure dolor in hendrerit in vulputate velit esse molestie consequat, vel illum dolore eu feugiat nulla facilisis at vero eros et accumsan et iusto odio dignissim qui blandit. Lorem ipsum dolor sit amet, consecte adipiscing elit, sed diam nonummy nibh euismod ut laoreet dolore magna aliquam erat volutpat dolore eu feugiat nulla facilisis feugait nulla facilisi.

THE TOP STORY

Lorem ipsum dolor sit amet, consect adipiscing elit, sed diam nonummy nibh euismod tincidunt ut laoreet dolore magna aliquam erat volutpat. Ut wisi enim ad minim veniam, quis nostrud exerci tation ullamcorper suscipit lobortis nisl ut aliquip ex ea commodo consequat.

Lorem ipsum dolor sit amet, consect adipiscing elit, sed diam nonummy nibh euismod tincidunt ut laoreet dolore magna aliquam erat volutpat. Ut wisi enim ad minim veniam, quis nostrud exerci tation ullamcorper suscipit lobortis nisl ut aliquip ex ea commodo consequat.

Duis autem vel eum iriure dolor in hendrerit in vulputate velit esse molestie consequat, vel illum dolore eu feugiat nulla facilisis at vero eros et accumsan et iusto odio dignissim qui blandit praesent luptatum zzril delenit augue duis dolore te feugait nulla facilisi. Lorem ipsum dolor sit amet, consectetuer adipiscing elit, sed diam nonummy nibh euismod tincidunt ut laoreet dolore magna aliquam erat volutpat.

Ut wisi enim ad minim veniam, quis nostrud exerci tation ullamcorper suscipit lobortis nisl ut aliquip ex ea commodo consequat. Duis autem vel eum iriure dolor in hendrerit in vulputate velit esse molestie consequat, vel illum dolore eu feugiat nulla facilisis at vero eros et accumsan et iusto odio dignissim qui blandit praesent luptatum zzril delenit augue duis dolore te feugait facilisi.Duis autem vel eum iriure dolor in hendrerit in vulputate velit esse molestie consequat, vel illum dolore eu feugiat nulla facilisis at vero eros et accumsan et iusto odio dignissim qui blandit luptatum zzril delenit augue duis dolore te feugait nulla facilisi. Lorem ipsum dolor amet, consectetuer adipiscing elit, sed diam nonummy nibh euismod tincidunt ut laoreet dolore magna aliquam erat volutpat.

Ut wisi enim ad minim veniam, quis nostrud exerci tation ullamcorper suscipit lobortis nisl ut aliquip ex ea commodo consequat. Duis autem vel eum iriure dolor in hendrerit in vulputate velit esse molestie consequat, vel illum dolore eu feugiat nulla facilisis

This story is important

Ut wisi enim ad minim veniam, quis nostrud exerci tation ullamcorper suscipit lobortis nisl ut aliquip ex ea commodo consequat. Duis autem vel eum iriure dolor in hendrerit in vulputate velit esse molestie consequat, at vero eros et accumsan et iusto odio dignissim qui praesent luptatum zzril delenit augue duis dolore te feugait nulla facilisi.

Nam liber tempor cum soluta nobis eleifend option congue nihil imperdiet doming id quod mazim placerat facer possim assum. Lorem ipsum dolor sit amet, consectetuer adipiscing elit, sed diam nonummy nibh euismod tincidunt nisl ut aliquip ex ea commodo consequat.vel illum dolore eu feugiat nulla facilisis at vero eros et accumsan et iusto odio dignissim qui blandit praesent luptatum zzril delenit augue duis dolore te feugait nulla facilisi nam liber tempor soluta.

Nam liber tempor cum soluta nobis eleifend option congue nihil imperdiet domin et iusto odio dignissim qui blandit luptatum zzril delenit augue duis dolore te feugait nulla.

Photographs

Newspapers must accommodate a wide variety of photographs of differing size and degree of importance.

In a typical newspaper, the front page alone often contains more photos than are found in an entire newsletter issue.

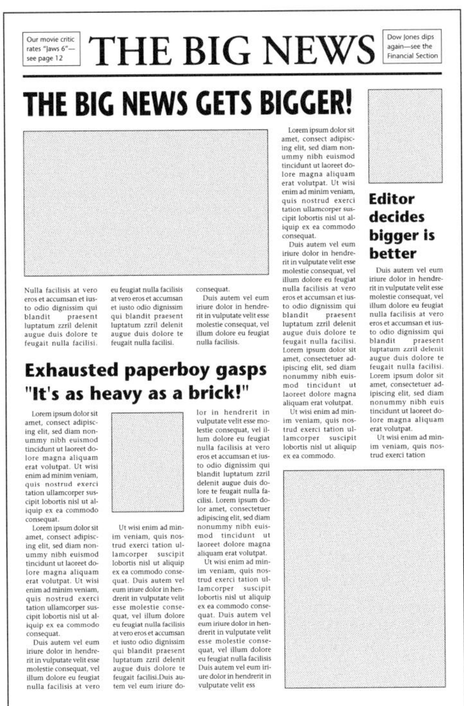

Our movie critic rates "Jaws 6"—see page 12

THE BIG NEWS

Dow Jones dips again—see the Financial Section

THE BIG NEWS GETS BIGGER!

Nulla facilisis at vero eros et accumsan et iusto odio dignissim qui blandit praesent luptatum zzril delenit augue duis dolore te feugait nulla facilisi. eu feugiat nulla facilisis at vero eros et accumsan et iusto odio dignissim qui blandit praesent luptatum zzril delenit augue duis dolore te feugait nulla facilisi. consequat.

Duis autem vel eum iriure dolor in hendrerit in vulputate velit esse molestie consequat, vel illum dolore eu feugiat nulla facilisis.

Lorem ipsum dolor sit amet, consect adipiscing elit, sed diam nonummy nibh euismod tincidunt ut laoreet dolore magna aliquam erat volutpat. Ut wisi enim ad minim veniam, quis nostrud exerci tation ullamcorper suscipit lobortis nisl ut aliquip ex ea commodo consequat.

Duis autem vel eum iriure dolor in hendrerit in vulputate velit esse molestie consequat, vel illum dolore eu feugiat nulla facilisis at vero eros et accumsan et iusto odio dignissim qui blandit praesent luptatum zzril delenit augue duis dolore te feugait nulla facilisi. Lorem ipsum dolor sit amet, consectetuer adipiscing elit, sed diam nonummy nibh euismod tincidunt ut laoreet dolore magna aliquam erat volutpat.

Ut wisi enim ad minim veniam, quis nostrud exerci tation ullamcorper suscipit lobortis nisl ut aliquip ex ea commodo.

Editor decides bigger is better

Duis autem vel eum iriure dolor in hendrerit in vulputate velit esse molestie consequat, vel illum dolore eu feugiat nulla facilisis at vero eros et accumsan et iusto odio dignissim qui blandit praesent luptatum zzril delenit augue duis dolore te feugait nulla facilisi. Lorem ipsum dolor sit amet, consectetuer adipiscing elit, sed diam nonummy nibh euis tincidunt ut laoreet dolore magna aliquam erat volutpat.

Ut wisi enim ad minim veniam, quis nostrud exerci tation

Exhausted paperboy gasps "It's as heavy as a brick!"

Lorem ipsum dolor sit amet, consect adipiscing elit, sed diam nonummy nibh euismod tincidunt ut laoreet dolore magna aliquam erat volutpat. Ut wisi enim ad minim veniam, quis nostrud exerci tation ullamcorper suscipit lobortis nisl ut aliquip ex ea commodo consequat.

Lorem ipsum dolor sit amet, consect adipiscing elit, sed diam nonummy nibh euismod tincidunt ut laoreet dolore magna aliquam erat volutpat. Ut wisi enim ad minim veniam, quis nostrud exerci tation ullamcorper suscipit lobortis nisl ut aliquip ex ea commodo consequat.

Duis autem vel eum iriure dolor in hendrerit in vulputate velit esse molestie consequat, vel illum dolore eu feugiat nulla facilisis at vero

Ut wisi enim ad minim veniam, quis nostrud exerci tation ullamcorper suscipit lobortis nisl ut aliquip ex ea commodo consequat. Duis autem vel eum iriure dolor in hendrerit in vulputate velit esse molestie consequat, vel illum dolore eu feugiat nulla facilisis at vero eros et accumsan et iusto odio dignissim qui blandit praesent luptatum zzril delenit augue duis dolore te feugait facilisi.Duis autem vel eum iriure dolor in hendrerit in vulputate velit esse molestie consequat, vel illum dolore eu feugiat nulla facilisis at vero eros et accumsan et iusto odio dignissim qui blandit luptatum zzril delenit augue duis dolore te feugait nulla facilisi. Lorem ipsum dolor amet, consectetuer adipiscing elit, sed diam nonummy nibh euismod tincidunt ut laoreet dolore magna aliquam erat volutpat.

Ut wisi enim ad minim veniam, quis nostrud exerci tation ullamcorper suscipit lobortis nisl ut aliquip ex ea commodo consequat. Duis autem vel eum iriure dolor in hendrerit in vulputate velit esse molestie consequat, vel illum dolore eu feugiat nulla facilisis Duis autem vel eum iriure dolor in hendrerit in vulputate velit ess

Arrange multiple photographs so that each is placed appropriately in relation to the others and to the page design as a whole. Also, be on the lookout for embarrassing juxtapositions if a photo must appear between two articles. The reader should not have to guess which article the photo is meant to accompany. A picture of the President, for instance, should not inadvertently appear alongside an article about an arrested felon.

Whereas most newsletter photographs are usually simple head shots, newspaper photos include a variety of subjects, shapes, and sizes. Like headlines, the relative size of a photo should be indicative of its importance.

Teasers

Because of a newspaper's greater size and complexity, it's even more important to provide front-page teasers to attract readers to the inside.

Attention must be drawn to special features and high-interest articles inside. Readers also want clear direction to specific items such as classified listings, calendars of events, and other sections.

Our movie critic rates "Jaws 6"—see page 12

THE BIG NEWS

Dow Jones dips again—see the Financial Section

THE BIG NEWS GETS BIGGER!

More of what you like

Exhausted paperboy gasps "It's as heavy as a brick!"

Price gets bigger too

WEATHER

Ut wisi enim ad minim veniam, quis nostrud exerci tation ullamcorper suscipit lobortis nisl ut aliquip ex ea commodo consequat. Duis autem vel eum iriure dolor in hendrerit in vulputate velit esse molestie consequat, at vero eros et accumsan et iusto odio dignissim qui praesent luptatum zzril delenit augue duis dolore te feugait nulla facilisi.

WHAT'S INSIDE			
Bridge	C-5	Lifestyles	E-6
Business	B-6	Markets	A-7
Classifieds	D-5	Movies	A-12
Comics	C-3	Obituaries	B-5
Crossword	C-5	Sports	G-1
Editorials	B-4	Stocks	F-2
Finance	F-1	Weather	A-1
Humor	E-5	World News	A-2

Keep teasers brief; front-page space is too precious to use extravagantly. Don't, for instance, put the entire weather report on the front page. Instead, merely supply a short summary and list the section and page number where the full report can be found.

Article Jumplines

Another peculiarity of newspapers is the large number of articles continued on inside pages.

Long articles are often broken into several segments placed on subsequent pages. Each segment requires jumplines to help the reader locate the continuation. This presents a challenge to the designer. Jumplines must be easily noticed, but also easily distinguished from headlines and subheads.

Article doesn't quite fit

Ut wisi enim ad minim veniam, quis nostrud exerci tation ullamcorper suscipit lobortis nisl ut aliquip ex ea commodo consequat. Duis autem vel eum iriure dolor in hendrerit in vulputate velit esse molestie consequat, at vero eros et accumsan et iusto odio dignissim qui praesent luptatum zzril delenit augue duis dolore te feugait nulla facilisi.

Nam liber tempor cum soluta nobis eleifend option congue nihil imperdiet doming id quod mazim placerat facer possim assum. Lorem ipsum dolor sit amet, consectetuer adipiscing elit, sed diam nonummy nibh euismod tincidunt nisl ut aliquip ex ea commodo consequat.vel illum dolore eu feugiat nulla facilisis at vero eros et accumsan et iusto odio dignissim qui blandit praesent luptatum zzril delenit augue duis dolore te feugait nulla facilisi nam liber tempor soluta.

Nam liber tempor cum soluta nobis eleifend optional congue nihil imperdiet domin. Duis autem vel iriurent

(Continued on p. 7)

Advertisements

Advertising is a necessary ingredient and, in fact, pays the bills for most newspapers.

It's often impossible to be sure of the number and sizes of advertisements you'll run until the last minute. Many newspapers adhere to the specifications of the Standard Advertising Units to simplify page makeup (check this with your local newspaper). These include a variety of standard ad sizes that can be used as building blocks in assembling pages.

It's a good idea to use a mix of advertisements and editorial material in your pages, to ensure that ads get noticed. Many readers will automatically bypass a page that contains ads only. If you can, though, keep editorial material together on a page. A checkerboard of advertisements and articles will frustrate readers.

For more about design and placement of advertisements, see Chapter 8.

Evaluation Checklist

Each of the chapters in this section will end with a list of questions. Pose these questions to yourself after you've completed a first draft of your publication. They will help you spot problem areas.

Newsletters

- Is your newsletter's nameplate distinctive? Does it identify subject matter and editorial focus in any way?
- Are volume numbers, issue numbers, and dates clearly identified?
- Do headlines compete with the nameplate or with each other?

- Is the source of your newsletter clearly identified by a logo, address, and telephone information?
- Is there a table of contents or some other form of teaser which directs the reader's attention inside?
- Are articles clearly separated from each other?
- Will it be possible to use the basic design for this newsletter in future issues?

Tabloids And Newspapers

- Does the front page include teasers to invite readers inside?
- Are headlines and photos sized and placed with their relative importance in mind?
- Can readers quickly locate article continuations on inside pages?
- Is the same column structure used throughout the publication?
- Does the back cover induce readers to examine the rest of the publication?

Advertisements 8

Design flexibility and pragmatism are important ingredients in effective advertisements.

Good design is particularly crucial in advertising, for the ironic reason that most viewers are content to ignore advertisements. Few media have such a built-in reluctance on the part of the reader. It requires that ads be visually striking, even flashy, to attract attention.

Unfortunately, flashiness does not always lend itself to good organization. Poorly organized ads—many of them quite attractive—abound. They succeed in attracting attention but fail to promote any awareness of the product. Here are just a few of the things that can go wrong:

- *Too many focal points.* The best ads have one dominant visual element. Readers forced to divide their attention will probably lose attention instead.
- *No integration of text and visuals.* An isolated visual may make readers look, but it won't cause them to read seemingly unrelated headlines and body copy. Make sure your headlines tie in with your visual elements and the eye travels a logical path when moving from picture to headline to copy. If the path seems haphazard, the ad needs restructuring.
- *Missing information.* Once you've hooked your readers, don't frustrate them by withholding crucial information. If the size of the ad precludes giving all the necessary information, include instructions for finding out more.

You'll probably find that if you concentrate on organization in your ads, the problem of visual interest will take care of itself. Well-arranged graphics and text are inherent focal points.

Small Ads

Small ads must compete with other page elements for attention.

A small ad is any advertisement that takes up only a portion of a page. Small ads have a built-in limitation—they're forced to compete with adjacent material for the viewer's attention. The adjacent material can be copy, headlines, or other advertisements. There's no way for the ad designer to know in advance.

The placement of your ad is largely beyond your control, so you should try to design ads that work reasonably well in any placement. You can so test the effectiveness of your ad by printing it at actual size, cutting it out, and superimposing it against some sample pages from the target publication. Try different placements. In particular, place it over ads of identical size. Does it stand out or get overwhelmed by the rest of the page? Does it compare favorably or unfavorably to the other small ads? Don't expect your ad to "win"—that is, draw the reader's attention first—every time, or even a majority of the time. Remember, most readers consider ads a distraction. The operative question should be, is your ad good enough to compete? If most of the other advertisements are overshadowing it, the answer is no.

Grids

Use a grid to plan your advertisements.

Don't abandon the concept of a grid just because you're dealing with smaller blocks of space. Organization is still all-important. Grids will help you decide the correct position and proper amount of space for each element.

The first step is to create a flexible grid. In the sample grid below, a standard vertical rectangle has been divided into 6 columns, with each column divided into 13 equal units.

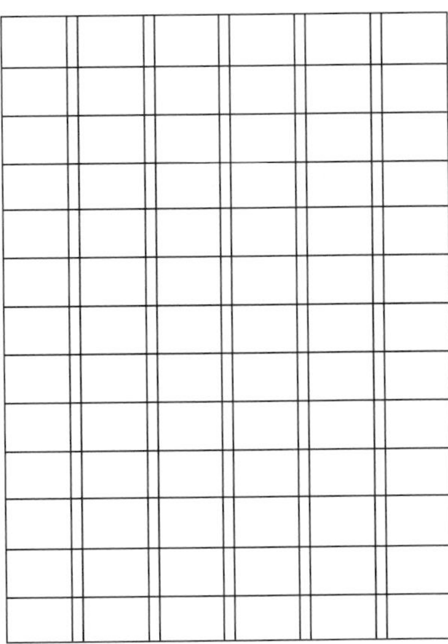

Err on the side of elaborateness when constructing your grid. Obviously, a quarter-page ad will not contain six text columns, but overdividing the space keeps your options open. The actual ad might contain three equal columns two units wide; two columns three units wide; one column four units wide, flanked by an empty column on each side—the list of possibilities is endless. A two-column grid, on the other hand, offers an extremely finite set of possible arrangements.

From the grid shown, a number of ways to mix text and graphics are possible. For example, you can divide the space from top to bottom into four areas: a two-unit-high headline area extending across the top of the page; below that, an area for visuals also extending the width of the page; then, three two-column-wide text blocks four units high, and at the bottom of the page, a two-unit-high response area. The response area would contain your firm's logo, address, and, perhaps, a coupon.

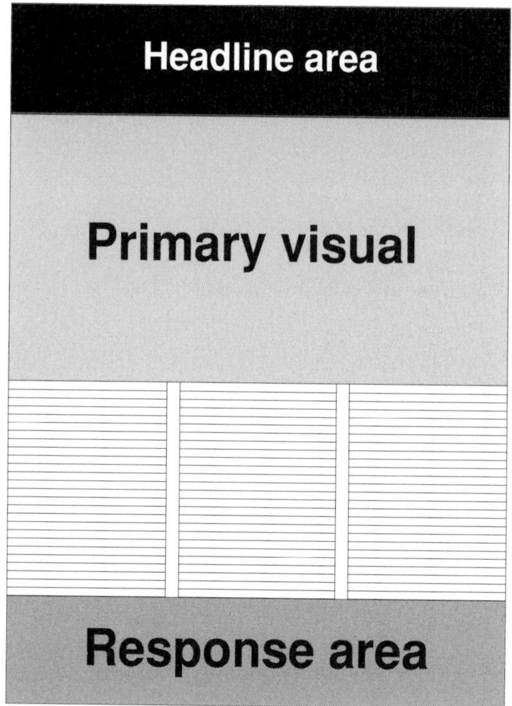

Simple sketches such as the one shown here can help you choose promising possibilities without having to perform the actual layouts.

If you have an idea of what the content of your ad will be, use that knowledge to refine your grid. For example, if your primary visual is meant to set a certain tone rather than depict a product, you might want it to appear before the headline.

If your intended primary visual is vertically oriented, your arrangement should be adjusted accordingly.

Primary visual

Headline area

Response area

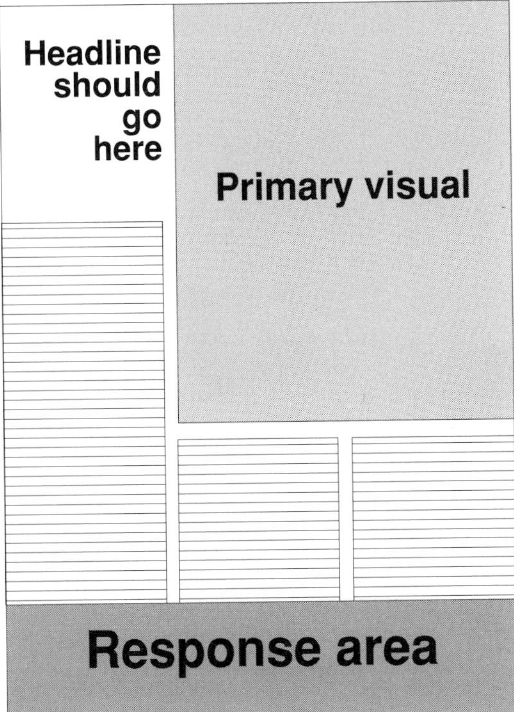

Likewise, if you intend to use several visual elements, make room for them in your grid. The combination of a large *atmosphere*—or *premise*—photograph, a column of premise copy, and a row of product photos with prices can make for an interesting design.

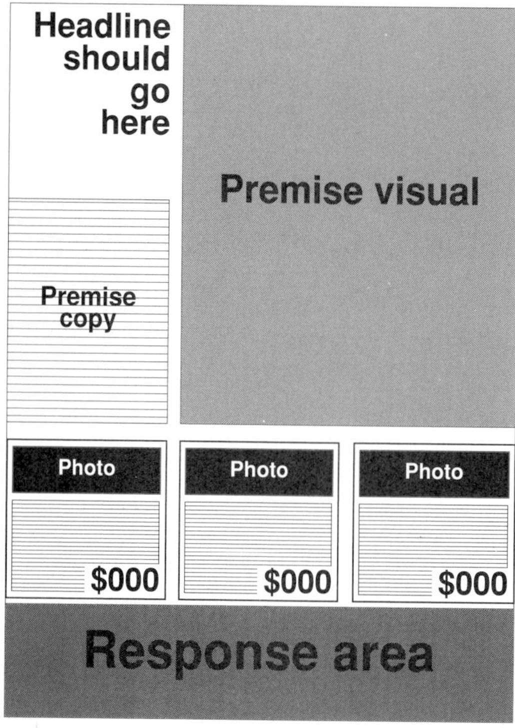

Once you've settled upon a satisfactory grid, the actual layout process becomes very straightforward.

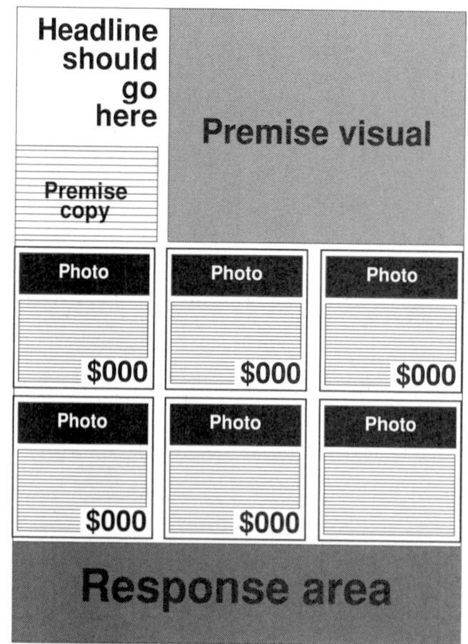

Templates For Small Ads

Templates can save you time and effort when designing small ads.

Create and save ad templates for various sizes (half-page, one-third-page, quarter-page, and so forth) to save yourself time. Design all of them to reflect a strong family resemblance, with consistent treatments of headlines, borders, artwork, and buying information. Besides making the design process easier, templates will promote reader recognition—your ads will become more noticeable through familiarity.

Borders

Strong borders separate your advertisement from the page elements that surround it.

A strong border can keep your ad from blending into its surroundings. The type of border you choose will often be determined by the shape of the ad. A vertically oriented ad should generally have strong top and bottom rules.

Fetter's Office Cleaning Service
We clean more offices than anyone else in the metropolitan area—and there's a reason we're so popular. In the dirty world of business, you don't want to trust your work area to just anyone. Give us a call.
(417) C•L•E•A•N•U•P

Generally, the smaller the advertisement, the thinner your rules should be. Small text-based ads in thick boxes aren't very effective—the border eclipses the text rather than frames it.

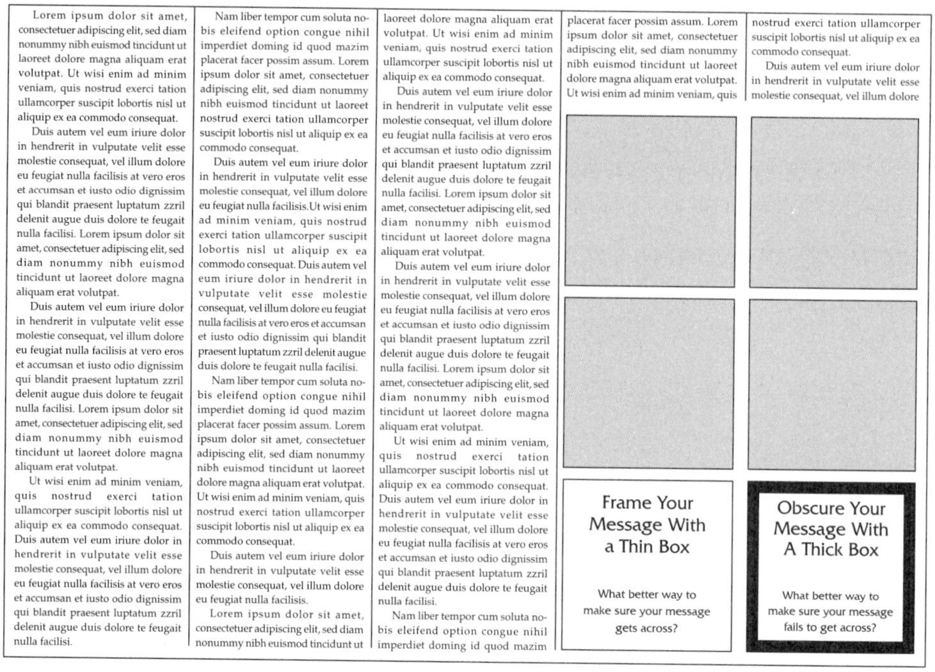

Lorem ipsum dolor sit amet, consectetuer adipiscing elit, sed diam nonummy nibh euismod tincidunt ut laoreet dolore magna aliquam erat volutpat. Ut wisi enim ad minim veniam, quis nostrud exerci tation ullamcorper suscipit lobortis nisl ut aliquip ex ea commodo consequat.

Duis autem vel eum iriure dolor in hendrerit in vulputate velit esse molestie consequat, vel illum dolore eu feugiat nulla facilisis at vero eros et accumsan et iusto odio dignissim qui blandit praesent luptatum zzril delenit augue duis dolore te feugait nulla facilisi. Lorem ipsum dolor sit amet, consectetuer adipiscing elit, sed diam nonummy nibh euismod tincidunt ut laoreet dolore magna aliquam erat volutpat.

Duis autem vel eum iriure dolor in hendrerit in vulputate velit esse molestie consequat, vel illum dolore eu feugiat nulla facilisis at vero eros et accumsan et iusto odio dignissim qui blandit praesent luptatum zzril delenit augue duis dolore te feugait nulla facilisi. Lorem ipsum dolor sit amet, consectetuer adipiscing elit, sed diam nonummy nibh euismod tincidunt ut laoreet dolore magna aliquam erat volutpat.

Ut wisi enim ad minim veniam, quis nostrud exerci tation ullamcorper suscipit lobortis nisl ut aliquip ex ea commodo consequat. Duis autem vel eum iriure dolor in hendrerit in vulputate velit esse molestie consequat, vel illum dolore eu feugiat nulla facilisis at vero eros et accumsan et iusto odio dignissim qui blandit praesent luptatum zzril delenit augue duis dolore te feugait nulla facilisi.

Nam liber tempor cum soluta nobis eleifend option congue nihil imperdiet doming id quod mazim placerat facer possim assum. Lorem ipsum dolor sit amet, consectetuer adipiscing elit, sed diam nonummy nibh euismod tincidunt ut laoreet nostrud exerci tation ullamcorper suscipit lobortis nisl ut aliquip ex ea commodo consequat.

Duis autem vel eum iriure dolor in hendrerit in vulputate velit esse molestie consequat, vel illum dolore eu feugiat nulla facilisis.Ut wisi enim ad minim veniam, quis nostrud exerci tation ullamcorper suscipit lobortis nisl ut aliquip ex ea commodo consequat. Duis autem vel eum iriure dolor in hendrerit in vulputate velit esse molestie consequat, vel illum dolore eu feugiat nulla facilisis at vero eros et accumsan et iusto odio dignissim qui blandit praesent luptatum zzril delenit augue duis dolore te feugait nulla facilisi.

Nam liber tempor cum soluta nobis eleifend option congue nihil imperdiet doming id quod mazim placerat facer possim assum. Lorem ipsum dolor sit amet, consectetuer adipiscing elit, sed diam nonummy nibh euismod tincidunt ut laoreet dolore magna aliquam erat volutpat. Ut wisi enim ad minim veniam, quis nostrud exerci tation ullamcorper suscipit lobortis nisl ut aliquip ex ea commodo consequat.

Duis autem vel eum iriure dolor in hendrerit in vulputate velit esse molestie consequat, vel illum dolore eu feugiat nulla facilisis.

Lorem ipsum dolor sit amet, consectetuer adipiscing elit, sed diam nonummy nibh euismod tincidunt ut laoreet dolore magna aliquam erat volutpat. Ut wisi enim ad minim veniam, quis nostrud exerci tation ullamcorper suscipit lobortis nisl ut aliquip ex ea commodo consequat.

Duis autem vel eum iriure dolor in hendrerit in vulputate velit esse molestie consequat, vel illum dolore eu feugiat nulla facilisis at vero eros et accumsan et iusto odio dignissim qui blandit praesent luptatum zzril delenit augue duis dolore te feugait nulla facilisi. Lorem ipsum dolor sit amet, consectetuer adipiscing elit, sed diam nonummy nibh euismod tincidunt ut laoreet dolore magna aliquam erat volutpat.

Duis autem vel eum iriure dolor in hendrerit in vulputate velit esse molestie consequat, vel illum dolore eu feugiat nulla facilisis at vero eros et accumsan et iusto odio dignissim qui blandit praesent luptatum zzril delenit augue duis dolore te feugait nulla facilisi. Lorem ipsum dolor sit amet, consectetuer adipiscing elit, sed diam nonummy nibh euismod tincidunt ut laoreet dolore magna aliquam erat volutpat.

Ut wisi enim ad minim veniam, quis nostrud exerci tation ullamcorper suscipit lobortis nisl ut aliquip ex ea commodo consequat. Duis autem vel eum iriure dolor in hendrerit in vulputate velit esse molestie consequat, vel illum dolore eu feugiat nulla facilisis at vero eros et accumsan et iusto odio dignissim qui blandit praesent luptatum zzril delenit augue duis dolore te feugait nulla facilisi.

Nam liber tempor cum soluta nobis eleifend option congue nihil imperdiet doming id quod mazim placerat facer possim assum. Lorem ipsum dolor sit amet, consectetuer adipiscing elit, sed diam nonummy nibh euismod tincidunt ut laoreet dolore magna aliquam erat volutpat. Ut wisi enim ad minim veniam, quis nostrud exerci tation ullamcorper suscipit lobortis nisl ut aliquip ex ea commodo consequat.

Duis autem vel eum iriure dolor in hendrerit in vulputate velit esse molestie consequat, vel illum dolore

Frame Your Message With a Thin Box

What better way to make sure your message gets across?

Obscure Your Message With A Thick Box

What better way to make sure your message fails to get across?

You can also define borders with backgrounds. Often, this type of border supplies enough visual interest to make additional visuals unnecessary; a simple centered headline might be enough to get the reader's attention.

Come to Grumper's Furniture and see some real wild stuff.

White Space

Use white space to further isolate and highlight your advertisement.

White space is chronically underused in the world of design, particularly in newspapers. This makes white space a powerful tool in advertising—an ad that uses white space liberally is a novelty, and novelties tend to get noticed.

One way to include white space in your design is to place the borders of your ad within the allotted space. The resulting border of white space will clearly separate your ad from its neighbors.

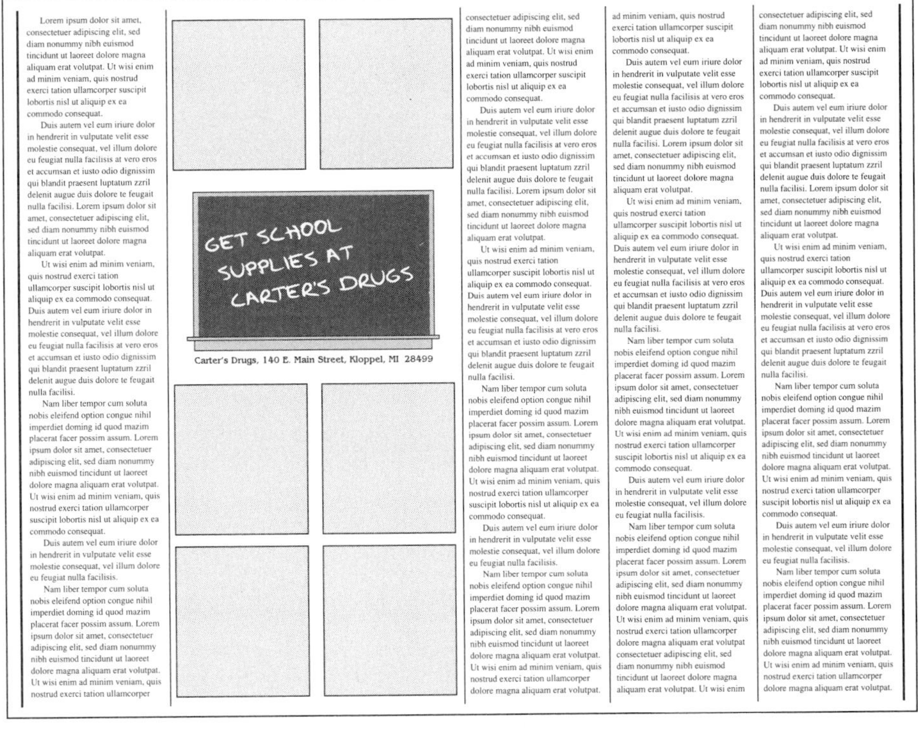

You can make small ads look larger by letting part of the ad break through the border, into the surrounding white space.

White space within ads can be created by using a multicolumn grid, indenting body copy, and allowing headlines to begin in the vertical band of white space to the left of the ad.

We're not just a bunch of dim bulbs.

Lorem ipsum dolor sit amet, adipiscing elit, sed diam nonummy nibh euismod tincidunt ut laoreet dolore magna aliquam erat volutpat. Ut wisi enim ad minim veniam, quis nostrud exerci tation ullamcorper suscipit lobortis nisl ut aliquip ex ea commodo consequat.

Duis autem vel eum iriure dolor in hendrerit in vulputate velit molestie consequat, vel illum dolore eu feugiat nulla facilisis at vero eros et accumsan et iusto odio dignissim qui blandit praesent luptatum zzril delenit augue duis dolore te feugait nulla facilisi.

Lorem ipsum dolor sit amet, elit, sed diam nonummy nibh euimod tincidunt ut laoreet dolore magna aliquam erat volupat. Ut wisi enim ad minim veniam.

Headlines

Headlines should be designed to draw attention.

In most small ads, the headline should be the dominant element. You'll want to set it at a large size and use a distinctive typeface.

Reversed type can be used to draw attention to your headline.

Everything Must Go!

After 40 years of serving the Van Nuys area, the Cobb-Hendricks Used Furniture Outlet is going out of business. Prices are dropping dramatically in an effort to empty our inventory. Our prices have never been this low! Beds, living room sets, dining room sets, sofas, chairs, and pianos are 50–70% off. So stop by and get a great deal on furniture—but hurry. After Wednesday, we'll just be a memory.

Cobb-Hendricks Used Furniture Outlet
3707 Siddown Avenue
Van Nuys, California 12345

Another effective technique is to place a dark-to-light gradient fill behind the headline and primary visual. The headline is set in reversed type, while the body text is black against a light background.

Plan Your Next Tropical Vacation

Lorem ipsum dolor sit amet, consectetuer adipiscing elit, sed diam nonummy nibh euismod tincidunt ut laoreet dolore magna aliquam erat volutpat. Ut wisi enim ad minim veniam, quis nostrud exerci tation ullamcorper suscipit lobortis nisl ut aliquip ex ea commodo consequat.

Duis autem vel eum iriure in hendrerit in vulputate velit esse molestie consequat, vel illum dolore eu feugiat nulla facilisis at vero ut wisi enim ad minim veniam, quis nostrud exerci tation ullamcorper suscipit lobortis nisl ut aliquip ex ea commodo consequat.

Autem vel eum hendrerit in vulputate velit esse molestie consequat, sed diam nonummy nibh euismod tincidunt.

Real World Travel
355 Roberson Way
Chapel Hill, NC 27516
919/944-3245

Choosing Headline Fonts

Find an interesting font to use for headline type. Avoid those printer-resident fonts like Times and Helvetica (or, if you're on a Windows platform, Times New Roman and Arial). They're okay for body text, but they don't have much character when set at large sizes. There are plenty of better choices, believe me! Explore your font menu. Because you're looking for headline type, examine each prospect at large sizes. You'll find that many typefaces that look generic when set as body text have real character when set at display size. If you can't find anything suitable, maybe it's time to do a little shopping. Fonts are cheap and plentiful these days—it's a worthwhile investment.

Headlines are often centered in newspaper ads, although that doesn't have to be the case. An alternate technique is to balance a strong flush-right headline with a smaller flush-left subhead. The headline can be catchy, to draw readers in, while the subhead can be more informative. (Anyone who's wrestled with the problem of making a single headline both catchy *and* informative will appreciate this technique.)

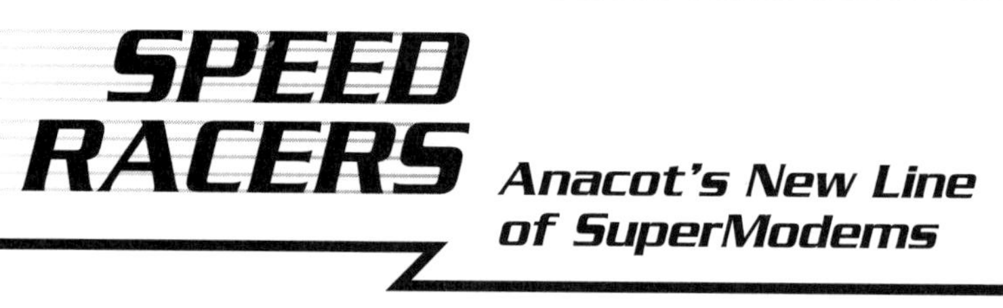

Screens

Screens add a two-color effect to your ads.

Using a screen within the border of your ad can prevent it from blending into a mostly white page. Screens also make good backdrops for black-and-white graphics.

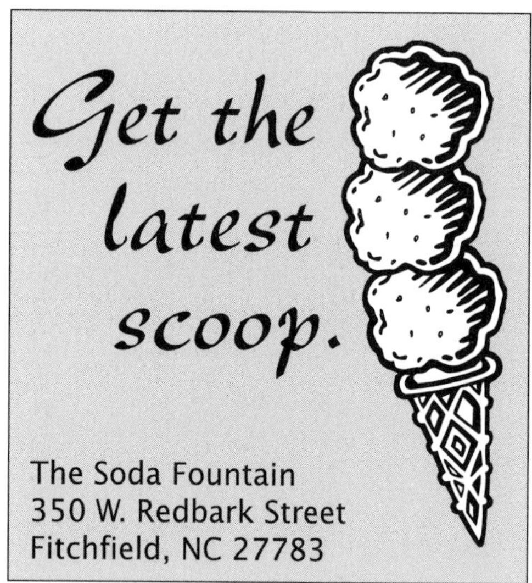

Buying Information And Prices

Use consistent type treatments for buying information and prices.

In general, the type size of a caption or price should be proportional to the size of the product illustration. Use large prices for large pictures and small prices for small pictures. However, you won't want to use a different type size for each product. Even the most product-filled ads need no more than a few type sizes. If you've got wildly varying sizes of artwork, try to divide the products into primary and secondary sets, and assign each set its own type sizes.

Remember that not every product advertised needs an illustration. Often, the best-looking ads simply list the available products, with a few representative photographs or drawings.

Logos And Contact Information

Advertisements should include all necessary purchasing information.

The logo of the firm running the ad should be prominent but not huge. Headlines and visuals should be proportionally larger. Logos will stand out well even at small sizes if surrounded by white space.

Clearly visible addresses, phone numbers, and other contact information make it easy for the reader to respond to the ad. You can use type size to indicate preferred modes of contact. If you'd rather receive phone calls than office visits, set the phone number in large, prominent type and the address in small, discreet type.

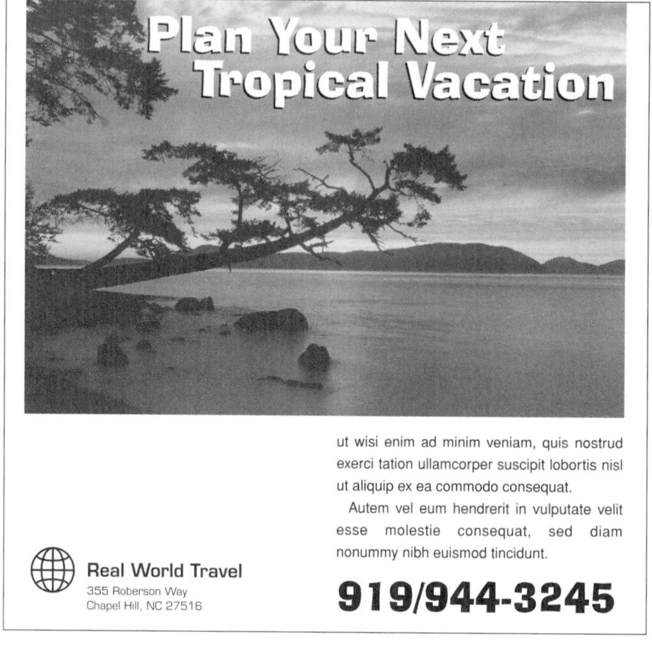

Small Ads In A Series

An increasingly popular trick is to create a series of similarly styled small ads and run them on successive pages of a publication, always in the same place. Although the ads should read well as a series, each individual ad should also function as a standalone item—just in case a reader notices one but not the others.

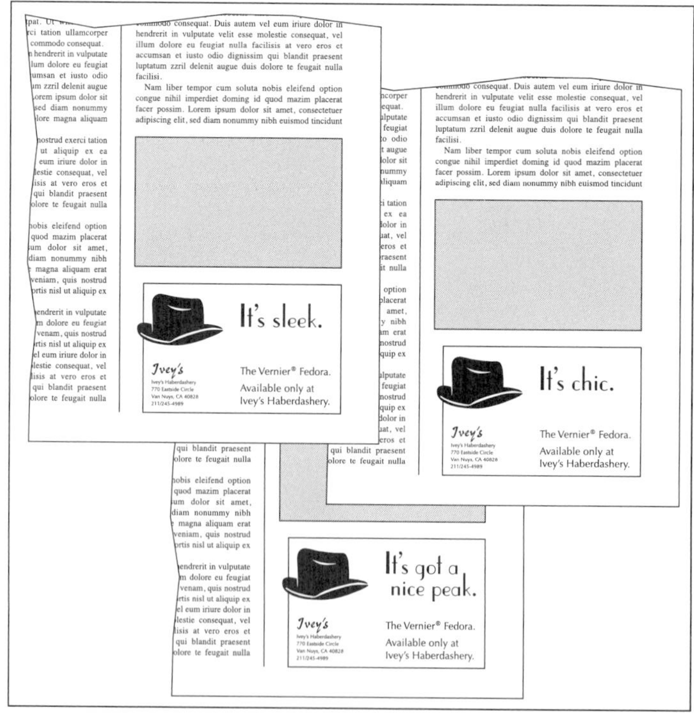

Full-Page Ads

From a design standpoint, there's no real difference between producing full-page ads and small ads. The same sorts of elements (headlines, copy, visuals, contact information) appear in both. However, full-page ads are generally more effective. They don't have to vie with adjacent material for the viewer's attention, so they're able to offer a more cohesive, complete message.

Now, before you ditch the small-ad concept entirely and sink your advertising budget into full-page ads, a few caveats. First of all, full-page ads are extremely expensive. For the same price as one full-page ad, you could run a small ad in several different publications. Although each individual small ad is less likely to be noticed, you could benefit dramatically from the increased circulation.

Second, you still don't have any control over what appears on the page *opposite* your ad. If it's another full-page ad, your reader may skip the entire spread after a single glance—most readers are interested in editorial content, not advertising.

Finally, it's important to remember that advertisements fail most often due to reader disinterest. It *helps* to have a prominent and well-designed ad, but even the most gorgeous ad for a new air conditioner is not going to tempt your average Siberian shopper. Before you shell out big bucks for a full-page ad, make sure that the target publication's demographic is made up of people who will probably be interested in your product. If there's no reason to expect good returns, you should probably be using small ads instead.

That said, it's difficult to ignore the power and effectiveness of a well-designed full page ad. They're particularly powerful in magazines, because the pages are trimmed on all four sides, and dramatic effects can be achieved with bleeds.

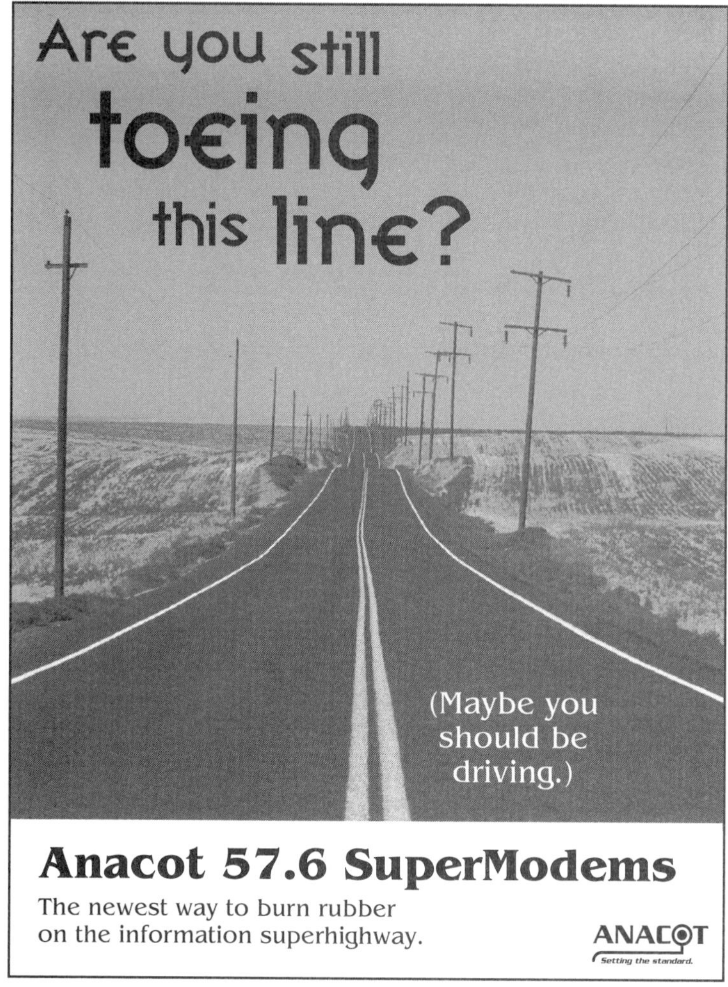

Classified Ads

Desktop publishing can produce attractive classified ads.

Often, advertisers don't realize they can submit their own camera-ready copy rather than leaving the ad preparation to the newspaper.

The addition of a strong, high-contrast headline and prominent border can make a big difference in the response you get to your help-wanted ad.

Because classified pages tend to be made up of gray space, the use of white space can be a real attention-getter. Indenting body copy creates strong vertical bands of white space around your ad.

A border can also add white space.

and originating its powers in such form, as to them shall seem most likely to effect their safety and happiness. Minimum.

DESKTOP PUBLISHING

Art/production person to help out three tired cowboys and one cowgirl who are working day and night to finish a graphic design book. Must have DTP experience, willing to work long hours, meet hot deadlines and like pizza. Must relocate to Denver, Colorado ASAP. Send resumé to *Laser Writing Inc.*, 20 W. Bond, Denver, CO 25982.

TRUTHSAYER. We hold these truths to be self evident, that all People are created equal, that they are endowed by their Creator with certain inalienable rights, that among these are Life, Liberty, and the Pursuit of Happiness.

NEW ASSISTANT KING. The history of the present King of Great Britain is a history of repeated injuries and usur-

We hold these truths to be self-evident, that all People are created equal, that they are endowed by their Creator with certain unalienable rights, that among these are Life, Liberty, and the Pursuit of Happiness. That to secure these rights, governments are instituted among Men and Women.

We hold these truths to be self-evident, that all People are created equal, that they are endowed by their Creator with certain unalienable rights, that among these are Life, Liberty, and the Pursuit of Happiness. That to secure these rights, governments are instituted among Men and Women.We hold these

SALES MANAGER

FOR EXPANDING COMPUTER SOFTWARE COMPANY

Supervisory or extensive retail experience required.

CALL TODAY!

1-800-333-4444

truths to be self-evident, that all People are created equal, that they are endowed by their Creator with certain unalienable rights, that among these are Life, Liberty, and the Pursuit of Happiness. That to secure these rights, governments are instituted among Men and Women.

We hold these truths to be self-evident, that all People are created equal, that they are endowed by their Creator with certain unalienable rights, that among these are Life, Liberty, and the Pursuit of Happiness. That to secure these rights, governments are instituted among Men and Women. We hold these truths to be self-evident.

LOREM IPSUM DOLOR

Consectetuer adipiscing elit, sed diam nonummy nibh euismod tincidunt ut laoreet dolore magna aliquam erat volutpat. Ut wisi enim ad minim veniam, quis nostrud exerci tation ullamcorper suscipit lobortis nisl ut aliquip ex ea commodo consequat.

DUIS AUTEM VEL EUM

Iriure dolor hendrerit vulputate velit esse molestie consequat, vel illum dolore eu feugiat nulla facilisis at vero eros et accumsan et iusto odio dignissim qui blandit praesent luptatum zzril delenit augue duis nostrud exerci tation ullamcorper suscipit dolor lobortis nisl ut aliquip commodo consequat et miriam.

A NEW HOUSE

3 bdrms., 2 bath, being offered by owners forced to relocate unexpectedly. Call 207/294-2428. No reasonable offer will be refused—we're desperate!

FACILIS ET VERO

Duis autem vel eum iriure dolor in hendrerit in vulputate velit esse moleste consequat, vel illum dolor eu feugiat nulla facilisis at veroros et accumsan et iusto dignisim qui blandit praesent luptatum zzril delenit augue duis dolore feugait nulla facilisi et suscipit lobortis.

CONSECTETUER ADIPISCING

Elit, sed diam nonummy nibh euismod tincidunt ut laoreet dolore magna aliquam volutpat. Ut wisi enim ad minim veniam, quis nostrud exerci tation ullam corper suscipit lobortis nisl ut aliquip ex ea comodo consequat. Duis autem vel eum iriure dolor in hendrerit in vulputate velit esse molestie consequat, vel illum dolore eu feugiat nulla facilisis. Ut wisi enim ad minim veniam, quis nostrud exerci tation ullamcorper suscipit lobortis.

ULLAMCORPER

Iriure dolor hendrerit vulputate velit esse molestie consequat, vel illum

Quality Considerations

It's entirely appropriate to prepare camera-ready newspaper ads using your laser printer. It's usually not necessary to go to the expense of having newspaper ads phototypeset, because the relatively coarse newsprint absorbs the ink to such a degree that the quality advantage offered by phototypesetting is lost. Although newspapers continue to improve their reproduction quality, the standard resolution for laser printers is also on the rise. The two factors tend to balance out, so, unless your printer is five or six years old, you're probably safe. (Even an old 300-dot-per-inch laser printer might suffice, as long as the ad contains no screens—low-resolution printers produce coarse, ugly screens.)

In addition, scanners and desktop publishing programs are rapidly improving in their ability to handle photographs. The quality produced on some laser printers approaches the quality of newspaper photo reproduction. Thus, it's entirely feasible that you prepare complete newspaper ads, including photographs, with your desktop publishing system and laser printer.

Magazine ads are another story, because glossy paper tends to show even the slightest imperfections. You should probably avoid sending camera-ready ads to magazines unless your printer is high-quality—1,000 dots per inch or better.

Evaluation Checklist

- Does your advertisement use borders, margins, and white space to set itself apart from adjacent page elements?
- Is your headline prominent and readable, without being overwhelming?
- Is there an obvious tie-in between your headline and your primary visual?
- Are captions and prices clearly connected to product photos or illustrations?
- Has all the necessary buying and contact information—address, phone numbers, business hours, credit terms, and so on—been included?
- Is your logo prominently featured and set off by white space?
- Are the treatments of repeating elements, such as prices and captions, consistent throughout the ad?
- Do your advertisements have a consistent look and feel to promote name recognition?

9 Sales Materials

Sales materials serve different needs than advertisements.

Sales materials—brochures, flyers, catalogs, and menus—are similar to advertisements in their primary purpose: Both are meant to coax readers into buying something. However, sales materials aren't meant to be encountered inadvertently, as ads are. Anyone who bothers to read a sales piece is almost certainly a prospective buyer. Rather than concern yourself with getting attention, your primary focus should be *keeping* it—and, hopefully, increasing it.

Because of this, the attention-getting tricks used in advertisements aren't as useful in sales materials—and in fact, they're often harmful. Think of an advertisement as the loud midway pitch of a vendor. It's directed to everyone within range, and meant only to draw customers closer. Once a potential customer approaches, the vendor stops *shouting* to a general audience and begins *talking* to a specific one, displaying and describing the available wares. Sales materials serve this latter role, offering a sales pitch that is at once more informative and more personal.

It should come as no surprise, then, that your sales materials reflect the nature of your organization much more than your advertisements do and, therefore, require more care in their design. A badly designed advertisement will probably be, at worst, ignored. A badly designed brochure will drive away your most likely customers. Don't make the mistake of skimping on your sales materials because they're being distributed to customers who are already "hooked," or you'll find yourself endlessly bemoaning the ones that got away.

There are several factors to consider when designing a sales piece:

- *The number, complexity, and cost of products and services being advertised.* Will the sales piece focus on a single item or accommodate a variety of products and services?
- *The targeted point in the purchase cycle.* Will the materials be designed for buyers who are merely interested in learning more or on the verge of making a purchase?
- *The focus of the appeal—pragmatic or emotional.* Should the product be depicted as a utilitarian item or as an enhancement to the buyer's lifestyle and self-image?
- *The appropriate overall style.* What tone does the target audience expect? Should the piece be sober and businesslike or informal and plain spoken? Is it more important to convey information or to project a certain image?

Answering these sorts of questions requires a certain amount of empathy with the potential consumers. Ask yourself: Why might *I* want this product? What further information would *I* want or need? Product research is a rather nebulous business. This is as good a way to start as any. To be thorough, you should canvass other views besides your own; try to spot patterns and trends among the opinions you receive.

Remember, too, that different people will approach your publications differently. Some readers flip through catalogs from cover to cover, others browse them randomly, and still others use them as references, looking up specific items of interest. Your materials should be tailored to accommodate all of these approaches.

Brochures

Organizations use brochures to convey information to potential customers or constituents.

Generally, brochure information falls into one of the following categories:

- *An organization's purpose, goals, and available products or services.* A health maintenance organization's brochures might describe its preventive medicine and long-term care plans, while a performing arts group's brochures might provide concert and instruction schedules.
- *A description of a product line or a single product.* An audio/video manufacturer might have separate brochures for compact disc players, videocassette recorders, and car stereo systems.
- *A description of a project being undertaken by an organization.* A college alumni association, for example, might prepare a brochure in conjunction with a fund drive to raise money for a new building.
- *Information which might be of assistance to an organization's patrons.* A bed-and-breakfast might offer brochures describing local areas of interest, sightseeing tours, and so on.

Small brochures are commonly produced by folding an 8½×11-inch sheet of paper into thirds and printing on both sides. Lengthier brochures take the form of staple-bound booklets, produced in any number of sizes. If your brochure's page count starts edging into the double-digit range, it's generally wise to include a small table of contents or an index. Readers who merely want to locate one specific item of interest should not be forced to skim through 20-odd pages.

Teasers

Teasers are brochures targeted to prospective buyers early in the decision-making process.

Teasers don't pretend to tell the whole story. Their purpose is to direct the reader to the next level of action, such as calling a toll-free telephone number.

Teasers are frequently printed on single sheets of paper, then folded into panels (to fit into a business envelope). They're inexpensively produced so that they can be distributed to as many prospective buyers as possible. Teasers are also displayed conspicuously in free-standing or countertop racks so that anyone can feel free to take one.

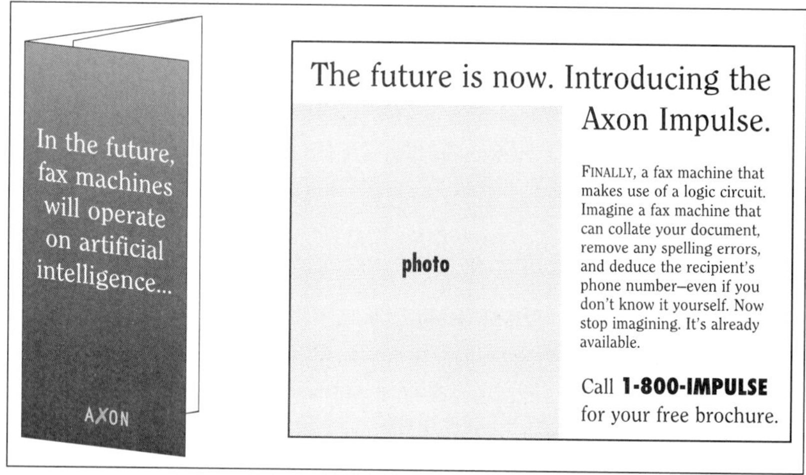

Tell-All Brochures

Tell-all brochures target qualified buyers.

Tell-all brochures are designed for the next level—serious potential buyers who are closer to the moment of truth. As the name implies, they provide much more information than teasers—they're designed to answer specific, detail-oriented questions.

Tell-all brochures usually take the form of booklets, printed on glossy paper using spot color or full color. This isn't a necessity, of course, but you need to be aware of the brochures your competitors are producing. If everyone else in the industry is using glossy full-color brochures, your matte one-color brochures will look like cheap leaflets in comparison—unless your design is truly inspired.

If your brochure is copy-heavy, use lots of text organizers to break up the gray space. Headlines, subheads, and bulleted lists should be employed. Even sidebars are not unheard of. If your brochure is product-oriented, you should include photos of the product. If it's a service brochure, illustrations might be more appropriate.

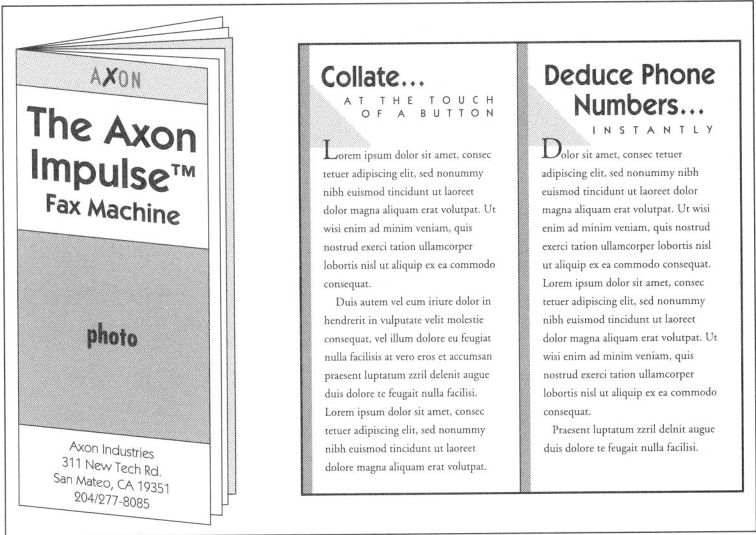

Impressers

Impressers approach the quality of small magazines in design sophistication.

Impressers follow up and reinforce the message at the crucial last phase before purchase. They combine sophisticated graphic design with high-quality printing and paper. An impresser brochure is frequently designed to be part of the product—the high quality of the brochure implies high quality in the product or service.

Impressers are appropriate when the products or services are either emotionally important to the buyer or in cases where benefits can't be measured until after the purchase is made. Examples include luxury items, such as expensive automobiles, complex technical products and services, and intangibles like public relations or financial services.

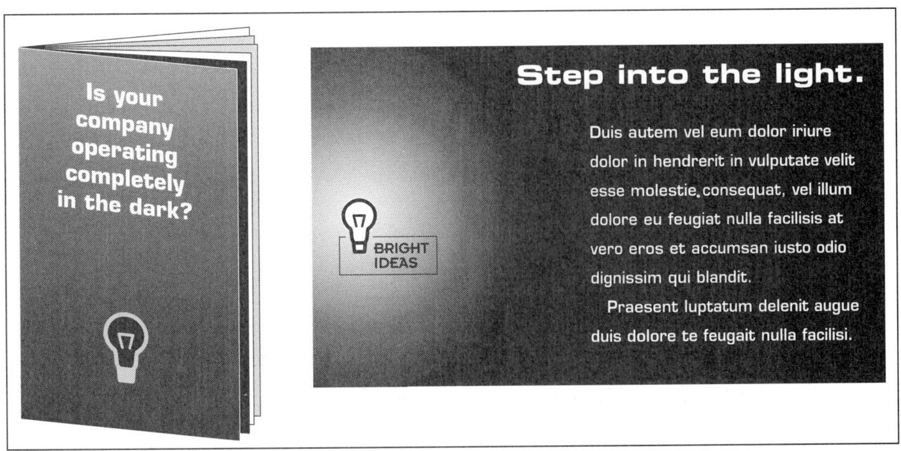

Brochures And Product Sheets

Brochures should be designed to have a long shelf life.

Full-color, multipage brochures are not the sorts of items you can afford to produce in small batches, bolstering your supply as the need arises. There's a fixed cost associated with setting up the printer, regardless of the size of the print run. You'll only get your money's worth if your print runs are large. As a result, your brochures should be designed to last a long time.

This can create a problem if your brochure is designed to cover an entire line of products. If even one product undergoes substantial revision, you'll be stuck reprinting the entire brochure, and throwing out the old copies. You can avoid this problem by supporting your brochures with detailed product sheets (see the "Product Sheets" section later in this chapter). Keep the brochure on a general level, covering only those aspects of the products that are unlikely to change significantly. Then, create a detailed product sheet for each individual item. These sheets can be revised and reprinted as necessary, at a fraction of the cost it would take to reprint your brochure.

Designing Brochures In A Series

Vary a distinct set of elements across a series of brochures to attain a unified look.

When creating a series of brochures, you'll want to define a distinct set of elements that will change from brochure to brochure. Your list should include some front-cover elements—readers can't be expected to open two identical-looking brochures to check for differences.

The most effective variable element is color. If you're using color printing, assign a distinctive spot color or color scheme to each brochure in the series. If your brochures are single-color, differentiating them may take a little more effort. For instance, if you decide to use a different black-and-white photo for each brochure cover, make sure the photos you choose are easy to tell apart. Scenes that are easily distinguished in color—for instance, rolling waves and rolling sand dunes—can look remarkably similar in black-and-white. The title of a brochure can also help set it apart from its brethren, if it's set prominently at large sizes.

Some design elements should not be considered candidates for variation. Keeping the following aspects consistent will help establish a unified look for your series:

USE VARIATION CONSISTENTLY!

Once you've determined a set of variable elements, make sure you vary them throughout your entire series. If you're using the cover photo to differentiate your brochures, don't use the same photo twice—even if it fits the content of both publications. If you're using spot color, pick a radically different shade for each brochure (color-impaired readers will not notice the difference between red and red-orange).

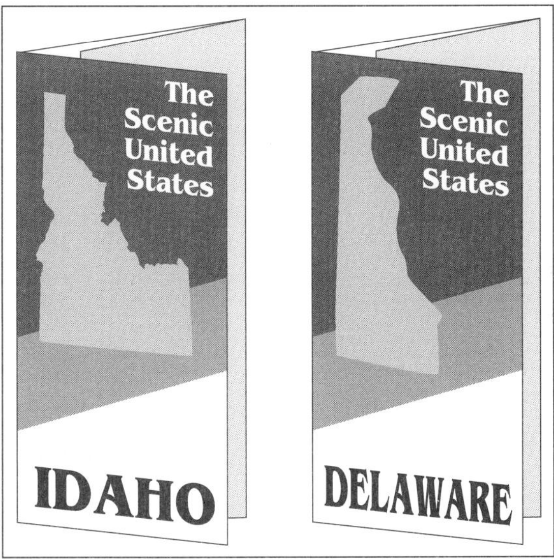

- Typefaces, type sizes, and type styles for headlines and body copy.
- Margins, borders, and graphic accents.
- Sizes and placements of photos or artwork.

Catalogs

Catalogs are similar to brochures, but they're usually longer and more product oriented.

While a brochure is used to display a single product or a product line, a catalog can display a firm's entire inventory. Catalogs are customarily produced once or twice a year. Because of their longevity, they're usually printed on expensive paper, and feature full-color printing. Page size is sometimes sacrificed for volume, which increases the perceived reference value of a catalog and contributes to its longevity. (Readers generally consider thick media, such as books and magazines, less disposable than thin media, such as brochures and newsletters.)

Covers

Catalog covers are often printed on a different paper stock than the inside pages.

A heavier, glossier paper stock can provide higher quality photo reproduction and better color saturation for your catalog's cover.

A single photo of the company's most popular product is often used on the cover to communicate an identity and promote sales.

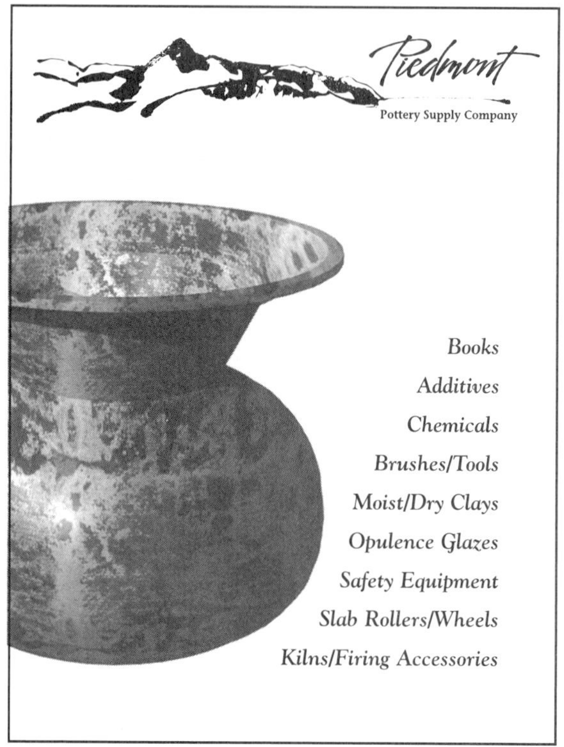

Piedmont
Pottery Supply Company
Books
Additives
Chemicals
Brushes/Tools
Moist/Dry Clays
Opulence Glazes
Safety Equipment
Slab Rollers/Wheels
Kilns/Firing Accessories

Alternately, the cover can also feature a collage of photos, calling attention to the diversity of products described inside.

Catalog titles are often designed like newsletter nameplates, with distinctive typographical treatments that remain the same for each new iteration of the catalog.

Inside Pages

The inside pages of a catalog must successfully integrate product visuals, captions, and prices.

The primary challenge when designing the interior spreads of a catalog is to successfully link product visuals with their corresponding captions and prices. A strong, ultraconsistent layout grid can solve this problem, but the result, while functional, is not very dynamic.

Most catalog designers use a more freewheeling approach to layout. Captions are tied to product visuals by proximity, and white space is used to separate individual products. This technique can be effective, but it's a pretty delicate operation. Too much white space between items can create a sparse, disconnected look, while too little can create a cluttered look.

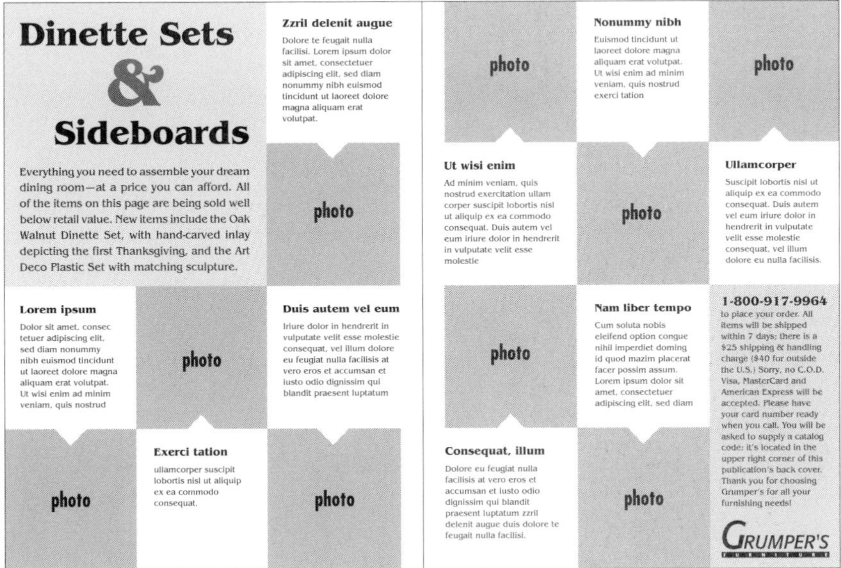

An alternative scheme is to group the visuals together and use alphanumeric references to link them to a separate list of captions. This scheme allows you to depict several small products in a single photo, rather than cluttering up the page with separate pictures.

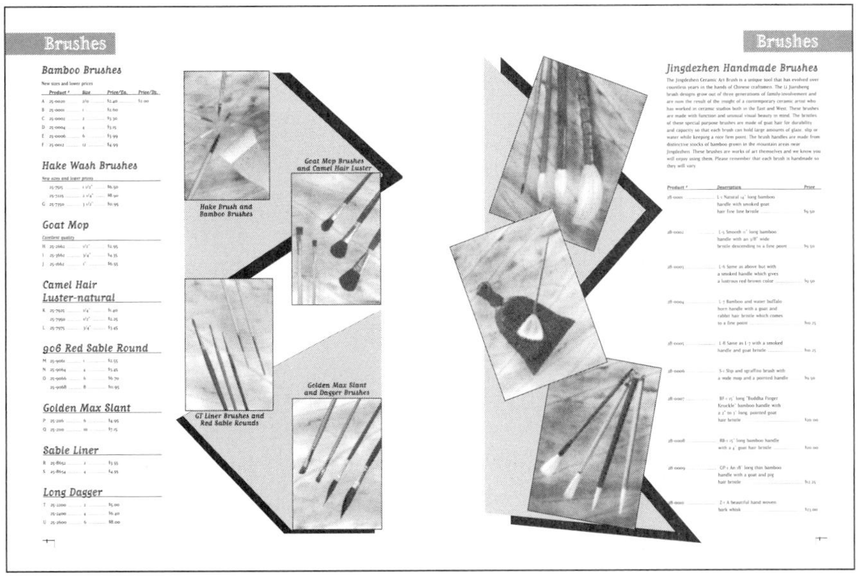

A catalog's inside front-cover spread can be used to describe the company and its policies. Frequently, there's a "Letter From the President" explaining the company philosophy.

Ordering Information

Ordering information and forms are typically printed as part of the catalog. However, response is encouraged by providing a separate, postage-paid, self-addressed order form inserted into the middle of the catalog.

Inviting readers to respond by offering easy-to-use order forms and placing toll-free telephone numbers in the catalog can greatly increase sales. It's a good idea to put your phone number in the same place on every spread of the catalog, to ensure that your readers will be able to find it quickly.

Order Forms

Order forms can be used as catalog inserts or as standalone sales materials.

The primary concern when producing an order form is ease of use. Instructions should be brief and concise. Areas designed to receive written information should be large and inviting, not small and cramped. Most important, the ordering process should be quick and relatively effortless.

For instance, don't force your customers to write out the full names of the products they want. If you have a small number of available products, list them all in a table. This allows your customers to place an order simply by specifying a desired quantity for each item. If your product list is too large for a table, assign each product a short alphanumeric code. Your customers can use the codes to specify the items they want. Make sure the codes are placed prominently beside the product listings in your catalog.

Don't feel, however, that order forms need to be purely functional. In fact, if your catalog is fancy or flashy, a drab and businesslike order form will seem distinctly out of place. Instead, let the style of the order form mirror the style of your catalog—be it elegant, informal, or downright wacky.

Order forms don't have to be part of a catalog. Sometimes they function well as standalone items, resembling small brochures. Try folding a single sheet of 8½×11 sheet of paper into thirds. Use one panel for the cover, two more panels for brief product descriptions, and the entire reverse side of the page for the order form. While perhaps not offering as much detail as an actual brochure would, the order form has an obvious benefit—customers who are interested in buying can do so, immediately!

Jeannine's Custom Wigs

Same person.
Different color.

Delivery within 7–10 days of order.
Sorry, no returns.
15% discount on orders of $50.00 or more.

Color	Qty	Price	Total
Red		$15.95	
Blonde		$14.95	
Dirty Blonde		$17.95	
Strawberry Blonde		$17.95	
Brown		$14.95	
Auburn		$14.95	
Russet		$15.95	
Blue with Purple Highlights		$20.95	
Black		$17.95	
Even Blacker		$18.95	

Name ______________ Diameter of Head (inches) ______

Address (include city, state, zip) ______________

Method of Payment: ☐ Check ☐ Money Order ☐ MasterCard ☐ Visa

Card number (if applicable) ______________

Product Sheets

Product sheets are generally used in conjunction with brochures.

Product sheets provide detailed information and specifications about a product or service, and they are usually printed on high-quality paper stock. The front side can display a large photograph of the product, a paragraph or two of explanatory material (often repeating the information contained in the company's full-line brochure), and an outline of the product features and benefits.

Information on the back is generally more detailed, including specific product information, related accessories and supplies, photos displaying the product being used, and/or cutaway diagrams.

Product sheets are often three-hole punched, so they can be inserted into binders or added to proposals.

Like brochures, product sheets can be created for an entire series of products within a single product line. Use the same techniques described in the section "Designing Brochures In A Series" to create a unified yet easily differentiable set of product sheets.

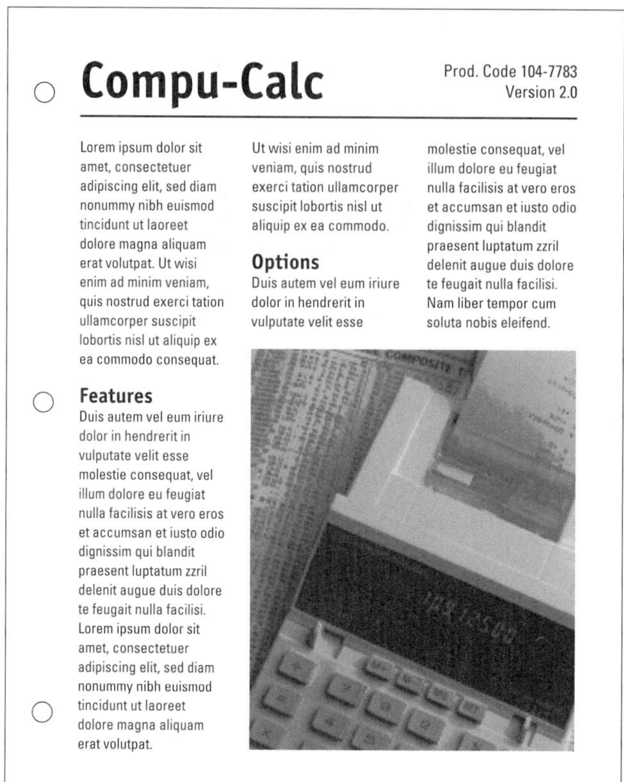

Compu-Calc

Prod. Code 104-7783
Version 2.0

Lorem ipsum dolor sit amet, consectetuer adipiscing elit, sed diam nonummy nibh euismod tincidunt ut laoreet dolore magna aliquam erat volutpat. Ut wisi enim ad minim veniam, quis nostrud exerci tation ullamcorper suscipit lobortis nisl ut aliquip ex ea commodo consequat.

Features

Duis autem vel eum iriure dolor in hendrerit in vulputate velit esse molestie consequat, vel illum dolore eu feugiat nulla facilisis at vero eros et accumsan et iusto odio dignissim qui blandit praesent luptatum zzril delenit augue duis dolore te feugait nulla facilisi. Lorem ipsum dolor sit amet, consectetuer adipiscing elit, sed diam nonummy nibh euismod tincidunt ut laoreet dolore magna aliquam erat volutpat.

Ut wisi enim ad minim veniam, quis nostrud exerci tation ullamcorper suscipit lobortis nisl ut aliquip ex ea commodo.

Options

Duis autem vel eum iriure dolor in hendrerit in vulputate velit esse molestie consequat, vel illum dolore eu feugiat nulla facilisis at vero eros et accumsan et iusto odio dignissim qui blandit praesent luptatum zzril delenit augue duis dolore te feugait nulla facilisi. Nam liber tempor cum soluta nobis eleifend.

Flyers

Flyers are typically used to advertise a special, limited-time promotion of a single product or service.

Flyers contain time-sensitive information printed on one side of a sheet of paper. They're ideal when you have only a small budget and need to get the information out right away. They can be distributed in a number of different ways. You can mail them, send them as faxes, stack them on countertops, hang them on walls, or tuck them beneath windshield wipers.

Flyers are appropriate vehicles for promoting a drug store's specially priced vitamins, a nightclub's upcoming performance of a popular jazz musician, or a music store's sale on a certain label's compact discs.

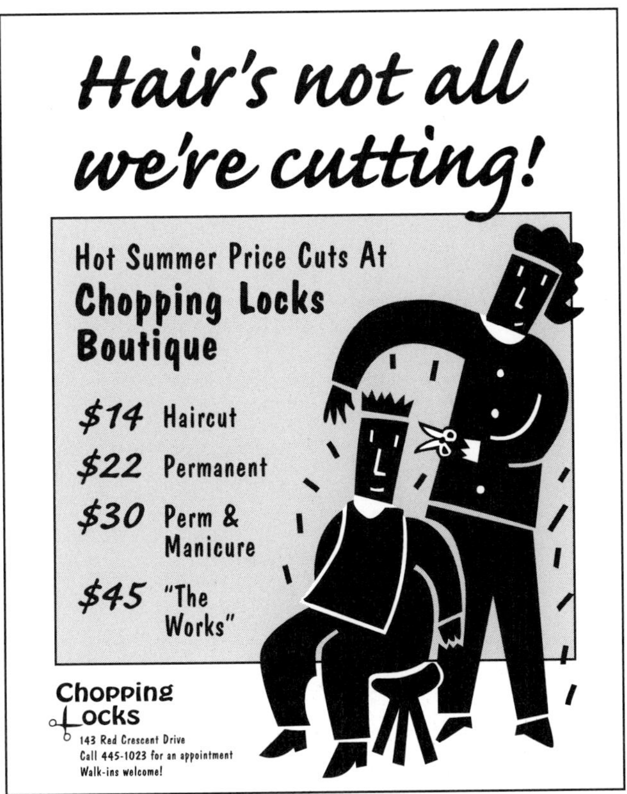

Flyers should be designed to capture an audience's attention. Use large headlines, clever catch phrases, and attention-getting visuals. Flyers are distributed much more indiscriminately than other sales materials, so it rarely pays to use expensive printing processes. Print them in one or two colors, on relatively cheap grades of paper. Low-cost colored paper will sometimes attract more attention than plain white paper, but don't pick overly dark colors that interfere with legibility. (For some reason, red seems to be popular color for flyers nowadays, but I wouldn't personally advise using it. The color may attract attention, but does anyone actually struggle through the barely-visible black text?)

Although most flyers are printed on standard 8½×11-inch paper, larger sizes are possible. Tabloid-sized 11×17-inch flyers can act as mini-billboards, providing high visual impact at a relatively low price.

Menus

A restaurant's menu is its most important advertising medium.

Designing menus requires special care. Menus are not mere lists of comestibles with prices. Their typography and design reflect the nature and ambiance of the restaurant. A fancy restaurant will not go far with a shoddy-looking menu. Customers will think to themselves, "Where *else* are they cutting corners?"

A menu is an excellent candidate for the application of desktop publishing technology. You can create menu templates that are easily updated when prices need to be changed or new items added. Indeed, many fine restaurants print new menus each day using color printers. This allows each menu to feature the daily specials and the freshest available produce.

Borders, typefaces, and visuals used in the menu's design play a major role in projecting the restaurant's character. Stylized serif typefaces and ornate borders can communicate an Old World atmosphere. A contemporary atmosphere is suggested by sparse, angular, or geometric sans serif type.

Menus present an ideal opportunity to use clip art to establish a mood. Clip art publishers offer a variety of country, urban, and atmosphere themes.

When creating your layout, remember that patrons will want to locate food categories quickly. Subheads set in a contrasting typeface, size, or style are easy to distinguish.

Categories can be separated by boxes, horizontal rules, or white space.

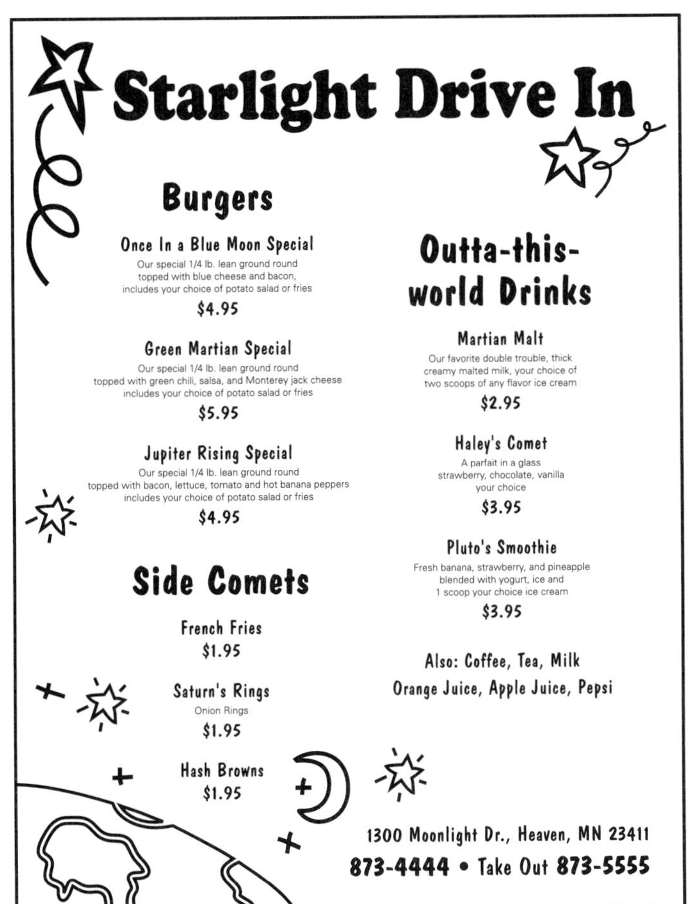

Starlight Drive In
Burgers
Once In a Blue Moon Special
Our special 1/4 lb. lean ground round topped with blue cheese and bacon, includes your choice of potato salad or fries
$4.95
Green Martian Special
Our special 1/4 lb. lean ground round topped with green chili, salsa, and Monterey jack cheese includes your choice of potato salad or fries
$5.95
Jupiter Rising Special
Our special 1/4 lb. lean ground round topped with bacon, lettuce, tomato and hot banana peppers includes your choice of potato salad or fries
$4.95
Side Comets
French Fries
$1.95
Saturn's Rings
Onion Rings
$1.95
Hash Browns
$1.95
Outta-this-world Drinks
Martian Malt
Our favorite double trouble, thick creamy malted milk, your choice of two scoops of any flavor ice cream
$2.95
Haley's Comet
A parfait in a glass strawberry, chocolate, vanilla your choice
$3.95
Pluto's Smoothie
Fresh banana, strawberry, and pineapple blended with yogurt, ice and 1 scoop your choice ice cream
$3.95
Also: Coffee, Tea, Milk
Orange Juice, Apple Juice, Pepsi
1300 Moonlight Dr., Heaven, MN 23411
873-4444 • Take Out 873-5555

One of the clichés of menu design is the use of separate columns for entrées and prices, with leader dots connecting each entrée to its corresponding price. Actually, this technique is rarely effective. The dots create a distracting horizontal pattern, and the prices gain an unwanted prominence over the cuisine. As an alternative, try placing prices discreetly after entrée descriptions. If your descriptions are suitably mouth-watering, the prices may not seem too terribly important!

Evaluation Checklist

Brochures

- Have you chosen an appropriate size and format?
- Does the front cover encourage readers to look further?
- Have you maintained page-to-page consistency throughout?
- Have you supplied all the information that prospective buyers need to make informed buying decisions?

Catalogs

- Does your catalog begin selling on the front cover?
- Have you paid as much attention to your catalog's nameplate as you would to a newsletter nameplate?
- Does your catalog contain information describing your company and its credentials?
- Have you made it easy for readers to respond by providing complete ordering information and a large, easy-to-use order form?

Order Forms

- Is your form easy to use? (See Chapter 11 for more on making easy-to-use forms.)
- Is the design style of your order form consistent with your catalog and with the nature of the merchandise?

Flyers

- Can readers glean your flyer's basic message at a glance?
- Have you edited your flyers to provide "who, what, when, where, and how" information in the fewest words possible?
- Have you avoided unnecessary clutter?

Menus

- Is the design style of your menu consistent with the spirit of your establishment?
- Can patrons quickly locate various food categories?
- Are prices clearly visible yet not overemphasized?

Product Sheets

- Do your product sheets share a common family resemblance through consistent use of typography, photo placement, and highlight color?
- Do your product sheets maintain the look established by the sales brochures they're designed to augment?

10 Business Communication

As you develop your design sense and become more familiar with the capabilities of desktop publishing, you'll continue to discover new applications. For in-house projects, you'll come to rely on your desktop system for design and production, rather than on professional service bureaus.

It's especially fitting for designers to develop their own business communication materials—letterhead, envelopes, business cards, and so on. Don't assume that these sorts of documents should only be handled by print professionals. If you've got a modicum of design sense, you should feel no qualms about handling the design yourself. Remember, you've got distinct advantages. You know your organization better than anyone, and you care enough about the results to spend whatever time is necessary to achieve perfection. Professionals, even thoroughly-briefed ones, will only have a vague sense of the image you wish to impart—and they can't be expected to spend days searching for the "perfect" look—they've got other clients besides you.

Letterhead

A good letterhead communicates practical information at a glance, yet it does not overshadow the more important message—namely, the letter.

Letterhead design is not as simple as it may seem. It's important to express something about the nature or character of your firm or association in your letterhead design, in addition to providing its name, address, and phone number as response information. A good design for a district attorney's letterhead would not translate well to the letterhead of a tanning salon.

There are several basic components of a letterhead:

- Firm or organization name
- Logo
- Motto or statement of business philosophy
- Street address and mailing address (if different)
- Telephone number(s)
- Telex and/or fax number
- Email address and/or Web address

Corporate and nonprofit letterheads often list officers or board members, as well. That's a lot of information to fit into a relatively small space—remember, most of your letterhead needs to be left blank for the message area.

Logo Size And Placement

The size of your logo must be proportional to the amount of supporting information.

Logos must be large enough to be noticed yet not so large that they visually overwhelm the letterhead. In the following example, the logo detracts from the message area.

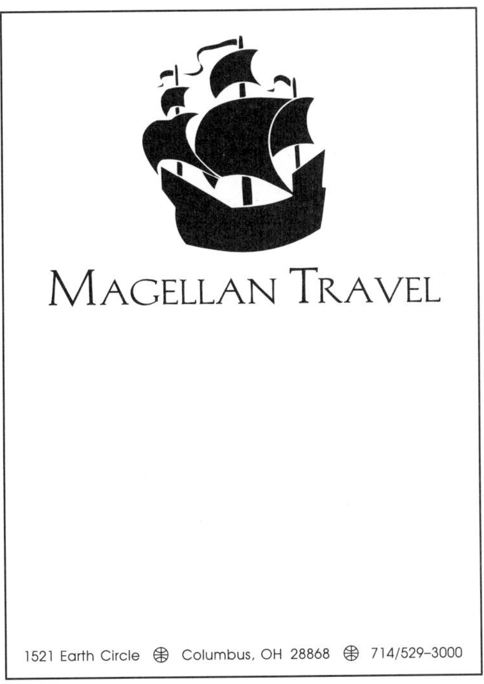

Placement can be flexible. Although logos are frequently centered above the letterhead, there is no reason why they can't be placed differently, as long as you observe basic rules of good design.

For example, logos can be set flush left or flush right at the top of the page.

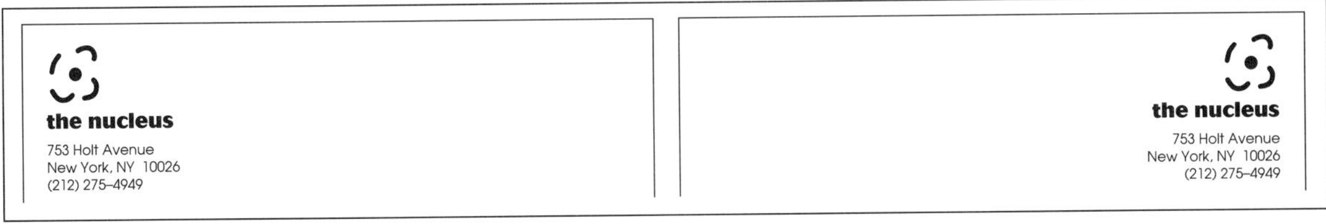

The letterhead can be designed on an asymmetrical grid. This will leave a vertical band of white space along the left-hand side of the letterhead.

Contact Information

Be sure to include all the information that the letter's recipient needs in order to respond.

Insufficient address and phone information can cause problems for your correspondents. One common mistake is to print a telephone number without the area code. That will put long-distance callers at a distinct disadvantage.

Placement of telephone and address information usually depends on logo placement. When the logo is centered at the top of the letterhead, telephone and address information is often centered in a smaller type size along the bottom.

When the logo is at the top left, contact information is commonly placed directly beneath the logo, beside the logo to the right, or at the bottom of the page. The information is usually aligned flush left, to match the logo.

Contact information is usually arranged as a set of stacked lines or as a single line with bullets separating the items (see previous examples). If you've got a great deal of information to include—telephone and fax numbers, as well as a separate street address and post office box number—another possibility is to divide the information into several small stacks and arrange them in adjacent columns. For instance, you might put the street address flush left on two lines, telephone and fax numbers centered on two lines in the middle, and the post office box number flush right.

753 Holt Avenue	PHONE: (212) 275–4949	P.O. Box 7982
New York, NY 10026	FAX: (212) 275–4870	New York, NY 10026

Mottos

You can include your company motto in your letterhead.

Mottos often run along the bottom of a letterhead, forming an umbrella over address and phone information. In these cases, the motto is typically set slightly larger and differentiated from the contact information by type style. Try using the italic version of a font for one of the elements and the normal face for the other.

"The Customer Comes First"

753 Holt Avenue New York, NY 10026 (212) 275–4949

"The Employees Come Dead Last"

753 Holt Avenue New York, NY 10026 (212) 275–4949

Message Area

The final challenge is to effectively set off the letterhead elements so they don't interfere with the contents of the document.

One way to isolate the message area is to box it.

You can also separate the two areas with a partial box or a rule. A screened column or panel, or a second color, can also be used to isolate supplementary information. This technique works well for listing board members or officers of an organization.

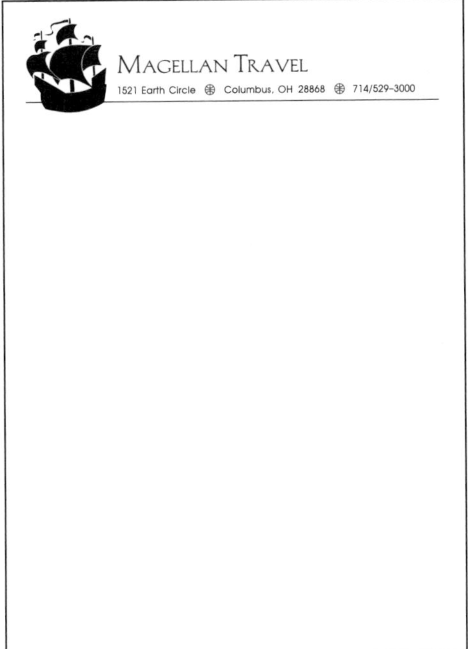

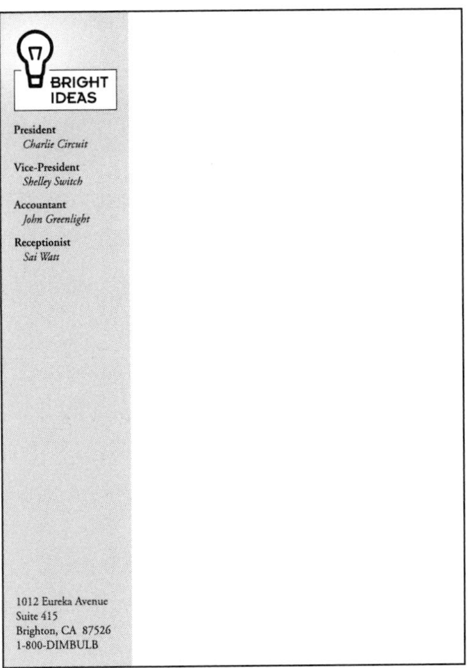

Envelope Design

Letterhead designs and logos—in a scaled down size—are repeated on the business envelope.

Some businesses use window envelopes, which eliminate the need to address separate envelopes or labels. In such cases, the letterhead must be designed so that the recipient's name and address will be positioned within the envelope window when the page is inserted.

Often a "family" of envelopes is created: a small, inexpensive envelope for sending invoices and paying bills; a Number 10 envelope printed on the same paper stock as the letterhead for standard correspondence; and a 9×12-inch envelope for formal proposals or oversized documents.

Occasionally, logo and address information are rotated 90 degrees and placed vertically along the side of the envelope. This isn't a conservative design, so banks and legal firms should probably shy away from it.

Business Cards

Business cards are not strictly functional—they often serve the function of sales materials.

On a business card, a lot of information must be presented in a relatively small amount of space—typically 3½×2 inches. The cardbearer's name and position need to be featured prominently, along with the name of the company and a logo. Addresses, phone and fax numbers, and online information should also be included.

Traditionally, the *quadrant* technique has been used as a solution to small space constraints. The firm's logo is placed flush left in the upper-left quadrant of the card, balanced by phone numbers set flush right in the upper-right quadrant. The street address is set flush left along the bottom of the card in the lower-left quadrant, and the post office box information is set flush right in the lower-right quadrant. These four elements form a framework for the individual's name and title, located in the center of the card.

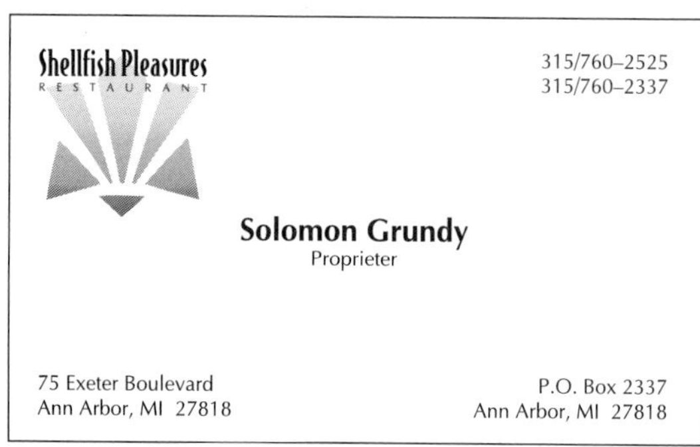

Unfortunately, this scheme rarely results in an attractive or effective layout. White space in the interior of the card quickly takes on a jumbled appearance, and there's no logical progression for the reader—important information is scattered willy-nilly.

It's better to keep contact information together, if you can. If your logo is roughly square, set it at the top left of the card, and put the text at the bottom right. The result is a well-balanced card with larger, less haphazard blocks of white space.

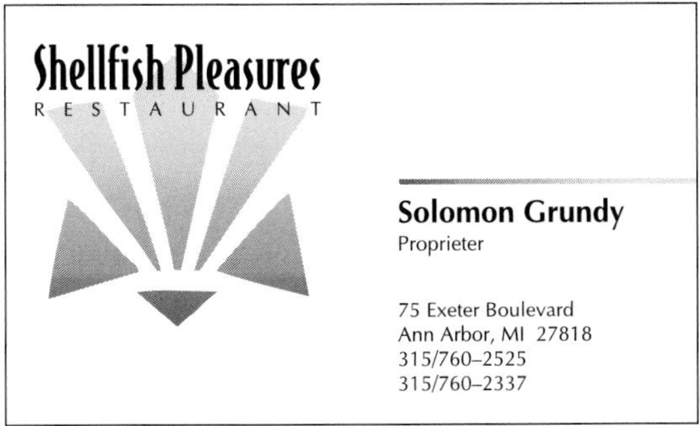

If your logo is long and thin, try setting it along the top of the card. Then, put your name in the center and your contact information at the bottom.

Vertical formats also work well. They command authority and lend a modern feel to your card.

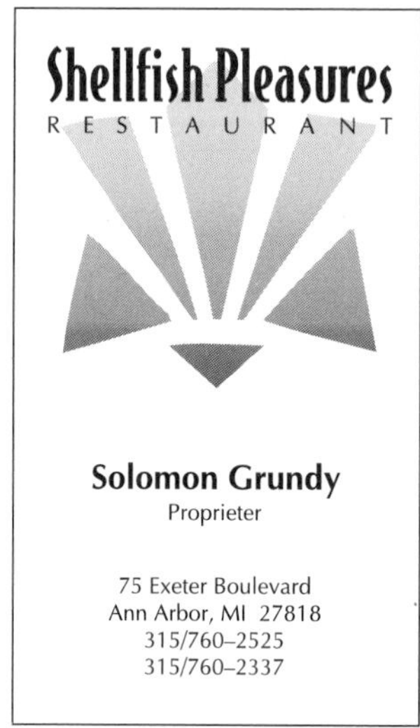

If you have even more information that you'd like to include on your business card—a motto, for instance, or a pager number—you might consider printing it on the back of your business card. It's a little more expensive to print on both sides, but it's worth it if you desperately need the space. A cluttered-looking card will cost your business plenty.

Color printing can help make your business card more flashy. You can use a second color to add accents to logos, graphics, or type. If you can't afford two colors, you might try printing your card in a single nonblack ink. It's a relatively inexpensive way to get the benefits of color, but you'll need to select a dark ink. Light colors can affect the legibility of small type.

Fax Cover Sheets

Fax transmissions are an important part of today's business world.

Well-designed cover sheets help ensure safe, efficient fax transmissions. It's important for the fax cover sheet to indicate the total number of pages sent. This helps the recipient know that the entire transmission has been received and nothing is missing. The following items should probably also be included:

- Recipient's name
- Sender's name
- Company name and logo
- Date of transmission
- Subject matter or summary of contents

Some fax cover sheets include space for a brief handwritten message.

Be careful when choosing typefaces for fax cover sheets. Because the quality of reproduction varies, it's important to choose a typeface that remains legible under any circumstances. Typefaces with thin strokes or detailed serifs tend to reproduce poorly and are not the most reliable choice for fax transmissions. Simple sans serif faces work best.

Resumes

A resume is direct response advertising in its purest form.

Good design is absolutely crucial for resumes. Although the actual text of your resume is a better indication of your talents and abilities, it's the design that determines the all-important first impression and provides the organizational structure which invites potential employers to read further. Don't assume that your merits will "speak for themselves"—if your resume is poorly designed, your merits may not get a chance to speak at all.

Changing Resume Trends

Today, the trend is toward less formal, more skill-oriented resumes.

Contemporary resumes focus more on what an individual has to offer a specific company, rather than a dutiful chronology of a person's education, career, and activities. Information is generally broken down with text organizers. White space, subheads, and graphic accents are used to separate categories. This allows prospective employers to locate relevant qualifications quickly, without having to play detective.

You should use two typefaces on your resume at most—one for subheads and one for body copy. Actually, the second font isn't strictly necessary. Many resumes use the italic version of the serif type in a larger type size for subheads. This softens the contrast between subheads and body copy.

Sell Yourself

Resumes are designed like advertisements—selling information precedes supporting or qualifying information.

Primary resume information describes the benefits of hiring you. Everything else is secondary and should be styled accordingly. Ideally, your resume should be customized to the recipient. Only include the work experience that a certain potential employer is likely to be interested in. This is where having an electronic version of a file can really come in handy—editing and updating becomes a matter of minutes, not hours.

GEORGE TCHOBANOGLOUS

662 Diego Place
Davis, California 95616
916/756-5747

Education

PhD., Civil Engineering, *Stanford University, 1969*
M.S., Sanitary Engineering, *University of California, Berkeley, 1960*
B.S., Civil Engineering, *University of the Pacific, 1958*

Present Position

Professor of Environmental Engineering, *Department of Civil Engineering, University of California, Davis.*
Research areas include solid waste management, innovative water and wastewater treatment systems, wastewater filtration, small wastewater treatment systems, on-site systems, and aquatic treatment systems.

Honors/Awards

Blue Key
Who's Who in America
Outstanding Teacher Award, 1980, School of Engineering, University of California, Davis
Gordon Maskew Fair Medal, 1985, Water Pollution Control Federation
Distinguished Alumnus of the Year for Public Service, 1985, University of the Pacific, Stockton, CA

Society Memberships

Association of Environmental Engineering Professors
Diplomat, American Association of Environmental Engineering Professors
American Society of Civil Engineers
Water Pollution Control Federation
American Water Works Association
International Association on Water Pollution Research and Control
California Water Pollution Control Federation
American Association for the Advancement of Science
Sigma Xi
World Mariculture Society
American Fisheries Association

Registration

Registered Civil Engineer in California

Employment

1976-Present	**Professor** *University of California, Davis, CA*
1971-1976	**Associate Professor** *University of California, Davis, CA*
1970-1971	**Assistant Professor** *University of California, Davis, CA*
1967-1969	**Acting Assistant Professor** *Stanford University, Stanford, CA*

Pay careful attention to typos, grammatical errors, and unwanted variations in letter and line spacing. It's difficult to convince an employer that you're detail-oriented if your resume is riddled with errors and inconsistencies. Your layout software should contain a spell checker and might even feature a grammar checker—make use of them.

Business Reports

Business reports are used to exhibit a company's current financial status and future plans. They usually contain a multitude of numerical data.

Designers of business reports should strive for a clean, conservative look. Although business reports are rarely seen by prospective customers, they're frequently seen by stockholders. Poor design or low print quality will not inspire much confidence.

A conservative design is not necessarily a dull design. It merely means you shouldn't be using elements like grunge typefaces, outlandish graphics, and rotated type. The easiest way to produce a professional look is to use an asymmetrical layout grid with plenty of white space. The asymmetry keeps the page dynamic-looking, avoiding the stodgy stick-in-the-mud impression conveyed by a balanced layout.

The Ferry Report

A Word From the President

Lorem ipsum dolor sit amet, consectetuer adipiscing elit, sed diam nonummy nibh euismod tincidunt ut laoreet dolore magna aliquam erat volutpat. Ut wisi enim ad minim veniam, quis nostrud exerci tation ullamcorper suscipit lobortis nisl ut aliquip ex ea commodo consequat.

Duis autem vel eum iriure dolor in hendrerit in velit esse molestie consequat, vel illum dolore eu feugiat nulla facilisis at vero eros et accumsan et iusto odio dignissim blandit praesent luptatum zzril delenit augue duis dolore te feugait nulla facilisi. Lorem ipsum dolor sit amet, consectetuer elit, sed diam nonummy nibh euismod tincidunt ut laoreet dolore magna aliquam erat volutpat. Ut wisi enim ad minim veniam, quis nostrud exerci tation ullamcorper suscipit lobortis nisl ut aliquip ex ea commodo consequat.

Lorem ipsum dolor sit amet, consectetuer adipiscing elit, sed diam nonummy nibh euismod tincidunt ut laoreet dolore magna aliquam erat volutpat. Ut wisi enim ad minim veniam, quis nostrud exerci tation ullamcorper suscipit lobortis nisl ut aliquip ex ea commodo consequat.

New Boat Designs

Nam liber tempor cum soluta nobis eleifend option congue nihil imperdiet doming id quod mazim placerat facer possim assum. Lorem ipsum dolor sit amet, consectetuer adipiscing elit, sed diam nonummy nibh euismod tincidunt ut laoreet dolore magna aliquam erat volutpat. Ut wisi enim ad minim veniam, quis nostrud exerci tation ullamcorper suscipit lobortis nisl ut aliquip ex ea commodo consequat.

Duis autem vel eum iriure dolor in hendrerit in vulputate velit esse molestie consequat, vel illum dolore eu feugiat nulla facilisis.

Lorem ipsum dolor sit amet, consectetuer adipiscing elit, sed diam nonummy nibh euismod tincidunt ut laoreet dolore magna aliquam erat volutpat. Ut wisi enim ad minim veniam, quis nostrud exerci tation ullamcorper suscipit lobortis nisl ut aliquip ex ea commodo consequat.

Ut wisi enim ad minim veniam, quis nostrud exerci tation ullamcorper suscipit lobortis nisl ut aliquip ex ea commodo consequat. Duis autem vel eum iriure dolor in hendrerit in vulputate velit esse molestie consequat, vel illum dolore eu feugiat nulla.

Seadogs and Sailors

Nam liber tempor cum soluta nobis eleifend option congue nihil imperdiet doming id quod mazim placerat facer possim assum. Lorem ipsum dolor sit amet, consectetuer autem vel eum iriure dolor in hendrerit in vulputate velit autem vel eum iriure dolor in hendrerit in vulputate velit esse molestie consequat, vel illum dolore eu feugiat nulla.

The Cape Hatteras Division

Copious white space indicates affluence. The implication is that your company is well-heeled enough to be unconcerned about printing costs. Of course, if your company is *extremely* concerned about printing costs, you're better off trying to convey professionalism with a tightly packed, no-nonsense style. (Which just goes to show, there's more than one way to skin a cat!)

Evaluation Checklist

Letterheads

- Does the design of your letterhead accurately reflect your firm's philosophy?
- Is the message area clearly set apart from the information area?
- Has all the necessary information been included, such as area codes, fax numbers, post office box numbers, and online addresses?
- Do the envelopes echo the style of the letterhead?

Business Cards

- Are the cardbearer's name and the company's name the most prominent items on the card?

- Has all relevant information been included: addresses, phone numbers, email accounts, and so forth?

Fax Cover Sheets

- Do your fax sheets clearly document the sender's name, recipient's name, transmission date, the total number of pages sent, and subject matter details?
- Will the typeface you've chosen retain legibility after being faxed? (Fax a copy to yourself, if you're unsure.)

Resumes

- Is information presented in order of importance to the reader?
- Have you used white space, subheads, and graphic accents (such as rules) to organize the information in your resume?
- Have you thoroughly checked your resume for typos, grammatical errors, and design inconsistencies?

Business Reports

- Do your typographical and design choices convey a sense of professionalism?
- Are charts and graphs easy to read and understand?
- Is the company name and logo featured prominently on both the cover and the inside pages?

11 Response Devices: Forms, Surveys, and Coupons

Adopt a pragmatic approach when designing response devices. The primary consideration should be ease of use. If you're reading this chapter at all, you're probably skimming it doubtfully while thinking to yourself: "Good grief, *forms*! What a one-way ticket to Dullsville *this* is going to be!"

Now, I'm supposed to contradict that thought and blather on about how wonderful forms can be, right? Well, no. The fact is, forms are generally pretty dry. There are exceptions, of course—and if you have a great idea for producing an exciting form, pursue it by all means, but don't despair if you don't. Most people don't want excitement from a form. They just want to fill it out *tout de suite*. If you really want to please your readers when designing response devices, concentrate on making them clear, concise, and easy to use.

This may sound like a humble aspiration for a designer to strive for, but, believe me, a well-designed form is a novelty. Many organizations don't even think of forms as "designed" documents. The job of creating a form is often given to someone with no design experience whatsoever. Actually, a good sense of design is not merely preferable but crucial. Confusing or unnecessarily laborious response devices are much more likely to fail in their primary purpose to elicit a response—readers won't bother, and who can blame them? Badly designed response devices are also a major headache for people who have to process the responses, because there's a greater chance that the information received will be inaccurate, incomplete, or both.

Elements Of Response Devices

Regardless of their specific function, response media are composed of similar basic parts:

- Title
- Instructions
- Response area
- Tables
- Addresses and phone numbers

Title

The title should clearly identify the form's purpose.

All response devices (except possibly coupons) should have a title to clearly identify their purpose. The title should be a prominent visual element. Set it in a distinctive typeface and/or a large size.

THE EXCEPTION TO THE RULE

Forms are generally dull and worthy documents, but *order forms* are a notable exception. Flashy, handsome-looking order forms can sometimes encourage readers to order more than they might have initially intended—a sales opportunity that no self-respecting marketing agent should pass up. For more on designing order forms, see Chapter 9.

Evaluation

Please circle one.

Strongly agree				Strongly disagree	General Session/Keynote Speaker
5	4	3	2	1	1. The information presented increased my knowledge of secondary education in Howard County.
5	4	3	2	1	2. The presentation was relevant and well presented.
5	4	3	2	1	3. I would recommend this speaker for future conferences.

Other comments or observations: __________

Session One/Title:

5	4	3	2	1	1. The information presented increased my knowledge of secondary education in Howard County.
5	4	3	2	1	2. The presentation was relevant and well presented.
5	4	3	2	1	3. The presentation will enable me to share the content with others.

Other comments or observations: __________

Session Two/Title:

5	4	3	2	1	1. The information presented increased my knowledge of secondary education in Howard County.
5	4	3	2	1	2. The presentation was relevant and well presented.
5	4	3	2	1	3. The presentation will enable me to share the content with others.

Other comments or observations: __________

Even if you're designing a form that will only be used in an interoffice capacity, by people who already know its function, it's a good idea to slug it with an appropriate title. Forms are rarely disposed of. They usually get stuffed away in filing cabinets for long-term reference, and it's much easier to organize and classify forms with clear, recognizable titles. The bureaucracy might seem manageable if you've only got one untitled form, but when the number of forms grows—and it invariably will, in a business environment—you'll quickly find yourself in a file clerk's worst nightmare.

Instructions

Clearly describe how to fill out and submit your response device.

Instructions should be set in a small type size, ideally near the title. Keep them as brief as possible without sacrificing information. Readers generally skim through instructions quickly and consider it a chore to reread them. Your instructions should take these criteria into account.

Coupon instructions should include payment options, for example, prepayment, COD shipment, and accepted credit cards. If personal checks are an option, specify to whom they should be made out. If items are to be shipped via United Parcel Service, customers should be reminded that a post office box address does not usually provide enough information for delivery.

Applications should indicate how and where the applicant should fill in needed information, and what to do with the document after completing it.

Surveys should clearly explain the rating scheme used—whether high numbers indicate agreement or disagreement with a given statement, for instance.

Don't skimp on instructions for interoffice forms, even if all the current users don't need them. New users will come along eventually. If your forms are self-explanatory, they won't be forced to ask questions, and you won't be forced to answer them.

Response Area

Readers record information in the document's *response area,* generally by filling in blanks or checking ballot boxes. Ballot boxes are preferable, because it takes much less time to draw a checkmark than to write an entire word or sentence.

Sleepytime Pillow Survey

Please take a few moments to fill out this survey. Your opinion is very important to us and these surveys help us better serve you. As an added incentive, all Sleepytime Pillow buyers who complete this survey will receive a set of Sleepytime Pillowcases absolutely free of charge. Sorry, you may not specify color.

Name ____________
Address ____________
____
Phone ____________
Date ____________
SSN ____________

1. How many Sleepytime Pillows do you own?
- ❒ 1
- ❒ 2
- ❒ 3
- ❒ 4 or more

2. How many hours do you sleep on a given night?
- ❒ less than 3
- ❒ 3–6
- ❒ 6–10
- ❒ more than 10

3. Do you ever let anyone borrow your Sleepytime Pillow?
- ❒ yes
- ❒ no
- ❒ absolutely not

6. What object would you say is most comparable, in terms of softness, to a Sleepytime Pillow?
- ❒ a cottonball
- ❒ a sponge
- ❒ a catcher's mitt
- ❒ a brick

7. Do you plan to buy another Sleepytime Pillow soon?
- ❒ yes
- ❒ no
- ❒ maybe

8. If someone stole your Sleepytime Pillow, would you respond with violence?
- ❒ yes
- ❒ no

Try to phrase your information requests as multiple-choice questions, and avoid blanks whenever possible. Even when a question has too many possible answers to list, you can provide ballot boxes for the most likely answers, and include an extra box labeled *Other* accompanied by a blank. Most readers will be saved a lot of effort.

Don't leave a lot of space between a ballot box and its accompanying label. Mentally matching up badly spaced boxes and labels becomes tedious and discourages respondents from completing the form.

1. What made you decide to buy a Sleepytime Pillow?

❒ Low price
❒ Softness
❒ Aesthetics
❒ Peer pressure

Blanks accommodate names, addresses, and other detailed information that might be required. Remember to provide sufficient line length and space between lines. It's in the best interest of everyone involved to provide adequate horizontal and vertical space to permit a comfortable, readable handwriting size.

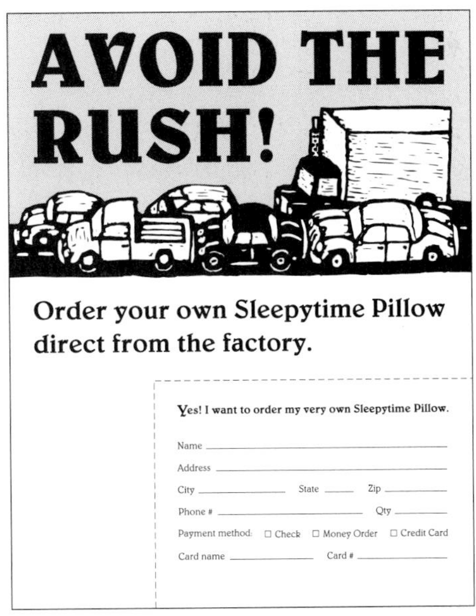

Incidentally, while it's better to err on the side of generosity when determining line length, don't go to extremes. Providing two full lines for a zip code, for instance, can mentally trip readers up (they might assume they skipped a question somewhere).

Tables

Tables are a special type of response area in which data is entered into cells cross-indexed by row and column. Tables are generally the most efficient type of response area, requiring the least user effort to elicit the most information, so they should be used whenever possible. For instance, if your form contains a sequence of multiple-choice questions with identical responses, you should probably consider replacing those questions with a table.

The Superhero Survey

1. Which superhero has the best costume?
❍ Superman ❍ Spider-Man ❍ Aquaman ❍ Wonder Woman ❍ Green Arrow

2. Which superhero is the most powerful?
❍ Superman ❍ Spider-Man ❍ Aquaman ❍ Wonder Woman ❍ Green Arrow

3. Which superhero has saved the entire world the most times?
❍ Superman ❍ Spider-Man ❍ Aquaman ❍ Wonder Woman ❍ Green Arrow

4. Which superhero has the most interesting super-powers?
❍ Superman ❍ Spider-Man ❍ Aquaman ❍ Wonder Woman ❍ Green Arrow

5. Which superhero seems the most heroic?
❍ Superman ❍ Spider-Man ❍ Aquaman ❍ Wonder Woman ❍ Green Arrow

6. Which superhero has the most fiendish arch-nemesis?
❍ Superman ❍ Spider-Man ❍ Aquaman ❍ Wonder Woman ❍ Green Arrow

The Superhero Survey

Which superhero...	Superman	Spider-Man	Aquaman	Wonder Woman	Green Arrow
... has the best costume?					
... is the most powerful?					
... has saved the entire world the most times?					
... has the most interesting super-powers?					
... seems the most heroic?					
... has the most fiendish arch-nemesis?					

Column headers for tables should be clear and concise. Typically, they're centered over the columns.

DON'S MASONRY
DON & RUSTY SPARROW

209 East Main Street
Carrboro, NC 27510

Job ____________________

Date ____________________

Masonry Units	Units Delivered	Left on Job	Units Laid	Unit Price		Amount
Face Brick – Regular						
Face Brick – Oversize						
Culls						
Solite Brick						
Fill Brick						
Block: 4"						
6"						
8"						
12"						
Caps						

TOTAL ________

Signature ____________________

This scheme works fine if the column heads are short. If they're not, or if you have an unusually large number of them, you'll soon find yourself running out of horizontal room. One possible fix, if the row heads are short, is to flip-flop the table so that rows become columns and vice versa. Another possibility is to rotate the column heads. Unless you're really crunched for space, though, don't rotate them a full 90 degrees—angles in the 45 through 60 degree range produce much more readable text, while saving a goodly amount of horizontal space.

	Ut wisi enim ad minim	Veniam, quis nostrud	Exercitation	Ullamcorper suscipit	Lobortis nisl ut aliquip	Ex ea commodo	Consequat
Lorem ipsum dolor sit amet							
Consectetuer adipiscing elit							
Sed diam nonummy nibh							
Euismod tincidunt ut laoreet							
Dolore magna aliquam erat							
Volutpat ex ea commodo							

In large tables, screening every other row or column helps respondents keep track of information.

PURCHASE ORDER

VENDOR # VENDOR REF # ORDER TYPE: RO#

VENDOR NAME DATE ORDERED

JOB #

SHIP TO: NAME

ATTN.

STREET

P.O. BOX

C-S-Z

QTY	PM#	VENDOR PART #	DESCRIPTION	SO#	UNIT COST

PURCHASING AGENT

TERMS

FOB POINT

SHIP VIA

CONF. NEEDED (N-original order, Y-confirming copy, X-no confirmation)

ORDER TAKEN BY

DATE REQUIRED

REFERENCES

Because tables often require the user to add up column totals, it's best to arrange a table as a single vertical block. The possibility of mathematical error increases when the user must deal with subtotals or add columns that aren't visually aligned.

Addresses And Phone Numbers

Include the four-digit extension to your zip code for carrier-route sorting. This information can expedite mail delivery and save your organization postage costs. Also, you might consider including the country name in your address—if your organization ever goes global, you'll be ready. (Even if you never go global, people might *think* you're global—hey, it couldn't hurt!)

Addresses for many large firms now include mail-stop information—their own internal zip codes. Make it easy for users to include complete delivery information; otherwise, order fulfillment and return communications could be seriously delayed.

Phone numbers should include the area code and extension numbers, if applicable.

Coupons

Coupons typically only take up a portion of a page and are bordered with a dashed line indicating that they're meant to be cut out. If you can afford to have the coupon perforated, do it—there are probably a fair number of readers out there who would rather give your coupon a miss than hunt up a pair of scissors. Coupons are easiest to detach, on average, when placed in the lower-right corner of a right-hand page. (My apologies to all the southpaws out there.)

Evaluation Checklist

Forms

- Does the form have a title?
- Are the directions clear and concise?
- Are information requests subdivided into clearly defined categories, where applicable?
- Have tables been used wherever possible?

Surveys

- Is the rating scheme clear?
- Have ballot boxes been used in place of blanks, whenever possible?
- Do the instructions tell the user how to submit a completed survey?

Coupons

- Is it clear where the coupon should be sent?
- Is there adequate space in which to write the needed information?
- Is the coupon large enough to attract notice yet small enough to avoid dominating the accompanying advertisement?

12 Common Design Pitfalls

Good design is easily sabotaged. Errors have exceedingly high visibility. Once spotted, they become the most prominent aspects of a document. Only virtually error-free documents are able to convey a straightforward, undiluted message. Even a minor layout flaw can turn the readers' attention toward the *design* of a document, when they should be concentrating on the *content*.

If that sounds like an exaggeration, consider an analogy from the world of film: imagine a panoramic landscape scene in which the camera tracks slowly over a hill, then launches into the sunset beyond, and, off to one side, a film crew member is seen standing, eating a sandwich. It may seem like a small flaw—the hill and sunset are still as glorious as ever, and the crew member only takes up a tiny portion of the screen for a few seconds. In reality, though, the entire scene is ruined. The viewers have been reminded—in the worst possible way—that they are merely watching a movie. Any chance of being "swept up into the story" has been dashed.

A Gallery Of Mistakes

This chapter lists and illustrates the most common errors that sabotage otherwise effective designs. Some of the errors result from an overuse of desktop publishing devices, whereas others are caused by a lack of attention to detail. Like the design concept checklist in Chapter 1, this list is meant to be used as a last-pass safeguard against careless mistakes.

Rivers Of White Space

Watch out for rivers of white space that can develop vertically or diagonally through justified text.

Rivers of white space are caused by gaps between words. They occur often when large type is justified in narrow columns. They're especially likely to occur if there are double spaces after periods.

Remedies include decreasing the type size, increasing the column width, or both. You can also reset the copy with a ragged (unjustified) right margin, although in narrow columns the right rag can get rather extreme.

Apartment Life

by Sid E. Slicker

I was so desperate to find a place to live when I first moved to New York, I signed a lease never having seen the apartment. Big mistake. The landlord, of course, gave a glowing description of the place, saying that it was "extremely well ventilated." It wasn't until I arrived at my new abode that I realized what he

meant: there were mammoth holes in the floor, ceiling and roof. I was despondent, needless to say, though at least I was sure my security deposit was safe; no further damage done to the apartment could possibly make it look any worse.

Apartment Life

by Sid E. Slicker

I was so desperate to find a place to live when I first moved to New York, I signed a lease never having seen the apartment. Big mistake. The landlord, of course, gave a glowing description of the place, saying that it was "extremely well ventilated." It wasn't until I arrived at my new abode that I realized what he meant: there were mammoth holes in the floor, ceiling and roof. I was despondent, needless to say, though at least I was sure my security deposit was safe; no further damage done to the apartment could possibly make it

Trapped White Space

Avoid "holes" in publications that disrupt the flow of information.

Trapping white space between elements on a page produces a visual hole in your layout. This confuses readers and interrupts the flow of the copy and graphics.

Fireside Reader

December 1998

Santa Considers the New Year

Lorem ipsum dolor sit amet, consectetuer adipiscing elit, sed diam nonummy nibh euismod tincidunt ut laoreet dolore magna aliquam erat volutpat. Ut wisi enim ad minim veniam, quis nostrud exerci tation ullamcorper suscipit lobortis nisl ut aliquip ex ea commodo consequat.

The elves take a much-needed coffee break.

Duis autem vel eum iriure dolor in hendrerit in vulputate velit esse molestie consequat, vel illum dolore eu feugiat nulla facilisis at vero eros et accumsan et iusto odio dignissim qui blandit praesent luptatum zzril delenit augue duis dolore te feugait nulla facilisi. Lorem ipsum dolor sit amet, consectetuer adipiscing elit, sed diam nonummy nibh euismod tincidunt ut laoreet dolore magna aliquam erat volutpat.

Ut wisi enim ad minim veniam, quis nostrud exerci tation ullamcorper suscipit lobortis nisl ut aliquip ex ea commodo consequat. Duis autem vel eum iriure dolor in hendrerit in vulputate velit esse molestie consequat, vel illum dolore eu feugiat nulla facilisis at vero eros et accumsan et iusto odio dignissim qui blandit praesent luptatum zzril delenit augue duis dolore te feugait nulla facilisi.

Nam liber tempor cum soluta nobis eleifend option congue nihil imperdiet doming id quod mazim placerat facer possim assum.

Rudolph's Nose Finally Goes Out

Diam nonummy nibh euismod tincidunt ut laoreet dolore magna aliquam erat volutpat. Ut wisi enim ad minim veniam, quis nostrud exerci tation ullamcorper suscipit lobortis nisl ut aliquip ex ea commodo consequat.

Duis autem vel eum iriure dolor in hendrerit in vulputate velit esse molestie consequat, vel illum dolore eu feugiat nulla facilisis. Lorem ipsum dolor sit amet, consectetuer adipiscing elit.

Ut wisi enim ad minim veniam, quis nostrud exerci tation ullamcorper suscipit lobortis nisl ut aliquip ex ea commodo consequat. Duis autem vel eum iriure dolor in hendrerit in vulputate velit esse molestie consequat, vel illum dolore eu

Solutions include increasing the size of display type, enlarging the illustration, or recomposing copy.

Inappropriate Column Spacing

Gutter width and type size need to be proportionate.

As type size increases, you need more space between columns (a wider gutter) to prevent the reader's eyes from moving horizontally across columns, instead of progressing down to the next line.

> As type increases, more space between columns is needed to prevent the reader's eyes from moving horizontally, across columns, instead of progressing down to the next line. Be careful that you do not overdo it, however. Overly generous column spacing causes distracting vertical bands of white space.
>
> As type increases, more space between columns is needed to prevent the

Be careful not to overdo it, however—overly generous column spacing creates distracting vertical bands of white space.

Whispering Headlines

Make headlines and subheads significantly larger and bolder than the text they introduce.

Gray pages result where there's not enough contrast between headlines and text. Whispering headlines fail to attract attention to the corresponding text.

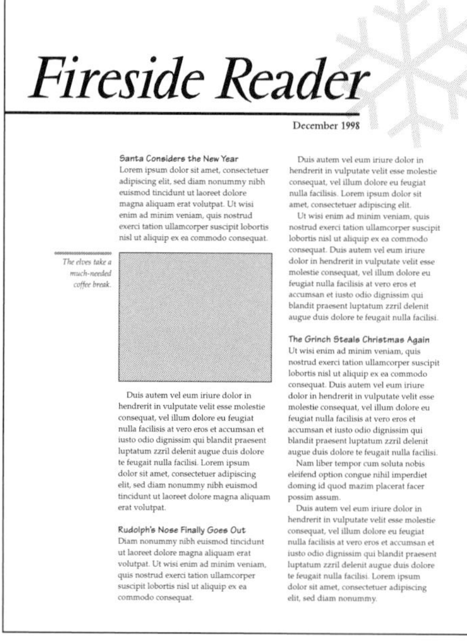

Fireside Reader

December 1998

Santa Considers the New Year

Lorem ipsum dolor sit amet, consectetuer adipiscing elit, sed diam nonummy nibh euismod tincidunt ut laoreet dolore magna aliquam erat volutpat. Ut wisi enim ad minim veniam, quis nostrud exerci tation ullamcorper suscipit lobortis nisl ut aliquip ex ea commodo consequat.

The elves take a much-needed coffee break.

Duis autem vel eum iriure dolor in hendrerit in vulputate velit esse molestie consequat, vel illum dolore eu feugiat nulla facilisis at vero eros et accumsan et iusto odio dignissim qui blandit praesent luptatum zzril delenit augue duis dolore te feugait nulla facilisi. Lorem ipsum dolor sit amet, consectetuer adipiscing elit, sed diam nonummy nibh euismod tincidunt ut laoreet dolore magna aliquam erat volutpat.

Rudolph's Nose Finally Goes Out

Diam nonummy nibh euismod tincidunt ut laoreet dolore magna aliquam erat volutpat. Ut wisi enim ad minim veniam, quis nostrud exerci tation ullamcorper suscipit lobortis nisl ut aliquip ex ea commodo consequat.

Duis autem vel eum iriure dolor in hendrerit in vulputate velit esse molestie consequat, vel illum dolore eu feugiat nulla facilisis. Lorem ipsum dolor sit amet, consectetuer adipiscing elit.

Ut wisi enim ad minim veniam, quis nostrud exerci tation ullamcorper suscipit lobortis nisl ut aliquip ex ea commodo consequat. Duis autem vel eum iriure dolor in hendrerit in vulputate velit esse molestie consequat, vel illum dolore eu feugiat nulla facilisis at vero eros et accumsan et iusto odio dignissim qui blandit praesent luptatum zzril delenit augue duis dolore te feugait nulla facilisi.

The Grinch Steals Christmas Again

Ut wisi enim ad minim veniam, quis nostrud exerci tation ullamcorper suscipit lobortis nisl ut aliquip ex ea commodo consequat. Duis autem vel eum iriure dolor in hendrerit in vulputate velit esse molestie consequat, vel illum dolore eu feugiat nulla facilisis at vero eros et accumsan et iusto odio dignissim qui blandit praesent luptatum zzril delenit augue duis dolore te feugait nulla facilisi.

Nam liber tempor cum soluta nobis eleifend option congue nihil imperdiet doming id quod mazim placerat facer possim assum.

Duis autem vel eum iriure dolor in hendrerit in vulputate velit esse molestie consequat, vel illum dolore eu feugiat nulla facilisis at vero eros et accumsan et iusto odio dignissim qui blandit praesent luptatum zzril delenit augue duis dolore te feugait nulla facilisi. Lorem ipsum dolor sit amet, consectetuer adipiscing elit, sed diam nonummy.

Claustrophobic Borders And Boxes

Provide sufficient breathing room between borders and text.

Squeezing text into boxes or wrapping it too tightly around illustrations or silhouetted photographs produces an unappealing claustrophobic feel.

A VERY TIGHT FIT

Lorum sum ipsum dolor sit amet, con; minimim venami quis nostrud laboris nisi ut aliquip ex ea com dolor . In reprehenderit in volupatate nonumy. Lorumque et ipsum dolor sit amet, con; minimim venami quis nostrud laboris nisi ut aliquip ex ea com dolor in reprehenderit in volu-patate nonumy. In reprehenderit in volupatate nonumy. laboris nisi. Lorum ipsum dolor sit amet, con; minimim venami quis nostrud laboris aliquip ex ea com dolor.

MUCH MORE COMFORTABLE

Lorum sum ipsum dolor sit amet, con; minimim venami quis nostrud laboris nisi ut aliquip ex ea com dolor . In reprehenderit in volupatate nonumy. Lorumque et ipsum dolor sit amet, con; minimim venami quis nostrud laboris nisi ut aliquip ex ea com dolor in reprehenderit in volu patate nonumy ibsen dipsum dong.

Jumping Horizons

Start text columns the same distance from the top of each page throughout a multipage document.

Jumping horizons occur when text columns start at different locations on a page. The up-and-down effect is disconcerting and destroys publication integrity.

PRODUCTS IN THE NEWS 23

Lorum ipsum dolor sit amet, con; minimim venami quis nostrud laboris nisi ut aliquip ex ea com dolor . In reprehenderit in volupatate nonumy. Lorum ipsum dolor sit amet, con; minimim venami quis nostrud laboris nisi ut aliquip ex ea com dolor in reprehenderit in volupatate nonumy. Lorum ipsum dolor sit amet, con. Minimim venami quis nostrud laboris nisi ut aliquip ex ea com dolor in reprehenderit in volupatate nonumy.

Lorum ipsum dolor sit amet, con; minimim venami quis nostrud.

Plastic Products

Lorum ipsum dolor sit amet, con; minimim venami quis nostrud laboris nisi ut aliquip ex ea com dolor . In reprehenderit in volupatate nonumy. Lorum ipsum dolor sit amet, con; minimim venami quis nostrud laboris nisi ut aliquip ex ea com dolor in reprehenderit in volupatate nonumy. Lorum ipsum dolor sit amet, con. Minimim venami quis nostrud laboris nisi ut aliq-

uip ex ea com dolor in reprehenderit in volupatate nonumy.

Ipsum dolor sit amet, con; minimim venami quis nostrud laboris nisi. Lorum ipsum dolor sit amet, con; minimim venami quis nostrud laboris nisi ut aliquip ex ea com dolor in reprehenderit in volupatate nonumy. Lorum ipsum dolor sit amet, con; minimim venami quis nostrud laboris nisi ut aliquip ex ea com dolor.

In reprehenderit in volupatate nonumy. Lorum ipsum dolor sit amet, con; minimim venami quis nostrud laboris nisi ut aliquip ex ea com dolor in reprehenderit in volupatate nonumy. Lorum ipsum dolor sit amet, con. Minimim venami quis nostrud laboris nisi ut aliquip ex ea com dolor in reprehenderit in volupatate nonumy. Lorum ipsum dolor sit amet, con; minimim venami quis nostrud laboris nisi. Lorum ipsum dolor sit amet, con; minimim venami quis nostrud laboris nisi ut aliquip ex ea com dolor in

reprehenderit in volupatate nonumy. Lorum ipsum dolor sit amet, con; minimim venami.

Metal Products

Lorum ipsum dolor sit amet, con; minimim venami quis nostrud laboris nisi ut aliquip ex ea com dolor .

In reprehenderit in volupatate nonumy. Lorum ipsum dolor sit amet, con; minimim venami quis nostrud laboris nisi ut aliquip ex ea com dolor in reprehenderit in volupatate nonumy. Lorum ipsum dolor sit amet, con.

Minimim venami quis nostrud laboris nisi ut aliquip ex ea com dolor in reprehenderit in volupatate nonumy.

Lorum ipsum dolor sit amet, con; minimim venami quis nostrud laboris nisi. Lorum ipsum dolor sit amet, con; minimim venami quis nostrud com dolor visi et laboris nisi ut aliquip ex ea com dolor in reprehenderit de selenium el de carbono in frujelica.

Overly Detailed Charts

Combine and simplify information presented in charts.

To highlight the important message of a chart, combine and simplify less important information. For example, a pie chart with more than six slices is confusing. Often, you can group the smaller slices together to simplify the chart.

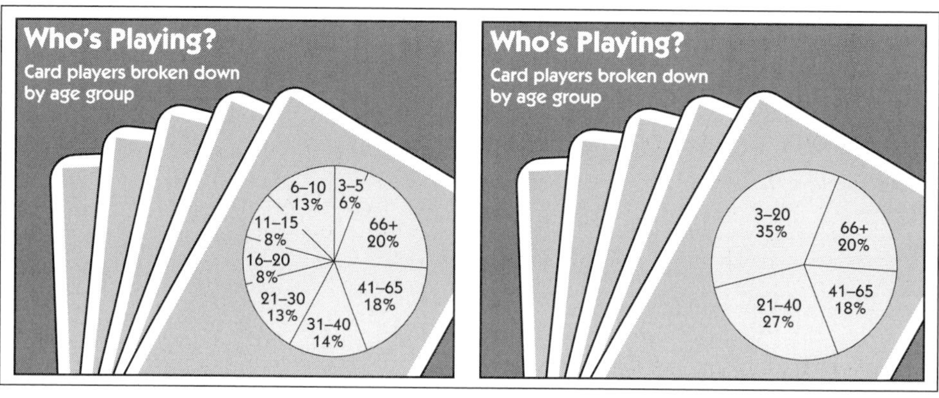

Buried Heads And Subheads

Avoid headlines and subheads isolated near the bottom of columns.

When only one or two lines of type follow a headline at the bottom of a page, the headline becomes visually buried, and the story appears to trail off into nowhere.

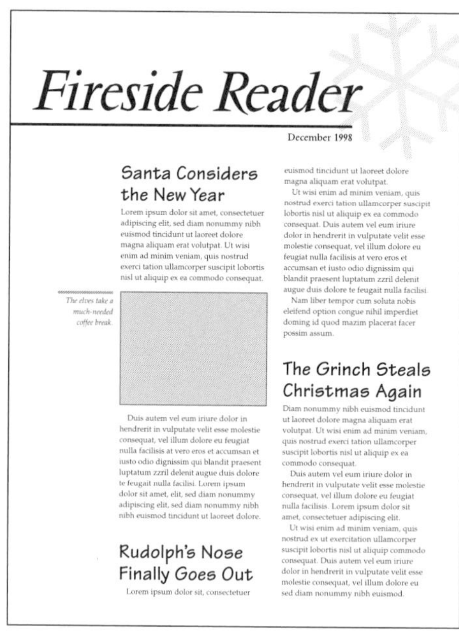

Fireside Reader

December 1998

Santa Considers the New Year

Lorem ipsum dolor sit amet, consectetuer adipiscing elit, sed diam nonummy nibh euismod tincidunt ut laoreet dolore magna aliquam erat volutpat. Ut wisi enim ad minim veniam, quis nostrud exerci tation ullamcorper suscipit lobortis nisl ut aliquip ex ea commodo consequat.

The elves take a much-needed coffee break.

Duis autem vel eum iriure dolor in hendrerit in vulputate velit esse molestie consequat, vel illum dolore eu feugiat nulla facilisis at vero eros et accumsan et iusto odio dignissim qui blandit praesent luptatum zzril delenit augue duis dolore te feugait nulla facilisi. Lorem ipsum dolor sit amet, elit, sed diam nonummy adipiscing elit, sed diam nonummy nibh nibh euismod tincidunt ut laoreet dolore.

Rudolph's Nose Finally Goes Out

Lorem ipsum dolor sit, consectetuer euismod tincidunt ut laoreet dolore magna aliquam erat volutpat.

Ut wisi enim ad minim veniam, quis nostrud exerci tation ullamcorper suscipit lobortis nisl ut aliquip ex ea commodo consequat. Duis autem vel eum iriure dolor in hendrerit in vulputate velit esse molestie consequat, vel illum dolore eu feugiat nulla facilisis at vero eros et accumsan et iusto odio dignissim qui blandit praesent luptatum zzril delenit augue duis dolore te feugait nulla facilisi.

Nam liber tempor cum soluta nobis eleifend option congue nihil imperdiet doming id quod mazim placerat facer possim assum.

The Grinch Steals Christmas Again

Diam nonummy nibh euismod tincidunt ut laoreet dolore magna aliquam erat volutpat. Ut wisi enim ad minim veniam, quis nostrud exerci tation ullamcorper suscipit lobortis nisl ut aliquip ex ea commodo consequat.

Duis autem vel eum iriure dolor in hendrerit in vulputate velit esse molestie consequat, vel illum dolore eu feugiat nulla facilisis. Lorem ipsum dolor sit amet, consectetuer adipiscing elit.

Ut wisi enim ad minim veniam, quis nostrud ex ut exercitation ullamcorper suscipit lobortis nisl ut aliquip commodo consequat. Duis autem vel eum iriure dolor in hendrerit in vulputate velit esse molestie consequat, vel illum dolore eu sed diam nonummy nibh euismod.

Floating Heads And Subheads

Position headlines and subheads close to the text they introduce, leaving plenty of room between them and the preceding text.

The impact and purpose of a heading is weakened if readers can't immediately identify which text it refers to.

Aliquip ex ea com dolor in reprehenderit in volupatate nonumy. Ipsum dolor sit amet, con com dolor nostrud.
Sensitivity to variations in spacing
Minimim venami quis nostrud. Laboris nisi lorum ipsum dolor sit. Aliquip ex ea com dolor in reprehenderit in volupatate nonumy ipsum dolor.
Aliquip ex ea com dolor in reprehenderit in volupatate nonumy. Ipsum dolor sit amet, con com dolor nostrud.
Sensitivity to variations in spacing
Minimim venami quis nostrud. Laboris nisi lorum ipsum dolor sit. Aliquip ex ea com dolor in reprehenderit in volupatate nonumy ispum dolor.

Box-itis And Rule-itis

Don't overuse boxes and rules.

Too many borders and lines make pages look compartmentalized and partitioned. Newsletters, in particular, often have this problem because of their highly modular designs. The result is a busy effect that interferes with reading.

Fireside Reader

Printed by the JingleBell Society of White Plains

December 1998

Santa Considers the New Year

Lorem ipsum dolor sit amet, consectetuer adipiscing elit, sed diam nonummy nibh euismod tincidunt ut laoreet dolore magna aliquam erat volutpat. Ut wisi enim ad minim veniam, quis nostrud exerci tation ullamcorper suscipit lobortis nisl ut aliquip ex ea commodo consequat.

The elves take a much-needed coffee break.

Lorem ipsum dolor sit amet, elit, sed diam nonummy adipiscing elit, sed diam nonummy nibh nibh euismod tincidunt ut laoreet dolore.

dolor in hendrerit in vulputate velit esse molestie consequat, vel illum dolore eu feugiat nulla facilisis at vero eros et accumsan et iusto odio dignissim qui blandit praesent luptatum zzril delenit augue duis dolore te feugait nulla facilisi.

Duis autem vel eum iriure dolor in hendrerit in vulputate velit esse molestie consequat, vel illum dolore eu feugiat nulla facilisis at vero eros et accumsan et iusto odio dignissim qui blandit praesent luptatum zzril delenit augue duis dolore te feugait nulla facilisi. Nam liber tempor cum soluta nobis eleifend option congue nihil imperdiet doming id quod mazim placerat facer possim assum.

The Grinch Steals Christmas Again

Diam nonummy nibh euismod tincidunt ut laoreet dolore magna aliquam erat volutpat. Ut wisi enim ad minim veniam, quis nostrud exerci tation ullamcorper suscipit lobortis nisl ut aliquip ex ea commodo consequat.

Duis autem vel eum iriure dolor in hendrerit in vulputate velit esse molestie consequat, vel illum dolore eu feugiat nulla facilisis. Lorem ipsum dolor sit amet, consectetuer adipiscing elit.

Ut wisi enim ad minim veniam, quis nostrud ex ut exercitation ullamcorper suscipit lobortis nisl ut aliquip commodo consequat. Duis autem vel eum iriure dolor

In This Issue

page 2 Mrs. Claus files for divorce

page 4 North Pole weather report

page 5 Frosty speaks out

page 6 Frosty finally stops talking

Rudolph's Nose Finally Goes Out

Lorem ipsum dolor sit, consectetuer euismod tincidunt ut laoreet dolore magna aliquam erat volutpat.

Ut wisi enim ad minim veniam, quis nostrud exerci tation ullamcorper suscipit lobortis nisl ut aliquip ex ea commodo consequat. Duis autem vel eum iriure

Likewise, too many horizontal rules can break up the natural flow of the page.

Printed by the JingleBell Society of White Plains

Fireside Reader

December 1998

Santa Considers the New Year

Lorem ipsum dolor sit amet, consectetuer adipiscing elit, sed diam nonummy nibh euismod tincidunt ut laoreet dolor magna aliquam erat volutpat. Ut wisi enim ad minim veniam, quis nostrud exerci tation aliquip ex ea commodo consequat.

The elves take a much-needed coffee break.

Duis autem vel eum iriure dolor in hendrerit in vulputate velit esse molestie consequat.

Ut wisi enim ad minim veniam, quis nostrud exerci tation ullamcorper suscipit lobortis nisl ut aliquip ex ea commodo consequat. Duis autem vel eum iriure dolor in hendrerit in vulputate velit esse molestie consequat, vel illum dolore eu feugiat nulla facilisis at vero eros et accumsan et iusto odio dignissim qui blandit praesent luptatum zzril delenit augue duis dolore te feugait nulla facilisi.

Nam liber tempor cum soluta nobis eleifend option congue nihil imperdiet doming id quod mazim placerat facer possim assum, vel illum dolore eu feugiat nulla facilisis at vero eros et accumsan et iusto odio dignissim qui blandit praesent luptatum zzril delenit augue duis dolore te feugait nulla facilisi.

Rudolph's Nose Finally Goes Out

Lorem ipsum dolor sit amet, consectetuer adipiscing elit, sed diam nonummy nibh euismod tincidunt ut laoreet dolore magna aliquam erat volutpat.

The Grinch Steals Christmas Again

Diam nonummy nibh euismod tincidunt ut laoreet dolore magna aliquam erat volutpat. Ut wisi enim ad minim veniam, quis nostrud exerci tation ullamcorper suscipit lobortis nisl ut aliquip ex ea commodo consequat.

Duis autem vel eum iriure dolor in hendrerit in vulputate velit esse molestie consequat, vel illum dolore eu feugiat nulla facilisis. Lorem ipsum dolor sit amet, consectetuer adipiscing elit.

Ut wisi enim ad minim veniam, quis nostrud exerci tation ullamcorper suscipit

Irregularly Shaped Text Blocks

Set type in novelty shapes only when doing so serves a purpose and the text retains its legibility.

It might be fun to set text in the shape of a diamond, cloud, or reindeer, but these special effects can diminish the overall effectiveness of your communication.

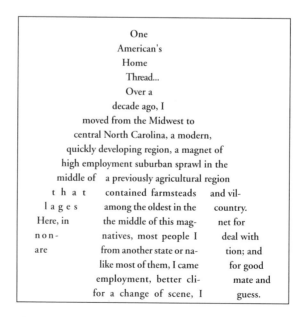

One
American's
Home
Thread...
Over a
decade ago, I
moved from the Midwest to
central North Carolina, a modern,
quickly developing region, a magnet of
high employment suburban sprawl in the
middle of a previously agricultural region
t h a t contained farmsteads and vil-
l a g e s among the oldest in the country.
Here, in the middle of this mag- net for
n o n - natives, most people I deal with
are from another state or na- tion; and
like most of them, I came for good
employment, better cli- mate and
for a change of scene, I guess.

Flush-left type is easiest to read. Lines without a consistent left margin take more time to read because readers lose track of each line's starting point.

Similar Typefaces

Strive for obvious contrast between different typefaces used in a single publication.

When using different typefaces for headlines and text, for example, go for contrast. Avoid typefaces that are similar.

This is Bookman.	**This is Helvetica Bold.**
Now is the time for all good men to come to the aid of their country. The history of the horse and buggy date back to a time when the modern car was not even a figment in	Now is the time for all good men to come to the aid of their country. The history of the horse and buggy date back to a time when the modern car was not even a figment in

Overuse Of Rotated Type

Rotated type works best in short banners or teasers.

Rotated, tilted, or angled type is difficult to read, especially if there's lots of copy or the type is set in a small point size. Readers are forced to tilt their heads, tilt the page, or even move on without reading.

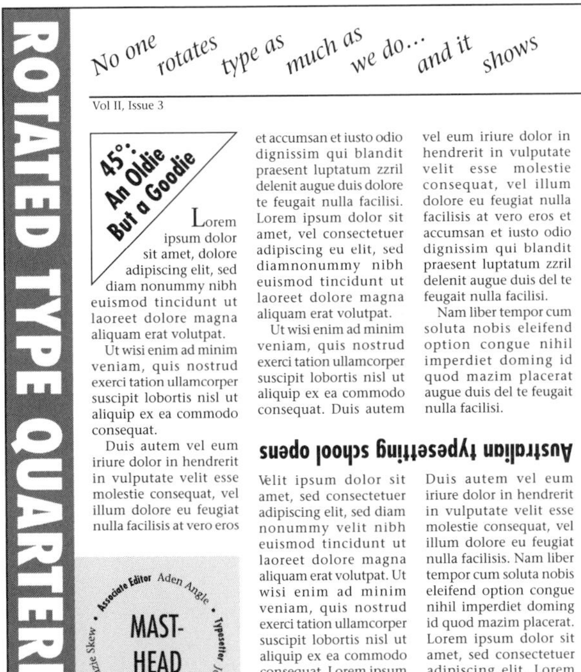

ROTATED TYPE QUARTERLY

No one rotates type as much as we do… and it shows

Vol II, Issue 3

45°: An Oldie But a Goodie

Lorem ipsum dolor sit amet, dolore adipiscing elit, sed diam nonummy nibh euismod tincidunt ut laoreet dolore magna aliquam erat volutpat.

Ut wisi enim ad minim veniam, quis nostrud exerci tation ullamcorper suscipit lobortis nisl ut aliquip ex ea commodo consequat.

Duis autem vel eum iriure dolor in hendrerit in vulputate velit esse molestie consequat, vel illum dolore eu feugiat nulla facilisis at vero eros et accumsan et iusto odio dignissim qui blandit praesent luptatum zzril delenit augue duis dolore te feugait nulla facilisi. Lorem ipsum dolor sit amet, vel consectetuer adipiscing eu elit, sed diamnonummy nibh euismod tincidunt ut laoreet dolore magna aliquam erat volutpat.

Ut wisi enim ad minim veniam, quis nostrud exerci tation ullamcorper suscipit lobortis nisl ut aliquip ex ea commodo consequat. Duis autem vel eum iriure dolor in hendrerit in vulputate velit esse molestie consequat, vel illum dolore eu feugiat nulla facilisis at vero eros et accumsan et iusto odio dignissim qui blandit praesent luptatum zzril delenit augue duis del te feugait nulla facilisi.

Nam liber tempor cum soluta nobis eleifend option congue nihil imperdiet doming id quod mazim placerat augue duis del te feugait nulla facilisi.

Australian typesetting school opens

Velit ipsum dolor sit amet, sed consectetuer adipiscing elit, sed diam nonummy velit nibh euismod tincidunt ut laoreet dolore magna aliquam erat volutpat. Ut wisi enim ad minim veniam, quis nostrud exerci tation ullamcorper suscipit lobortis nisl ut aliquip ex ea commodo consequat. Lorem ipsum dolor consect adipiscing elit nisl.

Duis autem vel eum iriure dolor in hendrerit in vulputate velit esse molestie consequat, vel illum dolore eu feugiat nulla facilisis. Nam liber tempor cum soluta nobis eleifend option congue nihil imperdiet doming id quod mazim placerat. Lorem ipsum dolor sit amet, sed consectetuer adipiscing elit. Lorem ipsum dolor sit amet, sed consectetuer elit.

MAST-HEAD

Associate Editor Aden Angle • Typesetter Johnny Bend • Editor-in-Chief Suzie Skew •

Underlining

Underlining undermines readability.

Use bold or italic type instead of underlining. More than a few underlined words cause visual clutter and confusion. Portions of the descenders often become lost in the underlining, making letters harder to identify and words harder to read.

FURTHER READING

Arnheim, Rudolf. Visual Thinking. Berkeley, CA: University of California Press, 1980.

Beaumont, Michael. Type: Design, Color, Character & Use. Cincinnati, OH: North Light Publishers, 1987.

Boom, Michael. Music through MIDI. Redmond, WA: Microsoft Press, 1987.

Busch, David D. The Hand Scanner Handbook: Mac & PC Editions. Homewood, IL: Business 1 Irwin, 1992.

FURTHER READING

Arnheim, Rudolf. *Visual Thinking.* Berkeley, CA: University of California Press, 1980.

Beaumont, Michael. *Type: Design, Color, Character & Use.* Cincinnati, OH: North Light Publishers, 1987.

Boom, Michael. *Music through MIDI.* Redmond, WA: Microsoft Press, 1987.

Busch, David D. *The Hand Scanner Handbook: Mac & PC Editions.* Homewood, IL: Business 1 Irwin, 1992.

Widows And Orphans

Watch for widows and orphans, which can cause unsightly gaps in text columns.

An *orphan* is a syllable or short word isolated at the bottom of a column, paragraph, or page.

The anchor is a means of securing, of holding fast, while the dolphin is capable of limitless movement. What adds to this tension is the way the dolphin is wrapped around the anchor. Is the dolphin lifting the anchor, or is the anchor holding down the dolphin?

A *widow* is a word or short phrase isolated at the top of a column or a page.

better.

What makes this emblem so appropriate? It encapsulates the the mission of the Aldine Press: to sustain tradition while encouraging progress in fact, to make them interdependent. As both a vehement classicist and an ardent innovator, Aldus used his creative resourcefulness in design and publishing technology to preserve the literature of the past.

You can banish widows and orphans from your layout by editing the text (the best solution), re-hyphenating line endings, or adjusting letter or word spacing.

Unequal Spacing

Strive for consistent spacing between the elements that make up a document.

Readers notice even the smallest variations in spacing. Inconsistent spacing can brand your work as careless and unworthy of serious notice, giving the impression that your message isn't important.

Pay attention to the relative space between headlines or subheads and text.

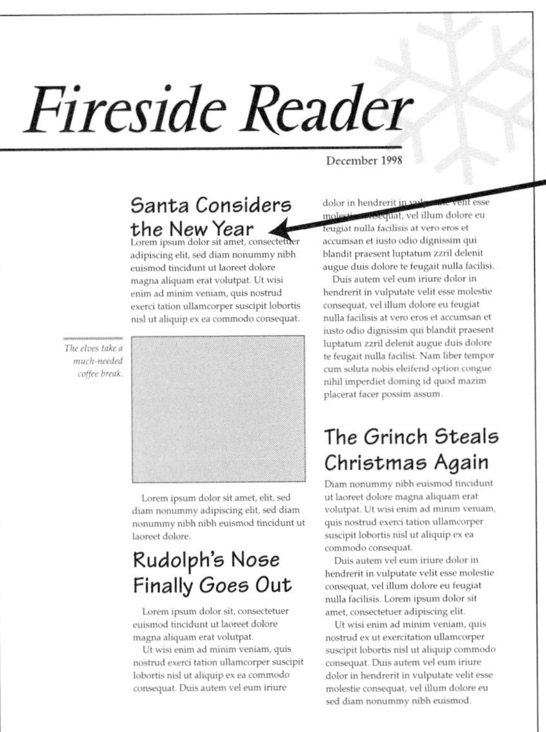

Fireside Reader

December 1998

Santa Considers the New Year

Lorem ipsum dolor sit amet, consectetuer adipiscing elit, sed diam nonummy nibh euismod tincidunt ut laoreet dolore magna aliquam erat volutpat. Ut wisi enim ad minim veniam, quis nostrud exerci tation ullamcorper suscipit lobortis nisl ut aliquip ex ea commodo consequat.

The elves take a much-needed coffee break.

Lorem ipsum dolor sit amet, elit, sed diam nonummy adipiscing elit, sed diam nonummy nibh nibh euismod tincidunt ut laoreet dolore.

Rudolph's Nose Finally Goes Out

Lorem ipsum dolor sit, consectetuer euismod tincidunt ut laoreet dolore magna aliquam erat volutpat.

Ut wisi enim ad minim veniam, quis nostrud exerci tation ullamcorper suscipit lobortis nisl ut aliquip ex ea commodo consequat. Duis autem vel eum iriure

dolor in hendrerit in [illegible] velit esse [illegible] consequat, vel illum dolore eu feugiat nulla facilisis at vero eros et accumsan et iusto odio dignissim qui blandit praesent luptatum zzril delenit augue duis dolore te feugait nulla facilisi.

Duis autem vel eum iriure dolor in hendrerit in vulputate velit esse molestie consequat, vel illum dolore eu feugiat nulla facilisis at vero eros et accumsan et iusto odio dignissim qui blandit praesent luptatum zzril delenit augue duis dolore te feugait nulla facilisi. Nam liber tempor cum soluta nobis eleifend option congue nihil imperdiet doming id quod mazim placerat facer possim assum.

The Grinch Steals Christmas Again

Diam nonummy nibh euismod tincidunt ut laoreet dolore magna aliquam erat volutpat. Ut wisi enim ad minim veniam, quis nostrud exerci tation ullamcorper suscipit lobortis nisl ut aliquip ex ea commodo consequat.

Duis autem vel eum iriure dolor in hendrerit in vulputate velit esse molestie consequat, vel illum dolore eu feugiat nulla facilisis. Lorem ipsum dolor sit amet, consectetuer adipiscing elit.

Ut wisi enim ad minim veniam, quis nostrud ex ut exercitation ullamcorper suscipit lobortis nisl ut aliquip commodo consequat. Duis autem vel eum iriure dolor in hendrerit in vulputate velit esse molestie consequat, vel illum dolore eu sed diam nonummy nibh euismod.

Keep an eye on the spacing between borders and text.

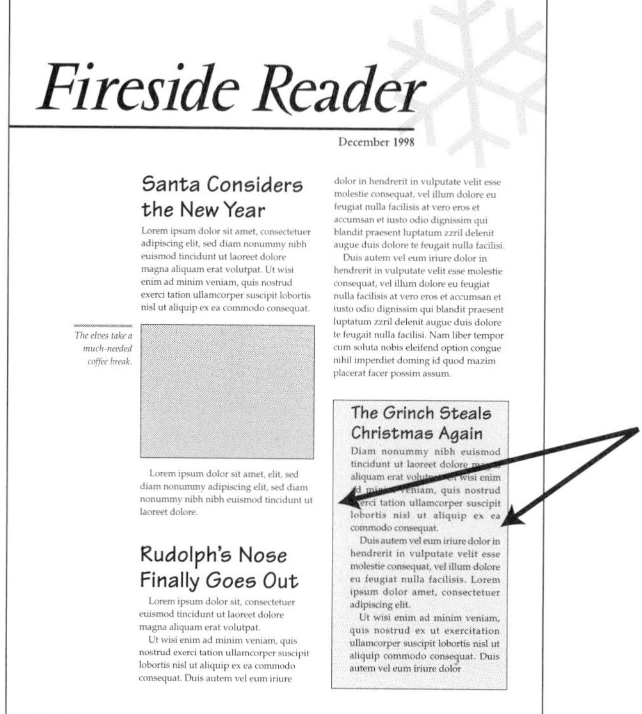

Fireside Reader

December 1998

Santa Considers the New Year

Lorem ipsum dolor sit amet, consectetuer adipiscing elit, sed diam nonummy nibh euismod tincidunt ut laoreet dolore magna aliquam erat volutpat. Ut wisi enim ad minim veniam, quis nostrud exerci tation ullamcorper suscipit lobortis nisl ut aliquip ex ea commodo consequat.

The elves take a much-needed coffee break.

Lorem ipsum dolor sit amet, elit, sed diam nonummy adipiscing elit, sed diam nonummy nibh nibh euismod tincidunt ut laoreet dolore.

Rudolph's Nose Finally Goes Out

Lorem ipsum dolor sit, consectetuer euismod tincidunt ut laoreet dolore magna aliquam erat volutpat.

Ut wisi enim ad minim veniam, quis nostrud exerci tation ullamcorper suscipit lobortis nisl ut aliquip ex ea commodo consequat. Duis autem vel eum iriure dolor in hendrerit in vulputate velit esse molestie consequat, vel illum dolore eu feugiat nulla facilisis at vero eros et accumsan et iusto odio dignissim qui blandit praesent luptatum zzril delenit augue duis dolore te feugait nulla facilisi.

Duis autem vel eum iriure dolor in hendrerit in vulputate velit esse molestie consequat, vel illum dolore eu feugiat nulla facilisis at vero eros et accumsan et iusto odio dignissim qui blandit praesent luptatum zzril delenit augue duis dolore te feugait nulla facilisi. Nam liber tempor cum soluta nobis eleifend option congue nihil imperdiet doming id quod mazim placerat facer possim assum.

The Grinch Steals Christmas Again

Diam nonummy nibh euismod tincidunt ut laoreet dolore magna aliquam erat volutpat. Ut wisi enim ad minim veniam, quis nostrud exerci tation ullamcorper suscipit lobortis nisl ut aliquip ex ea commodo consequat.

Duis autem vel eum iriure dolor in hendrerit in vulputate velit esse molestie consequat, vel illum dolore eu feugiat nulla facilisis. Lorem ipsum dolor amet, consectetuer adipiscing elit.

Ut wisi enim ad minim veniam, quis nostrud ex ut exercitation ullamcorper suscipit lobortis nisl ut aliquip commodo consequat. Duis autem vel eum iriure dolor

Consistently align captions and artwork.

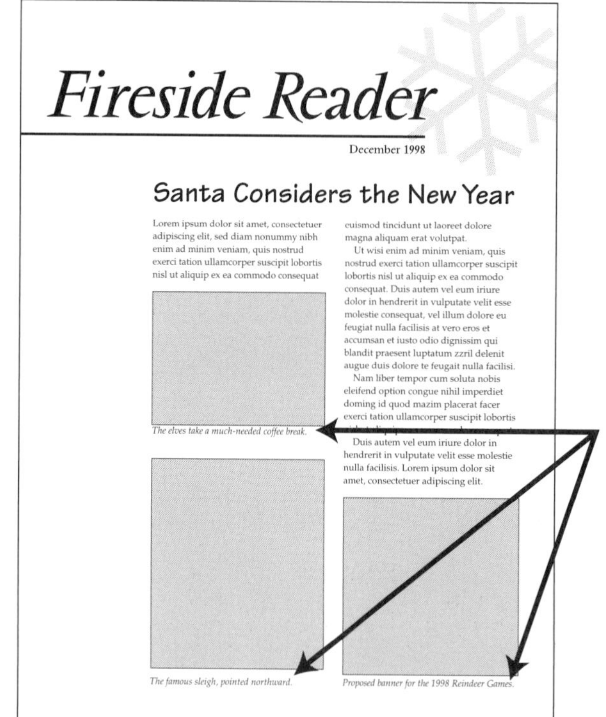

Fireside Reader

December 1998

Santa Considers the New Year

Lorem ipsum dolor sit amet, consectetuer adipiscing elit, sed diam nonummy nibh enim ad minim veniam, quis nostrud exerci tation ullamcorper suscipit lobortis nisl ut aliquip ex ea commodo consequat

The elves take a much-needed coffee break.

The famous sleigh, pointed northward.

euismod tincidunt ut laoreet dolore magna aliquam erat volutpat.

Ut wisi enim ad minim veniam, quis nostrud exerci tation ullamcorper suscipit lobortis nisl ut aliquip ex ea commodo consequat. Duis autem vel eum iriure dolor in hendrerit in vulputate velit esse molestie consequat, vel illum dolore eu feugiat nulla facilisis at vero eros et accumsan et iusto odio dignissim qui blandit praesent luptatum zzril delenit augue duis dolore te feugait nulla facilisi.

Nam liber tempor cum soluta nobis eleifend option congue nihil imperdiet doming id quod mazim placerat facer exerci tation ullamcorper suscipit lobortis

Duis autem vel eum iriure dolor in hendrerit in vulputate velit esse molestie nulla facilisis. Lorem ipsum dolor sit amet, consectetuer adipiscing elit.

Proposed banner for the 1998 Reindeer Games.

Pay attention to the spacing between artwork and text.

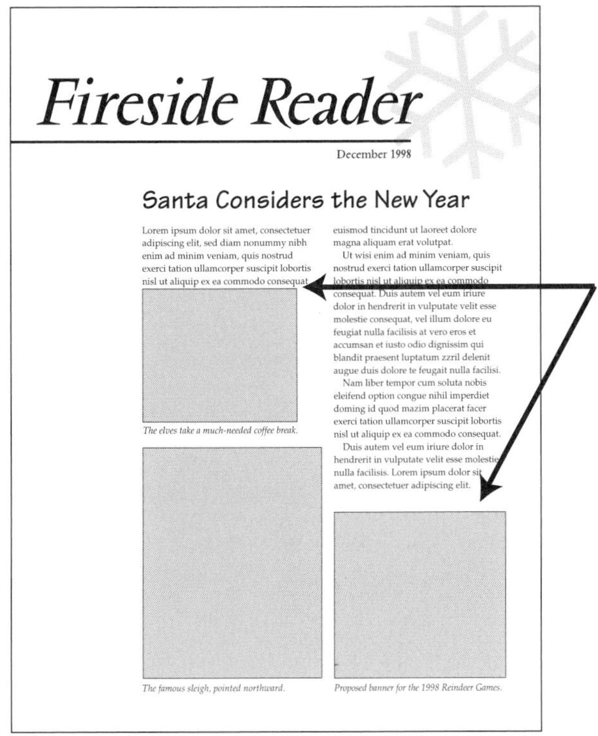

Fireside Reader

December 1998

Santa Considers the New Year

Lorem ipsum dolor sit amet, consectetuer adipiscing elit, sed diam nonummy nibh enim ad minim veniam, quis nostrud exerci tation ullamcorper suscipit lobortis nisl ut aliquip ex ea commodo consequat.

The elves take a much-needed coffee break.

euismod tincidunt ut laoreet dolore magna aliquam erat volutpat.

Ut wisi enim ad minim veniam, quis nostrud exerci tation ullamcorper suscipit lobortis nisl ut aliquip ex ea commodo consequat. Duis autem vel eum iriure dolor in hendrerit in vulputate velit esse molestie consequat, vel illum dolore eu feugiat nulla facilisis at vero eros et accumsan et iusto odio dignissim qui blandit praesent luptatum zzril delenit augue duis dolore te feugait nulla facilisi.

Nam liber tempor cum soluta nobis eleifend option congue nihil imperdiet doming id quod mazim placerat facer exerci tation ullamcorper suscipit lobortis nisl ut aliquip ex ea commodo consequat.

Duis autem vel eum iriure dolor in hendrerit in vulputate velit esse molestie nulla facilisis. Lorem ipsum dolor sit amet, consectetuer adipiscing elit.

The famous sleigh, pointed northward.

Proposed banner for the 1998 Reindeer Games.

Exaggerated Tabs And Indents

Make your tabs and indents proportionate with the type size and column width of your pages.

Default word processor and desktop publishing tab settings are often indented too deeply. Wide columns with large type usually require deeper tabs and indents than narrow columns with small type.

To guard against their editions being counterfeited, Renaissance publishers customarily put a printer's mark, or colophon, on the title page of each book. With a unique colophon, each book could be clearly identified as the work of a particular publisher or printer.

The choice of colophon, however, could not be a casual one. It had to represent what was distinctive about the publishing house. For the Aldine Press, Aldus Manutius mulled over the range of classical and Christian icons and finally chose the dolphin and anchor.

In the early Christian era, the dolphin and anchor represented the soul being

To guard against their editions being counterfeited, Renaissance publishers customarily put a printer's mark, or colophon, on the title page of each book. With a unique colophon, each book could be clearly identified as the work of a particular publisher or printer.

The choice of colophon, however, could not be a casual one. It had to represent what was distinctive about the publishing house. For the Aldine Press, Aldus Manutius mulled over the range of classical and Christian icons and finally chose the dolphin and anchor.

In the early Christian era, the dolphin and anchor represented the soul being

Excessive Hyphenation

Switch to manual hyphenation or adjust the hyphenation controls in your software when too many words are hyphenated.

Excessive hyphenation occurs in narrow columns of type. Solutions include reducing type size, increasing column width, manually hyphenating lines of text, or choosing unjustified, flush-left alignment.

> Five hundred years ago, Christopher Co-
lumbus was on his knees in throne rooms
throughout Europe, scrambling to finance
his first voyage to the New World. Mean-
while, his Venetian countryman Aldus Ma-
nutius—scholar, printer, and entrepre-
neur—was establishing what would be-
come the greatest publishing house in Eu-
rope, the Aldine Press. Like Columbus, Al-
dus Manutius was driven by force of in-
tellect and personality to realize a lifelong
dream.
>
> Aldus' greatest passion was Greek litera-
ture, which was rapidly gowing up in smoke
in the wake of the marauding army. It
seemed obvious to Aldus that the best way

> Five hundred years ago, Christopher
Columbus was on his knees in throne
rooms throughout Europe, scrambling to
finance his first voyage to the New World.
Meanwhile, his Venetian countryman
Aldus Manutius—scholar, printer, and entre-
preneur—was establishing what would
become the greatest publishing house in
Europe, the Aldine Press. Like Columbus,
Aldus Manutius was driven by force of
intellect and personality to realize a lifelong
dream.
>
> Aldus' greatest passion was Greek litera-
ture, which was rapidly gowing up in smoke
in the wake of the marauding army. It
seemed obvious to Aldus that the best way

Increasing the hyphenation zone in your software allows longer words at the end of each line, but this might result in excessive word spacing.

Manual hyphenation gives you control over which words are hyphenated and which are moved intact to the next line.

Cramped Logos And Addresses

Design your advertisements from the bottom up.

A firm's logo, address, phone number, and other identifying information are often difficult to read because they're treated as afterthoughts.

Having trouble establishing your corporate presence?

Owning a degree in business management doesn't always mean you have all the answers. You may have a great product, but without good name recognition, no one's going to notice it. And that means no one's going to buy it, either.

If your company's struggling to be noticed, you need to call Bright Ideas. We have fifty years' experience in improving corporate presence. Even the most obscure company name can become a household word after the Bright Ideas PR team works its magic.

John Q. Nobody, founder of Nobody Enterprises (and a satisfied Bright Ideas client), can vouch for the power of name recognition. "Before I went to Bright Ideas, we had no corporate presence at all. We couldn't even get a phone book listing. But BI retooled our image, and now everyone knows we're Nobody."

The power of Bright Ideas can work for you. Give us a callat 1-800-DIMBULB for a brighter future.

BRIGHT IDEAS

Having trouble establishing your corporate presence?

Owning a degree in business management doesn't always mean you have all the answers. You may have a great product, but without good name recognition, no one's going to notice it. And that means no one's going to buy it, either.

If your company's struggling to be noticed, you need to call Bright Ideas. We have fifty years' experience in improving corporate presence. Even the most obscure company name can become a household word after the Bright Ideas PR team works its magic.

The power of Bright Ideas can work for you. Give us a call at 1-800-DIMBULB for a brighter future.

1012 Eureka Avenue, Suite #415
Brighton, CA 87526
1-800-DIMBULB

To avoid that, build your documents around the logo and other vital information—or at least place those elements on the page first, instead of last.

Many designers create a single graphic file consisting of a properly spaced logo, address, and other information. That file can then easily be added to any ad, flyer, or other document in a single step.

Using Several Similar Visuals

Establish a visual hierarchy by altering the size and shape of photos and illustrations.

The size of an image should be a reflection of its relative importance. Avoid running every illustration at the same size and shape, or readers won't know where to look first.

Our movie critic rates "Jaws 6"—see page 12

THE BIG NEWS

Dow Jones dips again—see the Financial Section

THE BIG STORY

Duis autem vel eum iriure dolor in hendrerit in vulputate velit esse molestie consequat, vel illum dolore eu feugiat nulla facilisis at vero eros et accumsan et iusto odio dignissim qui blandit praesent luptatum zzril delenit augue duis dolore te feugait nulla facilisi.

Quat duis autem vel eum iriure dolor in hendrerit in vulputate velit esse molestie consequat, vel illum dolore eu feugiat nulla facilisis at vero eros et accumsan et iusto odio dignissim qui blandit praesent luptatum zzril delenit augue duis dolore te

Nam liber tempor cum soluta nobis eleifend option congue nihil imperdiet doming id quod mazim placerat facer possim assum. Lorem ipsum dolor sit amet, consectetuer adipiscing elit, sed diam nonummy nibh euismod tincidunt ut laoreet dolore magna aliquam erat volutpat. Ut wisi enim ad minim veniam, quis nostrud exerci tation ullamcorper suscipit lobortis nisl ut aliquip ex ea commodo consequat.

Duis autem vel eum iriure dolor in hendrerit in vulputate velit esse molestie consequat, vel illum dolore eu feugiat

The Big News Gets Bigger Yet Again

Duis autem vel eum iriure dolor in hendrerit in vulputate velit esse molestie consequat, vel illum dolore eu feugiat nulla facilisis at vero eros et accumsan et iusto odio dignissim qui blandit praesent luptatum zzril delenit augue duis dolore te feugait nulla facilisi. Ut wisi enim ad minim veniam, quis nostrud Lorem ipsum dolor sit amet, consectetuer adipiscing elit, sed diam nonummy nibh euismod tincidunt ut laoreet dolore magna aliquam erat volutpat.

Ut wi nim ad minim veniam, quis nostrud exerci tation ullamcor ritin vulputate velit esse molestie consequat, vel illum dolore eu feugiat nulla facilisis at vero eros et accumsan et iusto odio dignissim qui blandit praesent luptatum zzril delenit augue duis dolore te feugait nulla facilisi. Lorem ipsum dolor sit amet, consectetuer adipiscing elit, sed diam nonummy nibh euismod tincidunt ut laoreet dolore magna aliquam erat volutpat.

Ut wisi enim ad minim veniam, quis nostrud exerci tation lobortis nisl ut aliquip ex ea commodo, lobortis nisl ut aliquip ex commodo feugait nulla facilisi.

Exhausted paperboy gasps "It's as heavy as a brick!"

Lorem ipsum dolor sit amet, consect adipiscing elit, sed diam nonummy nibh euismod tincidunt ut laoreet dolore magna aliquam erat volutpat. Ut wisi enim ad minim veniam, quis nostrud exerci tation ullamcorper suscipit lobortis nisl ut aliquip ex ea commodo consequat.

Lorem ipsum dolor sit amet, consect adipiscing elit, sed diam nonummy nibh euismod tincidunt ut laoreet dolore magna aliquam erat volutpat. Ut wisi enim ad minim veniam, quis nostrud exerci tation ullamcorper suscipit lobortis nisl ut aliquip ex ea commodo consequat.

Duis autem vel eum iriure dolor in hendrerit in vulputate velit esse molestie consequat, vel illum dolore eu feugiat nulla facilisis at vero eros

Ut wisi enim ad minim veniam, quis nostrud exerci tation ullamcorper suscipit lobortis nisl ut aliquip ex ea commodo consequat. Duis autem vel eum iriure dolor in hendrerit in vulputate velit esse molestie consequat, vel illum dolore eu feugiat nulla facilisis at vero eros et accumsan et iusto odio dignissim qui blandit praesent luptatum zzril delenit augue duis dolore te feugait facilisi.Duis autem vel eum iriure dolor ummy nibh euismod tincidunt ut laoreet dolore magna aliquam erat volutpat.

Ut wisi enim ad minim veniam, quis nostrud exerci tation ullamcorper suscipit lobortis nisl ut aliquip ex ea commodo consequat. Duis autem vel eum iriure dolor in hendrerit in vulputate velit esse molestie consequat, vel illum dolore eu feugiat nulla facilisis Duis autem vel eum iriure dolor in hendrerit in vulputate velit ess

Price gets bigger too

Ut wisi enim ad minim veniam, quis nostrud exerci tation ullamcorper suscipit lobortis nisl ut aliquip ex ea commodo consequat. Duis autem vel eum iriure dolor in hendrerit in vulputate velit quod mazim placerat facer possim assum. Lorem ipsum dolor sit amet, consectetuer adipiscing elit, sed diam nonummy nibh euismod tincidunt nisl ut aliquip ex ea commodo consequat.vel illum do-

Too Many Typefaces

Avoid a potpourri of typefaces, sizes, and weights.

Including too many typefaces on a single page—one of the most common desktop publishing mistakes—makes your pages look amateurish and confusing.

Use a few carefully chosen typefaces, sizes, and weights to organize your information and create a hierarchy of importance. Each new typeface, size, or weight slows the reader down.

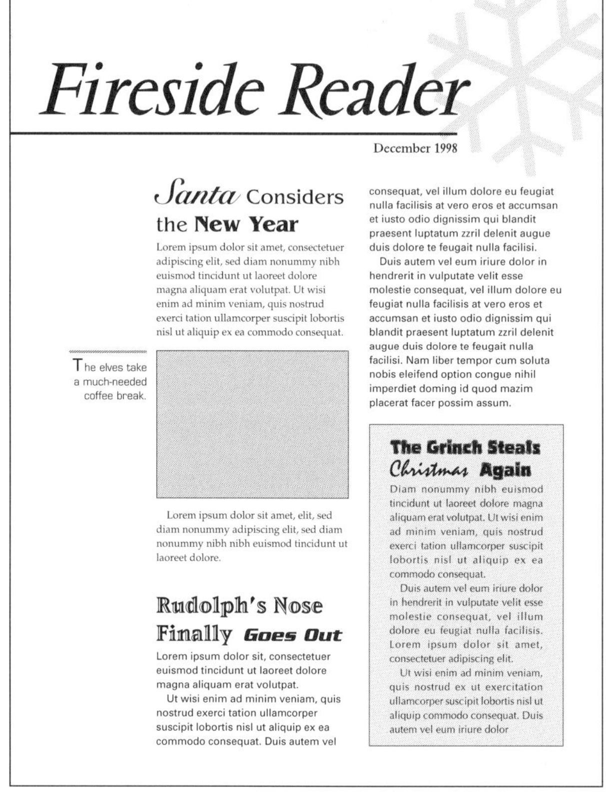

Fireside Reader

December 1998

Santa Considers the New Year

Lorem ipsum dolor sit amet, consectetuer adipiscing elit, sed diam nonummy nibh euismod tincidunt ut laoreet dolore magna aliquam erat volutpat. Ut wisi enim ad minim veniam, quis nostrud exerci tation ullamcorper suscipit lobortis nisl ut aliquip ex ea commodo consequat.

The elves take a much-needed coffee break.

Lorem ipsum dolor sit amet, elit, sed diam nonummy adipiscing elit, sed diam nonummy nibh nibh euismod tincidunt ut laoreet dolore.

Rudolph's Nose Finally Goes Out

Lorem ipsum dolor sit, consectetuer euismod tincidunt ut laoreet dolore magna aliquam erat volutpat.

Ut wisi enim ad minim veniam, quis nostrud exerci tation ullamcorper suscipit lobortis nisl ut aliquip ex ea commodo consequat. Duis autem vel

consequat, vel illum dolore eu feugiat nulla facilisis at vero eros et accumsan et iusto odio dignissim qui blandit praesent luptatum zzril delenit augue duis dolore te feugait nulla facilisi.

Duis autem vel eum iriure dolor in hendrerit in vulputate velit esse molestie consequat, vel illum dolore eu feugiat nulla facilisis at vero eros et accumsan et iusto odio dignissim qui blandit praesent luptatum zzril delenit augue duis dolore te feugait nulla facilisi. Nam liber tempor cum soluta nobis eleifend option congue nihil imperdiet doming id quod mazim placerat facer possim assum.

The Grinch Steals Christmas Again

Diam nonummy nibh euismod tincidunt ut laoreet dolore magna aliquam erat volutpat. Ut wisi enim ad minim veniam, quis nostrud exerci tation ullamcorper suscipit lobortis nisl ut aliquip ex ea commodo consequat.

Duis autem vel eum iriure dolor in hendrerit in vulputate velit esse molestie consequat, vel illum dolore eu feugiat nulla facilisis. Lorem ipsum dolor sit amet, consectetuer adipiscing elit.

Ut wisi enim ad minim veniam, quis nostrud ex ut exercitation ullamcorper suscipit lobortis nisl ut aliquip commodo consequat. Duis autem vel eum iriure dolor

Misaligned Elements

Strive to keep all elements on separate pages aligned with each other.

Consistency in aligning design elements, such as subheads and illustrations can make the difference between a professional-looking document and a rag-tag disorderly one.

Align columns and graphics vertically. Subheads, rules, boxes, bullets, and other items can rest along the same baseline as the text they accompany.

SPORTS NEWS

The Authority On What's Sporty

Track Team's Coach Is Very Confident

Lorem ipsum dolor sit amet, consectetuer adipiscing elit, sed diam nonummy nibh euismod tincidunt ut laoreet dolore magna aliquam erat volutpat. Ut wisi enim ad minim veniam, quis nostrud exerci tation ullamcorper suscipit lobortis nisl ut aliquip ex ea commodo consequat.

Duis autem vel eum iriure dolor in hendrerit in nisl vulputate velit molestie mini consequat, vel illum dolore eu feugiat nulla facilisis at vero eros et accumsan et iusto odio dignissim qui blandit duis praesent zzril delenit augue duis dolore te feugait nulla facilisi. Lorem ipsum dolor sit amet, consectetuer vel illum doloreadipiscing

Coach Fargus

The hurdles event is one of the team's strengths, says Fargus

elit, sed diam nonummy euismod magna aliquam iusto odioerat erat volutpat.

Ut wisi enim ad minim veniam, quis nostrud execi tation ullam corper susc pit lobortis nisl aliquip ex commodo consequat. Duis autem vel eum iriure dolor in hendrerit in vulputate velit esse molestie consequat, vel illum eu feugiat nulla at ver eros et accumsan iusto odio dignissim qui blandit present duis dolore te feugait null.

Nam liber tempor cum soluta nobis eleifend option congue nihil imperdiet doming id quod mazim placerat facer poss assium. Lorem ipsum dolor sit amet.

Lack Of Contrast Between Text And Other Elements

Strive for as much contrast between type and background as possible.

Without sufficient contrast, it's hard to distinguish text from backgrounds. Beware of overly dark screens or screened graphics placed behind text, or color combinations that can affect readability.

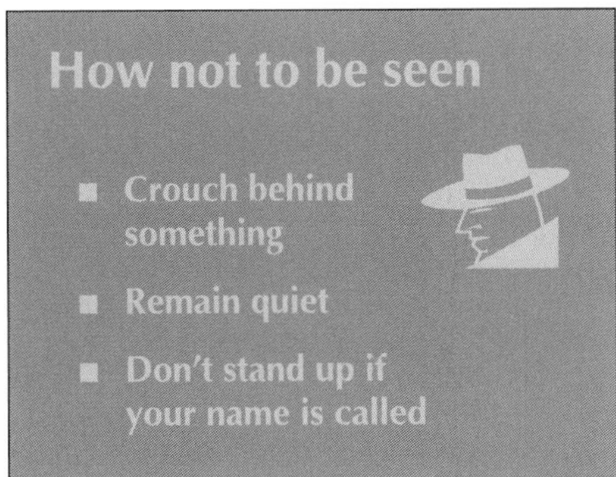

How not to be seen
Crouch behind something
Remain quiet
Don't stand up if your name is called

Unnecessary Special Effects

Overusing special type and graphic effects serves no effective purpose.

There's no substitute for clean, concise design. Using special effects for their own sake makes pages look frivolous and over-designed. Some computer-generated effects make information much more difficult to process and understand.

Graphic Gimmickry

Don't substitute or overshadow content with graphics and photos.

Graphics and photos should support the content of a document, making complicated information easier to understand. Access to a large library of art—whether it's clip art, photos, scans, or freehand illustrations—doesn't mean that you should flood your document to show your artistic skill. Using too many elements clutters the page.

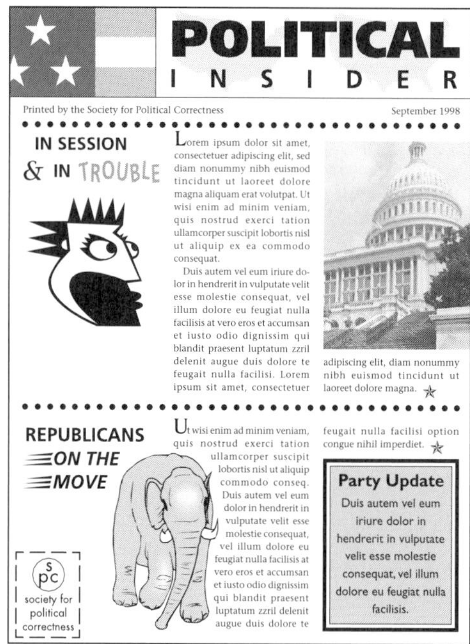

POLITICAL INSIDER

Printed by the Society for Political Correctness — September 1998

IN SESSION & IN TROUBLE

Lorem ipsum dolor sit amet, consectetuer adipiscing elit, sed diam nonummy nibh euismod tincidunt ut laoreet dolore magna aliquam erat volutpat. Ut wisi enim ad minim veniam, quis nostrud exerci tation ullamcorper suscipit lobortis nisl ut aliquip ex ea commodo consequat.

Duis autem vel eum iriure dolor in hendrerit in vulputate velit esse molestie consequat, vel illum dolore eu feugiat nulla facilisis at vero eros et accumsan et iusto odio dignissim qui blandit praesent luptatum zzril delenit augue duis dolore te feugait nulla facilisi. Lorem ipsum sit amet, consectetuer adipiscing elit, diam nonummy nibh euismod tincidunt ut laoreet dolore magna.

REPUBLICANS ON THE MOVE

Ut wisi enim ad minim veniam, quis nostrud exerci tation ullamcorper suscipit lobortis nisl ut aliquip commodo conseq. Duis autem vel eum dolor in hendrerit in vulputate velit esse molestie consequat, vel illum dolore eu feugiat nulla facilisis at vero eros et accumsan et iusto odio dignissim qui blandit praesent luptatum zzril delenit augue duis dolore te feugait nulla facilisi option congue nihil imperdiet.

Party Update

Duis autem vel eum iriure dolor in hendrerit in vulputate velit esse molestie consequat, vel illum dolore eu feugiat nulla facilisis.

spc society for political correctness

Shoehorning

Jam-packing every tidbit of information into the smallest available area will cause readers to fatigue.

Shoehorning makes information difficult to find and tiresome to read. Look for ways to include white space in your design.

Printed by the Society for Political Correctness

September 1998

IN SESSION & IN TROUBLE

Ut wisi enim ad minim veniam, quis nostrud exercitation ullam corper suscipit lobortis nisl ut aliquip commodo conseq. Duis autem vel eum dolor in hendrerit in vulputate velit esse molestie consequat, vel illum dolore eu feugiat nulla facilisis at vero eros et accumsan et odio dignissim qui blandit praesent luptatum zzril delenit augue duis dolore te feugait nulla facilisi option congue nihil imperdiet.

Duis autem vel eum iriure dolor in hendrerit in vulputate velit esse molestie consequat, vel illum dolore eu feugiat nulla facilisis at vero eros et accumsan

et iusto odio dignissim qui blandit praesent luptatum zzril delenit augue duis dolore te feugait nulla facilisi. Lorem ipsum sit amet, consectetuer adipiscing elit, diam nonummy nibh euismod tincidunt ut laoreet dolore magna.Lorem dolor sit amet, consectetuer adipiscing, sedl diam nonummy euismod tincidunt ut laoreet dolore magna aliquam erat volutpat. Ut wisi enim ad minim veniam, quis nostrud exerci tation ullamcorper suscipit lobortis nisl ut aliquip ex ea commodo consequat. Duis autem vel eum iriure dolor in hendrerit in vulputate velit. Lorem ipsum del solo.

REPUBLICANS ON THE MOVE

Ut wisi enim ad minim veniam, quis nostrud exercitation ullam corper suscipit lobortis nisl ut aliquip commodo conseq. Duis autem vel eum dolor in hendrerit in vulputate velit esse molestie consequat, vel illum dolore eu feugiat nulla facilisis at vero eros et accumsan et odio dignissim qui blandit praesent luptatum zzril delenit augue duis dolore te feugait facilisi option congue nihil imperdiet.

Duis autem vel eum iriure dolor inhendrerit in vulputate velit esse molestie consequat, vel illum dolore eu feugiat nulla facilisis at vero eros et accumsan et iusto odio dignissim qui blandit praesent luptatum zzril delenit augue duis dolore te feugait nulla facilisi. Lorem ipsum sit amet, consectetuer, diam nonummy nibh euismod tincidunt ut laoreet dolore magna.Lorem dolor sit amet, consectetuer adipiscing, sedl diam nonummy euismod tincidunt ut laoreet dolore magna aliquam erat volutpat. Ut wisi enim ad minim veniam, quis nostrud exerci tation ullamcorper suscipit lobortis nisl ut aliquip ex ea commodo consequat. Duis autem vel eum iriure dolor in hendrerit in vulputate velit.

Party Update

Duis autem vel eum iriure dolor in hendrerit in vulputate velit esse molestie consequat, vel illum dolore eu feugiat nulla.

Lorem ipsum del solo. Lorem ipsum sit amet, consectetuer, diam nonummy nibh euismod tincidunt ut laoreet dolore magna.Lorem dolor sit amet, consectetuer adipiscing, sedl diam nonummy tincidunt ut laoreet dolore magna aliquam erat volutpat. Ut wisi enim ad minim veniam, quis nostrud exerci tation ullamcorper suscipit lobortis nisl ut aliquip ex ea commodo consequat. Duis autem vel eum iriure dolor in hendrerit in vulputate velit. Lorem ipsum

Too Much Gray

Unless your reader is very devoted, a text-heavy page will discourage reading.

Remember that gray pages send a visual signal that a page will be time-consuming. No matter how compelling your content is, readers will be discouraged from reading your document.

POLITICAL INSIDER

Printed by the Society for Political Correctness

September 1998

In Session & In Trouble

Ut wisi enim ad minim veniam, quis nostrud exercitation ullam corper suscipit lobortis nisl ut aliquip commodo conseq. Duis autem vel eum dolor in hendrerit in vulputate velit esse molestie consequat, vel illum dolore eu feugiat nulla facilisis at vero eros et accumsan et odio dignissim qui blandit praesent luptatum zzril delenit augue duis dolore te feugait nulla facilisi option congue nihil imperdiet.

Duis autem vel eum iriure dolor in hendrerit in vulputate velit esse molestie consequat, vel illum dolore eu feugiat nulla facilisis at vero eros et accumsan et iusto odio dignissim qui blandit praesent luptatum zzril delenit augue duis dolore te feugait nulla facilisi. Lorem ipsum sit amet, consectetuer adipiscing elit, diam nonummy nibh euismod tincidunt ut laoreet dolore magna.Lorem dolor sit amet, consectetuer adipiscing, sedl diam nonummy euismod tincidunt ut laoreet dolore magna aliquam erat volutpat. Ut wisi enim ad minim veniam, quis nostrud exerci tation ullamcorper suscipit lobortis nisl ut aliquip ex ea commodo consequat. Duis autem vel eum iriure dolor in hendrerit in vulputate velit.

Duis autem vel eum dolor in hendrerit in vulputate velit esse molestie consequat, vel illum dolore eu feugiat nulla facilisis at vero eros et accumsan et odio dignissim qui blandit praesent luptatum zzril delenit augue duis dolore te feugait nulla facilisi option congue nihil imperdiet.

Duis autem vel eum iriure dolor in hendrerit in vulputate velit esse molestie consequat, vel illum dolore eu feugiat nulla facilisis at vero eros et accumsan et iusto odio dignissim qui blandit praesent luptatum zzril delenit augue duis dolore te feugait nulla facilisi. Lorem ipsum sit amet, consectetuer adipiscing elit, diam nonummy nibh euismod tincidunt ut laoreet dolore magna.Lorem dolor sit amet, consectetuer adipiscing, sedl diam nonummy euismod tincidunt ut laoreet dolore magna aliquam erat volutpat. Ut wisi enim ad minim veniam, quis nostrud exerci tation ullamcorper suscipit lobortis nisl ut aliquip ex ea commodo consequat. Duis autem vel eum iriure dolor in hendrerit in vulputate velit.

Republicans on the Move

Lorem ipsum sit amet, consec tetuer adipiscing elit, diam nonummy euismod tincidunt ut laoreet dolore magna.Lorem dolor sit amet, consectetuer adipiscing, sedl diam nonummy euismod tincidunt ut laoreet dolore magna aliquam erat volutpat. Ut wisi enim ad minim veniam, quis nostrud exerci tation ullamcorper suscipit lobortis nisl ut aliquip ex ea commodo consequat. Duis autem vel eum iriure dolor in hendrerit in vulputate velit.

Duis autem vel eum dolor in hendrerit in vulputate velit esse molestie consequat, vel illum dolore eu feugiat nulla facilisis at vero eros et accumsan et odio dignissim qui blandit praesent luptatum zzril delenit augue duis dolore te feugait nulla facilisi option congue nihil imperdiet.

Duis autem vel eum iriure dolor in hendrerit in vulputate velit esse molestie consequat, vel illum dolore eu feugiat nulla facilisis at vero eros et accumsan et iusto odio dignissim qui blandit praesent luptatum zzril delenit augue duis dolore te feugait nulla facilisi. Lorem ipsum sit amet, consectetuer adipiscing elit, diam nonummy nibh euismod tincidunt ut laoreet dolore magna.Lorem dolor sit amet, consectetuer adipiscing, sedl diam nonummy euismod tincidunt ut laoreet dolore magna aliquam erat volutpat. Ut wisi enim ad minim veniam, quis nostrud exerci tation ullamcorper suscipit lobortis nisl ut aliquip ex ea commodo consequat. Duis autem vel eum iriure dolor in hendrerit in vulputate velit.

Ut wisi enim ad minim veniam, nostrud exercitation ullam corper suscipit lobortis nisl ut aliquip commodo conseq. Duis autem vel eum dolor in hendrerit in vulputate velit esse molestie consequat, vel illum dolore eu feugiat nulla facilisis at vero eros et accumsan et odio dignissim qui blandit praesent luptatum zzril delenit augue duis dolore te feugait nulla facilisi option congue nihil imperdiet et corpus callosum.

Moving On

If you're using this chapter as an all-points checkup for your document and still haven't found any errors, congratulations! You've avoided the standard glitches, which puts your document way above average.

Unfortunately, an error-free document is not necessarily an effective one—it merely has more *potential* to be effective. In our final chapter, we'll take a look at some sample documents—some of them riddled with errors, others teetering on the brink of success—and show how they can be improved, through the application of basic design concepts and a smattering of common sense.

13 Redesign

The redesign process is nearly identical to the design process. The only real difference is your starting point. Rather than dreaming up possible designs, you begin by evaluating the existing design.

What you definitely *don't* want to do is open up the original document and start shoving textblocks and graphics around, hoping to hit upon a better arrangement. For those particular page elements, it's unlikely that a better arrangement exists because they were chosen and sized with a specific design in mind. Rearranging them is like trying to improve the appearance of an ugly jigsaw puzzle by interlocking the pieces differently—barring a miracle, your chances for success are nil.

Instead, get a hard copy of the original document and submit it to a thorough inspection. Read it through from start to finish. Try to pretend you're a first-time reader. Evaluate each page element on its own merits and on its relationship to the overall design. Ask yourself these sorts of questions:

- Is the reading process intuitive or unnecessarily cumbersome?
- Are the most prominent elements also the most important?
- If each page (or spread) was viewed as a separate unit, would it be apparent that all of them came from the same document?
- Do any elements seem inappropriate or out of place?
- When you *view* (as opposed to *read*) the document, what adjectives leap to mind as possible descriptors?

Your thorough scrutiny will produce one of three results. In the worst-case scenario, you'll decide that the original layout was completely off the mark and start the design process from scratch. Don't be too depressed by this outcome. You've saved yourself a lot of effort by realizing early the futility of a partial overhaul. Actually, a fresh start can be very liberating—you might not realize how strong your preconceptions are until you've deliberately discarded them.

In the best-case scenario, you'll decide that the document is nearly a success, with only a few discreet problem areas—an overly-formal headline font, perhaps, or a cluttered-looking corner. Pinpoint the problem elements, then delete, restructure, or replace them.

In the final (and most common) scenario, you'll have a mixed bag of impressions. Some page elements seem effective, others don't—but the "good" elements don't necessarily work well together. Or perhaps your document is attractive on a page-by-page basis, but the overall package is inconsistent, conveying no clear theme.

At this point, it's time to grab your sketchpad and draw some sample layouts, using a few harmonious pieces from the previous design to begin each sketch. Basically, you're going back to the design process, but you've got a head start—the original document has become a "grab bag" of design ideas. Quite often, one or two borrowed elements will suggest a framework for an entirely new design. Don't try to preserve too much of the original layout—you'll only end up re-creating the former flawed design.

Think of it this way. The design concepts you preserve are points, and a good design is a straight line that connects them. If you start with one or two predefined points, you'll always be able to produce a straight line. If you use three or more predefined points, however, your design must "bend" to connect them, and that's backward—if anything, your page elements should bend to fit your design.

Redesign Gallery

The remainder of this chapter is devoted to a gallery of redesigned documents. Each before-and-after example is thoroughly annotated, cataloging the defects of the old design and the advantages of the new one. I've tried to provide examples which encompass all of the "redesign scenarios"—some of the documents receive a complete overhaul, while others require only minor changes.

As you peruse the gallery, try to focus on design concepts rather than specific document types. A suggestion for producing a great-looking brochure might apply equally well to your newsletter. Remember, most good design tips are not document-specific.

THE ROAD NOT TAKEN

Often, the redesigner is faced with a tough choice: the original draft contains two utterly brilliant, utterly incompatible ideas. Unable to bear the thought of discarding either one, the designer attempts to shoehorn them together, usually with disastrous results.

Here's a better plan: Use one of the ideas in the redesign, and put a copy of the original document in your clip file. Next time you turn to the ol' clip file for inspiration, that second brilliant idea—the "road not taken"—will be ready and waiting for you.

Newsletters

Make sure the design of your newsletter matches the tone of its content. In the newsletter below, the comical dinosaur graphic and the article titles seem to be striving for a sense of fun—but the design is extremely conservative.

Original

The scattered nameplate is difficult to read—is it "The Fossil Record" or "Fossil The Record?"

The museum's logo is overpowered by the larger dinosaur above it.

The Official Newsletter of the 

July 1996

DEM BONES, DEM BONES...

Lorem ipsum dolor sit amet, consectetuer adipiscing elit, sed diam nonummy nibh euismod tincidunt ut laoreet dolore magna aliquam erat volutpat. Ut wisi enim ad minim veniam, quis nostrud exerci tation ullamcorp suscipit lobortis nisl ut aliquip ex ea commodo consequatvelit esse molestie consequat. Duis autem vel eum iriure dolor in hendrerit in vulputate velit esse molestie consequat, vel illum dolore eu feugiat nulla facilisis at vero eros et accumsan et iusto odio dignissim qui blandit praesent luptatum zzril delenit augue duis dolore te feugait nulla facilisi. Lorem ipsum dolor sit amet, consectet adipiscing elit, sed diam nonummy nibh euismod tincidunt ut laoreet dolore magna aliquam erat volutpat.

Ut wisi enim ad minim veniam, quis nostrud exerci tation ullamcorper suscipit lobortis nisl ut aliquip ex ea commodo consequat. Duis autem vel eum iriure dolor in hendrerit in vulputate velit esse molestie consequat, vel illum dolore eu feugiat nulla facilisis at vero eros et accumsan et iusto odio dignissim qui blandit praesent luptatum zzril delenit augue duis dolore nulla facilisi.

Nam liber tempor cum soluta nobis eleifend option congue nihil imperdiet doming id quod mazim placerat facer possim assum. Lorem ipsum dolor sit amet, consectetuer adipiscing elit, sed diam nonummy nibh euismod tincidunt ut laoreet dolore magna aliquam erat volutpat. Ut wisi enim ad minim veniam, quis nostrud exerci tation ullamcorper suscipit lobortis nisl ut aliquip ex ea commodo consequat. Duis autem vel eum iriure dolor in hendrerit in vulputate velit esse molestie consequat.

Duis autem vel eum dolor in hendrerit in vulputate velit esse molestie consequat, vel illum dolore eu feugiat nulla facilisis.

The words "In This Issue" are too big—except for the nameplate, they're the largest words on the page.

IN THIS ISSUE

COELACANTH MAKES QUITE A COMEBACK

Lorem ipsum dolor sit amet, consectetuer adipiscing elit, sed diam nonummy nibh euismod tincidunt ut laoreet dolore magna aliquam erat volutpat. Ut wisi enim ad minim veniam, quis nostrud exerci tation ullamcorp suscipit lobortis nisl ut aliquip ex ea commodo consequatvelit esse molestie consequat. Duis autem vel eum iriure dolor in hendrerit in vulputate velit esse molestie consequat, vel illum dolore eu feugiat nulla facilisis at vero eros et accumsan et iusto odio dignissim qui blandit praesent luptatum zzril delenit augue duis dolore te feugait nulla facilisi. suscipit lobortis. Lorem ipsum dolor sit amet, consectet adipiscing elit, sed diam nonummy nibh euismod tincidunt ut laoreet dolore magna minim veniam, quis aliquam erat volutpateu feugiat.

Ut wisi enim ad minim veniam, quis nostrud exerci tation ullamcorper suscipit lobortis nisl ut aliquip ex ea commodo consequat. Duis autem vel eum iriure dolor in hendrerit in vulputate velit esse molestie consequat, vel illum dolore eu feugiat nulla facilisis at vero eros et accumsan et iusto odio dignissim qui blandit praesent luptatum zzril delenit augue duis dolore nulla facilisi.

Nam liber tempor cum soluta nobis eleifend option congue nihil imperdiet doming id quod mazim placerat facer possim assum. Lorem ipsum dolor sit amet, consectetuer adipiscing elit, sed diam nonummy nibh euismod tincidunt ut laoreet dolore magna aliquam erat volutpat. Ut wisi enim ad minim veniam, quis nostrud exerci tation ullamcorper suscipit lobortis nisl ut aliquip consequat. Nam liber tempor cum soluta nobis congue nihil imperdiet.

A looser, more unconventional design makes the newsletter's informality explicit.

Redesigned

IN THIS ISSUE

THE FOSSIL RECORD

Official Newsletter of the Lithicus Museum / July 1996

Page space has been saved by incorporating the table of contents into the nameplate.

Dem bones, dem bones...

Lorem ipsum dolor sit amet, consectetuer adipiscing elit, sed diam nonummy nibh euismod tincidunt ut laoreet dolore magna aliquam erat volutpat. Ut wisi enim ad minim veniam, quis nostrud exerci tation ullamcorp suscipit lobortis nisl ut aliquip ex ea commodo consequatvelit esse molestie consequat. Duis autem vel eum iriure dolor in hendrerit in vulputate velit esse molestie consequat, vel illum dolore eu feugiat nulla facilisis at vero eros et accumsan et iusto odio dignissim qui blandit praesent luptatum zzril delenit augue duis dolore te feugait nulla facilisi. Lorem ipsum dolor sit amet, consectet adipiscing elit, sed diam nonummy nibh euismod tincidunt ut laoreet dolore magna aliquam erat volutpat.

Ut wisi enim ad minim veniam, quis nostrud exerci tation ullamcorper suscipit lobortis nisl ut aliquip ex ea commodo consequat. Duis autem vel eum iriure dolor in hendrerit in vulputate velit esse molestie consequat, vel illum dolore eu feugiat nulla facilisis at vero eros et accumsan et iusto odio dignissim qui blandit praesent luptatum zzril delenit augue duis dolore nulla facilisi.

Nam liber tempor cum soluta nobis eleifend option congue nihil imperdiet doming id quod mazim placerat facer possim assum. Lorem ipsum dolor sit amet, consectetuer adipiscing elit, sed diam nonummy nibh euismod tincidunt ut laoreet dolore magna aliquam erat volutpat. Ut wisi enim ad minim veniam, quis nostrud exerci tation ullamcorper suscipit lobortis nisl ut aliquip ex ea commodo consequat. Duis autem vel eum iriure dolor in hendrerit in vulputate velit esse molestie consequat.

Duis autem vel eum dolor in hendrerit in vulputate velit esse molestie consequat, vel illum dolore eu feugiat nulla facilisis.

Headlines are now half-buried in their corresponding stories—a visual pun on the newsletter's content, perhaps?

Coelacanth makes quite a comeback

Lorem ipsum dolor sit amet, consectetuer adipiscing elit, sed diam nonummy nibh euismod tincidunt ut laoreet dolore magna aliquam erat volutpat. Ut wisi enim ad minim veniam, quis nostrud exerci tation ullamcorp suscipit lobortis nisl ut aliquip ex ea commodo consequatvelit esse molestie consequat. Duis autem vel eum iriure dolor in hendrerit in vulputate velit esse molestie consequat, vel illum dolore eu feugiat nulla facilisis at vero eros et accumsan et iusto odio dignissim qui blandit praesent luptatum zzril delenit augue duis dolore te feugait nulla facilisi. suscipit lobortis. Lorem ipsum dolor sit amet, consectet adipiscing elit, sed diam nonummy nibh euismod tincidunt ut laoreet dolore magna minim veniam, quis aliquam erat volutpateu feugiat.

Ut wisi enim ad minim veniam, quis nostrud exerci tation ullamcorper suscipit lobortis nisl ut aliquip ex ea commodo consequat. Duis autem vel eum iriure dolor in hendrerit in vulputate velit esse molestie consequat, vel illum dolore eu feugiat nulla facilisis at vero eros et accumsan et iusto odio dignissim qui blandit praesent luptatum zzril delenit augue duis dolore nulla facilisi.

Nam liber tempor cum soluta nobis eleifend option congue nihil imperdiet doming id quod mazim placerat facer possim assum. Lorem ipsum dolor sit amet, consectetuer adipiscing elit, sed diam nonummy nibh euismod tincidunt ut laoreet dolore magna aliquam erat volutpat. Ut wisi enim ad minim veniam, quis nostrud exerci tation ullamcorper suscipit lobortis nisl ut aliquip consequat. Nam liber tempor cum soluta nobis congue nihil imperdiet.

LITHICUS MUSEUM

The empty column on the far left opens up the page somewhat, and provides a good place for the museum's logo.

Nameplates

The best nameplates use a distinctive type treatment to promote name recognition. The heavy monoweight typeface used in the nameplate below is hardly memorable, and its readability is hampered by a distracting pattern of thin horizontal lines.

Original

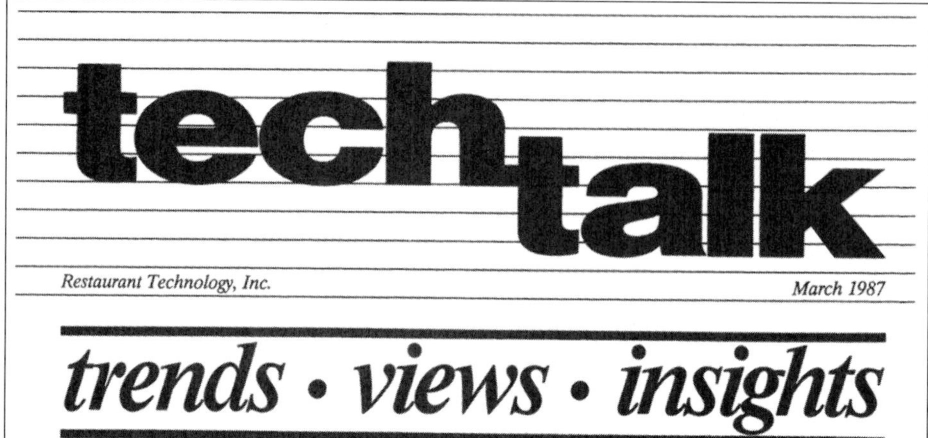

The subhead is far too large and contributes little to the message.

The slender, condensed serif face used in this nameplate has a lot more character and takes up less room, creating valuable white space on the page. The title is framed by simple rules, adding to the sense of minimalist elegance.

Redesigned

A publication of Restaurant Technology, Inc. *July 1987*

ity aspects of the business, you must maintain adequate controls and properly plan for the arrival of your guests or your reborn efforts will be in vain.

plan, the *basics* of your business have not changed. After all, that's why we're returning to them . . . they're the foundation on which the business was built.

The subhead has been eliminated and replaced by the less obtrusive "Restaurant Technology" slugline.

Advertisements

Inappropriate graphics can be worse than no graphics at all. The clip art in the ad below suggests that the lab assistant will be performing chemical experiments and analyzing slides—but the duties listed in the job description are mostly clerical.

Original

Relegating design elements to the corners of an ad can leave a disconcerting hole in the center.

Thin sans serif type with tight leading is difficult to read.

A simple stylized picture of a flask suggests a laboratory environment without misleading the applicant about the nature of the work.

Redesigned

Screening a small ad can help it stand out from adjacent ads.

The text of the ad reads more naturally without the ellipses.

Make an effort to integrate text and visuals when designing advertisements. The photograph in the advertisement below may connote air travel, but it doesn't visibly tie in with the ad's "cheap airfare" theme.

Original

WE OFFER THE CHEAPEST AIRFARE IN THE BUSINESS

For the remainder of the year, Sputter Airlines is offering the cheapest flight rates to be found anywhere! $69 to anywhere in the continental U.S., $99 to anywhere in North America (including Alaska and Hawaii), $149 to selected parts of Europe (England, France, Spain, Germany, and Scandinavia), and $219 for India and the Orient.

We're so sure that our fares are the lowest, we're willing to put money on it! If you can find cheaper airfare to the same location, we'll not only match the price, we'll beat it by $10! We call that our "Ten-Dollar Guarantee." (Written proof of the competing offer is required. Coupon specials and other forms of giveaways are not considered viable offers, and will not be honored with the Ten-Dollar Guarantee. Void where prohibited.)

So why take chances with some bargain airline? Come to the name you know, and get the lowest price available. We guarantee it!

SPUTTER

The largest chunk of white space in the ad is the area between the text columns—hardly a desirable focal point!

Most people won't find the image of a grounded airplane reassuring—it conjures up images of flight delays.

The disclaimer text at the end of the second paragraph interrupts the ad's positive message.

The company's name is never displayed prominently—it only appears once in the body copy (hyphenated, no less), and the logo at the bottom of the ad is small and cramped.

A vague, humorous headline connects the photograph to the rest of the ad. The first paragraph of the body text has been enlarged to serve as a lead-in to the rest of the copy.

Redesigned

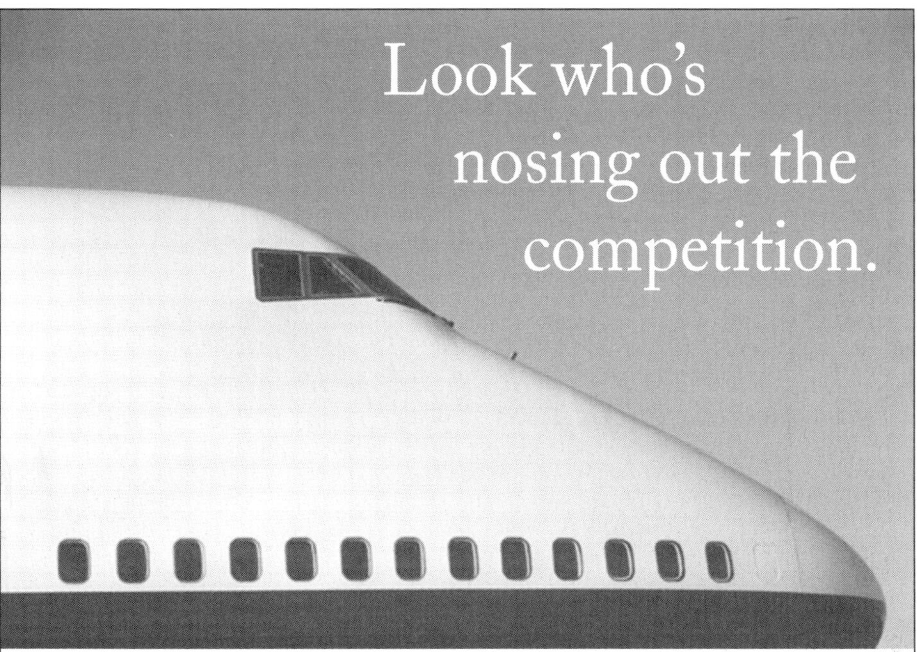
Look who's
nosing out the
competition.

Bleeding the photo rather than boxing it makes the ad seem larger.

For the remainder of the year,
Sputter Airlines is offering the cheapest flights
to be found anywhere. Guaranteed.

$69 to anywhere in the continental U.S., $99 to anywhere in North America (including Alaska and Hawaii), $149 to selected parts of Europe (England, France, Spain, Germany, and Scandinavia), and $219 for India and the Orient.

We're so sure that our fares are the lowest, we're willing to put money on it!

If you can find cheaper airfare to the same location, we'll not only match the price, we'll beat it by $10. We call that our "Ten-Dollar Guarantee."*

So why take chances with some bargain airline? Come to the name you know, and get the absolute lowest price available. We guarantee it.

*Written proof of the competing offer is required. Coupon specials and other forms of giveaways are not considered viable offers, and will not be honored with the Ten-Dollar Guarantee. Void where prohibited.

SPUTTER

Using a condensed typeface creates more white space within the ad, aiding readability.

The disclaimer text has been moved to the bottom of the page, and set in smaller type. A discreet asterisk signals its existence without interrupting the flow of the copy.

The company's logo has been enlarged and framed by white space.

Brochures

This brochure's informal tone is completely inappropriate for selling luxury items. Prominently-displayed phrases like "On Sale" and "Get Ready to Save!!!" put emphasis on price—but buyers of gold pocket-watches are probably more interested in the quality of the merchandise.

Original

Important ordering information is scattered all over the page—phone numbers at the top, restrictions at the bottom, and discount information near the right margin.

Fine Timepieces On Sale From Hannaford

To place orders, call toll-free 1-800-833-3328
For inquiries, call 1-617-535-5950
All prices are subject to change without notice.

Prices in effect from May 21, 1997 thru August 31, 1997

THE TRADITIONAL TIMEPIECE
Features the classic look of days gone by. Black roman numerals on a white face, in a 24-karat gold case with gold chain attached. $395.00

THE MODERN TIMEPIECE
Successfully blends the classic look with today's modern needs. Black arabic numerals on a white face, in a 24-karat gold case. Smaller dial inset on face displays seconds. $395.00

THE SILVER TICKER
Tastefully displays the elegance of silver. Silver numerals on a black face, in a sterling silver case with silver chain attached. $325.00

THE MACHINERY-LOVERS' SPECIAL
Lets the beauty of the watchmaker's craft show through. A transparent face allows the owner to watch the delicately-calibrated inner workings do their stuff. Comes in a 24-karat gold case with gold chain attached. $395.00

"Shoehorning" (using every bit of available space on the page) creates a claustrophobic feel.

THE MINIMALIST TIMEPIECE
Features a daring blend of past and present style. The handsome 24-karat gold case and chain echo the look of the Traditional Timepiece, but the inner white face is blank. $385.00

THE MYOPIC TIMEPIECE
Adapts the Modern Timepiece for the visually impaired. Larger arabic numerals make reading easier. $395.00

THE BRONZE BOMBSHELL
Features the look and feel of the watches carried by American soldiers in World War I. Lovingly recrafted, the watch features a case and chain made from actual bombshells. $295.00

Get ready to save!!!
10% off orders of $500 or more
20% off orders of $1000 or more

The "Restrictions and Extra Charges" paragraph looks like another item in the list of merchandise.

RESTRICTIONS AND EXTRA CHARGES
Watches and cases not sold separately. C.O.D. only. There is a 10% shipping and handling charge for orders within the continental U.S. (15% for orders outside the U.S.) This charge does not count toward the price needed for a discount.

Hannaford Timepieces, P.O. Box 2241, 3 Bourbon Street, Peabody MA 97874

A typographic overhaul and a generous use of white space give the brochure a formal, refined tone.

Redesigned

Fine Timepieces from Hannaford

on sale from May 21–August 31, 1997

Photographs of actual merchandise replace the frivolous clip-art graphic.

The Modern Timepiece

The Traditional Timepiece features the classic look of days gone by. Black roman numerals on a white face, in a 24-karat gold case with gold chain attached *(see above photo)*. $395.00

The Modern Timepiece successfully blends the classic look with today's modern needs. Black arabic numerals on a white face, in a 24-karat gold case. Smaller dial inset on face displays seconds *(see photo at right)*. $395.00

The Silver Ticker tastefully displays the elegance of silver. Silver numerals on a black face, in a sterling silver case with silver chain attached. $325.00

The Machinery-Lovers' Special lets the beauty of the watchmaker's craft show through. A transparent face allows the owner to watch the delicately-calibrated inner workings do their stuff. Comes in a 24-karat gold case with gold chain attached. $395.00

The Minimalist Timepiece features a daring blend of past and present style. The handsome 24-karat gold case and chain echo the look of the Traditional Timepiece, but the inner white face is blank. $385.00

The Myopic Timepiece adapts the Modern Timepiece for the visually impaired. Larger arabic numerals make reading easier *(see photo at right)*. $395.00

The Bronze Bombshell features the look and feel of the watches carried by American soldiers in World War I. Lovingly recrafted, the watch features a caseand chain made from actual bombshells. $295.00

The Myopic Timepiece

Precious space has been saved by combining the names and descriptions of the watches into single paragraphs.

Ordering Information

To place orders, call toll-free **1-800-833-3328**

For inquiries, call **1-617-535-5950**

There is a ***10% discount*** on orders of $500 or more. There is a ***20% discount*** on orders of $1000 or more.

All prices are subject to change without notice. Watches and cases not sold separately. C.O.D. only. There is a 10% shipping and handling charge for orders within the continental U.S. (15% for orders outside the U.S.) This charge does not count toward the price needed for a discount.

Hannaford Timepieces
P.O. Box 2241
3 Bourbon Street
Peabody MA 97874

All of the information needed to place an order has been moved to the bottom of the page.

Catalogs

Catalogs and price lists without illustrations present a unique set of design challenges. Type must be handled skillfully to avoid visual monotony.

Original

Using the same font for the titles and the copy doesn't provide enough differentiation, even though the titles are larger and boldfaced.

Often, a symmetrical layout with justified text provides too little contrast to fully engage the reader.

All-caps titles don't lend themselves to browsing—word recognition is much slower without ascenders and descenders.

NORMAN ROCKWELL
323 MAGAZINE COVERS
By Finch. 456 pages. Huge 12 X 15 1/4. This magnificent, large-format, full color volume spans the artist's long and prolific career, reproducing 323 of his cover paintings for the SATURDAY EVENING POST, LADIES HOME JOURNAL and other magazines. Published at $85.00. Only $45.00

GREAT MAGAZINE COVERS OF THE WORLD
By Kery. 184 pages. 9 1/4 X 12. A panorama of more than 500 great magazine covers (most reproduced in full color) from 20 countries, spanning a century and a half of magazine publishing around the world. Includes examples from 200 19th and 20th century magazines. Published at $65. Only $45.00

VASARELY
150 pages. 9 1/4 X 13. 180 illustrations, including 64 full color plates. Masterful reproductions and a text by the artist combine to form an authoritative yet personal study of one of the major figures of modern art. Published at $60.00. Only $35.00

CHAGALL BY CHAGALL
Sorlier. 262 pages. 11 1/4 X 12. 285 illustrations, including 83 full color plates. Illustrated autobiography. Published at $50.00. Only $40.00

MAXFIELD PARRISH
By Ludwig. 223 pages. 9 X 12. 184 illustrations, 64 in full color. Published at $25.00. Only $18.00

THE GREAT BOOK OF FRENCH IMPRESSIONISM
By Kelder. 448 pages. 12 X 14 1/4. Over 200 illustrations, including 200 full color plates and 16 spectacular full color fold-outs. Huge, exquisitely produced treasury of French Impressionist art, packed with full-page reproductions. Examines the lives and works of all the major Impressionists and Post-Impressionists. Published at $100.00. Now $59.00

CARL FABERGE: GOLDSMITH TO
THE IMPERIAL COURT OF RUSSIA
By Snowman. 100 pages. 8 1/4 X 10 1/2. Over 185 photos, 111 in full color. Originally published at $35.00. Only $22.00

CONTEMPORARY PAINTING
By Vogt. 135 pages. 7 1/2 X 10 1/2. Over 50 in full color. Penetrating analysis of World War II European and American art. Including paintings by Jaspar Johns, Andy Warhol, Roy Lichtenstein, Jackson Pollock, others. $19.95. Now $14.95

TWENTIETH CENTURY MASTERS
OF EROTIC ART
By Smith. 212 pages. 9 X 12. 190 full color plates presents erotic works by such top-ranking artists as Picasso, Segal, Dali, Ernst, Rauschenberg, Rivers, Warhol, Schiele and others, many of which have never been displayed in public exhibitions. $30.00. Now $20.00

LEONARDO DA VINCI
538 pages. 11 X 14 1/2. Huge. 1,635 illustrations, including many large full color plates. Originally published in Italy by the Instituto Geografico De Agostini, this new edition is the most lavish, authoritative ever produced. Published at $60. Now $50.00

REMBRANDT PAINTINGS
By Gerson. 527 pages. 11 X 14 1/2. Huge. Over 730 illustrations, including many large full color plates. Complete, authoritative and beautiful presentation of the great master's work. Written by one of the world's foremost Rembrandt authorities. The book was thirty years in the making in Amsterdam, and is lavishly illustrated with spectacular reproductions. Published at $60.00. Only $50.00

ENGLISH CAMEO GLASS
By Grover. 480 pages. 8 X 11. A wealth of rare firsthand material and over 1,000 color and black and white plates makes this book an invaluable reference. Published at $50.00. Now $25.00

20,000 YEARS OF WORLD PAINTING
By Jaffe. 416 pages. 9 X 13. Historical survey from early to modern art. 1,000 reproductions in full color. Was $50.00. Now $20.00

STAINED GLASS
By Seddon & Stephens. 205 pages. 473 full color photos. 11 X 14. Covers stained glass from the beginning to the present. Was $39.95. Now $19.95

THE COMPLETE BOOK OF EROTIC ART
By Kronhausen. 781 black and white plates. Extraordinary collection of the world's erotic art from Japan, China, India, Renaissance masters and modern greats. Originally published in 2 Volumes at $50.00. New, Complete 1 Volume Edition only $25.00

COLLECTING POLITICAL AMERICANA
By Sullivan 1980. 250 pages. 8 X 11. 400 illustrations. Packed with reading. Out of print. $15.95. Now $10.00

DIAMONDS
Myth, magic and reality. Revised edition. Over 420 full color illustrations. Beautiful and informative look at the world's most magnificent and mysterious stone. Tells how to recognize and appreciate quality stones, more. 288 pages. Large. 10 1/4 X 12. Originally published at $50.00. Only $29.00

THE GREAT BOOK OF JEWELS
By Heninger. 206 full color plates. 94 black and white photos. The most spectacular, lavishly illustrated, comprehensive volume ever published on jewels and jewelry. Nearly 300 photos specially made for this volume, many gems not available for public inspection before. Includes bibliography, table of gemstones: much more. Huge. 11 1/4 X 13 3/4. Published at $69.50. Now $29.95

10

Subtle changes in spacing and typeface create contrast and promote readability.

Redesigned

Norman Rockwell
323 Magazine Covers
By Finch. 456 pages. Huge 12 X 15 1/4. This magnificent, large-format, full color volume spans the artist's long and prolific career, reproducing 323 of his cover paintings for the SATURDAY EVENING POST, LADIES HOME JOURNAL and other magazines. Published at $85.00. Only $45.00

Great Magazine Covers of the World
By Kery. 184 pages. 9 1/4 X 12. A panorama of more than 500 great magazine covers (most reproduced in full color) from 20 countries, spanning a century and a half of magazine publishing around the world. Includes examples from 200 19th and 20th century magazines. Published at $65. Only $45.00

Vasarely
150 pages. 9 1/4 X 13. 180 illustrations, including 64 full color plates. Masterful reproductions and a text by the artist combine to form an authoritative yet personal study of one of the major figures of modern art. Published at $60.00. Only $35.00

Chagall by Chagall
Sorlier. 262 pages. 11 1/4 X 12. 285 illustrations, including 83 full color plates. Illustrated autobiography. Published at $50.00. Only $40.00

Maxfield Parrish
By Ludwig. 223 pages. 9 X 12. 184 illustrations, 64 in full color. Published at $25.00. Only $18.00

The Great Book of French Impressionism
By Kelder. 448 pages. 12 X 14 1/4. Over 200 illustrations, including 200 full color plates and 16 spectacular full color fold-outs. Huge, exquisitely produced treasury of French Impressionist art, packed with full-page reproductions. Examines the lives and works of all the major Impressionists and Post-Impressionists. Published at $100.00. Now $59.00

Carl Faberge: Goldsmith to the Imperial Court of Russia
By Snowman. 100 pages. 8 1/4 X 10 1/2. Over 185 photos, 111 in full color. Originally published at $35.00. Only $22.00

Contemporary Painting
By Vogt. 135 pages. 7 1/2 X 10 1/2. Over 50 in full color. Penetrating analysis of World War II European and American art. Including paintings by Jaspar Johns, Andy Warhol, Roy Lichtenstein, Jackson Pollock, others. $19.95. Now $14.95

Twentieth Century Masters of Erotic Art
By Smith. 212 pages. 9 X 12. 190 full color plates presents erotic works by such top-ranking artists as Picasso, Segal, Dali, Ernst, Rauschenberg, Rivers, Warhol, Schiele and others, many of which have never been displayed in public exhibitions. $30.00. Now $20.00

Leonardo Da Vinci
538 pages. 11 X 14 1/2. Huge. 1,635 illustrations, including many large full color plates. Originally published in Italy by the Instituto Geografico De Agostini, this new edition is the most authoritative ever produced. Published at $60. Now $50.00

Rembrandt Paintings
By Gerson. 527 pages. 11 X 14 1/2. Huge. Over 730 illustrations, including many large full color plates. Complete, authoritative and beautiful presentation of the great master's work. Written by one of the world's foremost Rembrandt authorities. The book was thirty years in the making in Amsterdam, and is lavishly illustrated with spectacular reproductions. Published at $60.00. Only $50.00

English Cameo Glass
By Grover. 480 pages. 8 X 11. A wealth of rare firsthand material and over 1,000 color and black and white plates makes this book an invaluable reference. Published at $50.00. Now $25.00

20,000 Years of World Painting
By Jaffe. 416 pages. 9 X 13. Historical survey from early to modern art. 1,000 reproductions in full color. Was $50.00. Now $20.00

Stained Glass
By Seddon & Stephens. 205 pages. 473 full color photos. 11 X 14. Covers stained glass from the beginning to the present. Was $39.95. Now $19.95

The Complete Book of Erotic Art
By Kronhausen. 781 black and white plates. Extraordinary collection of the world's erotic art from Japan, China, India, Renaissance masters and modern greats. Originally published in 2 Volumes at $50.00. New, Complete 1 Volume Edition only $25.00

Collecting Political Americana
By Sullivan 1980. 250 pages. 8 X 11. 400 illustrations. Packed with reading. Out of print. $15.95. Now $10.00

Diamonds
Myth, magic and reality. Revised edition. Over 420 full color illustrations. Beautiful and informative look at the world's most magnificent and mysterious stone. Tells how to recognize and appreciate quality stones, more. 288 pages. Large. 10 1/4 X 12. Originally published at $50.00. Only $29.00

The Great Book of Jewels
By Heninger. 206 full color plates. 94 black and white photos. The most spectacular, lavishly illustrated, comprehensive volume ever published on jewels and jewelry. Nearly 300 photos specially made for this volume, many gems never available for public inspection before. Includes bibliography, table of gemstones: much more. Huge. 11 1/4 X 13 3/4. Published at $69.50. Now $29.95

Reference Art Books PHONE TOLL-FREE / 1-800-238-8288

The two-column format is retained, but the text is set ragged-right to break up the symmetry. Vertical downrules are used to separate the columns.

Using a bolder sans-serif font for the titles provides contrast to the body copy, and setting them with initial caps rather than all caps increases readability. See how much easier it is to browse the titles?

The "Reference Art Books" logo (taken from the front cover) has been reversed and repeated on each page, along with the firm's toll-free phone number. In general, try to make user response as easy as possible.

Flyers

When working with text-heavy documents, readability should be your primary concern. In the question-and-answer flyer below, small text in a wide text column makes reading difficult.

Original

The question marks are redundant—the headline and content clearly communicate the Q&A format.

Answers to Questions Frequently Asked About Tri-Steel Homes

1. What is the Tri-Steel concept and why is it different from conventional wood frame construction?

The Tri-Steel concept is based upon the utilization and superior quality and strength of steel to form the frame or shell of the home. This allows the home to be stick built on site, but with steel instead of wood and bolts and fasteners instead of nails and staples.

The superior strength of steel means that the frame spacing can be on 6-foot and 8-foot centers instead of 16-inch and 24-inch centers. Plus, we can utilize 9 inches of insulation on the sides and also provide consistent quality, less maintenance, and much greater strength than is possible with conventional construction. In addition, this gives you much greater flexibility inside the home since none of the walls need to be load bearing. Also important, the entire shell can often be dried-in within 4 to 5 days by an inexperienced crew.

2. How are Tri-Steel homes unique?

Our homes utilize an engineered and computer designed steel structural system. You can choose from a wide selection of contemporary slant wall designs which stand out among conventional wooded structures or numerous conventional-looking straight wall designs ranging from conservatively gabled roof lines to ultra-modern units allowing clerestory window placement.

3. What are some of the advantages of Tri-Steel homes?

Tri-Steel homes can cost less to erect and can go up much faster. They are exceptionally energy efficient, require almost no exterior maintenance, and are tremendously flexible in their design. In addition to these areas of savings, they offer the strength and durability of steel to withstand extreme weather conditions, termites and fire. The quality of steel is consistently high. Pre-engineered framing components ensure your home goes up one way—the right way! Special snow or wind loads are possible with very little extra cost. The also meet Seismic 4 earthquake specifications—the highest rating required.

4. Have these homes been tried and proven?

Absolutely! In terms of the history of home building, Tri-Steel homes are a new and unique concept; however, these homes have been in use throughout the South for over ten years. Tri-Steel has thousands of structures all across the nation and we are constantly receiving letters from satisfied homeowners attesting to the beauty, strength and energy savings of Tri-Steel structures.

The text and visuals are crowded.

Answers beginning with a single boldface word (e.g. "Yes!") look as if they might belong with the preceding boldface question.

5. Can I put up one of these homes myself and is construction assistance available?

Yes! The home is actually designed to be constructed independently by the buyer. No heavy lifting equipment or special tools are required. The steel beams are designed to bolt together—A to B, B to C—with prepunched holes so you are basically working with a giant erector set. No cutting or welding is required on the job site and complete instructions and drawings are included with the package. Tri-Steel can provide your choice of construction assistance. As part of the assistance available, we can consult with you over the phone, have your shell erected, or provide on-site supervision on a daily or weekly basis.

6. How much flexibility do I have choosing a home size?

Infinite! A virtually unlimited variety of home sizes are offered from 800 square feet on up. Our homes come in one, two of three level designs with slant of straight walls. We have hundreds of plans drawn and available for immediate mailing and we can also draw custom designs to meet virtually any floor plan or size requirements.

7. Can I add to the home at a later date?

Yes! Additional space may be added in the future at low cost and relative ease, allowing you to enlarge your home economically as your needs and income requires.

Tri-Steel
Structures
5800 Campus Circle, Irving, TX 75063
Telephone (214) 580-3400
© 1997, All Rights Reserved
TM

A two-column format is more inviting for the reader. Using a different typeface for the questions makes scanning for specific information easier.

Redesigned

Building a Tri-Steel home:

Questions & Answers

The logo no longer interrupts the text.

Illustrations have been omitted to allow larger type and more white space.

Oversized Qs and As with drop-shadow blocks mirror the title design.

Q *What is the Tri-Steel concept and why is it different from conventional wood frame construction?*

A The Tri-Steel concept is based upon the utilization and superior quality and strength of steel to form the frame or shell of the home. This allows the home to be stick built on site, but with steel instead of wood and bolts and fasteners instead of nails and staples.

The superior strength of steel means that the frame spacing can be on 6-foot and 8-foot centers instead of 16-inch and 24-inch centers. Plus, we can utilize 9 inches of insulation on the sides and also provide consistent quality, less maintenance, and much greater strength than is possible with conventional construction. In addition, this gives you much greater flexibility inside the home since none of the walls need to be load bearing. Also important, the entire shell can often be dried-in within 4 to 5 days by an inexperienced crew.

Q *How are Tri-Steel homes unique?*

A Our homes utilize an engineered and computer designed steel structural system. You can choose from a wide selection of contemporary slant wall designs which stand out among conventional wooded structures or numerous conventional-looking straight wall designs ranging from conservatively gabled roof lines to ultra-modern units allowing clerestory window placement.

Q *What are some of the advantages of Tri-Steel homes?*

A Tri-Steel homes can cost less to erect and can go up much faster. They are exceptionally energy efficient, require almost no exterior maintenance, and are tremendously flexible in their design. In addition to these areas of savings, they offer the strength and durability of steel to withstand extreme weather conditions, termites and fire. The quality of steel is consistently high. Pre-engineered framing components ensure your home goes up one way—the right way! Special snow or wind loads are possible with very little extra cost. The also meet Seismic 4 earthquake specifications—the highest rating required.

Q *Have these homes been tried and proven?*

A **Absolutely!** In terms of the history of home building, Tri-Steel homes are a new and unique concept; however, these homes have been in use throughout the South for over ten years. Tri-Steel has thousands of structures all across the nation and we are constantly receiving letters from satisfied homeowners attesting to the beauty, strength and energy savings of Tri-Steel structures.

Q *Can I put up one of these homes myself and is construction assistance available?*

A **Yes!** The home is actually designed to be constructed independently by the buyer. No heavy lifting equipment or special tools are required. The steel beams are designed to bolt together—A to B, B to C—with prepunched holes so you are basically working with a giant erector set. No cutting or welding is required on the job site and complete instructions and drawings are included with the package. Tri-Steel can provide your choice of construction assistance. As part of the assistance available, we can consult with you over the phone, have your shell erected, or provide on-site supervision on a daily or weekly basis.

Q *How much flexibility do I have choosing a home size?*

A **Infinite!** A virtually unlimited variety of home sizes are offered from 800 square feet on up. Our homes come in one, two of three level designs with slant of straight walls. We have hundreds of plans drawn and available for immediate mailing and we can also draw custom designs to meet virtually any floor plan or size requirements.

Q *Can I add to the home at a later date?*

A **Yes!** Additional space may be added in the future at low cost and relative ease, allowing you to enlarge your home economically as your needs and income requires.

Announcement-style flyers should be brief and eye-catching. Readers are likely to ignore large amounts of text.

Original

The most important words on the flyer, "CLASSIC CAR SHOW," are no larger than the rest of the copy.

The graphics seem to have been added as an afterthought. The noticeable difference in the cars' sizes is jarring.

Exclamation points at the end of each line make it seem as if the document is shouting at the reader.

The centered, all-caps text is difficult to read.

COME ONE COME ALL
TO THE
CLASSIC CAR SHOW!!!!

ALL MAKES - ALL MODELS
FROM THE ROARING 20'S
TO THE NIFTY 50'S!

AUTO BUFFS WON'T WANT
TO MISS THIS EXTRAVAGANZA!

TO BE HELD AT MCMILLAN PARK
SATURDAY, AUGUST 23
FROM 2:00 PM
TO 6:00 PM

IT'LL DRIVE YOU BUGGY!

Deleting all but the most relevant text—what, where, when—increases the flyer's readability. A catchy lead-in completes the makeover.

Redesigned

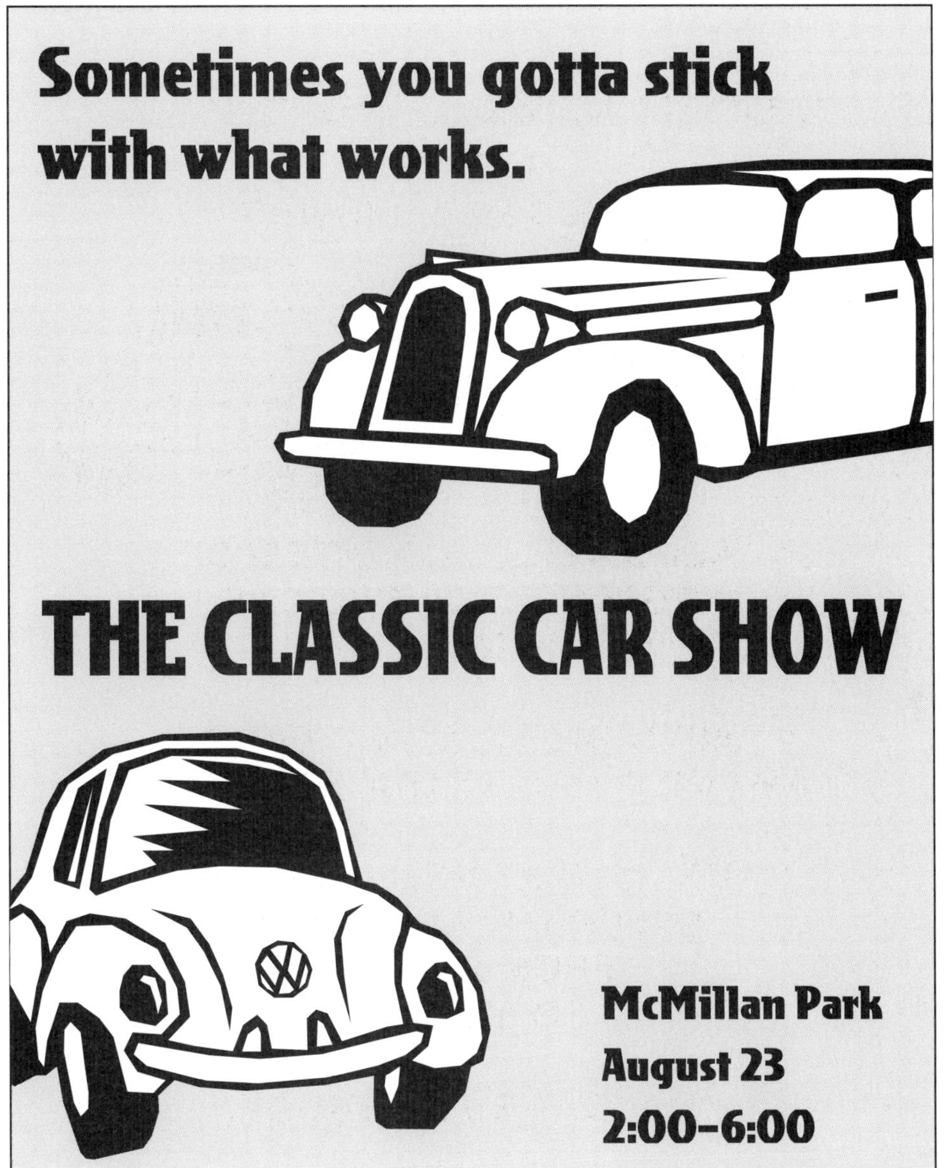

A decorative typeface serves as an attention-getter.

A light gray screen makes the graphics stand out.

The title of the event is now prominently featured in the center of the flyer.

Notice how the text progresses naturally from top left to bottom right.

Business Cards And Logos

An excessive amount of detail can be a hindrance when designing a pictorial logo. The eye is much better at processing and remembering simple images. The skull logo below may be anatomically correct, but it's not very memorable—and its detail will invariably be lost if the logo is faxed or shrunk.

Original

The company name is set in the same drab font as the rest of the text on the card.

The company motto is too small and contains a bad text break.

Morty Thanatos
Producer
127 Perish Blvd
Suite C
Hollywood, CA 90026
Phone: 815/983-4811
Fax: 815/983-4814
"We Make Your Horror Films More Horrible"
Death's Head Productions

A simpler, more exaggerated skull is easier to remember and will reproduce well at small sizes. Using a distinctive font for the company name also aids recognition.

Redesigned

Combining two of the address lines saves space, and gives the textblock a clean rectangular shape.

Enlarging and reversing the motto helps it stand out. The ragged edge of the reversed area is evocative of blood on a horror-movie poster.

Morty Thanatos
Producer
127 Perish Blvd., Suite C
Hollywood, CA 90026
Phone: 815/983-4811
Fax: 815/983-4814
Death's Head Productions
"We make your horror films more horrible"

Logos

Actually, the original design for this logo isn't bad, but there's always room for improvement. While most viewers will recognize the imagery for what it is—a white mountain against a night sky—others will merely see two shaded triangles. Also, the typeface is perhaps a little too ornate, given the simplicity of the rest of the design.

Original

Giving the mountain a jagged top, adding a moon to the sky, and moving the company name beneath the picture makes the "white mountain" image impossible to miss. To ensure that the text remains integrated with the visual, the gradient fill continues through the letters.

Redesigned

Letterheads

This project is a designer's worst nightmare—does all of this information *really* belong on the company letterhead? Probably not, but designers often have to make the best of what they're given. The layout below is an admirable attempt to organize the infoglut, but the overall feel is still rather cluttered.

Original

Closely set rules compartmentalize the logo.

A disconcerting variety of type sizes and rule thicknesses imparts a haphazard look to the design.

Categorizing the information with reversed subheads calls undue attention to the amount of information being included—something we'd rather downplay, if possible.

WHITE MOUNTAIN BREWERIES

Board of Directors

Amber Muggs
Chief Executive Officer

Ruiz Coldoné
Sales Director

Suds McKenzie
Vice President

Rex Stout
Production Director

Address/Phone

1130 Hop Street
White Mountain, CO
93437-1130
210/897-9947

Mailing Address

P.O. Box 1447
White Mountain, CO
93437-1447

A vertical orientation provides a column for company info that runs the full length of the letterhead. Generous line and paragraph spacing—made possible by the increase of available space—reduces the cluttered feel. In fact, there's even room for the company Web address!

Redesigned

WHITE
MOUNTAIN
BREWERIES

Amber Muggs
Chief Executive Officer

Suds McKenzie
Vice President

Ruiz Coldoné
Sales Director

Rex Stout
Production Director

1130 Hop Street
White Mountain, CO
93437-1447
210/897-9947

P.O. Box 1447
White Mountain, CO
93437-1447

www.wmbrew.com

The logo is framed by white space.

Although the letterhead still uses two typefaces (not counting the logotype), decreasing the variation in type size gives the text a more unified look.

Instead of subheads, small moon icons (borrowed from the logo) are used to separate information.

Company Reports

The low-contrast, gray tone of typewritten materials often neutralizes the effects of good writing, persuasive argument, and strong evidence. The information in the report below might be unimpeachable—but will employees stay awake long enough to read it?

Original

The limitation of a single typeface and type size makes it difficult to show relative importance.

CURRENT SNOOZE ALARM SALES

As stated previously, we believe that a high number of present users of snooze alarm technology will want to own TardiSnooz. Current sales of snooze alarms have never been higher, as the figures below show:

YEAR	# UNITS SOLD	$ RETAIL
1965	1,000	$ 12,000
1970	65,000	430,000
1975	220,000	2,800,000
1980	673,000	5,900,000
1985	1,220,000	11,760,000

A wide text column doesn't lend itself to speed-reading—an important consideration for business people.

A corresponding trend of employee tardiness has become evident, particularly in the last ten years. In fact, some researchers believe that snooze alarms have indeed played a large part in causing employee tardiness. According to Real Life Information in Palo Alto, California, "Snooze alarm technology is largely responsible for the dramatic rise in employee tardiness and late calls. Further, the admonishment thrust upon the average employee, compounded by the guilt, feelings of inadequacy and consequent resentment, creates an unresolved authority-figure conflict, resulting in sharply decreased productivity.... One solution to this problem is a mechanism whereby the employee can at least call in late with a feeling of efficiency and accomplishment, instead of languishing in a commuter-frustrated dissonance on his or her way to work."

Clearly, the above findings indicate the need for added features to snooze technology. This, coupled with the fall in wholesale modem chip prices, could make TardiSnooz our sale item of the decade.

PROJECTED TARDISNOOZ SALES

Based on a 1,000-piece consumer survey mailed last month (see attached data), we found consumers receptive, and indeed eager, to pay the slightly higher price that TardiSnooze would command. Below are projected sales figures, based on our survey:

Awkward spacing of data interrupts the flow of reading.

PROJECTED TARDISNOOZ SALES

YEAR	# UNITS PROJECTED		$ RETAIL
1990	34,000		$ 430,000
1991	81,000		970,000
1992	239,000		2,400,000
1993	310,000		3,700,000
1994	228,000	(Break-even)	2,200,000
1995	426,000	(Recession Projected)	4,450,000

When you examine the above figures, and consider that all we have to do is add a $.93 modem chip to our present alarms, the conclusion is inescapable to all but the most ardent critics that our company should move forward with plans to implement our new "Tardi-Snooz" line of products. Accordingly, our current line of products should be gradually and unobtrusively discontinued, with the intention of disavowing any knowledge of these offerings at the beginning of the next fiscal year.

This design isn't very complex, but it demonstrates the variety of options available to the desktop publisher, such as variations in typeface and type size, screens, bleeds, rules, graphics, and reversed type. The result is a high-contrast document that engages the reader's interest.

Redesigned

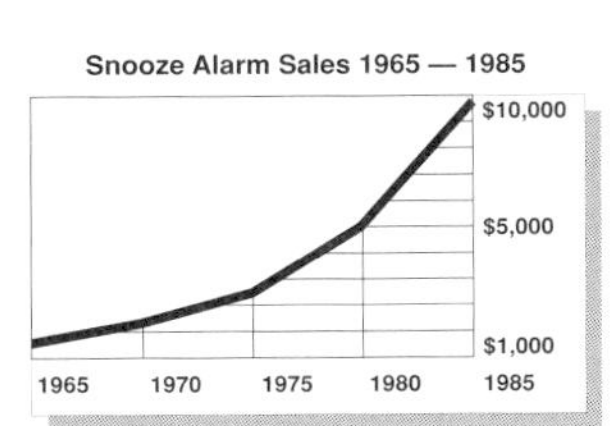

As stated previously, we believe that a high number of present users of snooze alarm technology will want to own TardiSnooz. Current sales of snooze alarms have never been higher, as the figures at left show.

A corresponding trend of employee tardiness has become evident, particularly in the last ten years. In fact, some researchers believe that snooze alarms indeed played a large part in causing employee tardiness. Real Life Information, a statistical analysis firm located in Palo Alto, California, has this to say about snooze alarm technology:

> *"Snooze alarm technology is largely responsible for the dramatic rise in employee tardiness and late calls. Further, the admonishment thrust upon the average by the guilt, feelings of inadequacy and consequent resentment, creates an unresolved authority figure conflict resulting in sharply decreased productivity.... One solution to this problem is a mechanism whereby the employee can at least call in late with feeling of efficiency and accomplishment, instead of languishing in commuter-frustrated dissonance on his or her way to work."*

Clearly, the above findings indicate the need for added features to snooze technology. This, coupled with the fall in wholesale modem chip prices, could make TardiSnooz our sale item of the decade.

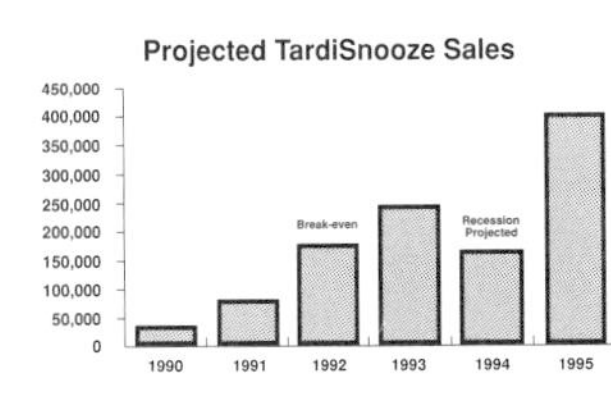

Based on a 1000-piece consumer survey mailed last month (see attached data), we found consumers receptive, and indeed eager to pay the slightly higher price that TardiSnooze would command. The graph at left shows the projected sales figures, based on our informal survey.

When you examine these figures, and consider that all we have to do is add a $.93 modem chip to our present alarms, the conclusion is inescapable to all but the most ardent critics that our company should move forward with implementing the new "Tardi-Snooz" line of products. Accordingly, our current line of products should be gradually and unobtrusively discontinued, with the intention of disavowing any knowledge of these offerings at the beginning of the next fiscal year.

Used consistently, the gray sink will unify the separate pages of the report.

Important research findings are set in larger italic type, to indicate their importance.

A narrow text column makes reading easier.

The text-based tables have been replaced by graphs, which show trends more clearly.

Surveys

Customers don't *have* to fill out surveys—the proprietor is asking for a measure of indulgence on the customer's part, so it's vital to make the process as simple as possible. The poorly-organized survey below bounces back and forth between multiple-choice questions and fill-in-the-blank questions, upsetting the reader's rhythm.

Original

"PLEASE TAKE A FEW MOMENTS..." is an appeal to the customer, not a title.

Arranging multiple-choice options in three columns makes browsing for the desired answer difficult.

The blanks following Questions 3 and 8 are too short to hold any information—it would be better to delete them entirely.

The answer ranges in Question 7 contain some overlap—if a customer visits the shop twice a month, should 1–2 or 2–3 to be selected?

PLEASE TAKE A FEW MOMENTS TO ANSWER THIS SURVEY

1. What is your primary reason for choosing Yummygummy doughnuts when you want doughnuts?
❑ taste ❑ texture ❑ price
❑ location of store ❑ service

2. How many doughnuts do you usually buy when you come to Yummygummy Doughnuts?
❑ 1 ❑ 2–3 ❑ half dozen
❑ full dozen ❑ more than a dozen

3. What would you say is your favorite type of doughnut? ____________
____

4. What would you say is your favorite beverage to drink when you're eating doughnuts? ________________________

5. Do you ever go to other doughnut places? ______ If the answer is yes, which ones? ________________________

6. Do you always get excellent service when you come to Yummygummy Doughnuts? _____ If the answer is no, what could be improved? ________________________

7. How many times a month would you say that you visit Yummygummy doughnuts?
❑ 0–1 ❑ 1–2 ❑ 2–3
❑ 3–4 ❑ 5 or more

8. Do you generally eat your doughnuts in the shop, or takeout? ______
____

9. Do you have any other comments that would help Yummygummy Doughnuts better serve you? ________________________

Rephrasing all of the questions as multiple-choice makes the document easier to complete. A two-column layout provides the needed vertical room to "stack" the checkboxes.

Redesigned

Customer Survey

yummYGummy doughnuts

Please take a few moments to complete this survey. Your opinions and preferences are very important to us. When you've finished answering the questions, please fold the survey in half and deposit it in the wooden box on the counter. Thank you for eating at Yummygummy!

What is your primary reason for choosing Yummygummy Doughnuts?

- ❒ taste
- ❒ texture
- ❒ price
- ❒ location of store
- ❒ service

How many doughnuts do you usually buy on a visit to Yummygummy Doughnuts?

- ❒ 1
- ❒ 2–5
- ❒ half a dozen
- ❒ a full dozen
- ❒ more than a dozen

What is your favorite type of doughnut?

- ❒ Old-fashioned
- ❒ Honey glazed
- ❒ Chocolate frosted
- ❒ Cinnamon
- ❒ Jelly
- ❒ Other ______________________

What beverage do you like to drink with your doughnuts?

- ❒ Coffee
- ❒ Milk
- ❒ Water
- ❒ Juice
- ❒ Soda
- ❒ Other ______________________
- ❒ None

What other doughnut shops do you patronize besides Yummygummy Doughnuts?

- ❒ Greebley's Doughnuts
- ❒ The Cop Corner
- ❒ Glazes & Sprinkles
- ❒ Other ______________________
- ❒ No other doughnut shops

Have you ever had any of the following problems with the service at Yummygummy Doughnuts?

- ❒ Slow service
- ❒ Rude service
- ❒ Mistakes with your order
- ❒ Incorrect change
- ❒ Other ______________________

How many times a month do you visit Yummygummy doughnuts?

- ❒ 0–1
- ❒ 2–3
- ❒ 4 or more

Where do you generally eat the doughnuts you order from Yummygummy?

- ❒ Inside the shop
- ❒ Outside the shop

Comments

____

____

____

____

A descriptive title and the addition of the company logo clearly identify the purpose of the document.

The instructions at the top of the page tell readers how to submit their completed surveys—an important detail that was overlooked in the original document.

Questions and answers are differentiated by type style.

Appendix: Prepress Tips And Techniques

Although computers are supposed to make document creation easier, sometimes technology only seems to complicate matters. This is especially the case if you're using an untested technique or trying out new hardware or software.

If you're working with color or digital photography, or if you plan to work with a service bureau for high-resolution output, the advice in this appendix may save you hours of frustration and a fair amount of money, too.

Image Databases

Image databases help you keep track of lots of different graphics.

If you work with lots of graphic files, you may find that keeping track of which images match which files can be a tricky process. Just as you can use a conventional database to sort and track information, you can use an image database to store a low-resolution screen image of your high-resolution digital photos and illustration files. Some image databases can show thumbnail views of groups of photos according to your specific instructions.

You can also use an image database to track how frequently you use a photo or illustration, as well as in which publications and situations. While they are currently used for more high-end publications, image databases are slowly becoming cheaper and easier to use, giving any desktop publisher the capability to track and sort images quickly and effectively.

Choosing The Right Paper

Paper plays a crucial role in how your documents appear.

High-end printing (especially if it involves photos or color) works best on higher-quality papers at fairly high output resolutions. Coarse papers don't hold ink well enough to create the crisp definition needed for high-resolution work. Finer papers hold ink more precisely, with less bleeding, running, and spreading.

Another consideration is the difference between coated (glossy) paper and uncoated (matte) paper. Publications that use lots of full-color illustrations and photos tend to benefit from glossy paper. There's less ink absorption, which yields more precise color reproductions. Then again, the slick look of glossy paper is sometimes too commercial for projects meant to reflect taste and refinement—uncoated paper in subtle off-white, brown, or gray shades can lend a certain stately authority to a document.

The paper thickness is also important. Using paper that is too thin may cause the inks to bleed through, wreaking havoc with type or images on the other side of the page. You'll also want to match the thickness of your paper to the format of your project—paper too stiff to bend is a poor choice for a booklet that requires users to flip through the pages, and business cards printed on onionskin command very little authority.

When planning your project's budget, the paper you intend to use is an important consideration. Size, thickness, coating, texture, and other factors, like availability and demand, can cause wide variations in paper prices.

Finally, don't forget the possibilities—or the pitfalls—offered by colored paper. It usually costs only slightly more than white paper, and the difference in impact can be significant. Of course, it's not always appropriate—bright yellow paper certainly gets attention, but setting an entire book in it is a surefire way to annoy your readers. Be aware of a given color's common associations (discussed in the *Do It In Color* section), and compare these with the mood or feel you're trying to convey. If your document is long or text-intensive, you should probably stick with good old-fashioned black-on-white—it's the most readable color combination. (You'll notice I'm using it now!)

The Role Of A Service Bureau

If you need your document printed at higher resolution than a laser printer can provide, it's time to visit a service bureau.

Most desktop publishers can't afford to lump the cost of a $50,000 imagesetter to output their high-resolution documents. For typeset quality output, it makes financial sense to use a service bureau.

Service bureaus vary widely in their prices and the amount of service offered. The cheapest option is to visit a copy shop or a small print house, but they generally only handle very small jobs, and their service reps are less knowledgeable about prepress arcana. Dedicated service bureaus feature experienced prepress technicians and state-of-the-art equipment, but, as you'd expect, the prices quickly skyrocket.

To find the right service bureau, call up each prospective candidate's customer service rep, and get answers to the following questions:

- *What file formats does the service bureau require or prefer?* You need to make sure that your system and documents are compatible with your prospective service bureau's standards. If they're not, don't buy a bunch of new software and utilities to fit that service bureau—shop around.

COLOR WOES

A recent widespread glitch in the separation software used by many color printers is the inability to separate TIFF files—unless you save your color graphics in EPS format, they print as black-and-white. The problem will no doubt soon be corrected, so this is less a warning about TIFF files than it is a general piece of advice: Be thorough when questioning prospective service bureau candidates. Problems like the one mentioned above are not the sorts of things you want to find out about *after* your document has gone to press.

Get specific when asking for and providing information—relay the names and version numbers of the software you intend to use, and ask about the graphic file formats they support. The most common formats for graphics are TIFF and EPS (all printers should be able to support these).

- *Can the service bureau make last-minute corrections?* You should know if your service bureau can make corrections for you and at what cost, if you happen to spot small errors in your document after it has already gone to press. The question will often depend on the material you've provided—application files are editable, while postscript files (copies of your document saved in electronic format) and camera-ready copy usually are not. If the service bureau you've chosen is using the same software as you are, it's much more likely that they'll be willing and able to make small corrections.
- *What is the average turnaround time?* If you've never used the service bureau before, allow for some extra time. It usually takes a while to iron out all the compatibility problems. Find out if they charge a premium for rush service, and ask for the best method of submitting jobs. If they use their own BBS, it may take a day or two to set up an account and password for you on their system, and provide you with the necessary communications software or configuration instructions. Also, find out if they offer delivery—free or otherwise—when the job is finished. These may seem like small considerations, but when you're on a tight deadline, little details like these can determine whether you squeeze under the wire or miss by inches.
- *How do they price their services?* Do they charge per page, per hour, or do they custom-quote each job? Depending on the nature of your project, some schemes may yield lower prices than others.

It's probably safest to find at least two good candidates for service bureaus, if your work is deadline-oriented. Service bureaus are hectic places, frequently beset by equipment problems, unexpected delays, and gigantic jobs that get dumped on them at a moment's notice. Don't be too surprised if your usually trusty service bureau is unable to promise the usual turnaround time for your latest job, due to unforeseen circumstances. If you've got the phone numbers and submission specs of a few backup service bureaus on hand, you won't be caught flat-footed.

Greasing The Wheels

While it's tempting to blame every problem, delay, and unexpected expense on your much-beleaguered service bureaus, the quality of their service is usually directly dependent upon how thorough and meticulous you've been when creating your files and supplying your print specs. Here are a few guidelines that will improve the chances of consistent, predictable results:

- *Ask for help.* Nobody knows everything about desktop publishing, and there's no shame in asking your service bureau or printer for advice on complex subjects, like scanning photos or defining electronic color trapping parameters. Actually, they'll probably be glad to hear you bring it up. Print technicians don't always mention every relevant issue to their customers, because they often find themselves in the futile position of talking over their clients' heads.
- *Remember, time is money.* When large files take longer than usual to print, you'll probably have to pay a surcharge for tying up a service bureau's equipment. Rush jobs cost extra as well, so plan ahead.
- *Streamline your documents as much as possible.* Large files can cost you time and money, so try to keep your files small. Don't use graphics, especially photos, digitized at a higher resolution than necessary—you'll just be wasting time processing image information you don't need. Likewise, don't use giant photos cropped to small sizes. Using a graphics program, crop graphics to the size you need.

  Also, if your layout program has a pasteboard (an off-the-page storage area for graphics and textblocks), delete everything on it before submitting the application file. Don't bloat your files with graphic elements that don't even show up on the finished output.
- *Run the numbers.* There are plenty of equations and rules that can guide you through esoteric calculations, such as how many steps to put in a graduated blend or at what resolution to scan a photo. Check with your service bureau early in the design process, and follow their instructions.
- *Mention special requests and possible problem areas as early as possible.* If you want all the photos in your document to be set as duotones, for instance, don't wait until the files are in their hands to mention it. The earlier you learn their requirements and preferences, the easier it is to conform to them. Likewise, if one of your graphics is in an unconventional format, ask about compatibility in advance—don't just wait and see what happens.

These tips basically boil down to accepting a measure of responsibility in the production of your document. Avoid dismissing concerns and small details with the haughty declaration of, "That's *their* problem." When they're unable to meet your deadline as a result, it quickly becomes *your* problem.

Getting Files From Here To There

Formerly—say, about 10 years ago—nearly all design jobs were submitted to service bureaus on diskettes, either by hand-delivery or snail mail. Nowadays, there are a number of online options as well. Many printers have private bulletin board services (BBSes) where you can post submissions. Most bureaus require you to set up an account with them, complete with password, before you're granted access. Jobs can also be sent as email attachments, though some sort of encoding is usually necessary to avoid the files becoming corrupted as they travel the information superhighway.

However you choose to submit your material, it's important to include everything your printer needs. Service bureaus generally accept either application files or postscript files. (If postscripts are required, make sure you get detailed specs from the service bureau—there are a lot of possible options to consider, and the slightest inconsistency can result in unreadable files.) Sometimes—*not always*—postscript files will contain embedded fonts and graphics, obviating the need to send copies of these support files to the printer. More often, though, you'll need to send everything. For example, if your file uses 2 typefaces, 12 pieces of clip art, and 5 scanned photos, you'll have 20 items to send to your service bureau (1 document file, 2 font folders, 12 clip-art files, and 5 photo files). Fortunately, most layout software will automatically move all the files necessary for printing to a specified spot on your hard disk, if you request it. (That sure beats trying to remember all those pesky file names—why *did* you name that file flubadub.tif, anyway?)

Incidentally, even if you're using a font that the printer probably already has (can you say, "Helvetica?") it's a good idea to send your copy to the printer anyway. Their copy of the font might have a different version number. It's even possible that, despite the identical name, their copy of the font was produced by a different manufacturer. (This is especially likely for fonts based on old printer's characters, like Garamond. Nearly every major font company produces its own slightly different version of Garamond.) Unless the printer is using the exact same fonts to output the document that you used to lay it out, slight differences in character width and kerning pairs can cause your text to reflow. Don't take chances—include everything.

Color Printing

Color printing, particularly four-color process printing, is extremely tricky, and a lot of things can go wrong. The following tips and techniques will help you avoid making some of the more frustrating mistakes. For more good advice, consult the "Color Caveats" section at the end of the *Do It In Color* section.

How Four-Color Printing Works

Four-color processing breaks each color in your document down into percentages of four component colors: cyan (a light blue), magenta (a pinkish purple), yellow, and black—referred to collectively as CMYK. A plate is generated for each ink color, and the inks are applied to the same sheet of paper—one after the other—as the sheet passes through the rollers. Imagine a photo of a grassy hillside. The cyan and yellow plates would show the hill quite distinctly (cyan and yellow create green shades when mixed), while the magenta and black plates would show very little of the hill (most greens don't use much of either color).

As you can imagine, getting the four ink applications to match up exactly is a little tricky. Paper, printing plates, and rollers can all slip out of alignment. If a single element isn't perfectly aligned with the others, your colors will print out of registration, with extremely ugly results. (Actually, the end result is not unlike those horrible old 3D posters that, when viewed with special glasses, showed Superman pivoting ineffectually back and forth. It's a look you should try to avoid, if possible.)

The Color Trap

Slight registration errors can be covered up with trapping.

Trapping is the process of determining how much overlap or spacing to leave between color elements to compensate for slight problems with alignment.

While trapping has traditionally been handled by the printer on a given job, most desktop publishing and illustration packages provide some means of electronic trapping control. As with most other aspects of color prepress and printing, the details of this process vary widely.

Poor trapping can be worse than no trapping at all, so it's best to consult your service bureau on the best way in which to proceed. If you decide to use your layout software's controls, make sure you know what you're doing, and consult the manual frequently.

Preparing Spot Color For Printing

Printing spot-color work is only slightly more involved than printing single-color work, but it requires that you plan and set up your document carefully. Your second color needs to be defined in your layout software's color palette and used consistently throughout. For instance, don't ever use process colors to simulate your spot color. Apply the actual spot color to each desired element.

You can print a spot color document in two ways. A *separation proof* creates two pages of output for each single page in your electronic document: one page showing all the black items and another showing the spot color items. A *composite proof* puts both colors on a single page, showing you how the final product will look. (Of course, unless you're using a color printer, your color elements will be rendered as grays.)

As with full-color documents, trapping is a concern, although it's less troublesome because there are only two plates to worry about. Discuss your options with your service bureau. Usually, the technicians will elect to handle the trapping issues themselves.

Color Matching

Color matching is the process by which the colors you choose for your computer-generated documents are matched to existing color standards. (It also refers to the process in which the final printed product is checked against a set of standard colors, as a final safeguard against inaccurate reproductions.)

There are a number of color matching standards. The most widely used is the Pantone Matching System (also known as PMS—obviously, the inventors weren't thinking too clearly when they named it). The Pantone system uses a swatch palette and an electronic color library to match colors with standard inks that printers use. Many other color matching systems besides Pantone are available; however, one of the prerequisites for your service bureau should be the use of a system you're comfortable with. Try not to flip back and forth between systems, or it will become nearly impossible to ensure consistency and quality. Your specific software package, color choices, and production and printing methods should play a major role in determining which matching system you choose. As always, consult your software manuals and your friendly neighborhood service bureau.

Happily, the disparity between color on the computer and color off the press is shrinking every day. Although they're still too expensive to be widespread, *color calibration* techniques have been developed to compensate for the differences between computer-generated and printed colors. Most desktop publishing programs include rudimentary color calibration utilities, but, for truly effective calibration, you currently still need special hardware and software devices. Well, maybe some day....

INDEX

M

N

O

P

Q

R

S

W

Z

LOOKING GOOD IN PRINT